Cuba
a country study

Federal Research Division
Library of Congress
Edited by
Rex A. Hudson
Research Completed
April 2001

On the cover: La Iglesia de San Francisco de Asís (Church of
  San Francisco) and the plaza fountain in La Habana Vieja
  (Old Havana), 1997
Courtesy Mark P. Sullivan

Fourth Edition, First Printing, 2002.

Library of Congress Cataloging-in-Publication Data

Cuba: a country study / Federal Research Division, Library of Congress ; edited by Rex A. Hudson — 4th ed.
    p. cm. — (Area handbook series, ISSN 1057–5294) (DA pam ;
550–152)
"Research completed April 2001."
Includes bibliographical references and index.
ISBN 0–8444–1045–4 (hc : alk. paper)
  1. Cuba. I. Hudson, Rex A., 1947– . II. Library of Congress. Federal Research Division. III. Series. IV. Series: DA pam ; 550–152

    F1758.C94875 2002
    972.91—dc21

                        2002018893

Headquarters, Department of the Army
DA Pam 550–152

For sale by the Superintendent of Documents, U.S. Government Printing Office
Washington, D.C. 20402

Foreword

This volume is one in a continuing series of books prepared by the Federal Research Division of the Library of Congress under the Country Studies/Area Handbook Program sponsored by the Department of the Army. The last two pages of this book list the other published studies.

Most books in the series deal with a particular foreign country, describing and analyzing its political, economic, social, and national security systems and institutions, and examining the interrelationships of those systems and the ways they are shaped by historical and cultural factors. Each study is written by a multidisciplinary team of social scientists. The authors seek to provide a basic understanding of the observed society, striving for a dynamic rather than a static portrayal. Particular attention is devoted to the people who make up the society, their origins, dominant beliefs and values, their common interests and the issues on which they are divided, the nature and extent of their involvement with national institutions, and their attitudes toward each other and toward their social system and political order.

The books represent the analysis of the authors and should not be construed as an expression of an official United States government position, policy, or decision. The authors have sought to adhere to accepted standards of scholarly objectivity. Corrections, additions, and suggestions for changes from readers will be welcomed for use in future editions.

Robert L. Worden
Chief
Federal Research Division
Library of Congress
Washington, DC 20540–4840
E-mail: frds@loc.gov

Acknowledgments

This fourth edition of *Cuba: A Country Study* supersedes the 1987 edition edited by James D. Rudolph. The authors acknowledge any general background information that the 1987 edition may have provided for the present volume, which is a completely new edition.

Enrique J. López is gratefully acknowledged for providing the section on telecommunications in chapter three. The book editor would also like to thank the chapter authors for reviewing and commenting on various chapters of this volume. Their shared expertise contributed greatly to its overall quality.

The authors are grateful to individuals in various agencies of the United States government and international organizations, including nongovernmental organizations (NGOs), as well as scholars affiliated with universities or other institutions, who offered their time, special knowledge, or research facilities and materials to provide information and perspective. None of these individuals is, however, in any way responsible for the work or points of view of the authors.

The book editor would also like to thank members of the Federal Research Division who contributed directly to the preparation of the manuscript. These include Sandra W. Meditz, who reviewed all textual and graphic materials, served as liaison with the sponsoring agency, provided numerous substantive and technical contributions, and prepared the index; Marilyn L. Majeska, who provided substantive editing and managed editing and production; Janie L. Gilchrist, who did the word processing and prepared the camera-ready copy; and Stephen C. Cranton, who provided automation and typesetting support.

The firm of Maryland Mapping and Graphics prepared the book's maps and charts based on the book editor's drafts, as well as the photographs and illustrations for the cover and chapter title pages.

Finally, the book editor acknowledges the generosity of the individuals and the United States Government, diplomatic, and international agencies and organizations who allowed their photographs to be used in this study.

Contents

List of Figures

Preface

Like its predecessor, published in 1987, this study is an attempt to examine objectively and concisely the dominant historical, social, environmental, economic, governmental, political, and national security aspects of contemporary Cuba. The views expressed are those of the authors and should not be construed as representing the views of the United States Government.

Chapter bibliographies appear at the end of the book and list sources thought by the chapter authors to be particularly helpful to the reader. Brief comments on sources recommended for further reading appear at the end of each chapter. To the extent possible, place-names follow the system adopted by the United States Board on Geographic Names (BGN). Measurements are given in the metric system; a conversion table is provided to assist readers unfamiliar with metric measurements (see table 1, Appendix). A glossary is also included.

The body of the text generally reflects information available as of April 2001. The introduction, in addition to providing historical perspective on Cuba's hemispheric relations, discusses significant events that occurred between the completion of research and mid-2002. The Country Profile generally reflects information contained in the chapters. Statistics contained in the tables or figures reflect the most current data available at the time.

Although there are many variations, Spanish surnames most often consist of two parts: a patrilineal name followed by a matrilineal name. In the instance of President Fidel Castro Ruz, Castro is his father's name, and Ruz is his mother's maiden name. In nonformal use, Cubans very often drop the matrilineal name. Thus, after the first mention the president is referred to simply as Castro. (His brother is referred to as Raúl Castro on second mention in order to avoid confusion.)

Some literature on Cuba refers to the Cuban Revolution as the guerrilla struggle that culminated in the fall of Fulgencio Batista y Zaldívar during the last days of 1958 and the first days of 1959. In this book, the Cuban Revolution refers to a historical process that began on January 1, 1959, and continues into the present. This definition, as well as the practice of uppercasing "Revolution" in this context, conforms with official Cuban government practice and with much scholarly literature.

Whenever possible, names, abbreviations, and acronyms of organizations or terms conform to official Cuban government use, as indicated in sources such as the Havana telephone directory, and official United States Government use, as compiled by the Foreign Broadcast Information Service (FBIS). For example, although the plural form of Committees for the Defense of the Revolution (CDRs) generally refers to the thousands of block CDRs, the national committee that heads these CDRs is listed officially in Cuban and United States Government reference sources as the Committee for the Defense of the Revolution (Comité de Defensa la la Revolución—CDR). Thus, the singular of the abbreviation is used to distinguish the national committee from the block CDRs.

Table A. *Selected Acronyms and Abbreviations*

Acronym or Abbreviation	Organization or Term
AIC	Agrupación Independiente de Color (Independent Colored Association)
AIDS	acquired immunodeficiency syndrome
AIE	Ala Izquierda Estudiantil (Student Left Wing)
ALADI	Asociación Latinoamericana de Integración (Latin American Integration Association)
ANAP	Asociación Nacional de Agricultores Pequeños (National Association of Small Farmers)
ANPP	Asamblea Nacional del Poder Popular (National Assembly of People's Power)
AT&T	American Telephone and Telegraph Company
BCC	Banco Central de Cuba (Cuban Central Bank)
BFI	Banco Financiero Internacional (International Financial Bank)
BNC	Banco Nacional de Cuba (Cuban National Bank)
BRR	Brigadas de Respuesta Rápida (Rapid Response Brigades)
Cadeca	Casas de Cambio (Exchange Houses)
Caricom	Caribbean Community and Common Market
Caritas	Catholic Relief Services
CCDRN	Comité Cubano Pro Derechos Humanos y Reconciliación Nacional (Cuban Committee for Human Rights and National Reconciliation)
CCPDH	Comité Cubano Pro Derechos Humanos (Cuban Committee for Human Rights)
CDA	Cuban Democracy Act
CDR	Comité de Defensa de la Revolución (Committee for the Defense of the Revolution)
CEA	Centro de Estudios sobre América (Center for American Studies)
CEATM	Comité Estatal de Abastecimiento Técnico-Material (State Committee for Technical and Material Supply)
CEB	Comunidades Eclesiásticas de Base (Ecclesiastical Base Communities)
CEPAL	Comisión Económica para América Latina
CETSS	Comité Estatal de Trabajo y Seguridad Social (State Committee on Labor and Social Security)
CIEM	Centro de Investigaciones de la Economía Mundial (Center for the Study of the World Economy)
CIGB	Centro de Ingeniería Genética y Biotecnología (Center for Genetic Engineering and Biotechnology)
Cimex	Compañía Importadora-Exportadora (Import-Export Company)
CIPS	Centro de Investigaciones Psicológicas y Sociológicas (Center for Psychological and Sociological Research)
CIS	Commonwealth of Independent States
CMEA (see Comecon)	
CNN	Cable News Network

Table A. *(Continued)* Selected Acronyms and Abbreviations

Acronym or Abbreviation	Organization or Term
Comarna	Comisión Nacional para la Protección del Medio Ambiente y la Conservación de los Recursos Naturales (National Commission for Environmental Protection and Conservation of Natural Resources)
Comecon	Council for Mutual Economic Assistance
CPA	Cooperativas de Producción Agropecuaria (Agricultural-Livestock Cooperatives)
CTC	Central de Trabajadores de Cuba (Cuban Workers Federation)
Cubalse	Empresa para Prestación de Servicios al Cuerpo Diplomático (Diplomatic Corps Service Company)
Cubana	Empresa Consolidada Cubana de Aviación (Consolidated Cuban Aviation Company)
Cubanacán	Corporación de Turismo y Comercio Internacional (International Tourism and Trade Corporation)
DA	Departamento América (America Department)
DAAFAR	Defensa Antiaérea y Fuerza Aérea Revolucionaria (Antiaircraft Defense and Revolutionary Air Force)
DCI	Dirección de Cédula de Identidad (Directorate for Identity Cards)
DCI	Dirección de Contra Inteligencia (Directorate of Counterintelligence)
DCPI	Dirección de Cuadros, Personal y Instrucción (Directorate of Cadres, Personnel, and Instruction)
DEP	Dirección de Establecimientos Penales (Directorate of Penitentiary Establishments)
DEU	Directorio Estudiantil Universitario (University Students Directorate)
DGG	Dirección General de Guardafronteras (General Directorate of Border Guards)
DGI	Dirección General de Inteligencia (General Intelligence Directorate)
DGSP	Dirección General de Seguridad Personal (General Directorate of Personal Security)
DGTE	Dirección General de Tropas Especiales (General Directorate of Special Troops)
DI	Dirección de Información (Information Directorate)
DI	Dirección de Inteligencia (Directorate of Intelligence)
DPEI	Departamento de Prevención y Extinción de Incendios (Directorate for the Prevention and Extinction of Fires)
DPNR	Dirección de la Policía Nacional Revolucionaria (National Revolutionary Police)
DRI	Dirección de Relaciones Internacionales (International Relations Directorate)
DSE	Departamento de Seguridad del Estado (Department of State Security)
DT	Dirección Técnica (Technical Directorate)
ECAM	Escuela de Cadetes Interarmas General Antonio Maceo (General Antonio Maceo Joint-Service School)
ECLAC	Economic Commission for Latin America and the Caribbean

Table A. *(Continued)* Selected Acronyms and Abbreviations

Acronym or Abbreviation	Organization or Term
EEC	European Economic Community
EJT	Ejército Juvenil de Trabajo (Youth Labor Army)
ELN	Ejército de Liberación Nacional (National Liberation Army)
EMCC	Escuelas Militares Camilo Cienfuegos (Camilo Cienfuegos Military Schools)
EMPA	Escuela Militar de Pilotos de Aviación (Aviation Pilots Military School)
ETA	Euzkadi Ta Azkatasuna (Basque Fatherland and Freedom)
ETECSA	Empresa de Telecomunicaciones de Cuba, S.A. (Telecommunications Company of Cuba)
EU	European Union
FAR	Fuerzas Armadas Revolucionarias (Revolutionary Armed Forces)
FARC	Fuerzas Armadas Revolucionarias de Colombia (Revolutionary Armed Forces of Colombia)
FEEM	Federación de Estudiantes de la Enseñanza Media (Federation of Secondary School Students)
FEU	Federación Estudiantil Universitaria (Federation of University Students)
FY	fiscal year
FMC	Federación de Mujeres Cubanas (Federation of Cuban Women)
FNLA	Frente Nacional de Libertação de Angola (National Front for the Liberation of Angola)
FSB	Federal'naya Sluzhba Bezopasnosti (Federal Security Service)
FSLN	Frente Sandinista de Liberación Nacional (Sandinista National Liberation Front)
FTAA	Free Trade Area of the Americas
GATT	General Agreement on Tariffs and Trade
GDP	gross domestic product
GNB	Grupo Nueva Banca (New Banking Group)
GNP	gross national product
GONGO	government-operated nongovernmental organization
GSP	global social product
GTP	Guerra de Todo el Pueblo (War of All the People)
HIV	human immunodeficiency virus
IAEA	International Atomic Energy Agency
IDI	Instituto de la Demanda Interna (Domestic Consumer Demand Institute)
IISS	International Institute for Strategic Studies
ITM	Instituto Técnico Militar (Military Technical Institute)
Juceplan	Junta Central de Planificación (Central Planning Board)
KGB	Komitet Gosudarstvennoi Bezopastnosti (Committee for State Security)
LAFTA	Latin American Free Trade Association
LCC	Laboratorio Central de Criminología (Central Laboratory of Criminology)

Table A. (Continued) Selected Acronyms and Abbreviations

Acronym or Abbreviation	Organization or Term
MCR	Movimiento Cívico Revolucionario (Civic Resistance Movement)
MGR	Marina de Guerra Revolucionaria (Revolutionary Navy)
MINFAR	Ministerio de las Fuerzas Armadas Revolucionarias (Ministry of the Revolutionary Armed Forces)
MNR	Milicias Nacionales Revolucionarias (National Revolutionary Militias)
MPLA	Movimento Popular de Libertação de Angola (Popular Movement for the Liberation of Angola)
MPS	Material Product System
MTT	Milicias de Tropas Territoriales (Territorial Troops Militia)
NAFTA	North American Free Trade Agreement
NATO	North Atlantic Treaty Organization
NGO	nongovernmental organization
NPT	Nuclear Non-Proliferation Treaty
OAS	Organization of American States
OCES	Organisation of the Eastern Caribbean States
ONE	Oficina Nacional de Estadísticas (National Statistical Office)
OPJM	Organización de Pioneros José Martí (Organization of José Martí Pioneers)
PCC	Partido Comunista de Cuba (Communist Party of Cuba)
PLA	Chinese Popular Liberation Army
PNR	Policía Nacional Revolucionaria (National Revolutionary Police)
PPC	Partido del Pueblo Cubano (Cuban People's Party)
PPC Orthodox	Partido del Pueblo Cubano (Ortodoxo) (Cuban People's Party) (Orthodox)
PRC	People's Republic of China
PRC	Partido Revolucionario Cubano (Cuban Revolutionary Party)
PRC Authentic	Partido Revolucionario Cubano (Auténtico) (Cuban Revolutionary Party (Authentic)
PRI	Partido Revolucionario Institucional (Institutional Revolutionary Party)
PSP	Partido Socialista Popular (People's Socialist Party)
PUND	Partido de Unidad Nacional Democrático (Democratic National Unity Party)
S.A.	*sociedades anónimas* (quasi-private companies)
SELA	Sistema Económica Latino Americana (Latin American Economic System)
SIGINT	signals intelligence
SMA	Servicio Militar Activo (Active Military Service)
SMO	Servicio Militar Obligatorio (Obligatory Military Service)
SNA	System of National Accounts
SNTAF	Sindicato Nacional de Trabajadores Agrícolas y Forestales (National Trade Union of Agricultural and Forestry Workers)
SPE	Sistema de Perfeccionamiento Empresarial (System for Managerial Improvement)

Table A. *(Continued) Selected Acronyms and Abbreviations*

Acronym or Abbreviation	Organization or Term
SUPV	Sistema Unificado de Prevención y Vigilancia (Unified Prevention and Vigilance System)
TGF	Tropas Guardafronteras (Border Guard Troops)
TSP	Tribunal Supremo Popular (Supreme Court of Cuba)
UBPC	Unidades Básicas de Producción Cooperativa (Basic Units of Cooperative Production)
UJC	Unión de Jóvenes Comunistas (Union of Young Communists)
UMAP	Unidades Militares de Ayuda a la Producción (Military Units in Support of Production)
UNCHR	United Nations Commission on Human Rights
UNDP	United Nations Development Programme
Uneca	Unión de Empresas de Construcción del Caribe (Union of Caribbean Construction Enterprises)
UNITA	União Nacional para la Independência Total de Angola (National Union for the Total Independence of Angola)
URC	Unión Revolucionaria Comunista (Communist Revolutionary Union)
USTEC	United States-Cuba Trade and Economic Council

Table B. Chronology of Important Events

Period	Description
PREHISTORY	
c. 1000 B.C.–c. 1000 A.D.	Ciboney Indians migrate to central-western Cuba.
c. 800–c. 1450	Successive migrations of Arawak Indians (sub-Taino and Taino) largely displace Ciboney.
FIFTEENTH CENTURY	
October 27, 1492	Christopher Columbus discovers and explores Cuba.
SIXTEENTH CENTURY	
1508	Sebastián de Ocampo circumnavigates and explores the island.
1511–24	Diego Velázquez de Cuéllar conquers the Indians and establishes various settlements, including Baracoa, the first settlement, established in 1512.
1515	Santiago de Cuba is established as the Cuban capital.
1519	San Cristóbal de Habana is relocated from its original site on the Gulf of Batabanó on the south coast to its present location on the north coast.
1522–33	The last major indigenous peoples' uprising is suppressed.
1523–24	Blacks are brought from Africa to work the mines and fields.
1538	La Habana (hereafter Havana) becomes the seat of government.
	Santiago de Cuba is selected formally as the capital of the island.
1553	The governor's seat moves from Santiago de Cuba to Havana.
1555	French pirate Jacques de Sores captures and burns part of Havana.
1592	Philip II declares Havana to be a city.
1595	Cattle raisers install sugar mills on their lands and begin sugar production.
SEVENTEENTH CENTURY	
1607	Havana is formally established as the capital of Cuba, and the island is organized into two governing regions.
1628	Dutch pirate Piet Heyn captures the Spanish fleet off the northern coast of Cuba.
1662	The English capture and ransack Santiago de Cuba.
EIGHTEENTH CENTURY	
1715	Political administration is centralized following the Bourbons' assumption of power in Spain.
	Bourbon reforms begin to be introduced into Cuba.
August 17, 1917	More than 500 armed *vegueros* (tobacco farmers) march into Havana to protest the Spanish tobacco monopoly.
1723	The first Cuban printing press is established.
1728	The University of Havana (Real y Pontificia Universidad de San Jerónimo de La Habana) is founded.
1733	Havana assumes jurisdiction over all Cuban administrative units.
1748	Havana is established as a bishopric.

Table B. (Continued) Chronology of Important Events

Period	Description
1762	The English capture and occupy Havana and the western half of the island. Havana becomes an open port.
1763	Havana is traded back to Spain for Florida under the Treaty of Paris, which ends the Seven Years' War.
1789	Cuba is divided into two ecclesiastical jurisdictions, one in Santiago and the other in Havana. Free slave trade is authorized by royal decree.
1790	Cuba's first newspaper is established.
1791	Haitian sugar and coffee planters flee to Cuba.
1792	The Economic Society of Friends of Cuba (La Sociedad Económica de Amigos del País) is founded.
1793	Cuba's first public library is established.
NINETEENTH CENTURY	
1808	Thomas Jefferson attempts to purchase Cuba from Spain.
1809	Joaquín Infante organizes the first independence conspiracy.
1812	José Antonio Aponte organizes a conspiracy of slaves and free blacks.
1814	Ferdinand is restored to the Spanish throne.
1817	England and Spain sign a treaty proclaiming the end of legal slave trade effective 1820.
1818	A Spanish royal decree opens Cuban ports to free international trade.
December 2, 1823	The United States issues the Monroe Doctrine.
1828–30	The Aguíla Negra (Black Eagle) Conspiracy is organized.
1830s	Spain imposes harsher authoritarian controls.
1837	The first railroad in Latin America commences operation in Cuba, linking Havana with Bejucal and Güines.
1844	A slave conspiracy, called La Escalera (the ladder) because suspects are tied to ladders and whipped, is suppressed.
1848	President James Polk attempts to purchase Cuba.
1854	The United States issues the Ostend Manifesto, calling for the purchase of Cuba.
1865	The Reformist Party (Partido Reformista), Cuba's first political party, is organized.
October 10, 1868	The Grito de Yará begins the Ten Years' War between Cuba and Spain.
April 10, 1869	Rebels fighting Spain hold a Constituent Assembly in Guáimaro, where they adopt Cuba's first constitution and elect Carlos Manuel de Céspedes as their president.
February 11, 1878	The Pact of Zanjón, signed with Spain, ends the Ten Years' War but does not win independence for Cuba. The country is organized into six provinces: Pinar del Río, La Habana, Matanzas, Santa Clara, Puerto Príncipe, and Santiago de Cuba.
March 15, 1878	The Protest of Baraguá: General Antonio Maceo rejects the Pact of Zanjón and calls for the abolition of slavery.
May 1878	The Ten Years' War officially ends, after the remaining Cuban forces surrender.

Table B. (Continued) Chronology of Important Events

Period	Description
1879–80	La Guerra Chiquita (The Little War), a short-lived rebellion against Spain, takes place.
October 7, 1886	Spain abolishes slavery in Cuba.
1892	José Martí forms the Cuban Revolutionary Party (Partido Revolucionario Cubano—PRC) in Tampa, Florida.
May 19, 1895	Cuba's foremost hero, poet, and visionary, José Martí, is killed on the battlefield at Dos Rios in eastern Cuba.
December 7, 1896	Antonio Maceo, one of the most successful guerrilla leaders, is killed at the Battle of Punta Brava in western Cuba.
February 15, 1898	The battleship U.S.S. *Maine*, anchored in Havana Harbor, blows up and sinks, killing 260 officers and crew.
April 25, 1898	The United States declares war on Spain, beginning the Spanish-American War (1898).
December 10, 1898	The United States and Spain sign the Treaty of Paris, ending the Spanish-American War and granting Cuba its independence.
January 1, 1899	The United States occupies Cuba militarily, installing General John R. Brooke as the first United States military governor.
TWENTIETH CENTURY	
June 21, 1901	The Cuban constitution is drafted, incorporating the United States-imposed Platt Amendment, which gives the United States the right to intervene in Cuba.
Republican Period	
May 20, 1902	The United States military occupation ends when the republic is proclaimed and Tomás Estrada Palma (president, 1902–06) is sworn in as Cuba's first elected president.
May 22, 1903	Cuba and the United States sign the Permanent Treaty, which incorporates the Platt Amendment.
July 2, 1903	The follow-up United States-Cuban Treaty is signed, whereby Cuba agrees to lease the United States military bases in the port cities of Guantánamo and Bahía Honda for an indefinite period.
1904	Cuba holds its first elections for national Congress.
August 1906	The August War (Guerrita de Agosto), a Liberal Party (Partido Liberal) uprising set off by Estrada Palma's fraudulent election, hastens United States intervention.
1906–09	The second United States intervention takes place, with Charles Magoon serving as governor of the island.
1908	Liberal Party candidate José Miguel Gómez (president, 1909–13) wins election to a four-year term.
1912	A short-lived racial uprising, led by the Independent Colored Association (Agrupación Independiente de Color), prompts the dispatch of United States Marines to Cuba.
1912	Conservative Mario García Menocal (president, 1913–21) is elected to a four-year term.
April 7, 1917	Cuba declares war on Germany.
1917	The Liberal Party leads a short-lived uprising in Oriente and Camagüey.
1920	The sugar boom collapses.
1920	Liberal Alfredo Zayas y Alfonso (president, 1921–25) wins election to a four-year term as president.

Table B. *(Continued) Chronology of Important Events*

Period	Description
February 1923	United States representative General Enoch Crowder is sent to Cuba to "reform" the political process.
1924	Gerardo Machado y Morales (president, 1925–33) is elected to his first four-year presidential term.
August 16, 1925	The Communist Party of Cuba (Partido Comunista de Cuba—PCC) is founded in Havana.
1927	The anti-Machado University Students Directorate (Directorio Estudiantil Universitario) is founded.
1930	The clandestine ABC organization is established.
1931	Carlos Mendieta and former President García Menocal organize a short-lived uprising in Pinar del Río.
	Machado's army crushes the expedition from the United States led by Carlos Hevia and Sergio Carbó.
1933	The United States becomes involved in mediating between Machado and various groups seeking to overthrow his government.
August 12, 1933	The army ousts Machado; Carlos Manuel de Céspedes y Quesada (president, 1933) becomes provisional president.
September 4, 1933	The Revolt of the Sergeants, led by Fulgencio Batista y Zaldívar (president, 1940–44, 1952–59), hastens the fall of Céspedes.
	Dr. Ramón Grau San Martín (president, 1933–34, 1944–48) becomes president of a revolutionary government.
January 1934	Colonel Batista overthrows Grau's regime and appoints Colonel Carlos Mendieta (president, 1934–35) as provisional president.
May 29, 1934	The United States abrogates the Platt Amendment by signing the Treaty of Relations between Cuba and the United States.
1934	The Cuban Revolutionary Party (Authentic) (Partido Revolucionario Cubano—PRC) (Auténtico) is organized.
December 11, 1935	A general strike forces the resignation of President Mendieta, who is replaced by José A. Barnet y Vinageras (president, 1935–36).
May 1936	Miguel Mariano Gómez y Arias (president, 1936) is "elected" president.
December 1936	Federico Laredo Bru (president, 1936–40) becomes president for a four-year term.
1939	Grau San Martín is elected president of the Constitutional Assembly.
1938	The PCC is recognized as a legal political party.
1939	The Workers' National Federation (Confederación Nacional Obrera), created in 1925, is reorganized into the Cuban Workers Federation (Confederación de Trabajadores de Cuba—CTC).
1940	A progressive constitution is drafted. General Batista is elected president for a four-year term.
December 9, 1941	Cuba declares war on the Axis powers.
1943	General Batista legalizes the PCC and established diplomatic relations with the Soviet Union, which is allied to the United States.

Table B. (Continued) Chronology of Important Events

Period	Description
1944	The PCC changes its party name to Popular Socialist Party (Partido Socialista Popular—PSP).
	Grau San Martín is elected president.
1947	Eduardo Chibás forms the Orthodox branch of the Cuban People's Party (Partido del Pueblo Cubano—PPC) Orthodox (Ortodoxo).
1948	Carlos Prío Socarrás (president, 1948–52) is elected president.
1951	Chibás commits suicide.
March 10, 1952	Batista seizes power through a military coup.
April 1952	Diplomatic relations with the Soviet Union are broken.
1953	Resistance is organized and led primarily by Auténticos and university students.
July 26, 1953	Fidel Castro Ruz launches the ill-fated Moncada Barracks attack.
November 1, 1954	Batista is "reelected" president for a four-year term.
May 15, 1955	Fidel Castro is released from prison and departs for the United States.
December 2, 1956	Castro's eighty-three-member *Granma* expedition lands in Oriente Province.
March 13, 1957	Members of the Directorate (Directorio) and the Auténticos attack the Presidential Palace unsuccessfully.
1957	Police kill Directorio leader José Antonio Echeverría.
	Castro consolidates his guerrilla operations in the Sierra Maestra.
1958	The Castro-organized general strike collapses.
	A military offensive against the guerrillas fails.
	The United States gradually withdraws support for the Batista regime, suspending arms shipments to it on March 14.
	A rigged election produces the victory of Batista's candidate, Andrés Rivero Agüero.
	Increased demoralization and corruption lead to the gradual collapse of Cuba's armed forces.
	Batista and his close associates escape to the Dominican Republic.
Revolutionary Period	
January 1, 1959	Fidel Castro assumes command and begins consolidation of power.
January 7, 1959	The United States recognizes the Castro government.
January 1959	Trials and executions of former Batista regime officials begin.
May 17, 1959	The first Agrarian Reform Law is promulgated, expropriating farmlands of more than 404 hectares and forbidding foreign land ownership.
1959	Castro becomes prime minister and replaces Manuel Urrútia Lleo with his hand-picked candidate, Oswaldo Dorticós Torrado.
February 1960	The Central Planning Board (Junta Central de Planificación—Juceplan) is created to plan and direct the economy.
May 7, 1960	Cuban-Soviet diplomatic relations resume.

Table B. (Continued) Chronology of Important Events

Period	Description
October 19, 1960	The United States declares an embargo on trade with Cuba, except for medical supplies and most foodstuffs.
January 3, 1961	The United States breaks diplomatic relations with Cuba.
April 17–19, 1961	Cuban forces defeat the United States-sponsored Bay of Pigs invasion.
December 2, 1961	Castro declares himself to be a Marxist-Leninist.
January 31, 1962	Cuba is expelled from the Organization of American States (OAS—see Glossary).
October 14, 1962	The Cuban Missile Crisis begins when United States reconnaissance aircraft photograph Soviet construction of intermediate-range missile sites in Cuba.
October 22–November 20, 1962	The Cuban Missile Crisis brings the United States and the Soviet Union to the brink of nuclear conflict.
November 21, 1962	President John F. Kennedy ends the quarantine measures against Cuba.
November 6, 1965	The Freedom Flights Program begins, allowing 250,000 Cubans to come to the United States by 1971.
November 2, 1966	The Cuban Adjustment Act allows 123,000 Cubans to apply for permanent residence in the United States.
August 1967	After a one-year suspension, flights resume to take United States citizens out of Cuba
October 9, 1967	Ernesto "Che" Guevara is executed in Bolivia.
1975	The United States reports the presence of Cuban soldiers and advisers in Angola to support the Marxist group, the Popular Movement for the Liberation of Angola (Movimento Popular de Libertação de Angola—MPLA).
October 1975	Cuba begins deployment of 35,000 combat troops to support the Marxist regime in Angola.
February 24, 1976	Cuba's new socialist constitution is promulgated, making Castro head of government as president of the Council of Ministers, commander of the armed forces, and first secretary of the PCC. The PCC is institutionalized within the formal governmental structure.
April 1977	Cuba undertakes internationalist military assistance to several African countries.
April 27, 1977	Cuba and the United States sign agreements on fishing rights and maritime borders.
September 1977	Cuba and the United States open interests sections in each other's capitals.
January 1978	Cuba begins deployment of 20,000 troops to Ethiopia.
August 30, 1979	The United States Senate announces discovery of a Soviet "combat brigade" of 3,000 troops in Cuba.
April 1980	About 10,000 Cuban refugees seeking asylum enter the Peruvian Embassy in Havana, starting a mass exodus of Cubans to Peru and the United States. Castro allows 125,000 Cubans to leave for the United States in the Mariel Boatlift.
April 19, 1982	The United States bans travel to Cuba by United States citizens and allows the 1977 fishing accord to lapse.

Table B. (Continued) Chronology of Important Events

Period	Description
1983	United States Assistant Secretary of State Thomas O. Enders meets with the head of the Cuban Interests Section in Washington, Ramón Sánchez-Parodi, to request that Cuba take back thousands of Cubans (who came to the United States via the 1980 Mariel Boatlift) because of their criminal conduct in Cuba.
	Cuba informs the United States it is willing to discuss the return of some Cubans who came to the United States illegally in 1980, but only as part of overall negotiations on "normalizing of migration" between the two countries.
July 31, 1984	Cuban and United States officials start discussions in New York about immigration issues, including the possible return of 1,000 Cuban refugees (*Marielitos*) from the 1980 Mariel Boatlift.
December 14, 1984	Cuba and the United States conclude a migration pact under which Cuba agrees to accept the return of *Marielitos*.
May 20, 1985	Radio Martí begins broadcast news and information from the United States to Cuba.
1985	Twenty-three Cuban *Marielitos* are returned to Havana. These are the first of more than 2,700 unwanted Cubans the United States wishes to return as part of an agreement with Fidel Castro's government.
	Havana suspends all immigration proceedings between Cuba and the United States in response to the start-up of Voice of America's Radio Martí. Cuban-Americans are prohibited from visiting Cuba.
October 4, 1985	President Reagan bans travel to the United States by Cuban government or PCC officials or their representatives, as well as most students, scholars, and artists.
1986	The United States and Cuba agree to negotiate the revival of the 1984 immigration agreement that enabled the United States to deport several thousand Cubans with histories of crime or mental illness who had arrived in the United States as part of the Mariel Boatlift of 1980. Talks collapse when the United States refuses to recognize Cuba's right to broadcast over an AM frequency in the United States to match Radio Martí transmissions.
	Cuba allows seventy political prisoners, many of whom had been in prison for more than twenty years, to leave the country and fly to Miami.
May 18, 1986	Farmers' markets (legal since 1980) are banned.
July 1, 1986	Cuba suspends service on its convertible currency (see Glossary) debt.
1987	Private home ownership is banned.
	Cuba agrees to release 348 political prisoners at request of Roman Catholic Church in the United States.
November 19, 1987	The Cuban government, in a policy reversal, agrees to restore an immigration pact with the United States by which 2,600 Cubans, whose criminal records make them ineligible for United States residence, are to be deported from the United States and up to 27,000 Cubans are to be allowed to emigrate to the United States each year.

Table B. (Continued) Chronology of Important Events

Period	Description
March 1988	United Nations Commission on Human Rights (see Glossary) unanimously agrees to accept an unexpected invitation from Havana to investigate human rights in Cuba. Even though UN specialists encounter harsh penal systems in Cuban prisons, they find no evidence to support United States charges of torture and executions. The official UN investigation concludes that abuses have declined.
April 21, 1988	John Cardinal O'Connor, Archbishop of New York, meets with Fidel Castro in Havana. It is the first visit by a Roman Catholic cardinal to Cuba since 1959.
1989	The UN issues a report on the human rights situation in Cuba, suggesting that although there have been big improvements in church-state relations and treatment of political prisoners, basic political liberties are still widely denied.
	Division General Arnaldo Ochoa Sánchez, a highly decorated war hero, is arrested on corruption charges; American officials say the action suggests dissension at the highest levels of the Cuban military; Cuba's Transportation Minister, Diocles Torralba González, a friend of Ochoa's, is also relieved of his duties; Ochoa is accused of being involved in illicit sales in Angola.
	Minister of Interior General José Abrantes Fernández is replaced as the top security officer following official charges that high military officers in Cuba are involved in drug trafficking. The Ministry of Interior is reorganized.
	Cuba announces that a firing squad has executed four Cuban Army officers convicted by court martial of conspiring to ship tons of cocaine and marijuana to the United States. The four include Ochoa Sánchez,
1990	The Castro regime announces a series of austerity measures, the "special period in peacetime" (hereafter Special Period—see Glossary).
March 23, 1990	TV Martí, an anti-Castro, United States-taxpayer-funded station, is launched, but the signal is jammed by the Cuban government.
1991	Switzerland, which sponsors United States diplomats in Havana, offers to sponsor the Cuban Interests Section in Washington to ensure that both countries have diplomatic representation in each other's capital.
	The deteriorating economic situation in Cuba prompts a large increase in the number of Cubans seeking to leave their country.
	Cuba announces the lifting of restrictions on travel abroad; anyone aged twenty or over is to be allowed to leave and visit other countries, provided that the host nation gives them a visa.
	The Fourth Party Congress is held and resolves to allow members of religious groups to join the party.
September 1, 1991	In order to remove a major obstacle to increased United States economic aid to the Soviet Union, President Mikhail S. Gorbachev declares that he will withdraw Soviet troops from Cuba and end the US$2-billion-a-year trade subsidy that Moscow gives Havana.
1992	The government of President Castro steps up efforts to crush internal opposition.

Table B. (Continued) Chronology of Important Events

Period	Description
	In a rare exception to the economic blockade of Cuba, the Bush administration grants permission to the American Telephone and Telegraph Company (AT&T) to expand telephone services between Cuba and the United States; Cuba rejects AT&T's proposal.
	Russia and Cuba agree to the withdrawal of a former Soviet infantry brigade that has been on the island since the Cuban Missile Crisis in 1962.
	Cuba and Russia sign trade accords for new ties based on mutual benefits; Cuba is to trade sugar for Russian oil at world market prices.
August 14, 1993	Cuba ends the ban on the use of dollars.
1994	The Clinton administration ends the United States' open-door policy toward Cuban refugees, who will be detained for an indefinite period after they arrive in the United States.
August 1994	Following Castro's declaration of an open migration policy, a new boat-lift begins. The United States stops refugees aboard rafts and boats off the Florida coast and begins detaining them at its Guantánamo Bay Naval Station.
September 9, 1994	Cuba and the United States reach agreement under which Cuba pledges to stop citizens from fleeing in small boats and the United States promises to accept at least 20,000 Cuban immigrants a year.
late September 1994	Farmers' markets are reinstated.
1994	The flood of Cuban refugees ends as the Cuban government implements terms of agreement reached with the United States aimed at halting the exodus.
	The Clinton administration gives United States telecommunications companies permission to establish direct telephone links with Cuba.
December 1994	Cuba establishes a new currency, the convertible peso (see Glossary).
May 2, 1995	Cuba and the United States issue a joint communiqué reaffirming their commitment to promote safe, legal, and orderly migration. Under this accord, Cubans interdicted at sea or who enter the Guantánamo Bay Naval Station illegally are returned to Cuba provided that they do not have any concerns about possible official Cuban retaliation.
February 24, 1996	Cuban Air Force MiG jet fighters shoot down two small unarmed aircraft belonging to Brothers to the Rescue, a Miami-based Cuban exile group, in international waters, killing four persons.
November 19, 1996	Pope John Paul II receives Fidel Castro at the Vatican and accepts an invitation to visit Cuba.
February 12, 1997	The White House approves licenses for ten press organizations interested in establishing bureaus in Havana; Cuba approves only the Cable News Network (CNN).
January 11, 1998	National and provincial parliamentary elections are held.
January 21–25, 1998	Pope John Paul II visits Cuba.

Table B. *(Continued)* *Chronology of Important Events*

Period	Description
February 25, 1999	Cuba suspends about 80 percent of its telephone links to the United States in retaliation for the withholding by five United States telecommunication firms of US$19 million in payments owed to the Telecommunications Company of Cuba (Empresa de Telecomunicaciones de Cuba, S.A.—ETECSA).
November 25, 1999	A five-year-old Cuban boy, Elián González, is rescued in the Straits of Florida.
TWENTY–FIRST CENTURY	
March 2000	Tough new legislation aimed at combating political dissent and protecting the Cuban economy becomes effective. Decree–Law 88, the Law for the Protection of the National Independence and Economy of Cuba, provides a penalty of up to twenty years' imprisonment for a series of offenses, including providing information to the United States government; owning, distributing, or reproducing material produced by the United States government or any other foreign entity; and collaborating, by any means, with foreign radio, television, press, or other foreign media, for the purpose of destabilizing the country and destroying the socialist state.
June 28, 2000	Elián González, accompanied by his father, returns to Cuba after an intense seven-month legal and political battle over the child's custody.
March 21–24, 2001	A conference of American and Cuban scholars, entitled "Bay of Pigs: Forty Years After," is held in Havana, and many declassified United States and Cuban documents on the invasion are released.
April 12–15, 2001	Chinese President Jiang Zemin pays a state visit to Cuba.
June 12, 2001	United States Secretary of State Colin L. Powell says that China had delivered arms to Cuba.
July 14, 2001	United States President George W. Bush confirms support for tougher economic and travel sanctions against Cuba.

Country Profile

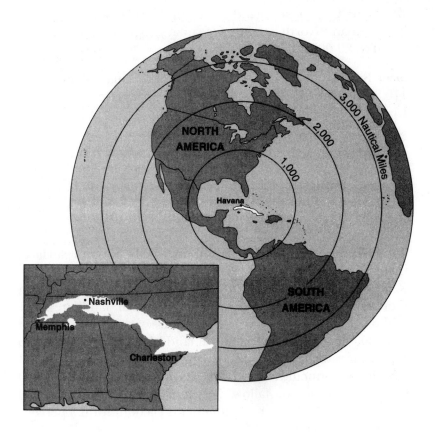

Country

Official Name: Republic of Cuba (República de Cuba).

Short Name: Cuba.

Term for Citizen(s): Cuban(s).

Capital: La Habana (hereafter, Havana).

Independence: May 20, 1902 (from Spain on December 10, 1898, but administered by United States from 1898 to 1902).

Geography

Location: Caribbean island south of Florida between Caribbean Sea and North Atlantic Ocean at geographic coordinates 21°30'N, 80°00'W.

Size: Slightly smaller than Pennsylvania. Square kilometers: 110,860, including Isla de Cuba (104,945 square kilometers), Isla de la Juventud (2,200 square kilometers), and adjacent keys (3,715 square kilometers).

Length of Coastline: 5,746 kilometers.

Maritime Claims: As signatory to Law of the Sea Treaty, Cuba claims twelve-nautical-mile territorial sea and 200-nautical-mile exclusive economic zone.

Topography: Plains cover about two-thirds of land surface, three principal mountain ranges the rest. Tallest peak, Pico Real del Turquino, at 1,974 meters, is in Sierra Maestra mountain chain. About 60 percent of total land area (11 million hectares) used for agriculture. About 12 percent (800,000 hectares) of agricultural land highly productive deep and permeable soils; 22 percent marginal for agriculture. Of remaining noncultivated land, 21 percent (or 2,311,000 hectares) pasture or fallow, and 25.7 percent (or 2,831,600 hectares) forested. Human settlements account for 6.3 percent (or 694,000 hectares).

Principal Rivers: Most important hydrographic basins: Cauto, Zaza, and Sagua la Grande. Average length of major rivers: ninety-three kilometers. Cuba's longest river: 370-kilometer Cauto, flowing from eastern mountains to southern coast.

Climate: Tropical, warm, and humid. Annual mean temperatures average 25° Celsius (C). Havana's average annual rainfall: 1,146.1 millimeters; days with rain: ninety-six. Average monthly temperatures in Havana range from 27° C in July and August to 22° C in January and February; average temperature: 24.5° C. Relative humidity: 79 percent. Island averages 1,400 millimeters of rainfall a year, although annual amount varies greatly from year to year. Two well-established dry and rainy seasons:

monthly rainfall averages between thirty-two and ninety-nine millimeters during dry season, from December to April; between 200 and 260 millimeters during rainy season, from May through November. Hurricane season: July to November; months of most frequent storms: September and October.

Society

Population: Total population (1999): 11,106,000 people. July 2001 estimate: 11,184,023. Net estimated migration rate (2000): -1.52 migrant(s) per 1,000 population. Illicit emigration continuing problem. Estimated 3,800 Cubans took to Florida Straits in 1999, 40 percent of whom (1,520) were interdicted by United States Coast Guard. Population density (1998): 100.3 inhabitants per square kilometer. Annual population growth rates in late 1990s less than 0.5 percent a year, down from 0.67 in 1995. Estimated population growth rate (2000): 0.39 percent. Population projection (2010): 11,516,000. Relatively high current median age (30.2 years) projected to increase further (to 38.7 years) by 2010. Country primarily urban, with 78 percent of population residing in cities and towns; 22 percent rural. Largest city: Havana, with 2.2 million inhabitants (1996). Estimated birth rate (2000): 12.68 births per 1,000 population. Estimated life expectancy at birth (for both sexes combined, 2000): 76.21 years (73.84 for males and 78.73 for females).

Ethnic Groups: According to 1981 Cuban census, 66 percent of population is "white" and 34.0 percent "nonwhite," latter including black (12.0 percent), mulatto or mestizo (21.9 percent), and Asian (0.1 percent). Since 1959 Revolution, nonwhite share of population has increased significantly. Percent of population classified as white declined from 73 percent in 1953 to 66 percent in 1981, whereas share of mulattos rose from 14 percent to 22 percent (black percentage remained almost same).

Official Language: Spanish (Español).

Education and Literacy: Adult literacy rate (people age fifteen and older who can read and write) in 1995: 95.7 percent (males: 96.2 percent; females, 95.3 percent). In late 1990s, Cuba had eighteen teachers per 1,000 population; and 12,223 schools, including 9,481 primary schools, 1,891 secondary schools, and thirty-two higher education institutions. In 1995–96 academic year, student enrollment in primary, secondary, and higher education was, respectively, 933,000, 639,000, and 111,000.

Health: Estimated infant mortality rate (2000): 7.51. Total fertility rate (1996): 1.54 children born per woman. Estimated total fertility rate (2000): 1.6. Major causes of death per 100,000 population (1996): heart disease, 206; malignant neoplasms (cancers), 37; cerebrovascular disease, 72; infectious and parasitic diseases, 53; accidents, 51; influenza and pneumonia, 40. Health personnel total 339,943, including 62,624 physicians and dentists, of whom 28,855, or 46 percent, are family doctors (1997). Total also includes 81,333 nurses and more than 56,342 mid-level technicians. Ratio of population to physicians (1997): 214, one of world's lowest, down from 1,393 in 1970. Physicians train in twenty-three medical schools, ten of which are located in Havana, and four dentistry schools. Health infrastructure includes 283 hospitals, 440 Polyclinics, 161 medical posts, 220 maternity homes, 168 dental clinics, and other facilities (1997). Forty-eight hospitals in Havana, and sixty-four in rural areas. Other facilities: 196 nursing homes for elderly (sixty-three of which provide only day services) and twenty-seven homes for disabled. Total number of hospital beds, including military hospitals (1997): 66,195; social assistance beds: at least 14,201. Only 2,155 cases diagnosed as human immunodeficiency virus (HIV) positive, 811 of which were known to have developed into full-blown acquired immunodeficiency syndrome (AIDS) (1999).

Religion: No official religion. Nearly 90 percent of population nominally Roman Catholic in prerevolutionary Cuba, but number of practicing Roman Catholics probably less than 10 percent. Estimated half of all Cubans agnostic, slightly more than 40 percent Christian; less than 2 percent practiced Afro-Cuban religions. Limited membership in other religions, including Judaism. Religiosity estimates may be considerably higher, however, if due credit is given to the cultural relevance of informal religions, particularly of syncretic Afro-Cuban rites, which historically were minimized.

Economy

Overview: State-controlled economy. Some reforms implemented in 1990s. Central control complicated by existence of informal, mostly dollar economy. Compared with 1990, living standards for average Cuban without dollars remain at depressed level.

Gross Domestic Product (GDP): During 1989–93, GDP declined by 35 percent because of lost Soviet aid and domestic inefficiencies. GDP grew by 0.7 percent in 1994, 2.5 percent in 1995, 7.8 percent in 1996, 2.5 percent in 1997, and 1.2 percent in 1998. Cumulative GDP growth rate over 1993–98 period was about 16 percent, compared with contraction of 35 percent between 1989 and 1993. GDP growth rate in 2000: 5.6 percent.

Per Capita GDP and Minimum Wage: Average monthly earnings of Cuban workers in main economic sectors, in pesos per month (for value of peso, see Glossary), from highest to lowest (1989): culture and arts, 223; science and technology, 217; transportation, 211; administration, 201; construction, 201; public health, social security, and tourism, 195; education, 191; finance and insurance, 190; agriculture, 186; industry, 186; forestry, 184; communications, 176; community and personal services, 164; and commerce, 163. Within industrial sector, average monthly earnings ranged from 237 pesos per month for workers in electricity production and distribution to 141 pesos per month for workers in apparel industry.

Inflation: In early 1990s, Cuba had very high levels of suppressed inflation (expressed through physical shortages and rampant black markets).

Employment and Unemployment: Self-employment in more than 100 occupations, primarily those related to transportation, home repair, and personal services, became legal in September 1993, and number of authorized occupations expanded to 140 in July 1995. Making such employment legal allowed approximately 208,000 workers to engage in self-employment, fewer than 5 percent of economically active population of 4.5 million workers. By March 1996, number had fallen to 160,000, as result of new taxes introduced that year. Restrictions on self-employment remain quite severe. State-sector employment in 1989 was roughly 4.1 million workers, of whom 3.5 million were civilian employees and 600,000 were classified as other state employees. During 1990s state-sector employment fell sharply, reflecting severe dislocations suffered by state enterprises and sharp reductions in size of armed forces. By 1996 overall state employment was roughly 3.2 million workers, 22 percent lower than in 1989. State civilian employment was 24 percent lower in 1997 than in 1990. From 1989 to 1996, nonstate-sector employment, particularly in agricultural sector, increased more than four-fold, from about 230,000 in 1989 to more than 1 million in 1996, absorbing large portion of workers shed by state sector.

Agriculture: Liberalized agricultural markets introduced in October 1994. In 1997 Cuba had 6,686,700 hectares of agricultural land, of which 3,701,400 hectares were cultivated. In 1997 state directly controlled 24.4 percent of agricultural land; nonstate sector controlled 75.6 percent. Besides sugar-cane, which accounted for 48 percent of cultivated land in 1997, state enterprises specialize in production of rice, citrus, coffee, and tobacco, as well as livestock, and market their output. Sugar production fell from 8.1 million tons in 1989 to 3.2 million tons in 1998.

Mining: Metal commodities produced in Cuba include chromite, cobalt, copper, crude steel, and nickel. Other nonfuel industrial mineral products include cement, gypsum, lime, ammonia, salt, silica sand, and sulfur. World's eighth leading producer of nickel in 1998, but produces only about 4 percent of world's total nickel mine production. Nickel most important metal to Cuban economy and export sector. Ministry of Basic Industry responsible for mineral and petroleum sectors.

Industry: In 1986 Cuba's manufacturing sector consisted of 827 enterprises of widely varying sizes, employing 726,000 workers. Industries with largest number of enterprises were nonelectrical machinery (150 enterprises), sugar (148), and foodstuffs (145). Majority of largest manufacturing plants (those employing more than 4,000 workers) were part of sugar industry; other industries having plants with more than 4,000 workers were textiles (three), mining and nonferrous metallurgy (one), apparel (one), fishing (one), and beverages and tobacco (one). In addition to sugar and nickel mining industries, significant contributors to national product in 1989 included beverages and tobacco, foodstuffs, nonelectrical machinery, chemical products, electricity generation, and construction materials.

Energy: Poorly endowed with energy resources, Cuba relies on imports to meet energy requirements. Coal not found in commercial quantities; hydroelectric resources limited by low-volume rivers; and oil and natural gas deposits inadequate to meet demand. Biomass (in form of bagasse) an important energy source for sugar industry. In 1988 Cuba met 70 percent of energy requirements with liquid fuels (crude oil, light oil products, and heavy oil products), about 29 percent with biomass, and remaining 1 percent with other energy sources such as coal, coke, and hydroelectricity. Domestically produced oil amounted to nearly 1.7 million tons in 1998. Combined electric-generation capacity in 1997: 4.33 gigawatt hours. Real generating capacity may be only 1,200 megawatts. Electricity production in 1998: 15.274 billion kilowatt hours. Electricity consumption in 1998: 14.205 billion kilowatt hours.

Services: In 1995 services included trade (hotels and restaurants); electricity, gas, and water; community, personal, and social services; finance (including business and real estate); and transport (including communications and warehousing).

Trade Balance: Cuba ran deficit in services trade in 1989–91 but has recorded surpluses in every year beginning in 1992. During 1993–95, surpluses were quite sizable, averaging around US$250 million. Income generated by tourism rose by 535 percent between 1990 and 1997; it first exceeded US$1 billion mark in 1995, reached nearly US$1.4 billion in 1996, and exceeded US$1.5 billion in 1997. Tourism surpassed nickel to become second largest source of revenue in 1991 and overtook sugar exports in 1994.

Imports: Over 1989–93 period, merchandise imports fell from 8.1 billion pesos to slightly more than 2.0 billion pesos, or by 75 percent. By 1998 they had risen to 4.2 billion pesos.

Exports: Exports, like imports, began to recover in 1994, rising to about 1.3 billion pesos that year and 1.9 billion pesos in 1996, falling to 1.8 billion pesos in 1997 and 1.4 billion pesos in 1998. Principal export destinations in 1999: Russia, accounting for about 25 percent of exports; Netherlands, 23 percent; Canada, 16 percent.

Balance of Payments: Unpaid debt and accrued service payments resulting from Cuba's suspension of payment on convertible currency effective July 1, 1986, amounted to nearly US$6.1 billion in 1987, US$6.5 billion in 1988, and US$6.2 billion in 1989. Outstanding debt grew from nearly US$8.8 billion in 1993 to more than US$11.2 billion at the end of 1998.

Budget Deficit: Budget deficit fell to pre-crisis level of -1.6 billion pesos in 1994, -766 million pesos in 1995, -569 million pesos in 1996, -459 million pesos in 1997, and -560 million pesos in 1998. Budget deficit as share of GDP was 39.5 percent in 1993, 12.6 percent in 1994, 5.8 percent in 1995, 4.0 percent in 1996, 3.1 percent in 1997, and 3.8 percent in 1998.

External Debt: Cuba's overall debt to Soviet Union and Eastern Europe in 1989 estimated at nearly US$27 billion (using official exchange rate of 1 ruble=US$1.58) and at US$30.2 billion in 1990 (using official exchange rate of 1 ruble= US$1.78). Because value of ruble vis-à-vis United States dollar fell sharply in 1990s, so did value of Cuban debt in United States dollar terms. Outstanding debt grew from nearly US$8.8 billion in 1993 to about US$9.1 billion in 1994, US$10.5 billion in 1995, and US$11.2 billion in 1998.

Official Exchange Rate: Value of peso dropped precipitously in 1990s as Cuban citizens expressed very strong preference for holding United States dollars to obtain goods and services not available through centrally planned first economy. In mid-1994 peso reached probably its lowest point when it was exchanged at about 150 pesos for one United States dollar. In second half of 1990s, unofficial exchange rate fluctuated in range of twenty to twenty-two pesos for one United States dollar. By January 2001, peso valued at twenty-two to dollar.

Foreign Investment: By end of 1998, 345 joint ventures had been created. Foreign investment for 1985–95 period totaled about US$2.1 billion.

Fiscal Year (FY): Calendar year.

Transportation and Telecommunications

Air and maritime transportation services provide access to almost every location in Cuba. Infrastructure of ports, airports, and warehouses supports extensive foreign trade.

Roads: Estimated 60,858 kilometers of highways, including 29,4820 kilometers of paved roads and 31,038 kilometers of unpaved roads. Main highway: Central Highway, mostly two-lane highway running for 1,200 kilometers from Pinar del Río in west to Santiago de Cuba in east. Multilane National Expressway being constructed, with 650 kilometers, from Pinar del Río in west to near Sancti Spíritus in east, completed.

Railroads: Standard-gauge railroads, 4,807 kilometers. Railroad transportation neglected since 1959 in favor of truck transport. Poorly maintained railroad system consists of one main axis running length of island, connecting all of major urban centers, economic zones, and ports, either directly or through branches. About one-third of railroads carry both passengers and freight, with rest dedicated to transport of sugarcane. Central railroad line under major reconstruction since late 1970s; equipment last updated with diesel locomotives manufactured in former Soviet Union and Czechoslovakia. Service has been reduced since early 1990s, and fuel shortages and frequent equipment breakdowns have made system largely unreliable.

Ports: Most important of eleven main ports capable of handling general export and import cargoes: Antilla, Cienfuegos, Havana, Mariel, Matanzas, Nuevitas, and Santiago de Cuba. Only major deep-water ports: bays of Cienfuegos, Havana, Mariel, Matanzas, Nipe, Nuevitas, and Santiago de Cuba. Havana by far most important port. In addition, eight bulk sugar loading terminals, one supertanker terminal at Matanzas, and several other smaller import facilities, as well as specialized port facilities for fishing fleet. Number one in sugar export, port of Cienfuegos capable of handling one-third of Cuba's sugar production through its bulk sugar terminal. Its pier for handling oil and oil byproducts allows berthing of ships up to 50,000 tons. Guantánamo Bay, leased by United States for naval base, separated from rest of Cuba by twenty-nine-kilometer boundary.

Pipelines: In late 1980s, Cuba completed an oil import facility at port of Matanzas and a pipeline linking it with new refinery built in Cienfuegos.

Air Transport and Airports: Ten of seventeen civilian airports handle international flights, with nine linked to nine largest tourist resorts. Main international airports include Camagüey, Ciego de Ávila, Cienfuegos, Havana, Matanzas, Santiago de Cuba, and Varadero. Main national airports that handle primarily domestic flights: Baracoa, Bayamo, Cayo Largo, Guantánamo, Holguín, Manzanillo, Moa, Nicaro, Nueva Gerona, and Santa Clara. Cuba's flag carrier: Consolidated Cuban Aviation Company (Empresa Consolidada Cubana de Aviación—Cubana). Of estimated 170 airports in 1999, seventy-seven paved and ninety-three unpaved.

Telecommunications: Domestic telephone countrywide trunk system coaxial cable; Havana and Isla de la Juventud have fiber-optic distribution. Country has two microwave radio relay installations (United States-built installation is old, with capacity of 960 channels; Soviet-built installation is newer, with capacity of 1,920 channels). Both analog and digital mobile cellular service established. Telephone density very low: 4.5 to 5.5 telephone lines per 100 inhabitants. Number of main telephone lines in use in 1995: 353,000. Existing lines and systems not suitable for speed, bandwidth, and applications of modern telecommunications. Number of mobile cellular telephones in use in 1995: 1,939. About 70,000 new telephone lines being installed per year, with emphasis on public telephones throughout Cuba. International telephone system uses satellite earth station Intelsat. Telecommunications Company of Cuba, S.A. (Empresa de Telecomunicaciones de Cuba, S.A.—ETECSA) is the state-owned telecommunications company. Principal foreign investor: STET, Italy's largest telecommunications concern.

Government and Politics

Administrative Subdivisions: Fourteen provinces (*provincias*) listed from west to east: Pinar del Río, La Habana, Ciudad de La Habana, Matanzas, Villa Clara, Cienfuegos, Sancti Spíritus, Ciego de Ávila, Camagüey, Las Tunas, Granma, Holguín, Santiago de Cuba, and Guantánamo. Special Municipality (*município especial*): Isla de la Juventud (Isle of Youth). Number of municipalities in national territory: 169.

Government: Communist state with one party, Communist Party of Cuba (Partido Comunista de Cuba—PCC). Current government of Fidel Castro Ruz in power since January 1, 1959. Castro president (chief of state and head of government) since December 2, 1976. As chief of state, Castro president of thirty-one-member Council of State and thirty-nine-member Council of Ministers. Cuba's most important executive institution: seven-member Executive Committee of Council of Ministers. Six vice presidents of Council of State among Cuba's most important politicians. Fidel Castro's formally designated successor: General of Army Raúl Castro Ruz, first vice president of Council of State and Council of Ministers and minister of Revolutionary Armed Forces (Fuerzas Armadas Revolucionarias—FAR). Provincial government consists of fourteen provincial assemblies, each headed by an Executive Committee, each with president and at least seventy-five members. Municipal government consists of 169 municipal assemblies, each headed by a president, who heads one of 169 executive committees.

Legislature: Under 1992 constitution, all formal legislative powers (including powers of amending constitution) vested in 601-member unicameral National Assembly of People's Power

(Asamblea Nacional del Poder Popular—ANPP; hereafter, National Assembly). National Assembly meets only two or three times annually for two or three days. National Assembly elects Council of State to make all decisions on behalf of National Assembly when latter not in session (most of time).

Judiciary: Minister of Justice administers all courts, which are all subordinate to National Assembly and Council of State and lack independence. Office of State Prosecutor (Fiscalía General de la República), overseeing all law enforcement, also subordinate to National Assembly and Council of State. Members of five-chamber Supreme Court of Cuba (Tribunal Supremo Popular—TSP) nominated for terms by minister of justice and confirmed by National Assembly, except for TSP's president and vice president (nominated by president of Council of State) and military chamber members (nominated jointly by ministers of justice and FAR). Each province has four-chamber provincial courts exercising jurisdiction over most types of crimes. Each municipality has municipal courts handling minor crimes.

Electoral System: National Assembly seats elected directly from slates approved by special candidacy commissions; members serve five-year terms. National elections last held January 11, 1998, when single official slate received 89.7 percent of vote and 601 seats; only 5 percent of voters voided their ballots or voted blank. In 1998 National Assembly elections, overall results slightly more favorable to government than in 1993, reflecting trend toward economic stabilization and recovery during intervening years. Results also more favorable to government in La Habana Province, where single slate received 88.4 percent of votes cast and percentage of null or blank ballots fell to 7 percent. Next elections to be held in 2003.

Politics: Under 1992 Electoral Law, Cuba has multi-candidate single-party elections with no effective campaigning at municipal level and entirely uncompetitive rules but some campaigning at provincial and national levels. At all levels, political regime sharply constrains freedom of political association. Cubans not free to associate in political party other than Communist Party of Cuba (PCC) to contest elections. Candidates running for office in different provinces and municipalities on official slate cannot associate into formally constituted "factions." Public authorities and PCC retain right to shape associational patterns at all levels. To be elected, candidate must receive more than half of valid votes cast. No candidate failed to be elected in 1993 and 1998 national elections.

Political Party: PCC remains only party, still Marxist-Leninist, but now also follower of José Martí. Political Bureau party's leading decision-making institution and Cuba's most important decision-making entity. Party congresses govern PCC by adopting party's statutes and its programs, and choosing membership of Central Committee and Political Bureau. Party congresses meet approximately every five years, Central Committee Plenum at least once a year, and Political Bureau once a week. Party membership 800,000 members by time of Fifth Party Congress in 1997.

Mass Media: Principal daily newspaper: *Granma*, official organ of PCC. Official organ of Union of Young Communists (Unión de Jóvenes Comunistas—UJC): *Juventud Rebelde*, weekly. Long-standing newsmagazine: *Bohemia*. Television remains principal source of communication for entertainment and news, although costs of production for television led government to reduce number of channels and of hours of transmission in 1990s. Number of television broadcast stations in 1997: fifty-eight. Number of televisions in 1997: 2.64 million. Radio became one of Cuba's more dynamic mass mediums in 1990s. Number of radio broadcast stations in 1998: AM 169, FM fifty-five, shortwave, one. Number of radios in 1997: 3.9 million.

Foreign Relations: Collapse of Soviet Union and communist governments of Central and Eastern Europe in 1989–90 left Cuba with no international allies. During 1990s, Cuban economic relations with Central and Eastern Europe plummeted. Cuban economic relations with Russia focused principally on barter trade, at market prices, exchanging sugar for petroleum. Consistent with its general policy on non-servicing of any debts, Cuba refused to service its large accumulated international debt to Russian Federation. Russian ground troops, stationed in Cuba since 1962 Cuban Missile Crisis, departed in 1992. Cuban relations with China recovered only gradually from the sharp bilateral split that had become manifest in 1966. With collapse of European communism, however, political relations warmed more quickly between these two remaining communist governments. Between 1989 and 1991, Cuba repatriated its overseas troops from all countries to which they had been deployed. In 1992 it announced that it had stopped providing military support to revolutionary movements seeking to overthrow governments in other countries. Traditional tension in United States relations with Castro regime continued through 1990s, aggravated by Cuba's encouragement of unauthorized emigration to United States in 1994, unilateral United States efforts to tighten economic embargo against Cuba, Cuba's human rights violations, and, in 1999–2000, dispute over custody of Cuban boy rescued off coast of Florida. Cuban policy has been most effective within Anglophone Caribbean. Admitted to Caribbean Tourism Organisation in 1992, Cuba in 1994 became founding member of Association of Caribbean States.

National Security

Armed Forces: Total active armed forces members in 2000: 58,000. Revolutionary Armed Forces (FAR) includes ground forces, Revolutionary Navy (Marina de Guerra Revolucionaria—MGR), and Antiaircraft Defense and Revolutionary Air Force (Defensa Antiaérea y Fuerza Aérea Revolucionaria—DAAFAR). Army, including conscripts and ready reserves, totals 45,000; MGR, 3,000; DAAFAR, 10,000. Army reserves: 39,000. Ready reserves serve forty-five days per year to fill out active and reserve units.

Military Service: Two years compulsory military service for young men beginning at age seventeen (registration at age sixteen); women volunteers serve three years.

Paramilitary Forces: Youth Labor Army (Ejército Juvenil de Trabajo—EJT): 65,000. Civil Defense (Defensa Civil): 50,000. Territorial Troops Militia (Milicias de Tropas Territoriales—MTT): 1 million. State Security: 20,000, including Ministry of

Interior's Special Troops (Tropas Especiales). Border Guard Troops (Tropas Guardafronteras—TGF): 6,500.

Defense Relations: Has long maintained contacts with armed forces of many developing world nations, including those in Latin America, as well as with Canada and Western Europe. International contacts broadened in 1990s. Ties with Chinese Popular Liberation Army (PLA) most important relationship with foreign military service to develop since Soviet Union's demise.

Defense Budget: Figures vary. According to the International Institute for Strategic Studies' *Military Balance 1999–2000,* defense expenditures amounted to estimated US$720 million in 1997 and estimated US$750 million in 1999, and defense budget in 1999 amounted to only P650 million, or US$31 million. Military expenditures approximately 4 percent of GDP (1995), according to the *World Factbook 2000,* or 1.6 percent, according to the *Encyclopaedia Britannica.* Military expenditures 2.2 percent of Gross National Product (GNP—see Glossary) (1995), or 2.3 percent (1997), according to *World Military Expenditures and Arms Transfers, 1998.*

Military Units: Army divided into three Regional Commands: Western (most important), Central, and Eastern, each with three army corps. Army units include four or five armed brigades, nine mechanized infantry brigades (three mechanized infantry, one armored, one artillery, and one air defense artillery regiment), one airborne brigade, fourteen reserve brigades, and one border brigade. Navy has four operational flotillas. Cubañas headquarters of Western Naval District, Holguín of Eastern Naval District. Naval bases at Cienfuegos, Cabañas, Havana, Mariel, Punta Movida, and Nicaro.

Foreign Forces: As of 1999, United States: 1,080 personnel stationed in Guantánamo (United States Navy: 590; United States Marines: 490). Russia: 810 personnel (signals intelligence); military advisers: an estimated ten military personnel.

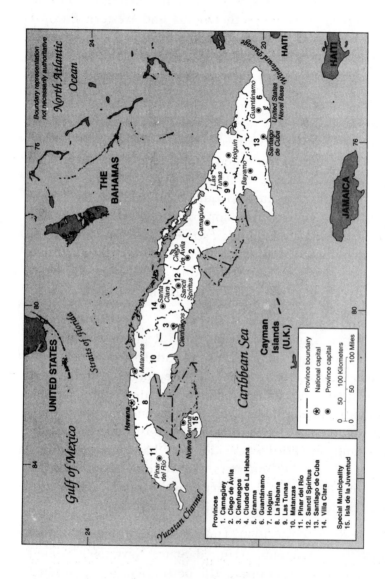

Figure 1. Administrative Units, 1999

Introduction

THE WORLD'S SEVENTH LARGEST island, with a total land surface of 110,860 square kilometers (about the size of Pennsylvania), the independent republic of Cuba is the largest and westernmost island in the West Indies, lying less than 150 kilometers south of Key West, Florida. Despite being an island country, it is, in terms of population (more than 11.1 million in 2001), the ninth largest country in Latin America and the sixty-seventh largest in the world, according to the United States Bureau of the Census.

Cuba's strategic location at the entrance to the Gulf of Mexico between North America, the Caribbean, and Central America has played an important part in its history since Christopher Columbus discovered the island in 1492. The Spaniards first used Cuba as an operational base for the conquest of Mexico; Mexico's Yucatán Peninsula lies only about 150 kilometers to the west of the island. During almost four centuries of Spanish rule, the Spaniards also used the island's natural harbors as ports for treasure-laden ships sailing between the New World and Spain. Spain imposed oppressive trade restrictions on its Cuban colony, however, until forced to reevaluate its policy after Britain occupied Havana in 1762–63 and lifted the restraints on commerce.

Cuba has been of strategic interest to the United States at least since 1808, when President Thomas Jefferson called it "the key to the Gulf of Mexico." It was suddenly transformed in that century from an unimportant "ever-faithful isle" of Spain into the world's major sugar producer, attracting United States economic interests. Liberated from Spain by the United States in the Spanish-American War (1898), Cuba came under the tutelage of a new power. The United States granted the island independence and a degree of self-rule in 1902 but kept it dependent as a result of economic involvement and successive military interventions, as authorized by the Platt Amendment (see Glossary) of 1901. The corrupt and brutal dictatorship of Fulgencio Batista y Zaldívar (president, 1940–44, 1952–59), during which there were 20,000 political killings, ended with its overthrow on January 1, 1959, by a popularly supported guerrilla force led by Fidel Castro Ruz (president, 1976–), who has presided over his own brand of communist dictatorship ever since.

In addition to being separated from its northern neighbor by the Florida Straits, Cuba has been isolated socially, economically, politically, and diplomatically from the world's leading democracy for more than four decades by an embargo originally imposed by the United States in 1960 for Cold War reasons. Only one other country has been under embargo longer than Cuba, namely the Democratic People's Republic of Korea (more commonly known as North Korea), which the United States began embargoing in 1950.

This fourth edition of *Cuba: A Country Study* would be incomplete without a discussion of the embargo, which the Cubans have always called the blockade (*el bloqueo*), and of Cuba's diplomatic strategy to counter it. The embargo has had a significant impact on numerous aspects of the island country, including the history of the Castro regime, the health of the population, the economy, foreign policy and relations, and the armed forces. Moreover, Cuba in the new millennium cannot be adequately understood without taking into account the embargo and the reality that the island nation is no longer isolated in the world, that it has become gradually integrated into the world system, and that it has been undergoing significant social and economic changes since the end of the Cold War. For these reasons, and also because American public opinion has become increasingly critical of the embargo, this introduction assesses the overall effectiveness of the sanctions during the 1960–2001 period; summarizes Cuba's efforts to use diplomacy, "internationalism" (see Glossary), and trade relations in the Western Hemisphere to counter it; and shows how the evolution of international opinion toward Cuba has evolved in response to the embargo.

Since the end of the Cold War, Cuba's diplomatic efforts to counter the embargo have resulted in very significant progress toward the reintegration of the once-pariah island nation into the Caribbean and Latin American communities and the world in general, with the main exception of the United States. As a result of this development, the United States' embargo of Cuba has become paradoxical. According to embargo critics, it would be in the United States' national interest to have Cuba fully integrated into the world community rather than isolated and unconcerned with international opinion regarding the issue. The record shows that when Cuba was relatively isolated during the Cold War it lashed out by engaging in foreign adventurism and overt domestic repression. As Cuba has become more a part of the world community since the end of the Cold War, diplomatic concerns have increasingly constrained the Castro regime from engaging in foreign subversive activities and domestic repression. Although the regime lacks the funding to engage in foreign adventurism in any case, it no longer can risk jeopardizing its hard-won diplomatic relations by exporting revolution on even a small scale. Nor can it risk jeopardizing its economically vital tourism industry by repressing Cuban citizens in full view of thousands of foreign tourists.

Because the objective of the embargo is to keep Cuba isolated, the existing situation limits the enormous potential American social, economic, and political influences that scholars seem to agree could accelerate the process of change in Cuba. Scholars also seem to agree that change in Cuba comes only from outside the country. For this reason, the issue of how the United States can best promote change in Cuba is likely to need further consideration. By keeping United States influence out of Cuba and thereby allowing the Cuban regime to maintain itself in power, the embargo has, according to this argument, served as a sort of reverse Berlin Wall.

Less than a year before the real Berlin Wall began to be erected on August 13 (coincidentally Fidel Castro's birthday), 1961, Washington began to build its invisible barrier around the island nation in retaliation against the Castro regime's nationalization of all United States businesses and property. On January 22, 1962, the Organization of American States (OAS—see Glossary), meeting in Punta del Este, Uruguay, reluctantly voted by a two-thirds majority to expel Cuba from the OAS because the island nation had "voluntarily" placed itself outside the inter-American system. Only fourteen of the twenty-one members voted for the resolution, with Argentina, Bolivia, Brazil, Chile, Ecuador, and Mexico abstaining.

Cuba's foreign policy subsequently became more radical. The embargo, the disastrous Bay of Pigs invasion of April 1961, and the Cuban Missile Crisis of October 1962 set the confrontational tone for Cuba-United States relations for the rest of the twentieth century. Historian Jaime Suchlicki is critical of President John F. Kennedy for allegedly being confused and indecisive about the Bay of Pigs invasion and for being apologetic about the outcome. Had Kennedy lived, however, Cuba-United States relations might well have taken a turn for the better, a development that would have been anathema to the Cuban-American community at that time. Kennedy reportedly had second thoughts about the embargo, just as he had regrets about the Bay of Pigs fiasco. On November 17, 1963, he met with French journalist Jean Daniel and asked him to tell Castro that the United States was now ready to negotiate normal relations and to drop the embargo. According to Kennedy's press secretary, Pierre Salinger, "If Kennedy had lived, I am confident that he would have negotiated that agreement and dropped the embargo because he was very concerned with the role the Soviet Union was playing in Cuba and Latin America...."

The OAS adopted the United States-imposed embargo on July 26, 1964, as a result of Castro's policy of supporting "armed struggle" (the old Cuban euphemism for terrorism and insurgency) in selective Latin American countries. Within two months, every Latin American country except Mexico had broken diplomatic relations with Cuba, and the island nation became a pariah state. In 1967, at the time of Ernesto "Che" Guevara's fatal guerrilla foray in Bolivia, Cuba had diplomatic relations with only one country in Latin America—Mexico.

In the early 1970s, Cuba's rapprochement with Latin America and the Caribbean in the form of "internationalist" assistance, especially medical aid, began to improve the revolutionary nation's regional image, with diplomatic results that began to erode the embargo. Increasingly, Cuba gave precedence to bilateral relations, such as those between Cuba and Mexico, that enhanced the island's diplomatic and trade security over support for revolutionary movements. Diplomatic relations were revived with various Caribbean and South American nations.

By 1975 Havana had restored diplomatic relations with ten of Latin America's twenty-two nations. The OAS, impressed by Cuba's overt goodwill efforts and Castro's diplomatic and trade overtures but apparently downplaying his continuing covert support for revolution, lifted its twelve-year-old diplomatic and economic sanctions on the island nation on July 29, 1975, with the approval of sixteen countries, including the United States. On August 21, 1975, the administration of President Jimmy Carter eased the trade embargo in order to allow United States subsidiaries in third countries to trade with Cuba.

With hopes of a rapprochement, Cuba and the United States agreed on May 30, 1977, to establish interests sections in each other's countries, beginning September 1. During 1978, however, Cuba's military involvement in Angola's civil conflict dashed any hope that the United States gesture to liberalize the embargo would lead to normalization of bilateral relations. Prospects for improved relations between Havana and Washington further dimmed during 1978–79, as Cuba expanded its military involvement in Africa and increased its support for revolutionary movements in Central America and the Caribbean.

At the start of the 1980s, several events disrupted Cuba's normalization campaign and contributed to the downturn in Cuba's relations with Latin America. The downturn began with Castro's failure to condemn the Soviet invasion of Afghanistan. Second, Cuba's handling of refugee incidents involving the Peruvian and Venezuelan embassies in Havana was inept and led to the 1980 Mariel Boat-Lift and the flight of more than 100,000 refugees. Castro's attempt to use the Mariel Boat-Lift to force the United States to discuss normalization of relations further exacerbated the situation. In addition, Castro reverted to virulent revolutionary rhetoric and continued support for armed struggle, particularly in Central America, Colombia, and Chile. These actions led the administration of President Ronald Reagan to make new efforts to isolate Cuba.

In 1980–81 Cuba suffered major diplomatic setbacks. Its relations were suspended, downgraded, or otherwise damaged with Ecuador, Peru, and Venezuela because of Cuban subversive activities or breaches of diplomatic protocol, and Colombia and Costa Rica broke relations with Havana over Cuba's renewed emphasis on armed struggle. Cuba's involvement in Grenada in 1981 created considerable tension in the Eastern Caribbean and led two other countries—Jamaica and St. Lucia—to break relations. Upon taking office as prime minister of Jamaica that January, Edward Seaga expelled the 500 Cubans working on the island and declared the Cuban ambassador persona non grata. By late 1981, Cuba had become so ostracized that even longtime friend Mexico failed to invite Castro to the North-South Conference held in Mexico that October, despite his position as leader of the Nonaligned Movement (see Glossary).

The Malvinas/Falkland Islands War between Argentina and Britain in 1982 provided Cuba the opportunity that it needed to break out of its self-created diplomatic isolation and proved to be a watershed in Cuba's relations with Latin America. Cuba improved its standing in South America and specifically its relations with Argentina, Ecuador, Peru, and Venezuela by joining them in siding with the right-wing military regime in Argentina. The Cuban government overlooked its ideological differences with the Argentine junta in large part because trade relations with Argentina gave Cuba another conduit for circumventing the embargo; Argentina soon surpassed Mexico as Cuba's largest regional trading partner.

Cuba's relations with the Eastern Caribbean, however, reached a nadir in 1983. The joint United States/Eastern Caribbean intervention in Grenada on October 25 put an abrupt end to Cuban activities in Grenada. The only members of the thirteen-member Caribbean Community and Common Market (Caricom—see Glossary) to retain relations with Cuba were Guyana and Trinidad and Tobago, neither of which supported the joint United States/Eastern Caribbean military action against Grenada.

By the mid-1980s, as a result of Havana's new overtures to Latin America, Cuba was again enjoying a rapprochement of sorts with the region. Fortunately for Castro, the demise of right-wing authoritarian regimes and the transition to democratic government in several South American nations in the 1980s improved his prospects for courting the region in the wake of the Falklands/Malvinas War and for normalizing relations with more countries.

Cuba also had become more integrated into Latin American multilateral organizations, such as the Latin American Parliament and the Latin American Integration Association (see Glossary), the successor to the Latin American Free Trade Association (see Glossary). Havana finally bowed to Latin American pressure to support the Central American peace process in 1985 by belatedly endorsing the proposals initiated by the Contadora Support Group (see Glossary), which called for the removal of all foreign forces from Central America.

At the same time that Cuba began emerging from its diplomatic isolation in the mid-1980s, Castro overestimated his self-appointed role in Latin America as revolutionary statesman. His attempt to fill a regional leadership vacuum by rallying Latin American and other developing world nations around his proposals for a debtors' cartel, a repudiation of Latin America's US$360-billion foreign debt, and a "new world economic order" was a failure. Although he succeeded in persuading Peru's President Alán García Pérez to suspend his country's debt payments, Castro's grandstanding elicited mainly skepticism in Latin America and the broader arenas of the developing world.

In 1986 the Reagan administration renewed attempts to isolate Cuba in the Americas by further tightening the embargo. Cuba was able to continue reducing its diplomatic isolation, however, by using its "internationalist" workers to provide medical, educational, construction, and other assistance to numerous countries. Although, until the early 1990s, Cuba's "internationalist" support to a number of politically unstable countries in the developing world also included military, guerrilla, and security support, the small-scale Cuban aid to nations where Havana sought to cultivate relations created goodwill that led to the resumption of relations with numerous countries. Contrary to assertions that Cuba provided "internationalist" assistance only to "ideologically compatible" countries in the 1970s and 1980s, Cuba aided several right-wing regimes, such as Peru in June 1970, Nicaragua in December 1972, Honduras in September 1974, and the Dominican Republic in 1987.

In November 1987, as a result of the goodwill created by Cuba's "internationalist" aid and its diplomatic overtures in the Latin American region, the presidents of eight Latin American countries—Argentina, Brazil, Colombia, Mexico, Panama, Peru, Uruguay, and Venezuela (the so-called Group of Eight—see Glossary)—agreed at a meeting in Acapulco that Cuba should be invited to rejoin regional organizations, including the OAS. The Group of Eight's proposal was the first direct regional challenge to United States policy toward Cuba.

Despite the calls for reintegration of Cuba into the Latin American community, most countries in the region remained wary of the communist island state, and antagonism between Cuba and the United States was greater in 1987–88 than at any time in the previous ten years. The Castro regime voiced support for Costa Rican President Oscar Arias Sánchez's Esquipulas II accord for peace in Central America in 1987, but the sincerity of Havana's support of the peace process came under question when the plan began to stagnate in late 1988.

Tension between Cuba and the Soviet Union increased in 1989, and Cuba's economic slide began. Castro formally welcomed Soviet President Mikhail S. Gorbachev during his official visit to Cuba in March, but Cuba's special relationship with the collapsing Soviet Union was already all but over. Castro reportedly had defied Gorbachev's advice that Cuba should get on track to political pluralism and a free market.

During the Cold War, the international community and news media bestowed on Cuba and Castro greatly exaggerated global significance as minor global actors. But as Havana's once-close ideological allies in the former Soviet bloc distanced themselves from the Castro government in 1989–90, this inflated aura of importance declined markedly.

In 1989 skepticism about the Castro regime began increasing in the Americas as a result of the televised Havana trials of several Ministry of Interior officials and Division General Arnaldo T. Ochoa Sánchez, hitherto a national hero, on trumped-up charges of drug trafficking. The summary executions of Ochoa and three other pro-reform officers in July 1989 shocked democratic leaders in Latin America, Spain, and elsewhere. By lauding the installation in September 1989 of the de facto, short-term president of Panama, Castro also earned bad publicity for flouting Latin American and world criticism of the lack of a democratic system in Panama.

In an attempt to counter the fallout from the Ochoa affair and to improve his country's regional standing, Castro again made overtures suggesting his willingness for closer relations with Latin America, which he described publicly as Cuba's "common fatherland" and "common future." In October 1989, the Group of Eight, absent Panama, added its voice to those calling for Cuba's reincorporation into the OAS. Castro, who throughout the 1960s had referred to the OAS contemptuously as the "ministry of colonies," announced Cuba's willingness to rejoin the organization, if formally invited.

Reaching out diplomatically became more urgent for the island nation as its estrangement from its one-time allies in the former Soviet bloc became increasingly apparent during 1990. In that pivotal year, the Soviet Union and Eastern Europe, whose Council for Mutual Economic Assistance (Comecon— see Glossary) trade bloc accounted for as much as 85 percent of Cuba's trade during the 1980s, significantly reduced their ties to Cuba. The Soviet Union also substantially reduced its financial support, and Cuba found itself no longer an indispensable Soviet ally. The Soviet Union now regarded it as a drain on its diminishing resources and of questionable value as a Soviet proxy in conflicts in the developing world that were no longer of interest to Moscow.

As a result of Nicaragua's presidential election in December 1989, Cuba lost a key regional ally. Subsequently, the Castro government, as the only Marxist-Leninist regime in a region of democratically elected governments, increasingly stood out in 1990 as an anachronism. Although the OAS nevertheless voted that year to admit Cuba as a member, the United States vetoed the OAS vote.

In order to survive the loss of its longtime Soviet benefactor and to improve its standing in the world, Cuba put a higher priority in the 1990s on continuing to reintegrate itself into the Latin American community of nations (including the Caribbean region), on expanding its relations globally, and on developing its tourist industry. Cuba also began actively seeking to cultivate alternative relationships, not only with major developing world nations, particularly China, but also with wealthy capitalist countries, such as Japan.

Regionally, Cuba focused its efforts on the Eastern Caribbean. By 1990 Cuba had begun new diplomatic initiatives to improve its relations with Caricom and to obtain observer status on a number of Caricom standing committees, including health and education. Caricom's decision in 1990 to promote cooperative projects with Cuba facilitated Cuba's rapprochement with the English-speaking Caribbean.

By 1990 Latin America and Cuba's status in the region had also changed significantly. The democratically elected governments that had replaced military regimes in the region had opened diplomatic and trade relations with Cuba (often simply to demonstrate their independence of United States policy) and had admitted it into more inter-American organizations. In addition, Cuba appeared to have sharply curbed its support for armed struggle in South America and the Caribbean, although it continued to support the insurgency in El Salvador.

As Cuba pursued its foreign policy of expanding diplomatic relations, it continued its traditional domestic policy of repression. In defiance of the March 5, 1990, vote by the United Nations Commission on Human Rights in Geneva calling for continued scrutiny of human rights in Cuba, the Castro regime began to crack down on the nascent human rights movement that had flowered since 1989. By April 1990, while communist rule was collapsing in Eastern Europe, the regime had crushed the Cuban human rights movement led by dissident Gustavo Arcos Bergnes, president of the Havana-based Cuban Committee for Human Rights (Comité Cubano Pro Derechos Humanos—CCPDH).

A short time later, beginning on July 9, 1990, the Castro government damaged relations with Italy and Switzerland, as well as with traditional friends and important trading partners, such as Czechoslovakia, Mexico, and Spain (Cuba's principal Western creditor), by interfering with attempts by a few dozen Cuban asylum seekers to obtain sanctuary in the embassies or diplomatic residences of these nations in Havana. But despite these setbacks, Cuba was elected on October 18, 1990, for the first time since 1956, to a seat on the United Nations Security Council as one of the ten nonpermanent members. Cuba won the votes of all Latin American and Caribbean nations, as well as the largest number of votes cast for any of the aspirants to vacant seats (146 votes out of a possible 156).

In the wake of the democratic tidal wave that swept away Cuba's allies in Eastern Europe and the Soviet Union in 1989–91, Castro defiantly maintained that Cuba's "socialist" system was unique and would remain unaffected by the sudden demise of East European socialism and the rise of democratic reformism. While the Castro government pursued a policy of fostering foreign relations with most countries, it simultaneously sought to keep the Cuban population from being contaminated ideologically, not only by the democratic revolution that had overpowered his former communist allies but also by other outside influences, such as democracy in the Americas, globalization, and capitalism. Gorbachev's policy of glasnost (openness) was anathema to Castro, who openly sided with hard-line conservative Soviet leaders. In the early 1990s, Castro continued to insulate Cuba to a considerable extent from the political and ideological repercussions of the events in the communist bloc, aided by the nation's geographical distance from Eastern Europe and the former Soviet Union, the embargo-imposed isolation from the United States, and the government's highly effective repressive apparatus.

In 1991, as the full weight of the embargo finally began to be felt in Cuba, Castro faced one of the most critical years of his rule since the Bay of Pigs invasion thirty years earlier. Cuba's severe economic crisis and mounting international pressure on the Castro regime to democratize generated some overly optimistic predictions that 1991 would likely be Castro's last year in power.

On May 24, 1991, in the wake of the Cold War's end, the Castro regime completed withdrawing its military troops from Africa and began focusing on implementing the policy, adopted in 1989, of opening its economy and attracting foreign investment. To that end, Havana sharply shifted its efforts from building its Revolutionary Armed Forces (Fuerzas Armadas Revolucionarias—FAR) to developing an international tourism industry and expanding international relations. The new emphasis on tourism was in response to the country's precipitous economic deterioration resulting not only from the cutoff of Soviet aid and the breakup of economic and trade relations with East European countries and the Soviet Union, but also from Castro's unwillingness to radically restructure the economy to introduce free markets and private ownership. The continuation of the embargo, for its part, exacerbated the country's economic collapse.

Cuba's participation in the First Ibero-American Summit of civilian heads of state of nineteen Latin American nations and of Spain and Portugal held on July 18–19, 1991, in Guadalajara, Mexico, prompted Havana's rapprochement with Chile, Colombia, and other countries. Leaders in the region urged Castro to quicken the pace of reform in Cuba in return for closer relations and possible reincorporation into the OAS. On August 2, 1991, the Latin American Parliament voted 154 to twenty-seven, with thirty abstentions, for a resolution asking for an end to the embargo of Cuba. Cuba continued to make diplomatic advances in Latin America and the Eastern Caribbean during 1992.

Spurning the worldwide appeal to lift the embargo, the United States, in the apparent belief that the collapse of the post-Soviet Castro regime was imminent, intensified its embargo on October 15, 1992, with the passage of Representative Robert G. Torricelli's Cuban Democracy Act (see Glossary). This legislation, which President George Bush signed into law on October 23, tightens restrictions on humanitarian aid, specifically food, medicine, and medical supplies. In addition to prohibiting American subsidiaries in third countries from trading with Cuba, the Act prohibits any vessel that had engaged in trade with Cuba within the previous 180 days from entering into the United States to load or unload freight.

The Cuban Democracy Act outraged the international community. Many countries claimed that the Act violated both international law and United Nations resolutions that food and medicine cannot be used as weapons in international conflicts. Britain and Canada immediately barred United States subsidiaries located in their countries from complying with its provisions. On November 24, fifty-nine members of the United Nations General Assembly voted against the United States in favor of a resolution proposed by Cuba demanding that the law and the trade embargo be terminated. Only Israel and, by mistake, Romania, voted with the United States in opposing the measure. The European Union (EU—see Glossary), Canada, Argentina, Mexico, and Japan were particularly incensed over the Cuban Democracy Act.

Cuba again did well on the diplomatic front in 1993–94. At the Third Ibero-American Summit, held in Salvador, Brazil, on July 15–16, 1993, the leaders of Latin America, Spain, and Portugal called for an end to the United States trade embargo of Cuba. On November 3, the United Nations General Assembly voted by eighty-eight to four (Albania, Israel, Paraguay, and the United States), with fifty-seven abstentions, to condemn the embargo. In 1994 the leaders of Latin America, Spain, and Portugal became increasingly critical of the embargo and called for the United States to ease its stance. At the twenty-fourth General Assembly of the OAS in Brazil in early June, the foreign ministers of most OAS members called for the end of the embargo and the readmission of Cuba to the OAS. At the Ibero-American Summit meeting held in Cartagena, Colombia, on June 14, the leaders of nineteen Latin American nations and of Spain and Portugal approved a communiqué calling for the elimination of the unilateral United States economic and trade boycotts of Cuba and readmission of Cuba to the OAS.

Three months later, on September 10, 1994, the fourteen-member Rio Group (see Glossary) also called for incorporating Cuba fully into regional bodies and lifting the embargo of Cuba. In addition, the Rio Group urged "peaceful transition toward a democratic and pluralist system in Cuba." On October 26, the United Nations General Assembly again voted overwhelmingly to demand an end to the embargo against Cuba, with 101 in favor, two opposed (the United States and Israel), and forty-eight abstaining. In contrast to international opinion, in 1994 only 35 percent of Americans favored ending the embargo, while 51 percent opposed ending it, according to a September 1994 *Time*/Cable News Network (CNN) poll.

Throughout his regime, Castro has invoked the threat of United States military invasion of Cuba as justification for militarizing the island, and he has blamed the embargo for the hardships and privations caused by his own social, economic, and political policies. An independent countrywide survey conducted in Cuba in late 1994 and designed by the *Miami Herald* and CID/Gallup, the Costa Rican affiliate of the Princeton, New Jersey-based Gallup, found that the great majority (62 percent) of Cubans blamed the United States economic sanctions, rather than Cuba's political system, for economic difficulties.

On March 22, 1995, conservative members of the United States Congress, seeing no reason to change the status quo, proposed to tighten the embargo even more through passage of the Cuban Liberty and Democratic Solidarity Act (see Glossary; more commonly known as the Helms-Burton legislation). This legislation proposed augmenting the embargo extraterritorially by punishing foreign companies that do business with Cuba. Meeting in Quito, Ecuador, on May 22–23, the foreign ministers of the Rio Group unanimously condemned the bill. The bill's adoption by the Congress in October 1995 prompted the leaders of Latin American countries, Spain, and Portugal, all attending the Ibero-American Summit in Bariloche, Argentina, at the time, to issue a strong condemnation of United States policy toward Cuba. Shortly thereafter, on November 2, one hundred and seventeen members of the United Nations General Assembly voted to condemn the embargo; only the United States, Israel, and Uzbekistan voted in favor of it.

In retaliation for the shooting down by two Cuban MiG–29 fighter jets of two civilian planes piloted by four members of a Cuban exile group, Brothers to the Rescue, over international waters, within sight of Key West, on February 24, 1996, the United States Senate approved the conference report to the Helms-Burton legislation by a vote of seventy-four to twenty-two on March 5. Canada, Russia, the EU, and the fourteen-member Caricom strongly condemned the bill. Despite the international furor aroused by the bill, President William Jefferson Clinton signed the Helms-Burton legislation into law on March 12, thereby halting a series of liberalizing measures toward Cuba. The new law did not deter foreign companies from entering into joint ventures with Cuban state companies. Moreover, every six months for the remainder of his administration, President Clinton waived Title III, which would have allowed United States citizens to sue foreign companies for conducting business on confiscated American property in Cuba.

The Helms-Burton Act intensified international outrage over the embargo. On August 26, 1996, thirty-four members of the OAS passed a resolution declaring that the Helms-Burton Act "does not conform to international law." That October 28, the EU approved legislation forbidding compliance with the Helms-Burton Act. On November 12, the United Nations General Assembly voted by 138 to three (United States, Israel, and Uzbekistan) to condemn the embargo. (For the first time, all fifteen EU countries voted yes.) On November 28, Canada's Parliament passed legislation penalizing companies for obeying the Helms-Burton Act.

The Castro regime's repressive policies, however, continued to limit international solidarity with the island nation. For example, in May 1996 Cuba's failure to enact political reforms and economic liberalization led the EU to suspend discussions with Havana on an economic cooperation agreement. At the annual Ibero-American Summit, held in Santiago, Chile, on November 10–11, 1996, Latin American leaders pressed Castro to make democratic changes on the island, while they denounced moves by the United States to isolate Cuba. On December 2, the EU further conditioned improvement in political and economic relations with Cuba and developmental assistance on progress in human rights and fundamental democratic reforms in Cuba.

Cuba responded to the Helms-Burton Act by adopting a law in January 1997 that penalizes United States citizens who seek restitution of their expropriated properties under the Helms-Burton law. More significantly, the United States was also subjected to retaliatory legislation from its trade partners, and in 1997 the United Nations General Assembly voted 143 to three against the embargo of Cuba. Individual countries flouted the embargo. For example, in August 1997 France announced a trade agreement with Cuba.

During his visit to Cuba on January 21–25, 1998, Pope John Paul II criticized the embargo several times. The papal visit had a beneficial effect on Cuba's international image. Responding to the pope's call for the world to open up to Cuba and Cuba to open up to the world, numerous celebrities and senior officials and leaders of foreign governments visited Havana during the year. Several countries, including Guatemala, the Dominican Republic, and Spain, restored diplomatic relations with Cuba as a result of the papal visit.

Moreover, in the aftermath of the papal visit, the Castro government released many of its 1,320 political prisoners, leaving between 350 and 400 in prison. In April 1998, the United Nations Commission on Human Rights, for the first time in several years, voted down a United States-backed resolution condemning Cuba.

Acknowledging the impact of the pope's visit to Cuba, President Clinton, on March 20, 1998, eased controls on licensing procedures of direct humanitarian charter flights to Cuba, on resuming cash remittances up to US$300 per quarter for the support of close relatives in Cuba, and on developing procedures for streamlining and expediting licenses for the commercial sale of medicines and medical supplies and equipment to Cuba. President Clinton also agreed to work on a bipartisan basis with Congress on the transfer of food to the Cuban people. Havana, however, subsequently announced that it would refuse all direct American humanitarian aid as long as the United States maintained the embargo on Cuba.

Underscoring the mounting isolation of the United States on the Cuba embargo issue, the United Nations General Assembly on October 14, 1998, again passed a resolution calling for an end to the embargo. An overwhelming majority (157 votes, with twelve abstentions) pitted the United States and, symbolically at least, Israel against most of the world.

Despite the worldwide criticism of the embargo, on January 5, 1999, President Clinton declined the recommendation of twenty-four United States senators requesting that he establish a National Bipartisan Commission to review United States policy toward Cuba. At the same time, the president announced five minor changes in the embargo: broadening cash remittances, expanding direct passenger charter flights from New York and Los Angeles to Cuba, reestablishing direct mail service to Cuba, authorizing the sale of food and agricultural inputs to independent entities in Cuba, and expanding exchanges among academics, athletes, and scientists.

American public support for the embargo began to show signs of cracking. A Gallup poll released on May 24, 1999, showed that, in contrast to the 1994 *Time*/CNN poll, only 42 percent of those polled supported the embargo, while 51 percent favored ending it. The poll also found that 71 percent of Americans supported reestablishing diplomatic relations with Cuba.

On November 9, 1999, the United Nations General Assembly, by a vote of 155 in favor to two against (the United States and Israel), again adopted a resolution on the need to end the embargo of Cuba. Nevertheless, the island nation's poor human rights record continued to keep many countries at arm's length. Staunch traditional allies such as Canada and Mexico had tended to overlook the Castro government's human rights record, but that attitude began to change in the late 1990s, especially after Havana put a harsh new law on dissent into effect in February 1999. The legislation, which provides a maximum prison sentence of twenty years, includes penalties against unauthorized contacts with the United States and the import or supply of "subversive" materials, including texts on democracy, by news agencies and journalists. That March a court used the new antisedition law in sentencing four dissidents to prison terms of up to five years, despite Canadian Prime Minister Jean Chrétien's personal request to Castro in a meeting in Havana in April 1998 for their freedom. Beginning in April 1999, relations between Cuba and Canada—the largest foreign investor in Cuba and Cuba's second-largest trade partner, behind Spain—cooled over the Castro regime's continued crackdowns on dissident journalists and human rights activists. Canada had already halted its unsuccessful campaign to restore Cuba's membership in the OAS.

In general, human rights issues seemed not to interfere greatly with Cuba's relations with Latin America and the Caribbean. At the Ibero-American Summit held in Havana in November 1999, Mexico's President Ernesto Zedillo did what no Mexican leader had done before, when he made an implicit call for greater democracy in Cuba, but Cuban-Mexican relations remained unchanged. Nor were human rights a factor in Cuba's strong relations with Venezuela. These relations greatly strengthened after Hugo Chávez Frías, a leftist military officer and populist, was inaugurated as president in February 1999, an event attended by Castro. Nor did human rights issues prevent Paraguay, South America's only hold-out, from reestablishing full diplomatic relations with the island nation on November 8, 1999.

By providing small-scale "internationalist" aid, Cuba has continued to reap diplomatic dividends. In 1998 Cuba reportedly had 2,759 "internationalist" technical workers, professionals, and specialists in eighty-six countries. In late December 1998, in the aftermath of Hurricane Mitch, which devastated Central

America during the October 27 to November 1 period, Cuba dispatched about 600 medical doctors to aid the affected populations of Belize, Guatemala, Honduras, and Nicaragua. In the immediate aftermath of the flooding and mud slides that devastated a large area of Venezuela in December 1999, Cuba sent more than 400 health-care personnel to assist in the recovery efforts. In August 2000, Cuba aided El Salvador in combating an outbreak of dengue fever.

Despite Cuba's continuing condition as an embargoed nation, the only major country that Cuba was isolated from in 2001–01 was the United States, and the only Latin American countries still without diplomatic relations with Havana were El Salvador and Honduras. Relations between Cuba and the United States were still limited to Interests Sections in each other's capitals.

As a result of Havana's diplomatic and "internationalist" initiatives and the global propaganda value to Cuba of the United States embargo, the island nation today no longer stands alone in the court of world opinion. Growing international resentment of the embargo appears to have spurred many countries to open relations with Cuba. By 2000 Cuba's public renunciation of its longtime support for armed struggle and revolutionary military "internationalism" in the early 1990s and its diplomatic initiatives during the decade had allowed the island nation to upgrade its international standing, in the form of diplomatic relations with 172 members of the 187-member United Nations. With the important exception of the United States, Cuba was no longer seen as a rogue state but as a diplomatically accepted member of the world community.

In Latin America and the Caribbean, Havana had succeeded in reestablishing relations with twenty-nine countries and in improving relations with others, such as El Salvador and Honduras. Havana has twenty-three accredited missions in the region, and twenty-one Latin American and Caribbean countries have diplomatic posts in Havana. The Castro regime's diplomatic comeback in Latin America may be a far more significant Cuban achievement in the region than Cuba's short-lived revolutionary victories in Grenada and Nicaragua.

Viewed as a David against Goliath, Cuba is now seen internationally as a victim of a United States isolation strategy widely regarded as punitive and counterproductive, and, because it supposedly ignores the Cuban reality, as irrational. With increasingly large majorities, the United Nations General

Assembly has voted overwhelmingly every year since 1992 for resolutions condemning the unilateral economic sanctions. Only Israel has regularly stood with the United States in opposing United Nations resolutions condemning the embargo since 1992. Israel, however, is an active trading partner of Cuba, as well as a major investor, even though it lacks diplomatic relations with Havana.

The embargo is widely seen as having helped to keep the Castro regime in power by preventing Cubans from being influenced by new ideas about human rights, economics, and democracy, and by giving Castro a scapegoat on which to blame Cuba's economic problems. Many Cubans reportedly believe that his regime would not last a year if the embargo were lifted. Just as President Reagan's decision to let American students travel to Eastern Europe helped to bring down the Berlin Wall on November 7, 1989, the Castro regime, according to embargo critics, would be unlikely to withstand the ideological and socioeconomic impact of millions of United States visitors. Cuban-American visitors alone have had a profound impact on Cuban society. As sociologist Sergio Díaz-Briquets points out herein, "Many observers feel that the 1980 Mariel outflow was a direct result of family visits as many disaffected Cubans were deeply influenced by contacts with Cuban-American visitors and the perceptions of their experience abroad."

Despite Cuba's geographical proximity, United States citizens, unlike those of most other countries, have not been free to visit their island neighbor. United States law restricts travel to Cuba to all but a few American and foreign government officials traveling on official business (including representatives of international organizations of which the United States is a member), journalists regularly employed by a news-reporting organization, and Cuban-Americans, who are accorded the special right to make a once-a-year visit to family relatives. The United States ban on travel to Cuba was lifted on March 18, 1977, but it was reimposed on April 19, 1982, and has remained in effect since then.

The legal restrictions notwithstanding, as many as 154,000 United States residents, including about 124,000 Cuban-Americans and 30,000 others, such as journalists, humanitarian workers, and academics, reportedly visited Cuba legally during 2000. Estimates of United States citizens, including Cuban-Americans, who visited the island nation illegally in 2000 range from 22,000 to 80,000. Despite these numbers, Cuba remains largely terra incognita for its northern neighbor as a result of the embargo. It is not surprising, therefore, that, according to a February 1–4, 2001, poll by Gallup, 68 percent of Americans had an unfavorable opinion of Cuba, while only 27 percent had a favorable opinion.

The Castro government, however, has not helped its case with its poor human rights record, which has included sharp restrictions on basic rights, such as freedom of expression, association, assembly, and movement. Indeed, there has been a pattern of crackdowns following United States initiatives to ease the embargo, as if Castro were signaling that his government would prefer not to have the embargo lifted just yet.

Human rights issues relating to Cuba also continued to be of concern to several democratic governments in the Americas in 2000 and 2001. In late April 2000, Argentina and Chile voted "yes" in favor of a United Nations Commission on Human Rights vote censuring Cuba for its human rights record, while Mexico, Colombia, and Ecuador abstained. The final vote was twenty-one in favor, eighteen against, and fourteen abstaining.

In 2000–01, once-close relations between Cuba and Mexico and Spain appeared to be on a somewhat more formal footing because of the Castro government's continued hard line regarding human rights issues. At the Ibero-American Summit held in Panama on November 17–18, 2000, Castro criticized Mexico and Spain for supporting an El Salvador-proposed resolution against terrorism because it did not mention Cuba's complaints of Cuban-American-sponsored terrorism perpetrated in Cuba. (Throughout the 1990s, Cuban-American exiles boasted of paramilitary raids into Cuba, including a series of hotel bombings in Havana in 1997.) Cuba's refusal to sign the resolution strained ties with Spain.

Two weeks later, on December 1, 2000, Castro attended the presidential inauguration of Mexico's President-elect Vicente Fox. With Fox's inauguration, relations between Cuba and Mexico began on a new footing as the Institutional Revolutionary Party (Partido Revolucionario Institucional—PRI), which had ruled Mexico for seven decades and which historically was friendly to Cuba, relinquished the presidency to the opposition. Nevertheless, in 2001 Mexico's economic and commercial relations with Cuba continued, and bilateral relations remained friendly and cooperative.

Cuba's human rights record notwithstanding, international disapproval of the embargo has continued to increase. The continuation of the embargo has remained a significant irritant in the relations of Latin America and United States allies with Washington. The embargo has remained widely criticized internationally as a relic of the Cold War that lost its justification when Cuba ceased being a satellite of the former Soviet Union. It is also widely viewed as having been highly ineffective in achieving its main foreign policy goals, and as having failed to oust the Castro government and to keep Cuba from gradually reestablishing cultural, diplomatic, economic, and other ties with Latin America and the rest of the world.

In 2000 and 2001, there was no lack of support in Washington for continuing the embargo of Cuba. The embargo lobby continued to argue that economic sanctions should not be lifted until Castro allows free elections and open markets, releases all political prisoners, and restores civil liberties—conditions that were not made when the embargo was first imposed. Embargo proponents continued to argue that United States economic ties to Cuba would only boost the Castro regime politically and economically and not benefit the Cuban people. They continued to argue that sustained sanctions can work. Despite the annual Cuban-American visits to Cuba that are a major source of financial support for the Cuban economy in the form of remittances, Cuban-American activists in South Florida have continued to express outrage that American tourists have been visiting Cuba illegally and spending money there.

The forty years of embargo have been costly for Cuba. According to a Cuban complaint lodged with the United Nations General Assembly in October 1998, the United States' trade embargo on Cuba had cost the Caribbean island US$60 billion in lost revenues, severely undermining the country's economy. In April 2000, Cuba's public health minister told the Group of Seventy-Seven (see Glossary) Summit in Havana that the embargo had cost Cuba's health sector more than US$2 billion. Cuba also announced in April that the embargo had cost the country's world-renowned cigar industry US$1.1 billion in lost revenues.

Despite its economic losses from the embargo, Cuba has been able to circumvent it since 1991 by finding trading partners among the former socialist nations and among market-economy countries. Cuba's top four trading partners in 1999 were Spain, Canada, China, and Venezuela, in that order. In 2000 Venezuela, as a result mainly of crude oil and refined product exports to Cuba, jumped to the top spot, with Spain following at a close second, according to Cuba's Central Bank.

The pro-embargo lobby has found its stance under increasing scrutiny in the new millennium. The story of six-year-old Elián González, the ship-wreck survivor who lost his mother at sea and was cared for by relatives in Miami's Little Havana, put Cuba back in the news in early 2000 and created a widespread perception that Cuban-Americans in Miami were extremist. The backlash prompted lawmakers to reexamine United States policy toward Cuba.

After four decades of status quo in relations between Havana and Washington, the embargo was widely regarded in the United States as an archaic policy. Increasingly, the American public and lawmakers questioned whether a United States policy that was initially formulated and adopted at the height of the Cold War could still be relevant in the post-Cold War era. United States public opinion favored a reassessment by Washington of the 1960s-era policy framework of the embargo. A May 2000 Gallup poll showed that 48 percent of Americans favored ending the embargo, as opposed to 42 percent in favor of maintaining it. The same poll, perhaps influenced by the Elián controversy, found that 57 percent of Americans favored renewing diplomatic relations with Cuba (a 14 percent decline, however, since the May 1999 poll), while only 36 percent opposed resuming ties.

Embargo critics include those advocating an approach that calls for engaging Cuba in dialogue while lifting some United States sanctions that they believe hurt the Cuban people. Others call for lifting the embargo completely and restoring all relations. They argue that the embargo continues to provide Castro with a pretext not only for keeping Cuban society militarized (through mass militias) and under the tight control of the Communist Party of Cuba (Partido Comunista de Cuba—PCC), but also for exploiting United States-Cuban hostilities. Like the long-standing Platt Amendment authorizing United States military intervention in Cuba from 1901 until its abrogation in 1934 and the leasing "in perpetuity" of the Guantánamo naval base in 1903 and, since 1934, for less than US$4,000 in annual rent, the embargo has long turned public sentiment in Cuba as well as international opinion against the United States.

Lifting the embargo and restoring relations, critics argue, would be more likely to lead to a peaceful transition to democracy rather than violent civil conflict. Advocates of a policy change toward Cuba also point to the international consensus against the embargo, the suffering that it has caused the Cuban people, and lost opportunities to United States businesses interested in competing with Canadian and European companies operating in Cuba. Moreover, it is argued that lifting the embargo would not necessarily help the regime but instead would deprive Castro of one of his most important propaganda weapons.

On May 25, 2000, a proposed measure to permit the export of food, medicine, and medical products to Cuba marked a significant shift in Congress and reflected a growing impatience with the embargo's failure. In particular, business interests, including American farmers, alarmed that international competitors had been making major sales to countries under unilateral United States sanctions, were joining traditional opponents of the embargo. As a result of a growing desire by American farmers and business people to trade with Cuba, by 2000 the once-powerful but still influential embargo lobby had been reduced to the vocal right wing of the Cuban-American community in Florida, its allies in Congress, and other conservatives. Nevertheless, a Florida International University poll released in October 2000 found that, although only 25.8 percent of Cuban-Americans felt that the embargo had worked well, 64.2 percent of the Cuban-American population expressed strong support for its continuation.

The new congressional proposal of May 25, 2000, seemed to herald a gradual easing of the embargo, but its actual helpfulness to Cuba appeared to be minimal at best because of the conditions attached to it. For example, the proposal disallowed bartering, purchase of any Cuban goods by United States companies, or extension of any public or private credit to cash-strapped Cuba from the United States to finance purchases. In addition, under the Cuban Democracy Act, ships visiting Cuba would still be banned from docking at a United States port during the following six months.

Despite the prospects raised by the proposed exemption, a Cuban-American congressional representative from Florida forced removal of the trade provision from the agricultural spending bill on grounds that it was an unacceptable attachment to a spending bill. Furthermore, a House-approved measure that would have dropped enforcement of United States restrictions on travel to Cuba by Americans was replaced by a provision that codified the ban on American tourism to the island. Moreover, on June 20, 2000, the Senate voted, by fifty-nine to forty-one, to again defeat the proposed creation of a National Bipartisan Commission to study the effectiveness of the economic embargo of Cuba.

On November 9, 2000, the international community reiterated its contrary stance when the United Nations General Assembly passed, with 167 votes in favor, a nonbinding, Cuba-drafted resolution urging Washington to lift the embargo as soon as possible and all countries to refuse to comply with it. Only the United States, Israel, and the Marshall Islands voted against it, while four other countries abstained.

On March 10, 2001, Caricom went on record against Cuba's isolation from the integrational process linked with the creation of a Free Trade Area of the Americas (FTAA) zone. In an official statement, Caricom said that any policy of isolation and expulsion is counterproductive in the post-Cold War era.

The United States' tattered diplomatic prestige became evident with its ouster from the fifty-four-nation Commission on Human Rights on May 3, 2001. The unprecedented action reportedly reflected a growing frustration with America's allegedly noncooperative actions and attitudes toward international organizations and treaties, as well as its votes involving the Palestinians and countries like China, Cuba, and Iran. On May 19, President Bush specifically linked the Commission's vote on Cuba with the subsequent loss of the United States' seat.

Despite the favorable votes in the United Nations and other multinational fora over the embargo issue, Cuba's pariah status in organizations or pacts involving the United States continued. Cuba was the only country in the Americas to be excluded from the Summit of the Americas held in Québec, Canada, on April 20–22, 2001, when the agreement was approved, because only democratic countries are eligible to participate in the proposed FTAA.

Although its economic system survived the 1990s, the island nation underwent significant social and economic changes during the decade as the economy geared toward dollar-based tourism, dollar remittances, and foreign investment. Political scientist Jorge I. Domínguez observes herein that since the 1990s Cuba has been undergoing a gradual social and political transition of a still undetermined nature. He explains that a proto-civil society has grown as a consequence of government reforms (such as greater religious freedom), as many Cubans become largely independent of the state for their livelihood, and as younger, more dynamic, well-educated, and pragmatic leaders emerge in key institutions. Sergio Díaz-Briquets explains that the greater religious freedom "will inevitably contribute to the undermining of the ideological, social, political, and economic power of the Cuban totalitarian state." He adds that tourism and the dollarization of the domestic economy "will further accelerate a process of social change." And he points out that the presence of so many foreign visitors limits the regime's ability to suppress civil and political dissent.

In the first quarter of 2001, the Castro regime, apparently more confident from having surmounted the country's economic depression of the 1990s and angry over international criticism of its human rights practices, returned to the mass protests, hard-line rhetoric, and confrontational diplomacy that had characterized the island nation during the decades of the Cold War. Instead of consumer ads, billboards displayed the old "Socialism or Death" signs. The resurgence of the hard line has been attributed to the divisive effect of the regime's 1993 decision to allow the circulation of dollars and the regime's concern that discontent could get out of control unless redirected away from regime policies and toward the United States.

Legalization of dollars made it possible for taxi drivers, hotel workers, and other Cubans, including prostitutes, associated with the tourism industry and getting tipped or paid in dollars to earn far more than professionals, such as government officials, military officers, doctors, scientists, and university professors. Since dollars became legal, resentment has grown between those with access to dollars and those without. Cubans receiving remittances from relatives in the United States have also contributed to the growing inequalities.

Many Cubans reportedly also greatly resent the system of tourism apartheid that prevents Cubans from getting near tourist resorts for foreigners or entering hotels for foreign tourists (unless they are employees), that reserves first-class medical facilities for foreigners and high Cuban officials, and that compels many young Cuban women to prostitute themselves for dollars.

If its frequent, government-sponsored, anti-United States rallies held in Havana's open-air structure called the protest drome (*protestodromo*) are any indication, the regime appears to be fearful that this seething resentment could get out of control and, instead of being directed against the United States embargo and government, develop into mass protests against the Castro regime. In this regard, the embargo appears to serve the Castro regime well as a scapegoat and as a mechanism for bottling up growing resentment, at least for the short term. Mounting popular resentment may have the potential for unraveling the Castro regime and is reminiscent of the social discontent that erupted in the 1959 Revolution.

On July 14, 2001, President Bush announced plans to strengthen the embargo by enforcing limits on cash payments that Cuban-Americans may send to their relatives on the island and by preventing American tourists from visiting Cuba. On July 16, however, in an unexpected setback for the Cuban exile lobby and its Congressional allies, President Bush announced that he would continue the Clinton administration policy of waiving Title III of the Helms-Burton Act for six months at a time. On July 25, for the second successive year, the House voted, by 240 to 186, to approve a measure that would effectively lift the ban on most travel to Cuba, but the measure again died in the Senate.

Embargo critics believe that the politically charged embargo has long narrowed the perceptual lens through which United States policymakers view the prospects for effecting a peaceful transition to democracy in Cuba. For example, a related argument against the embargo is that, in the absence of relations between Cuba and the United States, Washington lacks the ability to influence the direction of the generational transition of Cuba's social, economic, and political system, or even the military, still dominated by aging generals of the generation of Fidel and Raúl Castro. According to this argument, whether post-Castro Cuba remains under a regime headed by the uncharismatic General of the Army Raúl Castro Ruz, the first vice president of the Council of State and Council of Ministers and minister of the Ministry of the Revolutionary Armed Forces (Fuerzas Armadas Revolucionarias—MINFAR), or instead somehow undergoes a gradual transition to democracy, the lifting of the embargo would allow Cuba to accelerate a process of change that the United States could influence for the better.

Additional groundwork for Raúl Castro's eventual succession as chief of state reportedly was made as a result of a reorganization of the FAR High Command in January 2001. Five generals—two FAR vice ministers and the commanders of the eastern, central, and western armies—were promoted to the rank of army corps general (*general de cuerpo de ejército*). Until then, Minister of Interior Abelardo Colomé Ibarra was the sole individual holding that rank.

Few Cubans reportedly believe that the Cuban Revolution will outlast Fidel Castro. According to Professor Jorge Domínguez, younger, more competent, and more urbane civilian members of the political elite who are more attuned to economic and political experimentation include Carlos Lage Dávila, secretary of the Executive Committee of the Council of Ministers; and Ricardo Alarcón de Quesada, president of the National Assembly of People's Power (Asamblea Nacional del Poder Popular). Although one of these civilian leaders might make a more credible figurehead president in a post-Fidel Castro transitional government than Raúl Castro, it appears unlikely that there will be any transition from communism to democracy in Cuba until the Cuban population is allowed to elect a president in a free and fair election.

Moreover, there are two important aspects of civil-military relations in Cuba that should be taken into account in any assessment of post-Fidel Castro Cuba. First, the military is well regarded by the Cuban population and is considered by many observers to be the most powerful institutional actor in the political system. Second, although it seems unlikely that the Cuban elites and the population in general would back a regime headed by Raúl Castro, a long-time ideological hardline military man who lacks political charisma and any international stature, he will likely succeed his brother, as long as he retains the support of the military.

In assessing the prospects for change in Cuba's relatively closed society, the impact of the information revolution is also an important consideration. The Cuban government's efforts to expand Cuba's ties with the nations of the world and its reported plans to create an information technology (IT) business on the island make its long-standing policy of trying to control the population's access to information increasingly untenable. Cuban authorities have long stifled Cuba's IT development. Because the Internet poses a serious threat to the Cuban government's information monopoly, Internet access is allowed only to businesses, foreigners, and about 40,000 officials of state entities. According to reports by foreign news media, Internet access in Cuba is forbidden to the average citizen. The Castro government denied these reports in early

March 2000, however, claiming that access to the Internet is limited only for technological and financial reasons.

As the leaks in its information monopoly proliferate, the regime is likely to find its policy of keeping the population isolated from the global revolution in IT to be a hopeless and highly counterproductive task. Despite the obstacles, a growing number of younger Cubans, ignoring official Internet prohibitions, have been able to purchase computers on the black market and to find a way to tap into official Internet links without permission. Cuba reportedly began to open a dozen cyber-cafes around Havana in 2001, but the US$5 per hour Internet access charge is likely to limit use of these facilities mainly to tourists and the relatively few Cubans who are paid in dollars.

Although this general review of the embargo issue suggests that the arguments in favor of lifting the embargo seem to greatly outweigh those against it, the matter is complicated by the Castro regime's unceasing hostility toward America and the regime's potential or actual military, intelligence, and terrorist threats to United States national security interests. In regard to the potential military threat, an unclassified United States Department of Defense report entitled "The Cuban Threat to U.S. National Security" concluded that the Cuban Armed Forces posed "a negligible conventional threat" to the United States or surrounding countries by the late 1990s. Although the greatly downsized and financially strapped Cuban Armed Forces may not pose a significant conventional threat, the report failed to take into account an Armageddon-type crisis, such as a scenario in which the regime were about to be overthrown. In that situation, the Castro brothers could order some unanticipated terrorist attack against the United States, possibly using MiGs. Furthermore, the Cuban military is highly defensive, with much of its equipment hidden in a vast system of caves and tunnels.

Russian President Vladimir Putin's visit to Cuba in December 2000 raised the specter of a new alliance between Havana and Moscow, but reportedly was mostly symbolic rather than a signal of a resumption of once-close relations between Cuba and the former Soviet Union. Rather than resume Russia's subsidizing of Cuba, Putin reportedly was more interested in getting the Castro government to repay Cuba's multibillion-dollar debt to Russia, as well as making an opening for large Russian companies that might be interested in investing on the island. Putin's visit reportedly failed to achieve a breakthrough in relations, a significant trade deal, or even an agreement by Castro to repay the debt.

President Putin's visit did, however, reportedly result in the signing by the Russian and Cuban defense ministers of a military and technical plan that calls for the parties to develop cooperation in such spheres as military personnel training, modernization of armaments, and military equipment. The agreement specifically concerns repair and modernization of Cuban planes made in the former Soviet Union. To that end, a Cuban military delegation headed by Army Corps General Julio Casas Regueiro, deputy minister of the FAR, visited Moscow in late April 2001.

Cuba's anti-United States intelligence activities have also apparently impeded reestablishment of diplomatic relations with the United States. While the Castro regime has overtly pursued a diplomatic strategy to win acceptance in the international community, it has a well-publicized record of using its diplomatic posts, including the United Nations, for intelligence activities against the United States and its North Atlantic Treaty Organization (NATO) allies.

The Cuban intelligence threat was also manifested in 2001 by cases of proven or alleged espionage by Cuban citizens residing in the United States. On June 8, 2001, a federal jury in Miami, concluding a six-month trial, convicted five Cuban agents of espionage against the United States. Five other indicted members of the spy ring, which was revealed in September 1998, pleaded guilty in exchange for cooperation and received lighter sentences. The leader of the ring, Gerardo Hernández, the only one charged and convicted in a murder conspiracy in the death of the four Brothers to the Rescue members whose planes were shot down on February 24, 1996, received a sentence of life imprisonment. Four others were able to flee to Cuba and avoid prosecution. Reflecting the anti-United States hostility of the Castro regime, *Granma International*, the English version of Cuba's official newspaper, on June 24, 2001, headlined the actions of the Cuban spies as "a heroic behavior in the entrails of the monster," a slogan that also appeared on a large poster behind Fidel Castro's podium when he addressed a crowd of 60,000 in Havana on June 23, along with photos of the five indicted Cubans, and on the T-shirts of many Cubans at weekly rallies in Havana. In addition, on September 22, 2001, the *Washington Post* reported the arrest by agents of the United States Federal Bureau of Investigation

(FBI) of a senior intelligence analyst for Cuban affairs, on charges of spying for the Castro regime.

Since 1964 Cuba's intelligence threat to the United States and NATO has been symbolized by the Russian-operated Lourdes electronic eavesdropping site, which has targeted the United States. On October 17, 2001, however, President Putin, reversing his earlier stance, announced that Russia will close the Lourdes facility in order to save the annual rental fee of US$200 million, which Castro had refused to cancel as partial payment for Cuban debts to Moscow. The Castro government angrily denounced Putin's decision.

Cuba's potential terrorist threat needs to be put in some context. According to Professor Jaime Suchlicki, one of the "major themes" of Cuba's international relations by the 1990s included continuous support of "movements of national liberation in Asia, Africa, the Middle East, and Latin America." By the early 1990s, the regime appeared to have largely ceased active support of revolutionary groups in the absence of subsidies and other support that it had received from the former Soviet Union. According to Professor Domínguez, Cuba announced in 1992 "that it had stopped providing military support to revolutionary movements seeking to overthrow governments in other countries." By most accounts, Cuba has promoted tourism, trade, and diplomacy instead of terrorism and revolutionary military internationalism since the early 1990s.

Nevertheless, the regime has reportedly continued ties with a number of international terrorist groups, and it has remained on the United States Department of State's list of nations sponsoring terrorism. According to the Department's *Patterns of Global Terrorism 2000*, published in April 2001, the island country continued to provide safehaven to members of several terrorist groups, as well as to several United States terrorist fugitives. Active terrorist groups with members taking refuge in Cuba include the Basque Fatherland and Freedom (Euzkadi Ta Azkatasuna—ETA) and Colombia's National Liberation Army (Ejército de Liberación Nacional—ELN) and Revolutionary Armed Forces of Colombia (Fuerzas Armadas Revolucionarias de Colombia—FARC).

Cuba also has continued to maintain ties to other state sponsors of international terrorism, according to the report. In addition, in May 1998 then Secretary of Defense William Cohen testified in Congress that Cuba possesses advanced biotechnology and is capable of mass-producing agents for biological warfare. The Castro regime also reportedly poses a cyberterrorism threat to the United States infrastructure, according to Admiral Tom Wilson, director of the Defense Intelligence Agency. During the public part of a hearing of the United States Senate Intelligence Committee on February 7, 2001, Admiral Wilson was widely reported to have told the committee, in response to a question concerning Cuba's capability for cyber warfare, that the FAR could start an "information warfare or computer network attack" that could "disrupt our military."

If Cuba is, as alleged by the Department of State report, secretly supporting international terrorism, the Castro regime could be seen by the United States as posing an unacceptable potential threat to vital United States national security interests in the post September 11, 2001, world. If Fidel Castro was willing to risk nuclear war between the former Soviet Union and the United States in October 1962, some have argued that he could become desperate enough to help Islamic terrorists use biological weapons against the United States. In the spring of 2001, Fidel Castro toured Iran, Libya, and Syria, and was quoted as telling Iranian university students that "Iran and Cuba, in cooperation with each other, can bring America to its knees." Like other nations on the list of state sponsors of terrorism, Cuba could find itself coming under increasing United States pressure to demonstrate that it deserves to be removed from the list by discontinuing to provide safehaven or other support to members of active terrorist groups.

A lack of Cuban cooperation in the antiterrorism war could impede progress toward reestablishing diplomatic relations with the United States. In his speech of September 22, 2001, Fidel Castro was unsparing in attacking the United States and its intention to wage a war in Afghanistan, contending that United States "fanaticism" was stronger than that of the terrorists who carried out the September 11 attacks. Moreover, Cuba was the only nation that failed to condemn terrorism at the United Nations General Assembly session on November 16, 2001. Instead, the Cuban foreign minister, Felipe Pérez Roque, used the forum to launch a propaganda attack against the United States. Echoing the propaganda of Osama bin Laden and the Taliban, he denounced the United States for waging an "ineffective, unjustifiable bombing campaign" in Afghanistan, which "has targeted children, the civilian population, and the International Red Cross hospitals and facilities as enemies."

Prior to the tragic terrorist attacks in the United States on September 11, 2001, many observers believed that the Castro regime would be able to maintain itself in power and continue to blame the island's socioeconomic problems on the embargo as long as the status quo, Cold War situation between Cuba and America prevailed. Major setbacks to the Cuban economy during the year, however, had, by late 2001, compelled the Cuban government to reiterate its readiness for normal relations with the United States. Tourism to the island, a critical source of dollars, fell sharply following the September 11 terrorist attacks. Another critical source of dollars, remittances from exiles in Miami, also declined sharply because of the post-September 11 economic downturn in the United States. President Putin's abrupt decision to close Russia's Lourdes listening post constituted another major loss of revenue. And on November 4, Hurricane Michelle, the island's worst storm in five decades, severely damaged crops that Cuba needed for export and domestic consumption. Creating a crack in the embargo, the aftermath of the storm prompted the first trade accords between Cuba and the United States in four decades, allowing four American companies to sell Cuba about US$20 million worth of wheat, corn, and other foodstuffs. Whether the trade deal heralds a thaw in relations remains to be seen.

Meanwhile, post-September 11 world sympathy for Cuba's financial plight and condemnation of the blockade remained unchanged, despite strong United Nations support for the United States-led war against terrorism. This fact was evident when the United Nations General Assembly again voted overwhelmingly on November 27 for an end to the United States trade embargo against Cuba. As in 2000, the vote was 167 to three (United States, Israel, and the Marshall Islands). At a time when vital national security interests of the United States were under threat by international terrorism, maintaining the status quo between Cuba and the United States no longer seemed feasible to many Americans. Thus, it remained a compelling argument, that, if Cuba were opened to unchecked United States influences through the lifting of the embargo, the Castro regime would be unlikely to keep the socioeconomic impact of American trade and millions of United States visitors, the IT revolution, and the forces of economic globalization from sweeping his communist system into the same dustbin of history now occupied by the former Soviet Union and its East European allies.

December 14, 2001

*　　*　　*

In the first half of 2002, it appeared that Castro himself was increasingly becoming a major liability in his own decades-long diplomatic offensive in Latin America. With his mind-set stuck in the Cold War and in his "untouchable" communist system of rule, Castro had succeeded in alienating even his long-time allies in the region. Despite having diplomatic relations with most countries and worldwide support for the lifting of the United States embargo, Cuba remained ostracized from the United States, and this ostracism adversely affected Cuba's relations with other countries, most notably Mexico.

As Mexico's relations with the United States and the global economy grew closer, President Vicente Fox distanced himself from Castro during the first half of the year, and Mexico's four-decades-old policy of neutrality toward Cuban human rights issues began to unravel. President Fox ended a good-will visit to Cuba on February 4 by meeting with several of the Cuban government's most prominent opponents and calling on the Castro government to pursue democratic reforms and increase human rights protections. Fox's visit and Castro's subsequent brief appearance at the United Nations development summit meeting in Monterrey, Mexico, in March set the stage for Castro's diplomatic debacle with President Fox a few weeks later.

At the United Nations Human Rights Commission meeting on April 19, Castro was especially piqued by Mexico's vote censuring Cuba. He called it a "despicable betrayal" because it allowed the measure to narrowly prevail by twenty-three to twenty-one votes. In apparent retaliation, Castro seriously damaged Cuban-Mexican relations by publicizing a humiliating tape recording that he had made of a private telephone conversation with Fox in which the Mexican president had tried to persuade Castro to cancel or cut short his attendance at the Monterrey summit the previous month in order not to "complicate" Mexican-United States relations. The audiotape was highly embarrassing to Fox because he had stated publicly that he did not ask Castro to cut short his attendance at the meeting.

For Cuba's annual May 1 commemoration, Castro continued his bitter campaign against his former Latin American allies by ordering several million Cubans to rally in the center of Havana to express condemnation of the "treasonous sycophants"—otherwise known as the democratic governments of Argentina, Chile, Costa Rica, Guatemala, Mexico, Peru, and Uruguay. These countries had joined in supporting a resolution critical of Cuba at the United Nations Human Rights Commission meeting on April 19.

Meanwhile, United States policy toward Cuba under the administration of President George W. Bush appeared reminiscent of the 1980s. President Bush committed his administration to a continuation of the traditional Cold War policy toward Cuba. Bush's call for Castro to open his country's political and economic system was part of the "Initiative for a New Cuba" launched as a result of a review that began in January. Bush said that he would veto further measures on trade with Cuba and on lifting the ban that empowers the United States Department of the Treasury to fine Americans traveling to Cuba.

In the annual publication entitled *Patterns of Global Terrorism—2001*, released by the United States Department of State's Office of the Coordinator for Counterterrorism on May 21, 2002, Cuba remained on the list of state sponsors of terrorism, despite signing all twelve United Nations counterterrorism conventions and the Ibero-American declaration on terrorism at the 2001 summit. Although the report did not mention anything about Cuba's biological weapons capabilities, in the March-June period of 2002 United States military and Department of State officials made conflicting statements as to whether Cuba possessed biological weapons. On March 19, Carl W. Ford, Jr., assistant secretary for intelligence and research of the Department of State, stated in testimony to the Senate Foreign Relations Committee that, "Cuba has at least a limited developmental offensive biological warfare research and development effort." On May 6, a week before former President Jimmy Carter's five-day visit to Cuba on May 12–17, Under Secretary of State John R. Bolton made a similar statement to a meeting of the conservative Heritage Foundation, indicating that Cuba is developing biological weapons and has "at least a limited offensive biological research and development effort" in germ warfare. Later that month, however, in response to Bolton's allegation that Cuba is developing biological weapons, Major General Gary Speer, acting commander in chief of the United States Southern Command, stated that he had seen no evidence that Cuba is producing biological weapons from its biomedical research program.

After being effusively welcomed by Castro, Carter began his historic visit to Cuba with a promise from Castro that he could visit any of the island's biotechnology research centers. Not being in Cuba on an arms-inspection mission, however, Carter toured only the Center for Genetic Engineering and Biotechnology (Centro de Ingeniería Genética y Biotecnología— CIGB) in Havana, a facility visited by thousands of foreign scientists, including 400 Americans in 2001.

Carter was the most prominent American political figure to visit Cuba in forty-three years of communist rule. As Cuban human rights advocates had hoped, his visit lent support to their campaign for greater political and economic freedom. By the time that he arrived in Cuba on May 12, dissident activists had openly collected 11,020 valid signatures on a petition calling for a national referendum to institute civil rights, the right to own and operate private businesses, electoral reform, and an amnesty for all political prisoners. Article 88 of the 1976 constitution allows any citizen who collects the signatures of at least 10,000 registered voters to petition the National Assembly for a referendum on any subject. The three-year-long petition drive was known as the Varela Project, after Félix Varela, a nineteenth-century Roman Catholic priest, philosopher, and Cuban independence activist. Although the petition was rejected when its creator, Oswaldo Payá, a dissident engineer, delivered it to the National Assembly on May 10, the Varela Project was the biggest peaceful challenge to date to the Cuban government. Despite being unsuccessful in its reform objectives, the Varela Project united more than 140 of Cuba's dissident groups in a single campaign and marked a historic victory over opposition divisiveness and apathy, as well as intimidation by the authorities.

As he had done for Pope John Paul II's visit in 1998, Castro accorded Carter the unprecedented privilege of having the country's news media broadcast the entire text of the former president's address to the Cuban people. In addition, the official newspaper, *Granma*, published Carter's entire speech in its May 16 issue, except for his comments about democracy. "Our two nations have been trapped in a destructive state of belligerence for forty-two years," Carter said in his twenty-minute address, which he delivered in Spanish. "And it is time for us to change our relationship and the way we think and talk about each other." Carter called on Castro to allow a national referendum to bring about broad reforms in political rights. He also praised the Varela Project and castigated Cuba's socialist system for denying basic freedoms.

As Cuban officials had hoped, Carter called in his speech for easing sanctions against the island nation. The next day, forty members of the United States Congress (half Democrats and half Republicans) called for unrestricted American travel and increased trade with Cuba. The continuation of the traditional policy toward Cuba was becoming increasingly unpopular in Congress, where a majority in the House and Senate reportedly favored lifting the travel ban. Nevertheless, a few days later President Bush announced that he would tighten sanctions. In a policy speech at the White House on May 20, Bush conditioned any easing of this policy on Cuba's adoption of democratic reforms, such as holding democratic elections; giving opposition parties the freedom to organize and speak, thereby allowing non-communist candidates to participate in the 2003 legislative elections; freeing all political prisoners; and allowing the development of independent trade unions.

President Bush's announced intention to expand a program to provide assistance to internal Cuban dissidents through American religious and nongovernmental organizations met with a cold reception among Cuban dissidents. A number of them reiterated their belief that aid offered by the United States government would compromise their efforts. Carter strongly warned against the proposed aid program and confirmed that the Cuban dissidents he met unanimously oppose the United States embargo on food and medicine and favor more interchange with Americans.

Having rejected the reform demands made by opposition figures and President Bush, Castro on June 12 launched a petition drive for a constitutional amendment to declare Cuba's socialist system "irrevocable." He defiantly staged a massive march through downtown Havana, while other marches were held in cities, towns, and villages throughout the island nation. Castro ordered the country's eligible voting population over sixteen years of age—totaling between 7 and 8 million of Cuba's 11 million population—to show their solidarity by signing a petition in favor of the proposed constitutional amendment. Castro's claim that 99.7 percent of registered voters signed his petition was reflective of the autocratic nature of his regime and suggested that the results were most likely rigged. Moreover, the fact that Castro felt compelled to go to such an extent to ratify his system of government seemed indicative of how worrisome the Varela Project and Jimmy Carter's visit must have been as a challenge to his rule. Just as the papal visit had resulted in a significant opening of religious freedom in Cuba, Carter's visit may have had a similarly profound impact on the human rights movement in Cuba.

Although the influx of dollars had created a vibrant underground economy, the country's economic outlook remained bleak in the first half of 2002, as tourism remained down and the sugar and nickel industries experienced continuing low prices. In June the government was preparing to close about half of the country's 156 decrepit sugar mills. The resulting dismissal of thousands of Cuban sugar workers was expected to add to the climate of tension on the island. Cuba's overall terms of trade were not expected to improve until sugar and nickel prices reversed their decline. Cuba also lost a third of its daily oil supply when Venezuela stopped shipping its inexpensive oil to Cuba in April 2002, forcing the island nation to spend millions of dollars more than planned on the world market. The negative economic trends could be reversed somewhat by a recovery in agriculture, remittances, and tourism, but the Castro regime's ratification of its "irrevocable" communist system of government effectively sentenced the country to continual suffering without any real prospect for change. The domestic opposition remained weak, but the population seemed be waiting for the moment when the maximum leader would pass from the scene, and the country could begin a long-awaited transition to democracy.

July 22, 2002

Rex Hudson

Chapter 1. Historical Setting

Statue of national hero Carlos Manuel de Céspedes in Arms Plaza (La Plaza de Armas), Havana, 1997
Courtesy Mark P. Sullivan

THE HISTORY OF CUBA began with the arrival of Christopher Columbus in 1492 and the subsequent invasion of the island by the Spaniards. Although aboriginal groups inhabited the island, they were soon eliminated or died as a result of diseases or the shock of conquest. As a result, the impact of indigenous groups on subsequent Cuban society was limited, and Spanish culture, institutions, language, and religion prevailed in Cuba. Colonial society developed slowly, with pastoral pursuits and agriculture serving as the basis of the economy. For the first three centuries after the conquest, the island remained only a neglected stopping point for the Spanish fleet that visited the New World and returned to Spain with the mineral wealth of continental America.

Cuba awakened dramatically in the nineteenth century. The growth of the United States as an independent nation, the collapse of Haiti as a sugar-producing colony, Spanish protective policies, and the ingenuity of Cuba's Creole business class all converged to produce a sugar revolution on the island. In a scant few years, Cuba was transformed from a sleepy, unimportant island into the major sugar producer in the world. Slaves arrived in increasing numbers. Large estates squeezed out smaller ones. Sugar supplanted tobacco, agriculture, and cattle as the main occupation. Prosperity replaced poverty. Spain's attention replaced neglect. These factors, mainly prosperity and Spain's involvement, delayed a move toward independence in the early nineteenth century. While most of Latin America was breaking with Spain, Cuba remained "the ever-faithful island."

Toward the end of the nineteenth century, all this began to change. Creole rivalry with Spaniards for the governing of the island, increased Spanish despotism and taxation, and the growth of Cuban nationalism all produced a prolonged and bloody war. By 1898 the United States, concerned about its economic interests on the island and its strategic interest in a future Panama Canal and aroused by an alarmist "yellow" press, focused its attention on Cuba. The emergence of the United States as the victorious power in the Spanish-American War (1898) ensured the expulsion of Spain, United States supremacy in the Caribbean, and tutelage over Cuban affairs.

In 1902 Cuba launched into nationhood with fewer problems than most Latin American nations. Prosperity increased during the early years. Militarism seemed curtailed. Social tensions were not profound. Yet corruption, violence, and political irresponsibility grew. Successive United States interventions and economic involvement weakened the growth of Cuban nationality and made Cuba more dependent on its northern neighbor.

The 1930s saw a major attempt at revolution. Prompted by a cruel dictatorship, the economic hardships of the world depression, and the growing control of their economy by Spaniards and North Americans, a group of Cubans led by students and intellectuals sought radical reforms and a profound transformation of Cuban society. In January 1934, after the overthrow of the regime of Gerardo Machado y Morales (president, 1925–33) and the short-lived first presidency of Ramón Grau San Martín (president, 1933–34, 1944–48), they were catapulted into power. Their revolution failed, however. The rise of militarism, the opposition of the United States, and divisions among Cuban political elites and within the revolutionary ranks returned the island to less turbulent times. Fulgencio Batista y Zaldívar (president, 1940–44; dictator, 1952–59) and the military emerged as the arbiters of Cuba's politics, first through de facto ruling and finally with the election of Batista to the presidency in 1940.

The end of World War II and the end of this early Batista era brought to power the inheritors of the 1933 revolution. With the election in 1944 of Grau San Martín and, four years later, his successor, Carlos Prío Socarrás (president, 1948–52), an era of democratic government, respect for human rights, and accelerated prosperity ensued. Yet political violence and corruption increased. Many saw these Auténtico administrations, that is, administrations belonging to the Cuban Revolutionary Party (Partido Revolucionario Cubano—PRC), more commonly known as the Authentic Party (Partido Auténtico), as having failed to live up to the ideals of the revolution. Others still supported the Auténticos and hoped for new leadership that could correct the vices of the past. A few conspired to take power by force.

Batista's coup d'état on March 10, 1952, had a profound effect. It led to doubts and disillusionment about the ability of the Cubans to govern themselves. It began a brutal dictatorship that resulted in the polarization of society, civil war, the over-

4

throw of the dictatorship, the destruction of the military and most other Cuban institutions, and the rise of a long totalitarian system led by a charismatic, anti-United States caudillo (see Glossary). Fidel Castro Ruz (president, 1976–) seized power on January 1, 1959, as the result of his successful guerrilla campaign against the Batista regime.

In power for four decades, Fidel Castro converted Cuba into a Marxist-Leninist society with no individual freedoms or private property and with a Soviet-style centrally planned economy (see Glossary) run by a vast and cumbersome bureaucracy that has stifled innovation, productivity, and efficiency. Despite massive Soviet aid, the Cubans sank to unprecedented levels of poverty, aggravated further by the collapse of communism in the former Soviet Union and Eastern Europe.

Cuba's alliance with the Soviets provided a protective umbrella that propelled Fidel Castro onto the international scene. Cuba's support of anti-United States guerrilla and terrorist groups, military intervention in Africa, and unrestricted Soviet weapons delivery to Cuba made Castro an important international player. Cuba's role in bringing to power a Marxist regime in Angola in 1975 and in supporting the Sandinista overthrow of the dictatorship of Nicaragua's Anastasio Somoza Debayle in July 1979 perhaps stand out as Castro's most significant accomplishments in foreign policy. In the 1980s, the United States expulsion of the Cubans from Grenada, the electoral defeat of the Sandinistas in Nicaragua, and the peace accords in Central America, including El Salvador, showed the limits of Cuba's "internationalism" and influence.

The collapse of communism in the early 1990s had a profound effect on Cuba. Without Soviet support, internationalism decreased significantly, and Cuba found itself in a major economic crisis. Minor adjustments, such as more liberalized foreign investment laws and the opening of private, but highly regulated small businesses and agricultural stands, were introduced. Yet the regime continued to cling to an outdated Marxist and *caudillista* (see Glossary) system, refusing to open the political process or the economy. Castro remained one of the last unyielding communist bulwarks bent on remaining in power and perpetuating his dynastic vision of a communist Cuba, led by his anointed successor, his brother General Raúl Castro Ruz, first vice president of the Council of State.

The Early Years, 1492–1520

The Indigenous Peoples

Knowledge about the early inhabitants of Cuba is sketchy. The people who inhabited the island at the time of Columbus's landing, estimated at about 60,000, had no written language. Most of them, although peaceful, were annihilated, absorbed, or died out as a result of the shock of conquest. Whatever information is available comes primarily from the writings of early explorers and from later archaeological discoveries and studies of village sites, burial places, and so forth. These sources indicate that at least three cultures—the Guanahatabey, the Ciboney, and the Taino—swept through the island before the arrival of the Spaniards.

The first of these, the Guanahatabey, was the oldest culture on the island. It was a shell culture, characterized by its use of shell gouge and spoon as its principal artifacts. The Guanahatabey might have come from the south of the United States, for their artifacts display certain similarities with those of some early inhabitants of Florida. Yet some archaeologists and anthropologists are more inclined to accept the theory that the Guanahatabey migrated from South America through the chain of islands in the West Indies until finally settling in Cuba. By the time of the Spanish arrival, they had retreated to the most western part of Cuba.

The Guanahatabey built no houses and lived mostly in caves. They were fruit pickers and food gatherers and did little fishing or hunting. They seem to have relied on mollusks as their principal foodstuff. Their civilization apparently was in decline by the time the Europeans arrived.

The second culture, the Ciboney, was part of the larger South American Arawak group. The Ciboney inhabited western Cuba and the southwestern peninsula of Hispaniola. It is generally agreed that the Ciboney, as well as the more advanced Taino, the other Arawak group found in Cuba, originated in South America and had island-hopped along the West Indies.

The Ciboney were a Stone Age culture and were more advanced than the Guanahatabey. They were highly skilled collectors, hunters, and fishermen and inhabited towns, usually near rivers or the sea. Some lived in caves while others had begun to inhabit primitive dwellings called *bajareques* or *barbacoas*. The Ciboney practiced some form of elementary agriculture, and their diet included turtles, fish, birds, and mollusks. Two of the more typical artifacts they developed included a stone digger *(gladiolito)* and a ball *(esferolito)*, both symbols of authority or high social status; they were also considered magical objects. The Ciboney fell prey to the more advanced Taino and became their servants, or *nabories.* Bartolomé de Las Casas, an early chronicler known as the "protector of the Indians," described the Ciboney as "a most simple and gentle kind of people who were held like savages."

The Taino was the second and more advanced Arawak group to enter the island. The Taino people occupied the central and eastern parts of Cuba, as well as most of Hispaniola, Jamaica, and Puerto Rico. The Taino made extensive use of pottery and stone artifacts that are reminiscent of Old World neolithic artifacts. The short, olive-skinned Taino people subjected their children to artificial cranium changes by binding the frontal or occipital regions of their heads during early childhood; hence, their faces and particularly foreheads were unusually wide. They preferred high and fertile terrain close to sources of fresh water and lived in small villages in round houses with conical roofs made up of bamboo and thatched palm called *caneyes* or rectangular ones called *bohios.*

The Taino developed a rather advanced economic system based on agriculture with commonly cultivated fields. The cultivation and preparation of *yuca* (manioc), a sturdy tuber, played a significant role in their society. After the *yuca*, which has a period of growth longer than a year, had been harvested, the Taino grated it, drained it of its poisonous juice, and baked it into unleavened bread called *cassava*, which the Spaniards labeled "bread of the earth." This bread was both nutritious and tasty and kept for several months, even in humid weather.

Tobacco, cotton, corn, and white and sweet potato were also an important part of the Taino economy. Tobacco was used for smoking as well as for religious ceremonies and for curing the ill. After the Spanish occupation, tobacco became an important item for export. Cotton was mostly used for hammocks, bags, and fishing nets. Both the manufacture of textiles and the making of pottery items were tasks performed by women, while men engaged in hunting, fishing, or agriculture. The Taino also developed a number of wooden artifacts, such as powerful canoes, which gave them great mobility by water.

Society was organized along distinct class lines. At the top was the chief, or *cacique*, who managed all the affairs of the community and ruled over a specific territory. The line of inheritance to become a *cacique* was not direct; the eldest son of the *cacique's* eldest sister became chief when the former *cacique* died. If the *cacique* did not have any sisters, then his eldest son would inherit the post. The *caciques* were aided by the *nitaínos*, a group of advisors who supervised communal work and seem to have been in charge of various sectors of the population. Aware of the *nitaínos'* importance in controlling the labor supply, the Spaniards used them later on as overseers on their plantations. Next to the *nitaínos* was the medicine man, or *behique*. The lower class was composed of the *nabories*, who did most of the work of the village.

The Taino believed in a supreme invisible being, and their religion was dominated by a series of gods represented by idols. Ancestor worship was common, and the Taino carved special idols resembling their ancestors. The souls of the dead were thought to reside in a nearby island and to return at night to hunt the living.

In terms of economic development, social organization, technological advances, and art, the native peoples of Cuba were far inferior to the more advanced civilizations of the mainland, such as the Maya and Aztec of Mexico or the Inca of Peru. The Ciboney and Taino left only a mild imprint on Cuba's later culture; the Guanahatabey left almost none. There was little mingling of races between Spaniards and Indians. A new society, first of Spaniards and then of Spaniards and blacks, supplanted the indigenous society. New institutions, new values, and a new culture replaced the old ones. Some Indian words, foods, and habits, as well as agricultural techniques, however, were retained by later generations. Retained also was the *bohio*, the typical and picturesque dwelling of many Cuban farmers, which still can be seen today and remains perhaps the most visible legacy of the native society.

For the most part, however, the Cuban native peoples' contribution to the development of a Cuban nationality must be considered minor. Nevertheless, for generations after the conquest, Native American warriors such as Hatuey, who fought the Spanish conquest in eastern Cuba, were glorified in the pages of Cuban history books and raised to the status of folk heroes. They represented for Cuban children a symbol of native resistance against the oppressive Spanish conquistador. The Indians' innocence and kindness were contrasted with the cruelty of the Spanish invaders. But for those present-day

Cubans in search of the roots of a uniquely Cuban national identity, this Indian heritage was not enough of a foundation. Unlike for the Mexicans, the glory of the Aztec past was not there for the Cubans to turn to. Instead, Cuban writers in search of the roots of Cuban nationality would later look to Spanish or Negro contributions and try to find in them the missing link with the past, but with little luck. The Spanish heritage was dismissed as part of the rejection of colonialism, and Negro contributions were never totally recognized, particularly by white Cuban society.

Spanish Conquest and Colonization

In the early sixteenth century, following Christopher Columbus's discovery of the island in 1492, the Spanish crown became increasingly intrigued with the possibility of finding gold in Cuba. Spanish officials, desirous of increasing their labor supply as well as exploring possible new sources of wealth, also began to look toward Cuba. Columbus's son, Diego Columbus, who had been appointed governor of the Indies in 1508 and lived in Hispaniola, was particularly interested in extending the territory under his control. As a preliminary step toward colonization, Nicolás de Ovando (governor of Hispaniola, 1502–9) sent an expedition headed by Sebastián de Ocampo that circumnavigated Cuba in 1508; he brought back tales of wealth and a more detailed picture of the island's fine terrain and harbors.

Finding a conquistador who combined military skill, administrative talent, and loyalty to the crown as well as to Diego Columbus himself was no easy task. The choice finally fell on Diego Velázquez de Cuéllar (governor of Hispaniola, 1511–21), Ovando's lieutenant and one of the wealthiest Spaniards in Hispaniola. Although not as heroic or daring as later conquistadors such as Francisco Pizarro, conqueror of Peru, or as cunning as Hernán Cortes, conqueror of Mexico, Velázquez had achieved a reputation for courage and sagacity because of his role in subduing Indian *caciques* in Hispaniola.

From the start, Velázquez faced an outraged and hostile Indian population. Led by Hatuey, a fugitive Indian chieftain from Hispaniola, the natives of eastern Cuba resolved to resist the Spanish onslaught. It was a futile gesture, for the peaceful Tainos lacked the military skills and weapons to face the better armed and trained Spaniards. Spanish horses and hounds, both unknown in Cuba, played a decisive role in terrorizing the indigenous peoples, who soon surrendered or fled into the mountains to escape the wrath of the conquistadors. Hatuey himself was captured, tried as a heretic and a rebel, and burned at the stake.

Velázquez set out to pacify the country and end the abuses against the Indians. He induced groups of Indians to lay down their weapons and work near the several new towns that he established throughout the island. Among these were Baracoa, Bayamo, Trinidad, Sancti Spíritus, La Habana (hereafter, Havana), Puerto Príncipe, and Santiago de Cuba.

In this task, Velásquez was decisively aided by the work of Bartolomé de Las Casas. The Dominican friar preceded the Spaniards into native villages on many occasions and succeeded in convincing the indigenous peoples to cooperate with the conquistadors. Las Casas, however, was horrified by the massacre of the natives and became an outspoken critic of the conquest of Cuba. He wrote extensively condemning the Spaniards' cruelty and claiming that the Indians were rational and free and therefore entitled to retain their lands.

To strengthen his own power and gain supporters both in Cuba and in Spain, Velázquez began to grant *encomiendas* (see Glossary), or contracts, whereby large landowners (*encomenderos*—see Glossary), who were favored conquistadors, supposedly agreed to provide protection and religious instruction to Indians in return for their labor. The crown used the *encomienda* concept as a political instrument to consolidate its control over the indigenous population. Many *encomenderos*, however, interested only in exploiting the resources of the island, disregarded their moral, religious, and legal obligations to the Indians. A conflict soon developed between the crown and the Spanish settlers over the control and utilization of the labor by the exploitative *encomenderos*, and also over the crown's stated objective to Christianize the natives and the crown's own economic motivations. In the reality of the New World, the sixteenth-century Christian ideal of converting souls was many times sacrificed for a profit. Christianization was reduced to mass baptism; and despite the crown's insistence that Indians were not slaves, many were bought and sold as chattels.

The Colonial Period, 1520–1898

Administration and Economy

As soon as the conquest was completed and the Indians sub-

*A view of El Castillo del Morro (Morro Castle) and the lighthouse from El Castillo de la Punta (Point Castle), 1997
Courtesy Mark P. Sullivan*

jugated, the crown began introducing to the island the institutional apparatus necessary to govern the colony. The governor, the highest representative of the crown on the island, ruled Cuba with almost complete authority over administrative, political, and judicial affairs. The governor was technically subject to the *audiencia* (see Glossary) in Santo Domingo and to a viceroy in New Spain, the highest royal official in the New World. In practice, however, he exercised great autonomy, particularly after the wealth of Mexico was discovered, diverting the crown's interests away from Cuba and its lack of resources.

Nominally responsible for the collection and expenditures of revenues and all financial affairs, the governor delegated these functions to several royal officials (*oficiales reales*—see Glossary) appointed directly by the crown. At first the seat of government remained in Baracoa, the first village founded by Velázquez. In 1515 it was transferred to Santiago, and finally in 1538 to Havana because of Havana's geographic location and excellent port. In 1607 Havana was formally established as the capital of Cuba, and the island was divided into two provinces

11

with capitals at Santiago and Havana. The governor-captain general at Havana ruled in military matters over the entire island, but the governor at Santiago was able to exercise considerable political independence.

Although the governor-captain was nominally subject to the viceroy of New Spain, the viceroy exerted little control over the affairs of the island. Of more direct influence, and a powerful check on the governor, was the *audiencia* of Santo Domingo. This tribunal heard criminal and civil cases appealed over the decisions of the governor. But it soon, as in Spain, became more than a court of law; it was also an advisory council to the governor and always exercised its right to supervise and investigate his administration.

At the local level, the most important institution was the *cabildo* (see Glossary), a town council, usually composed of the most prominent citizens. The *alcaldes* (judges) acted as judges of first instance, and, in the absence of the governor or his lieutenant, presided at meetings of the *cabildo*. They also visited the territories under their jurisdiction and dispensed justice in rural areas.

As royal government became better organized and more entrenched in Cuba, the powers and prerogatives of the *cabildo* were progressively curtailed. By the end of the colonial period, few responsible citizens wanted to become involved in local government. Those who did were more interested in their personal well-being than in the affairs of the colony. Peninsular Spaniards, or *peninsulares* (see Glossary; hereafter, Peninsulars), who bought their offices sought rewards for their investments and enriched themselves at the expense of public funds. Creoles (*criollos*), Spaniards born in the New World, also joined the Spanish bureaucracy in order to gain wealth and participate in other opportunities controlled by Peninsulars. They looked to local government as one of the few potential areas of employment in which they could succeed. Very few Creoles ever attained a position of importance in the political hierarchy of the island. As the bureaucracy grew in the colonial period, a latent hostility developed between Peninsulars and Creoles—a hostility that erupted into hatred and violence during the wars for independence in the nineteenth century.

In the early years, *cabildo* members were content to eke out an existence until such time as new opportunities might arise for them to migrate to better lands or until mineral wealth that would bring them instant wealth might be discovered in Cuba.

Those who expected to enrich themselves from Cuba's mineral resources were greatly disappointed. The island did not enjoy the large deposits of gold and other minerals that were later found in Mexico and South America. Gold found in the river banks did not represent any great wealth, although washing the gold did require a large labor supply as well as costly equipment. A handful of Spanish entrepreneurs controlled the business and used Indians as a labor supply. The crown was also involved from the earliest times in controlling mining operations. The Spanish monarchs took one-fifth of all production as a tax for the right of mining, especially when Indians in an *encomienda* arrangement did the mining.

Foodstuffs also were an important part of the economy. The Indian agricultural practices were taken over by the Spaniards, who continued to grow some of the native foodstuffs, particularly yuca. New crops and new grains from the Old World were also brought to the island. Sugarcane, which had been grown by the Spaniards in the Canary Islands, was also a part of the island's economy. As early as 1523, the crown instructed the Contracting House (Casa de Contratación—see Glossary) to lend money to settlers in Cuba to help finance the construction of a sugar mill. Other similar loans were made in later years, but it was not until the eighteenth century and particularly the nineteenth century that sugar assumed any importance. Lacking large amounts of capital, an adequate labor supply, and official encouragement, the sugar industry remained overshadowed in importance by the more lucrative and important business connected with the cattle industry and its derivative products.

Cattle-raising became one of the most prosperous businesses, especially in the seventeenth century. Although the activity called for daring horsemanship, it required no sustained effort, for Cuba's abundant pasture lands facilitated breeding. The cattle were let loose on Cuba's savannas, where they multiplied rapidly. They were used as a means of transportation as well as for feeding purposes. Salted meat became an important item sold to the Spanish ships that called at Cuba's ports. Perhaps the chief value of cattle lay in the hides. In the seventeenth and eighteenth centuries, as demand for leather grew in Europe, cattle hides became Cuba's chief export, yielding considerable profit.

Tobacco also made some modest gains, particularly in the seventeenth century. Because it was not too bulky and commanded high prices in Europe, tobacco was a favorite item for smuggling. By the eighteenth century, it became an important export item to the French. Throughout this period, the tobacco business remained in private hands. But under the administration of Charles III (1759–88), it was converted into a government monopoly. The crown advanced money to the growers, who sold their crops to the government at a fixed price. In the early nineteenth century, the value of tobacco as an export began to decline. By then the price of land had increased tremendously, partly as a result of the growth of sugar estates. Tobacco growers found themselves either squeezed out of their lands or selling them to the sugar capitalists. The crown's emphasis on coffee and sugar growing was also detrimental to the tobacco industry. In desperate need of capital, the Spanish monarchs encouraged the more lucrative sugar business as a source of revenue.

The economy was oriented toward importing the bare necessities, with little or no provision for domestic manufacturing. Spain followed a thoroughly mercantilist economic policy, encouraging Cuba's dependence on outside sources of supply for its needs and looking at the island as a producer of raw materials to satisfy the needs of the mother country.

Life and Society

In the early years, Cuba became the source of support for the conquest of nearby lands. It was from the island that Hernán Cortes's expedition sailed in 1519 to conquer the Aztec Empire. The conquest of Mexico meant temporary prosperity and great euphoria, but it also meant the decline of Cuba's importance. The days of boom soon gave way to years of bust. Farmers and adventurers all left the island in search of El Dorado in Mexico, or joined the ill-fated expedition of Pánfilo de Narváez of 1527 and Hernando de Soto in 1539 to conquer Florida. Exodus of population, decline of food production, and economic misery afflicted the island. Estates were abandoned by their owners and bought cheaply by less adventurous Peninsulars, humble folks willing to produce for the passing ships and live a modest existence.

For the next two centuries, Spain focused most of its attention on the continental colonies from which it obtained much-needed mineral wealth. A complex and at times cumbersome political and defense system developed to ensure the uninterrupted flow of this wealth. Cuba was relegated to a mere stopping point for passing ships. It remained valuable only because of its strategic location as the gateway to the New World, not because of its products.

Cuba's population diminished continuously throughout this period. The indigenous peoples continued to die out and there was little new influx of Spanish immigrants. An economy of scarcity and a hot, sickness-ridden tropical climate offered little incentive for new immigration. Those who did come to Cuba were mostly Spanish officials, soldiers, and members of the clergy; there were also many transient migrants on their way to Mexico or South America. By 1544 Cuba had a population of fewer than 7,000, composed of 660 Spaniards, some 5,000 native Americans, and 800 black slaves.

This early society was characterized by little social mobility as well as lack of interest in the arts or in education. Creoles were less educated and seemed less interested in a formal education than were their ancestors. Living in small towns, surrounded by an unknown and at times hostile environment, fearful of Indian or later of black rebellion, or of foreign attacks, most had little time for cultural activities and were mainly concerned with the daily problems of existence. Brutality, opportunism, corruption, and smuggling characterized this society. Violence and lack of observance of the law flourished as the struggle for survival became harsher. Whatever education existed was offered within the Roman Catholic Church.

Protected by the power of the state, the church grew in numbers and influence. By the mid-seventeenth century, there were about 200 friars and priests and about 100 nuns on the island. Churches were built in every new city, and church wealth increased through the continuous acquisition of lands donated to the church and through the collection of rents, as well as of the special tax called *diezmo*. With wealth came not only prestige and influence, but also the loss of the church's early missionary zeal. The priesthood began identifying with the wealthier classes to the neglect of Indians and blacks and became a conservative institution interested in preserving the status quo.

The uninterrupted arrival of blacks throughout the colonial period decisively influenced this developing society. African slavery existed in Spain, and the first slaves had come to Cuba with the early conquistadors. Later they were brought in greater numbers to pan for gold; they replaced the weaker indigenous groups. The importation of black slaves was costly, however. As gold reserves became exhausted, there was little need for a large and expensive labor supply, and so their importation slowed down. Not until the full-scale development of the sugar industry was there again a significant need for manpower. Thousands of black slaves entered Cuba in the nineteenth century, and by 1825 the black population had surpassed the white one.

The condition of the slaves, although not unbearable, was poor. Blacks were much more valuable than the Indians and seemed to have received better treatment. Yet Spanish officials complained to the crown that the blacks were given little food or clothing and that they were subjected to abusive corporal punishment, forcing many to escape into Cuba's mountains. These runaway slaves, called *cimarrones*, were a constant concern to the Spaniards because by their example they encouraged other slaves to escape captivity and to rebel. As early as 1538, black slaves rioted and looted Havana, while French privateers were attacking the city from the sea.

Although most blacks worked in rural areas, some performed a variety of jobs in the cities. A considerable number labored in artisan industries, in construction, in the wharves, and in domestic service. Some were able to obtain their own earnings and thus liberate themselves or pay the price of their manumission. Others were freed after they had performed services their master was willing to reward. The number of slaves decreased continuously until reaching the low figure of 38,879, out of a total population of 171,620 in 1774.

The opportunities for slaves to become free contributed to the development of a uniquely Cuban society. Spanish law, the Roman Catholic religion, the economic condition of the island, and the Spanish attitude toward blacks all contributed to aid their integration into Cuban society. While the black population in the British sugar-producing colonies in the Caribbean lived under the tight political control of a small, exploiting minority of overseers and government officials, blacks in Cuba coexisted with the rest of the population and lived mainly by farming and cattle grazing. Prior to the eighteenth century, the island avoided the plantation system with its concomitant large-scale capital investment, latifundios (large estates), and docile black slave labor force. Instead, society developed with little outside interference. Cuba thus began to find its own identity in a society that combined racial balance, small-scale agriculture, and folk-Catholicism within a Spanish framework.

The British Occupation, 1762–63

Of all the wars that ravaged the Caribbean, one in particular, the Seven Years War (1756–63), had a profound effect on Cuba. At first only France and Britain were at war, but soon Spain came in on the French side. Motivated by dynastic connections with France, by grievances against Britain and its colonies in the New World, especially in Central America, and by an awareness that if France lost the war Britain would be supreme in the Caribbean, Spain cast its lot with the French. Spain's entrance into the war proved disastrous because Spain lacked the naval power to confront the British or to prevent them from capturing Spanish possessions. In August 1762, the British destroyed a large Spanish naval force and captured Manila and Havana, only to trade the latter back to Spain for Florida in the Treaty of Paris in 1763.

Several factors converged in the late eighteenth century to bring Cuba out of its isolation and into the mainstream of world affairs and to give the sugar industry the boost it needed. These developments included the relaxation of Spanish trade restrictions, the emergence of the important and nearby United States market for Cuban products, and the devastation of Haiti's sugar and coffee estates following the rebellion of that country's slaves in the 1790s. But it was the British capture and occupation of Havana that really shocked Cuban society out of its lethargic sleep.

During the brief eleven months of British occupation, the oppressive Spanish trade restrictions were lifted, and Havana was thrown open to trade with Britain and particularly with the North American colonies. More than 700 merchant ships visited the port during those months, more than the number that had visited Havana in the preceding decade. British capital, as well as large numbers of low-priced slaves, entered the island, boosting sugar production. For the most part, Britain maintained Spanish administrative institutions, although an attempt was made to reform the judicial system by ending some of the existing privileges and streamlining judicial practices.

The impact of the occupation was long-range. It made the Cubans aware of the benefits of trading with the British and particularly with a close and growing market like the United States. The large quantities of British goods that entered the island gave the Cubans a taste for those products and increased their demands for freer trade. Similarly, the occupation focused the attention of North American entrepreneurs on Cuba's economic potential as an area for investment, a source of raw materials, and a market for British and North American products. Finally, Spain was forced to reexamine its policies toward Cuba. The island was no longer the stopping point of the fleets, but a bone of contention among European powers, one important enough to have merited a British effort at conquest. Spain had to look at its Caribbean possession and try to satisfy, or at least placate, the demands and aspirations of her tropical subjects.

The British occupation had given the island the initial economic boost it needed. When the slave uprisings and the destruction of properties took place in Haiti, Cuba was ready to become the sugar bowl of the Caribbean and soon replaced Haiti as the supplier of European sugar. Cuban planters pleaded with the Spanish crown for the easing of trade relations and for the free importation of slaves. Spain acceded to these pleadings in 1791.

In the years that followed, the sugar industry grew substantially. Annual production rose from 14,000 tons in 1790 to more than 34,000 tons in 1805, and the number of sugar mills grew to 478, more than twice as many as had existed prior to the British capture of Havana. Sugar also benefited from the close commercial relations that developed between Cuba and the United States. The wars of the French Revolution isolated Spain from her colonies, thus helping the growth of trade between Cuba and the United States. By the turn of the century, Cuba enjoyed substantial trade with the United States, and when Cuban ports were thrown open to free trade with all nations in 1818, commercial relations between the two grew even closer.

Sugar, Prosperity, and Unrest in the Nineteenth Century

Throughout the nineteenth century, sugar as well as coffee became increasingly important in the Cuban economy. Large cattle estates were subdivided and sold to enterprising Spaniards for sugar or coffee cultivation. Aware of the profit possibilities, the Spanish crown encouraged and aided the subdivisions of land. Prior to this time, much suitable land was often part of large estates, the owners of which could neither divide nor sell the land because it had been granted to them for use, not ownership. The crown agreed in 1819 to consider landowners all those who could prove they had been on the land for the past forty years. This measure facilitated the breakdown of large estates, contributed to the growth of the sugar industry, and benefited a new class of proprietors. These new landowners could sell their land at a profit, become sugar producers themselves, or lease their land to other less fortunate and smaller planters, who did not receive title to a piece of real estate. In 1827 Cuba had 1,000 sugar mills, 2,067 coffee estates, and 5,534 tobacco farms. By 1860 it is estimated that there were about 2,000 sugar mills, the greatest number in Cuban history. A prosperous and large class of rural proprietors who based their prosperity on the cultivation of sugar and tobacco had emerged.

Despite its rapid growth, the sugar industry's development was not without serious problems and setbacks. Overproduction, fluctuations in price, competition from the British islands in the Caribbean, and the appearance of a dreaded competitor, beet sugar, in the second decade of the century depressed the sugar market and slowed down Cuba's sugar boom. These problems were further complicated by the British-imposed legal suppression of the slave trade in 1821. This action deprived the island of a continuous source of labor. Moreover, Cuba lacked an appropriate network of internal transportation that could facilitate movement of sugar to the mills and the ports of embarkation.

In the 1840s, however, two events renewed the acceleration of the sugar industry. Coffee, which had come to occupy an important position in the island's economy, was seriously affected by a fall in prices that almost ruined coffee planters. Capital and labor fled from coffee into sugar, and much land was shifted to the growing of cane. The second event was the introduction of the railroad. Cane could now be brought from remote areas to the mills and then to the ports for shipment. What started out as a relatively small business grew into a powerful, capitalistic enterprise based on large landholding, slave labor, and mass production.

In the early decades of the century, most Cubans seemed content with their status. The new aristocracy of wealth that had developed around the sugar industry enjoyed its recently acquired wealth and feared that a repetition in Cuba of the continental wars would upset the social order upon which its prosperity depended. This "plantocracy" was willing to tolerate a limited number of political and economic reforms, so long as the status quo was not endangered. The status quo meant the presence of a foreign power to protect their position against the possibility of a black rebellion similar to the one in Haiti.

By the 1840s, there was real concern about preserving Cuba's colonial status. Still fearful of a slave rebellion, or even an actual end to slavery forced on a weak Spain by Britain, the plantocracy looked toward the United States for a possible permanent relationship. Painfully aware of the problems in the British Caribbean since the abolition of slavery and its impact on sugar production, the property owners saw in the United States, particularly in the southern states, a slave-owning society similar to Cuba's own plantation economy. A series of slave revolts in Cuba in the early 1840s increased apprehension and the desire for a permanent relationship with the United States.

United States interest in Cuba and in its strategic location grew, particularly after the war with Mexico and the acquisition of California. In the 1840s and 1850s, Presidents James K. Polk, Franklin Pierce, and James Buchanan attempted unsuccessfully to purchase Cuba from Spain. In 1854 three United States ministers to Europe signed a secret report, later known as the Ostend Manifesto (see Glossary), which called for the United States purchase of Cuba or, if this failed, the forceful wresting of the island from Spain.

The Ostend Manifesto was the high watermark of United States interest in acquiring Cuba peacefully in the 1850s. Other efforts, however, proved bolder. During the administrations of Zachary Taylor (president, 1849–50) and Millard Fillmore (president, 1850–53), pro-slavery elements were discouraged by the lack of official support. Some turned to filibustering expeditions, hoping that they might lead to the overthrow of Spanish power on the island. The principal filibusterer was Narciso López, a Venezuelan-born Spanish general. He lived in Cuba and became involved in a conspiracy and various expeditions to the island in an attempt to annex Cuba to the United States.

The failure of López's expeditions and his death in 1851 and the United States Civil War ended, at least temporarily, the clamor for annexation. The abolition of slavery in the United States deprived Cuban slaveholders of the reason for wanting to tie themselves permanently to their northern neighbor. Abraham Lincoln's coming to power also had a significant effect on the Cuban policy of the United States, for Lincoln and his advisers were willing, as long as Spain remained nonaggressive, to allow Cuba to stay under Spanish control. The expansionist attempts of the 1840s and 1850s thus gave way to the less aggressive era of the 1860s. The proponents of the acquisition of Cuba were not defeated, however, only silenced. What their brethren were unable to achieve in mid-century, the expansionists of the 1890s accomplished at the turn of the century when the United States occupied Cuba during the Spanish-American War and later exerted considerable political and economic influence over the affairs of the island.

Throughout the second half of the nineteenth century, Cuba continued to prosper. The progressive changes known as the Bourbon Reforms (see Glossary), initiated throughout Latin America by Charles III (King of Spain, 1759–88), quickened economic and political activities and started a complete transformation of Cuban society. Population increased, agricultural production and profits expanded, and contacts with various Spanish ports as well as with the rest of Europe became closer, leading to the introduction of new ideas into the colony. The old order began to decay. To the forefront of Cuban society came a new and active class of Creole *hacendados* (hacienda owners) and entrepreneurs, who based their prosperity on sugar, coffee, land speculation, and the slave trade.

It was only natural that members of this group would make their point of view felt concerning economic and social matters. As the century progressed and their power increased, they began questioning Spanish mercantilist policies. Their primary focus concerned their immediate economic interests. Yet at a time when Europe was undergoing profound intellectual changes resulting partly from the Enlightenment (see Glossary), their questioning of Spain's economic policies naturally led to the growth of a more critical attitude on the part of many Creole writers and intellectuals on the island. The desire for economic reforms was later translated into a desire for political and even social change. Intellectual activity flourished so intensely during the century that the period has come to be known as Cuba's Golden Century.

Many of the attitudes of prominent Creoles were influenced by ties with the international community and particularly by Spain's inability to satisfy the island's economic needs. It finally became clear that Spanish policy had little to offer in exchange for increased taxation, ineffective administration, and the exclusion of Creoles from responsible positions in government. The Cubans turned away from any hopes of reform and toward independence.

With the annexation movement faltering and the possibility of independence still remote, some Cubans turned to attempts at reform within the Spanish empire. Reformism (*reformismo*), a movement that had existed in Cuba since the beginning of the nineteenth century for the purpose of reforming Spanish institutions in Cuba, took new impetus in mid-century, partly as a result of the failure of a number of conspiracies aimed at expelling Spanish power and because of black uprisings against slavery on the island. Spain also seemed at the time to be following a more conciliatory policy toward Cuba.

In 1865 the reform movement was strong enough to organize the Reformist Party (Partido Reformista), the first such political party to exist on the island. The party was not a cohesive political organization. Some of its members had been previously involved with the annexation movement, and a few still flirted with the idea. Others wanted some form of political autonomy for Cuba within the Spanish empire. Still others called for the island's representation in the Cortes (see Glossary). A few felt that reformism could be a step that would eventually lead to complete independence. In general, the party advocated equal rights for Cubans and Peninsulars, limitation on the powers of the captain-general, and greater political freedom on the island. It also supported freer trade and gradual abolition of slavery, and called for an increase of white immigrants into Cuba. The slave trade was partially curtailed in 1865, and the Spanish governor issued a law abolishing slavery in Cuba on November 5, 1879. It was not until October 7, 1886, however, that a royal decree completely abolished slavery in Cuba.

The activities of the Reformists soon met with strong opposition from a group of Peninsulars, who formed the Unconditional Spanish Party (Partido Incondicional Español). Trying to prevent any economic or political change, especially if it affected their interests, the Peninsulars used their newspaper, the *Diario de la Marina*, to attack the reformers. They cautioned that any concessions from Spain could only strengthen the Creoles, weakening continuous Spanish control over Cuba.

The work of the Reformists and their clash with the Peninsulars had an impact on Spain. Following the successful movement for independence in Santo Domingo against Spanish rule in 1865, and at a time when Spain was experiencing renewed economic and political difficulties, the Spanish monarchy felt it would be best to moderate its policy toward Cuba. It therefore called for the election of a reform commission that would discuss changes to be introduced on the island.

The Information Board (Junta de Información) (1866–67), as the Reform Commission came to be known, was composed of twelve elected Creole reformers and four Peninsulars, reflecting Cubans' desire for reform. To appease the fears of the conservative elements within Cuba and to prevent the election of radical reformers, the Spanish government instructed the Cuban municipalities to set high property qualifications for voting. Yet to everyone's surprise, the reformers won a major victory in the elections. Of the sixteen Cuban commissioners, twelve were Creole reformers. The results of this election clearly indicated the Cubans' desire for reform, rather than a widespread Cuban desire for independence. It seems that a significant proportion of the white Creole population of the island still hoped, as late as the 1860s, for a modification of Spanish policy and the introduction of reforms that would permit them to continue within the Spanish empire.

Yet the hope for change was short-lived. The Spanish government, which had come to power as the Reform Commission began deliberations several months earlier, had decided to let the commission meet, but had no intention of implementing its recommendations. In early 1867, the government not only disbanded the Information Board and dismissed all of its recommendations, but also imposed new and irritating taxes. Furthermore, Spain sent to Cuba Francisco Lersundi (captain-general, 1867–69), a reactionary captain-general who prohibited public meetings and tightly censured reformist literature.

The failure of the Information Board in particular and of reformism in general gave new impetus to the independence movement. Aware that Spain would not permit any significant changes and that the island's destiny as well as their own would best be served by an independent Cuba, Creoles began preparing for complete separation from Spain.

Toward Independence, 1868–1902

The Ten Years' War, 1868–78

Although remaining in the Spanish fold, the "ever-faithful" island, as Cuba became known, grew away from the crown. The interests and views of the Creoles and Peninsulars increasingly clashed. Reconciliation seemed difficult; those who clamored for violence became more numerous, and, finally, war broke out. The wars for independence that followed lasted more than thirty years, from 1868 until the outbreak of the Spanish-American War, followed by the intervention of the United States in 1898. The wars were Cuba's belated reaction to the fight for independence waged throughout most of Latin America during the first quarter of the century.

This is not to say that Cubans made no attempts to separate from Spain in the first part of the century. As early as 1809, at a time of turmoil and rebellion against Spanish power in Latin America, several Cubans conspired to gain independence for Cuba. Lacking widespread popular support, however, the early attempts at independence were weakened by several factors. Among these were the growth of the sugar industry and of wealth in general, the fear of a black rebellion, and the increased sentiment in favor of annexation by the United States. Then, too, a number of Spanish royalists and troops settled in Cuba following their defeat in Latin America. Cuba became a heavily fortified garrison, the last significant bastion of Spanish power in the New World.

The international picture also was not favorable to the Cuban cause for independence. Fearful of European expansion into the New World and particularly of British and French designs on Cuba, the United States was quick to issue the Monroe Doctrine (1823), which warned in part that the nation would not tolerate the transfer of New World colonies from one European power to another. The United States seemed to have preferred Cuba under a weak Spain than under a mighty Britain. If anyone else were to have Cuba, some United States politicians and business interests reasoned, it would be its neighbor to the north.

The reasons for the war that broke out in 1868 in Cuba were many and complex. Throughout the nineteenth century, Spain had experienced increasing political instability, with liberal and reactionary governments alternating in power. Spanish policy changes were particularly reflected in the colony under the rule of such arbitrary and ruthless captain-generals as Miguel Tacón (1834–38) and Francisco Lersundi (1867–69), the latter sharing power with more moderate and understanding officials, such as Domingo Dulce and General Francisco Serrano.

The clash between Spanish economic measures and the desires of the Creole sugar slavocracy also contributed to the mounting tension. Throughout the nineteenth century, the planters had grown into a powerful and vocal group that could control or at least decisively influence the internal politics of the island. The planters now found themselves saddled with an imperial power whose protectionist policies were challenging their status by attempting to curtail their prerogatives and reduce their mounting importance. Naturally, they were not about to relinquish their position without a fight.

Throughout the century, the Cubans had also progressively developed a separate and distinct identity. Although many thought of Cuba as another province of Spain and demanded equal rights and representation, others longed for an independent nation. Writers, painters, and poets, by looking inward to portray themes of their homeland, helped to develop the roots of their nationality. Through their works, they fostered not only a pride in being Cuban and a love for Cuban subjects but also a sort of shame over the fact that the island remained a Spanish colony. While Spanish America, with the exception of Puerto Rico, had successfully overthrown Spanish power, Cuba was still clinging to its colonial ties.

The war broke out in 1868. It was organized and directed by radical Creole landowners in Oriente Province together with a group of lawyers and professionals. The peasants did the bulk of the fighting, however, with blacks joining the rebel ranks. The leadership of the movement was in the hands of the son of a wealthy landowner from Oriente Province, Carlos Manuel de Céspedes y Quesada.

Céspedes and his group were determined to strike a blow at Spanish control of Cuba. When they learned that the Spanish authorities had discovered their conspiratorial activities, the conspirators were forced to act. On October 10, 1868, Céspedes issued the historic call to rebellion, the "Grito de Yará," from his plantation, La Demajagua, proclaiming Cuba's independence. He soon freed his slaves, incorporated them into his disorganized and ill-armed force, and made public a manifesto explaining the causes of the revolt. Issued by the newly organized Revolutionary Junta of Cuba (Junta Revolucionaria de Cuba), the manifesto stated that the revolt was prompted by Spain's arbitrary government, excessive taxation, corruption, exclusion of Cubans from government employment, and deprivation of political and religious liberty, particularly the rights of assembly and petition. It called for complete independence from Spain, for the establishment of a republic with universal suffrage, and for the indemnified emancipation of slaves.

The manifesto was followed by the organization of a provisional government, with Céspedes acting as commander in chief of the army and head of the government. Céspedes's almost absolute power as well as his failure to decree the immediate abolition of slavery soon caused opposition within the revolutionary ranks. Facing mounting pressure, Céspedes conceded some of his power and called for a constitutional convention to establish a more democratic provisional government.

The war centered in eastern Cuba. Céspedes decreed the destruction of cane fields and approved the revolutionary practice of urging the slaves to revolt and to join the *mambises*, as the Cuban rebels were then called. Numerous skirmishes took place, but Cuban forces were unable to obtain a decisive victory against the Spanish army. Simultaneously, Céspedes made several unsuccessful attempts to obtain United States recognition of Cuban belligerency.

While Céspedes retained civilian leadership, the military aspects of the war were under the leadership of the Dominican Máximo Gómez. Unhappy with the treatment Dominicans had received from Spain during Spanish occupation of his own country (1861–65), and horrified by the exploitation of the black slaves, Gómez started to conspire with the Cuban revolutionaries and joined Céspedes after the Grito de Yará. His experience in military strategy was invaluable to the revolutionary cause, and he was soon promoted to the rank of general and later to commander of Oriente Province. A master of guerrilla warfare, Gómez alternated training the Cubans in that type of struggle with commanding his forces in numerous battles.

Antonio Maceo, a mulatto leader, supported Gómez's plans and actions. Under Gómez's direction, Maceo had developed into one of the most daring fighters of the Cuban army. Showing extraordinary leadership and tactical capabilities, Maceo won respect and admiration from his men, as well as fear and scorn from the Spanish troops. He kept tight discipline in his encampment, constantly planning and organizing future battles. Maceo enjoyed outsmarting and outmaneuvering the Spanish generals, and on successive occasions he inflicted heavy losses on them. Maceo's incursions into the eastern sugar zones not only helped to disrupt the sugar harvest but more importantly led to the freedom of the slaves, who soon joined the ranks of the Cuban army.

By 1872 Maceo had achieved the rank of general. His prominent position among revolutionary leaders soon gave rise to intrigue and suspicion. Conservative elements that supported the war effort began to fear the possibility of the establishment of a black republic with Maceo at its head. The example of Haiti still loomed in the minds of many. Dissension in the revolutionary ranks and fears of the blacks slowed down the revolutionary effort.

The war dragged on, with neither the Cubans nor the Spaniards able to win a decisive victory. Finally, on February 11, 1878, the Pact of Zanjón ended the Ten Years' War. Most of the generals of the Cuban army accepted the pact; Maceo, however, refused to capitulate and continued to fight with his now depleted army. On March 15, 1878, he held a historic meeting, known as the "Protest of Baraguá," with the head of the Spanish forces, Marshal Arsenio Martínez Campos, requesting independence for Cuba and complete abolition of slavery. When these conditions were rejected, he again resumed fighting.

It was, however, a futile effort. Years of bloodshed and war had left the Cuban forces exhausted. Aid from exiles decreased, and Maceo now faced the bulk of the Spanish forces alone. Realizing the hopeless situation, he left for Jamaica. From there he traveled to New York to raise money and weapons necessary to continue fighting. He soon joined the activities of Major General Calixto García, then organizing a new rebellion. This uprising in 1879–80, known as the Little War (La Guerra Chiquita), was also to end in disaster. Maceo was kept in exile for fear of antagonizing the conservative elements in Cuba, and García was captured soon after he landed on the island. Exhausted and disillusioned after the long, bitter struggle and faced with a powerful and determined Spain, the Cubans were in no mood to join this new and ill-prepared attempt.

After more than ten years of strife, the Cubans were unable to overthrow Spanish power on the island. The reasons for this failure are to be found partially in internal dissension, regionalism, and petty jealousies among the leaders, and partially in lack of internal organization and external support, which resulted in chronic shortages of supplies and ammunition. The odds against the Cubans were also almost insurmountable. They were fighting well-disciplined, well-organized, and well-equipped forces augmented steadily by reinforcements from Spain. The Spaniards also controlled the seas, preventing the smuggling of reinforcements and weapons from abroad. The Cubans were thus forced to carry on guerrilla operations in the hope of demoralizing the Spanish army or creating an international situation favorable to their cause.

The protracted war had a profound effect on Cubans. Many Creoles fought in parts of the island they had never even seen before. Gradually, regionalism collapsed and a common cause emerged; the little homeland (*patria chica*), with its stress on local loyalties, gave way to the fatherland. The war also forced many to take sides on issues, thus accelerating the process of popular participation and integration. Finally, the war provided numerous symbols that became part of Cuba's historical heritage. The national anthem and flag as well as the national weapon, the machete, came out of this war. In particular, the dedication of the *mambises*, who abandoned position and comfort to fight Spanish power, became for future generations an example of unselfish sacrifice for the fatherland.

The impact of the war was particularly felt in the economic realm. The destruction caused by the fighting did away with the fortunes of many Cuban families. Although the struggle was concentrated in eastern Cuba and many sugar plantations escaped the ravages of war, the continuous development of a landed slavocracy in Cuba suffered a severe blow. Numerous participants and sympathizers with the Cuban cause lost their properties. Most Peninsulars sided with Spain, and many estates passed from Creole to loyalist hands. Because they had backed the Spanish cause, some Creole loyalists also profited from the losses of their brethren. The growth and power of the Creole propertied class was to be further undermined in 1886 with the abolition of slavery.

With the first major attempt at independence having ended in partial disaster, many Cubans turned to *autonomismo* (autonomy movement). The movement, which advocated autonomous rule for Cuba under the Spanish monarchy, differed little from reformism. *Autonomismo* had its origins in the first half of the century but lost momentum during the periods of annexation and reformism. Now, after the end of the Ten Years' War, it coalesced into the Autonomous Liberal Party (Partido Liberal Autonomista). The founders of the party, former annexationists and reformists, called for a system of local self-government patterned on the British colonial model and requested numerous economic and political reforms, but within the Spanish empire.

It soon became clear, however, that Spain still intended no radical changes in its policies. By 1892 the much promised and awaited reforms were not forthcoming. Disillusionment and frustration began to take hold of those who still hoped for a continuous association with Spain. The party warned that unless Spain stopped its policy of repression and persecution, another rebellion would be inevitable. While the stage was being set for the decisive effort at independence, however, the forces that advocated independence were still racked by schism and indecision. The enthusiasm and prestige of the military leaders of the Ten Years' War were not sufficient to coordinate and direct the independence effort against Spain. This leadership vacuum came to be filled by a young poet and revolutionary, José Martí.

José Martí and the War for Independence, 1895–1902

José Martí realized very early that independence from Spain was the only solution for Cuba and that this could only be achieved through a quick war that would at the same time prevent United States intervention in Cuba. His fear of a military dictatorship after independence led in 1884 to a break with Máximo Gómez and Antonio Maceo, who were at the time engaged in conspiratorial activities. He withdrew from the movement temporarily, but by 1887 the three men were working together, with Martí assuming political leadership. In 1892 he formed the Cuban Revolutionary Party (Partido Revolucionario Cubano—PRC) in the United States and directed his efforts toward organizing a new war against Spain.

Martí's pilgrimage through the Americas in the 1880s and early 1890s helped to unite and organize the Cubans, and with Gómez and Maceo he worked tirelessly toward the realization of Cuban independence. So well had they organized the anti-Spanish forces that their order for the uprising on February 24, 1895, assured the ultimate expulsion of Spain from the island. The war, however, was not the quick and decisive struggle that Martí had sought. It took his life on May 19, 1895, dragged on for three more years, and eventually prompted the United States intervention (1899–1902) that he had feared.

After Martí's death, the leadership of the war fell to Gómez and Maceo, who were now ready to implement their plan to invade the western provinces. In repeated attacks, they undermined and defeated the Spanish troops and carried the war to the sugar heart of the island. From January to March of 1896, Maceo waged a bitter but successful campaign against larger Spanish forces in the provinces of Pinar del Río and La Habana (see fig. 1). By mid-1896 the Spanish troops were in retreat, and the Cubans seemed victorious throughout the island. Then came a change in the Spanish command: the more conciliatory Marshal Arsenio Martínez Campos was replaced by General Valeriano Weyler, a tough and harsh disciplinarian. Weyler's policy of concentrating the rural population in garrisoned towns and increasing the number of Spanish troops allowed the Spaniards to regain the initiative after Maceo's death on December 7, 1896, in a minor battle. Yet they were unable to defeat the Cuban rebels or even to engage them in a major battle. Gómez retreated to the eastern provinces and from there carried on guerrilla operations. He rejected any compromise with Spain. In January 1898, when the Spanish monarchy introduced a plan that would have made Cuba a self-governing province within the Spanish empire, Gómez categorically opposed the plan.

United States Involvement

In April 1898, the United States declared war on Spain. The reasons for United States involvement were many. A growing and energetic nation, the United States was looking for new markets for its budding industrial establishment. United States investments in Cuba were now threatened by the devastating war carried on by the Cubans. National security also demanded the control of the Central American isthmus and of its maritime approaches. A strong navy as well as naval bases would be essential to protect the future Panama Canal. The rich Spanish colony, located 145 kilometers from the Florida coast and dominating the sea-lanes to the isthmus, was a growing haven for investors and the dream of every expansionist in the United States. It now seemed ripe to fall into the hands of its northern neighbor.

Throughout the century, United States interest had wavered. Early on, United States policy makers supported a Cuba under a weak Spain rather than in the hands of other European powers. In mid-century, annexation became a temporary hope, only to be ended by the United States Civil War. In the 1870s and 1880s, United States investments grew in Cuba as a result of the war. Taking advantage of the bankruptcy of many Span-

José Martí
Courtesy Organization of
American States

ish and Cuban enterprises, United States capital acquired sugar estates and mining interests. When the expansion of European beet sugar production closed this market for Cuban sugar, the United States became the largest and most important buyer of the island's crop. The depressed world price of raw sugar ruined many Cuban producers and facilitated United States economic penetration. The McKinley Tariff of 1890, which placed raw sugar on the free list, led to an increase in Cuban-American trade and especially to the expansion of sugar production. Although by 1895 control of the economy was still largely in the hands of the Spaniards, United States capital and influence, particularly in the sugar industry, were dominant.

The ingredients for United States involvement were all present in 1898. All that was needed was the proper national mood and a good excuse to step in. The first was easily achieved. The United States wanted intervention. Aroused by stories of Spanish cruelty blown out of proportion by irresponsible "yellow journalists" and by a new sense of Anglo-Saxon "racial" responsibility toward the "inferior" people of the Latin world, large sectors of public opinion clamored for United States involvement and pressured President William McKinley to intervene. The excuse was provided by the explosion of the United States battleship *U.S.S. Maine* in Havana's harbor early in 1898.

The Spanish-American War was short, decisive, and popular. Such defenders of manifest destiny as Alfred T. Mahan, Theodore Roosevelt, and Henry Cabot Lodge seemed vindicated by an easy and relatively inexpensive war. United States business interests saw new commercial and investment opportunities as a result of the capture of Cuba, Puerto Rico, and the Philippines. United States strategic interests were also assured by the final expulsion of Spain from the New World in 1899 and the emergence of the United States as the dominant Caribbean power.

The defenders of imperialism, however, were not unchallenged. In the United States Congress, Senator Henry M. Teller won approval for the Teller Resolution, which pledged the United States to support an independent Cuba. Roman Catholic and labor leaders criticized the United States and called for the granting of complete independence to Cuba. Similarly, Cuban leaders complained that Cuba was not a part of the Treaty of Paris (1898), which ended the Spanish-American War, that their soldiers had been excluded from the cities by the United States Army, and that despite innumerable sacrifices independence still loomed more as a hope than a reality. Although Spain relinquished Cuba under the Treaty of Paris, Manuel Sanguily, a staunch defender of Cuba's sovereignty, denounced the fact that the most reactionary Spanish elements had been permitted to remain on the island and retain their possessions.

Those who criticized United States policies, however, were voices crying in the wilderness. This was the finest hour for United States expansionists, and they were not about to give up Cuba completely. It was not until 1902, after two years of United States occupation of the island, that the United States granted Cuba nominal independence, and only after Congress had defined the future relations of the United States and Cuba. On February 25, 1901, Senator Orville H. Platt introduced in Congress the Platt Amendment (see Glossary), which stipulated the right of the United States to intervene in Cuba's internal affairs and to lease a naval base in Cuba. The bill became law on March 2.

On June 12, 1901, a constitutional convention met in Havana to draft a constitution. On June 21, by a majority of one, it adopted the Platt Amendment as an annex to the Cuban constitution of 1901. The constitution also provided for universal suffrage, separation of church and state, a popularly elected but all-powerful president, and a weakened Senate and Chamber of Deputies.

Despite the opposition that it generated, the occupation did have a number of beneficial and generally supported results. The United States faced a difficult task indeed in governing Cuba. Famine and disease were rampant. Industrial and agricultural production were at a standstill. The treasury was empty. The Cuban revolutionary army was idle and impatient. With no experience in colonial affairs, the United States tackled the job. The military governors, Generals John Brooke (1899) and Leonard Wood (1899–1902), supported by a variety of Cuban secretaries, were the supreme authority, and under them were other United States generals in charge of every province. These were soon replaced by Cuban governors. A method of food distribution was established that proved effective. A system of rural guards, initiated earlier by General Leonard Wood in Oriente, was soon extended to all the provinces, providing employment to many soldiers after the Cuban army was disbanded.

The Wood administration gave particular attention to health and education. It built hospitals, improved sanitation and health conditions, and eradicated yellow fever, primarily through the work of the Cuban scientist Carlos J. Finlay, who discovered the mosquito vector of yellow fever. The Wood administration established a public school system and modernized the university. Wood also reorganized the judicial system, provided it with buildings and other facilities, and placed the judges on salary for the first time. In 1899 Wood proclaimed an electoral law that gave the franchise to adult males who were literate, owned property, or had served in the revolutionary army. Elections for municipal offices were held in June 1900, and in September, thirty-one delegates, mostly followers or representatives of the revolutionary army, were elected to the Constitutional Convention that drafted the constitution of 1901.

On May 20, 1902, the occupation ended. On that day, General Wood turned over the presidency to Tomás Estrada Palma (president, 1902–06), first elected president of the new republic and former successor to Martí as head of the PRC. It was a day of national happiness, as the Cubans plunged into a new era of political freedom and republican government. Optimism, however, was tempered by the shadow of the United States hanging over the new nation. Looking into the future, a few Cubans warned that the immediate task was to resist foreign encroachments. Many still remembered Martí's prophetic words: "Once the United States is in Cuba, who will get it out?"

The Republic, 1902–59

The Platt Amendment Years, 1902–34

Apparently highly favorable conditions accompanied Cuba's emergence into independence. There were no major social or political problems similar to those that other Latin American nations had experienced after their break with Spain. There was no large unassimilated indigenous population, and although blacks represented a significant proportion of the total population, there was no major racial conflict. The two groups had learned to live together since colonial times. In addition, no strong regionalism or powerful church challenged the authority of the state. Furthermore, the liberal conservative feud that plagued countries like Mexico during the nineteenth century was nonexistent in Cuba.

The economic situation was also favorable. The infusion of foreign capital, the increasing trade with the United States, and favorable sugar prices augured a prosperous future. Cuba and the United States signed a Commercial Treaty of Reciprocity in 1903 that guaranteed a 20 percent tariff preference for Cuban sugar entering the United States. In return, Cuba granted certain United States products preferential treatment. The treaty reinforced the close commercial relations between the two countries, but it also made Cuba further dependent on a one-crop economy and on one all-powerful market. Under the terms of the May 1903 Treaty of Relations (also known as the Permanent Reciprocity Treaty of 1903) and the Lease Agreement of July 1903, the United States also acquired rights in perpetuity to lease a naval coaling station at Guantánamo Bay, which has remained the United States Naval Station at Guantánamo Bay ever since.

Despite apparently favorable conditions, Martí's vision of a politically and economically independent nation failed to materialize in the postindependence years. Whether he would have been able to prevent the events that followed the War for Independence can only be conjectured. A process of centralization extended the great sugar estates of the colonial period, restraining the growth of a rural middle class and creating an agrarian proletariat of poor whites and mulattoes. Cuba became more and more commercially dependent on the United States, and the inclusion of the Platt Amendment into the Cuban constitution of 1901 established United States supervision of political developments in Cuba.

Another problem was Cuba's preservation of the colonial Spanish attitude that public office was a source of personal profit. Electoral fraud became a standard practice. Politics became the means to social advancement, a contest between factions for the spoils of office. *Personalismo* was substituted for principle; allegiance to a man or a group was the only way to ensure survival in the political arena. The Spanish legacy of political and administrative malpractice increased in the new nation too suddenly to be checked by a people lacking experience in self-government. The United States' dissolution of Cuba's veteran army prevented a repetition of the typical nineteenth-century Spanish-American experience. Nevertheless, many veterans took an active part in politics, and their influence was felt in the years following the establishment of the republic in 1902.

As successor to Spain as the overseer of the island's affairs, the United States unwittingly perpetuated the Cubans' lack of political responsibility. Cubans enjoyed the assurance that the United States would intervene to protect them from foreign entanglement or to solve their domestic difficulties, but the situation only encouraged an indolent attitude toward their own affairs and was not conducive to responsible self-government. In the early decades of the republic, the Cubans developed a "Platt Amendment mentality," which led them to rely upon the United States for guidance in their political decisions.

This civic indolence was also not conducive to the growth of Cuban nationalism. Although the Cubans were enclosed in a geographic unit and shared a common language, religion, and background, they lacked national unity and purpose. The influence of the United States weakened the forces of nationalism in the early part of the century. As the century progressed, another force, *españolismo,* became an important factor in keeping the nation divided. When Cuba became independent, Spaniards were guaranteed their property rights and were allowed to keep commerce and retail trade largely in their own hands. Immigration from Spain, furthermore, increased considerably, and by 1934 there were an estimated 300,000 Spaniards on the island. This influx constantly strengthened Spanish traditions and customs. Many Spaniards themselves remained divided, retaining the ways of their own native provinces, hoping for an eventual return to Spain and thus failing to assimilate into the mainstream of Cuban society.

A dangerous tendency to solve differences through violence also permeated the political atmosphere. In 1906 President Estrada Palma called for United States intervention to offset the so-called Little August War. Organized by José Miguel Gómez and his liberal followers, who were outraged by Estrada Palma's fraudulent reelection, this revolt aimed at preventing Estrada Palma from serving a second term in office. United States Marines were sent to end the conflict, initiating a new intervention that lasted from 1906 until 1909.

This second intervention differed significantly from the first. The United States was not eager to embark on a new period of rule in Cuba, and the provisional governor, Charles E. Magoon, turned to dispensing government sinecures, or *botellas,* to pacify the various quarreling factions. Magoon also embarked on an extensive program of public works, gave Havana a new sewerage system, and organized a modern army. These accomplishments, however, were partially overshadowed by extravagant spending that left Cuba with a debt where there once had been a surplus. Magoon also drew up an organic body of law for the executive and the judiciary, and for provincial and municipal government. He also provided an electoral law, as well as laws for a civil service and for municipal taxation. Evidently, the United States government considered enactment of fair legislation that would prevent civil wars to be one of the main purposes of the intervention. Having pacified the country and introduced this new legislative apparatus, the United States called for municipal and national elections. In 1908 the Liberals, members of the newly created Liberal Party (Partido Liberal), won a solid majority and elected their leader, José

United States troops marching in Havana, 1908
United States Marine tents in front of the Palacio de los Capitanes
Generales, the old palace of the Spanish governors, 1908
Courtesy Organization of American States

Miguel Gómez (president, 1909–13), to the presidency. The United States seemed willing to allow the democratic process to follow its course, and on January 28, 1909, the interventionist forces were withdrawn from the island.

The impact of this second intervention was far-reaching in other, less positive ways. It removed any pretense of Cuban independence, strengthened the Platt Amendment mentality, and increased doubts about the Cubans' ability for self-government. Disillusionment took hold among many leaders, intellectuals, and writers, and this feeling was transmitted to the mass of the population. Cynicism and irresponsibility increased and so did the resort to violence to solve political differences. Even hitherto peaceful racial relations were affected.

The 1908 electoral fiasco of a group of radical blacks, who had organized a political party called the Independent Colored Association (Agrupación Independiente de Color—AIC), increased the frustration of blacks. When the Cuban Senate passed a law prohibiting parties along racial lines, the AIC staged an uprising in 1912. The uprising alarmed Washington, which landed United States Marines in several parts of the island, over the protests of President José Miguel Gómez. Trying to avert another full-fledged intervention, Gómez moved swiftly and harshly. Government forces captured and executed most of the leaders and crushed the rebellion. The AIC collapsed soon after. It was to be the last time that a revolt along strictly racial lines would develop in Cuba.

The tendency to resort to violence was displayed in two other instances at this time. In 1912 veterans of the War for Independence demanded the ouster of pro-Spanish elements from bureaucratic positions and threatened to take up arms against the government of President Gómez. When the United States expressed "grave concern" over these events, the veterans rapidly renounced their violent tactics. The second incident occurred again in 1917. This time the Liberal Party rebelled to protest the fraudulent reelection of Mario García Menocal (president, 1913–1921). Led by former President Gómez, the rebels took control of Oriente and Camagüey provinces. But Menocal, supported by a warning from the United States that it would not recognize a government that came to power by unconstitutional means, moved troops into the areas controlled by the rebels and captured Gómez. The rebellion soon died out, and, although its leaders were arrested, they were later pardoned.

As a result of the economic downturn of the 1920s, various groups protested Cuba's economic dependence on the United States. In 1920, after a sharp drop in the price of sugar created a severe economic crisis, Cuba was subjected to financial chaos and social misery. The crisis accelerated the desire for change and led to a questioning of the existing order of society among intellectuals and writers and also among other groups that were barred from becoming productive members of society. This economic crisis led in particular to a resurgence of economic nationalism. Several groups demanded protective legislation for Cuban interests and questioned the close economic ties between the United States and Cuba. The Platt Amendment as well as the repeated interventions of the United States government in Cuba's internal affairs came under attack. Anti-United States feeling, xenophobia, and retrieval of the national wealth became the main themes of this blossoming nationalism. As the decade progressed, however, its scope was widened to include a call for social justice and for an end to political corruption and economic dependence on a single crop.

Liberal Alfredo Zayas y Alonso (president, 1921–24), as corrupt as his administration was, managed to take advantage of this nationalism to reassert Cuba's sovereignty vis-à-vis the United States and its special envoy, Enoch Crowder. Although his administration was overshadowed by graft and mismanagement, Zayas retrieved Cuba's credit, averted intervention, and through later negotiations secured definite title to the Isla de Pinos (now Isla de la Juventud) off the southern coast of Cuba after a two-decade delay imposed by the Platt Amendment.

The inability of Cuban society to absorb all university graduates accentuated the feelings of frustration in a generation that found itself with little opportunity to apply its acquired knowledge. In 1922 university students in Havana created the Federation of University Students (Federación Estudiantil Universitaria—FEU), occupied university buildings, and organized short-lived student strikes. The students obtained a series of academic and administrative reforms, larger government subsidies, and the establishment of a University Reform Commission composed of professors, students, and alumni.

The university reform movement, which had started as a crusade for academic reform, developed political overtones in 1928 when students began protesting the decision of President Gerardo Machado y Morales (president, 1925–29, 1929–33) to remain in power for another term. Claiming that his economic program could not be completed within his four-year term and that only he could carry it out, Machado announced his decision to reelect himself. In April 1928, a packed constitutional convention granted Machado a new six-year period of power without reelection and abolished the vice presidency. In November, through a fake election in which he was the only candidate, Machado was given a new term, to run from May 20, 1929, to May 20, 1935.

Whereas a similar attempt by Estrada Palma to remain in power had resulted in rebellion, Machado's decision at first brought about only a wave of national indignation against the invalidation of suffrage. The regime still enjoyed the support of the business and conservative sectors of society. Increased revenues had brought prosperity, and Machado's improved administration, especially in the field of public works, had gained him a strong following. The Cuban armed forces, organized two decades earlier during Gómez's administration, also strongly backed the regime. Machado had successfully won over the military through bribes and threats and had purged disloyal officers. He used the military in a variety of civilian posts both at the national and local levels, thus increasingly militarizing society. The few officers who were discontented with Machado's reelection seemed powerless and ineffective to oppose the regime. In the midst of growing domestic and international problems, the United States looked with indifference at events in Cuba and seemed unwilling to become involved in Cuban affairs as long as the Machado administration maintained order and stability and a friendly posture toward Washington. Machado, furthermore, prevented the growth of political opposition by winning control of the Conservative Party (Partido Conservador) and aligning it both with his own Liberal Party and with the small Popular Party (Partido Popular). Through bribes and threats, Machado was able to subordinate Congress and the judiciary to the executive's will.

Machado's decision to extend his presidency met with stern student opposition, resulting in riots and demonstrations in several towns throughout the island. Machado took immediate measures to prevent further opposition from that quarter. He temporarily closed the university, dissolved the FEU, and abolished the University Reform Commission. He also tightened political control. Several Spanish and European labor leaders were expelled from the country as undesirable aliens. Antigovernment newspapers were closed down, and the military took an increasingly growing role in surveilling and policing the population. Machado warned sternly that he would keep order and peace at any cost.

These measures, however, failed to control the students completely. In mid-1927, a small but active group organized the University Students Directorate (Directorio Estudiantil Universitario—DEU; hereafter, Directorio) to oppose the regime. The Directorio issued a manifesto defending the right of university students to discuss politics and attacking Machado's reelection attempts. When students demonstrated in front of the university, Machado rapidly retaliated. Following his orders, the University Council, composed of faculty and administrative officials, formed disciplinary tribunals and expelled most of the Directorio leaders from the university.

A clash with police that left Rafael Trejo, a student leader, dead was the turning point in the struggle against the regime. From that time on, many Cubans viewed the courageous student generation that battled Machado's police with admiration and respect. For some, the "generation of 1930," as these students were later known in Cuban history, seemed irresponsible and undisciplined, but for others it became the best exponent of disinterested idealism. Embattled by the first shock waves of the world depression and oppressed by an increasingly ruthless dictator, many Cubans, especially those among the less privileged sectors of society, turned in hope toward these young people. They placed their faith in a generation that, although inexperienced and immature, seemed incorruptible and willing to bring morality to Cuba's public life.

While the principal leaders of the Directorio were in jail in 1931, a small group formed a splinter organization, the Student Left Wing (Ala Izquierda Estudiantil—AIE). The AIE, however, became merely a tool of the Communist Party of Cuba (Partido Comunista de Cuba—PCC). The party, founded in 1925 and led in the early 1930s by Rubén Martínez Villena, a popular poet and intellectual, directed the organization's activities and used it to influence the student movement. Throughout most of his regime, the communists opposed Machado and advocated, as the only correct strategy to overthrow his government, the mobilization of the proletariat, culminating in a general strike. The PCC opposition, however, was ineffectual.

The DEU and the AIE were not the only groups opposing Machado. The Nationalist Union (Unión Nacionalista), headed by a War of Independence colonel, Carlos Mendieta, also condemned the regime in newspapers and in public demonstrations. In 1931 Mendieta and Menocal, the former president, organized a short-lived uprising in Pinar del Río Province. That same year, a group led by engineer Carlos Hevia and journalist Sergio Carbó equipped an expedition in the United States and landed in Oriente Province, only to be crushed by Machado's army. In New York, representatives of several anti-Machado organizations united and formed a revolutionary junta.

Most prominent, perhaps, of these anti-Machado groups was the ABC, a clandestine extremist organization composed of intellectuals, students, and the middle sectors of society, established in 1930. Led by several Cuban intellectuals who were Harvard graduates, the ABC undermined Machado's position through sabotage and terrorist actions, and in December 1932 published a manifesto in Havana criticizing the underlying structure of Cuban society and outlining a detailed program of economic and political reforms. Although the means to achieve its political and economic program were not clear, the ABC called for the elimination of large landholdings, nationalization of public services, limitations on land acquisitions by United States companies, and producers' cooperatives, as well as political liberty and social justice.

Such was the existing condition on the island when the United States, attempting to find a peaceful solution to Cuba's political situation, sent Ambassador Benjamin Sumner Welles in 1933 to act as mediator between government and opposition. By then, United States interests in Cuba had grown significantly. Investment was concentrated in land and in the sugar industry, but also extended into transportation, natural resources, utilities, and the banking system. World War I had accelerated this trend, making Cuba more and more dependent on its neighbor to the North. As economic dependence increased, so did political dependence. A new crop of Cuban businessmen, technocrats, and, naturally, politicians had developed who identified with their counterparts in the United States and sought political guidance from Washington and Wall Street. This "Platt Amendment complex" permeated large sectors of Cuban society, with the exception, perhaps, of some writers, intellectuals, and students who saw a danger in the close relationship for the development of a Cuban nationality and identified the *patria* with the workers, the poor, and the blacks. Their ranks were small, however, and economic prosperity drowned their voices. The fear of, or the desire for, United States involvement in Cuban affairs was the dominating theme, and many Cubans were willing to use the threat of or even actual intervention by the United States to further their narrow political and economic objectives.

Most political factions and leaders supported Sumner Welles's mediation, with the exception of the radicals and the Conservative followers of former President Menocal, the Directorio, and a few Cuban leaders. The Directorio strongly opposed the United States' action. The leaders of the "generation of 1930" saw themselves as representatives of the national will and heirs to Martí's legacy (see José Martí and the War for Independence, 1895–1902, this. ch.); their mission was to carry on the revolution that "the United States had frustrated in 1898." Finding inspiration and guidance in Martí's teaching and his vision of a just society in a politically and economically independent nation, they opposed United States supervision of Cuban affairs and the humiliating Platt Amendment.

Sumner Welles's mediation efforts culminated in a general strike, in dissension within the armed forces, and in several small army revolts that forced Machado to resign and leave the country on August 12, 1933. This general strike deepened the schism between the PCC and the anti-Machado groups. Although the party had played an important role in promoting the strike, it reversed itself just prior to Machado's fall and issued a back-to-work order, fearing that the general strike might provoke United States intervention or the establishment of a pro-United States government. The failure to support the anti-Machado struggle discredited the PCC, especially among the students. From that time on, the party, alienated from progressive and revolutionary forces within the country, found it easier to reach agreements and work with traditional conservative political parties and governments, even with military presidents.

Sumner Welles and the army appointed Carlos Manuel de Céspedes to succeed Machado. The son of Cuba's first president during the rebellion against Spain in the 1860s and a prestigious although uninspiring figure, Céspedes soon received United States support and the backing of most anti-Machado groups. He annulled Machado's constitutional amendments of 1928, restored the 1901 constitution, and prepared to bring the country back to normalcy.

Returning Cuba to normalcy seemed an almost impossible task amid the worldwide chaos of the early 1930s. The deepening economic depression had worsened the people's misery, and Machado's overthrow had released a wave of uncontrolled anger and anxiety. Looting and disorder were widespread in Havana, where armed bands sought out and executed Machado's henchmen. In rural areas, discontented peasants took over sugar mills and threatened wealthy landowners. Although the appointment of Céspedes as president did not end the crisis, it reduced political tensions and the level of armed conflict.

An Attempt at Revolution, 1933–34

Machado's overthrow marked the beginning of an era of reform. The revolutionary wave that swept away the dictatorship had begun to acquire the characteristics of a major revolution. Although it lacked a defined ideology, this revolution was clearly aimed at transforming all phases of national life. The leaders of the "generation of 1930" were the best exponents of this reformist zeal. Espousing the usual anti-United States and nonintervention communist propaganda and advocating measures of social and economic significance for the less privileged sectors of society, the students monopolized the rhetoric of revolution. Céspedes's refusal to abrogate the 1901 constitution, which was regarded as too closely modeled after the United States Constitution and ill-adapted to Cuba's cultural milieu, created a crisis. The Directorio, furthermore, linked Céspedes to the deposed dictator, pointing to his serving in Machado's first cabinet and living abroad as a diplomat.

In September 1933, the unrest in Cuba's political picture again came to a head. Unhappy with both a proposed reduction in pay and an order restricting their promotions, the lower echelons of the army, led by Sergeant-Stenographer Fulgencio Batista y Zaldívar, invited the Directorio to meet with them at Camp Columbia in Havana on September 4. Batista's contact with Directorio leaders dated back to the anti-Machado struggle, when he had served as stenographer during some of the students' trials. By the time the students arrived at Camp Columbia, army discipline had collapsed. Sergeants were in command and had arrested numerous army officers. After consulting with Batista and the army, the Directorio agreed to Céspedes's overthrow and named five men to form a pentarchy (a five-member civilian executive commission) to head a provi-

*Havana's Museum of the Revolution (Museo de la Revolución),
formerly the Presidential Palace (El Palacio Presidencial), home
of President Fulgencio Batista until 1959*

sional government. That same night, Céspedes handed over
the presidency to the five-member commission, which formally
took possession of the Presidential Palace.

September 4, 1933, was a turning point in Cuba's history. It
marked the army's entrance as an organized force into the running of government and Batista's emergence as self-appointed
chief of the armed forces and the arbiter of Cuba's destiny for
years to come. On that date, the students and the military, two
armed groups accustomed to violence, united to rule Cuba.
The marriage, however, was short-lived. A contest for supremacy soon began between the students and the military. Very few
expected the students to win.

The pentarchy's inability to rule the country became evident
at once. The group lacked not only the support of the various
political parties and groups, but also the support of the United
States. The Franklin Delano Roosevelt administration, sur-
prised and confused by events on the island, refused to recognize the five-member government and rushed naval vessels to
Cuban waters. When one member of the pentarchy promoted

Sergeant Batista to the rank of colonel without the required approval of the other four, another member resigned and the regime collapsed. In a meeting with Batista and the army on September 10, 1933, the Directorio appointed a university physiology professor, Dr. Ramón Grau San Martín (president, 1933–34, 1944–48), as provisional president.

The new president had no political experience to qualify him for the job at such a crucial time. He had won the admiration of the students when in 1928 he allowed the expelled Directorio leaders to read their manifesto to his class. At a time when other professors refused the students' request, Grau's gesture gained for him a following at the university. While he was in jail in 1931, Grau and students met again and cemented their relationship. When the pentarchy collapsed, their old professor was the students' first choice. A witty and intelligent man, Grau projected a controversial image. He appeared indecisive and powerless, yet he was actually cunning and determined.

With Grau, the "generation of 1930" was catapulted into power. The students held Cuba's destiny in their hands. It was a unique spectacle indeed. Amidst thunder from the left and the right, and opposition from most political parties and personalities, the Directorio held daily meetings to shape governmental policy.

The Directorio leaders advocated several reforms. Now that Machado had been overthrown, they wanted to wipe out all vestiges of his regime, including corrupt, pro-Machado army officers, politicians, office holders, and university professors. They called for a complete reorganization of Cuba's economic structure, including revision of the foreign debt, tax reforms, and a national banking and currency system removing Cuba from monetary and financial dependence on the United States. Aware that the Platt Amendment allowed for continuous United States interference, they sought its removal. The students also demanded agrarian reform and eventual nationalization of the sugar and mining industries. Finally, they wanted an autonomous university, sheltered from political interference.

Grau's regime was the high-water mark of the revolutionary process and of the intense nationalism of the generation of 1930. Nationalist sentiment rather than radical doctrines dominated the regime's consideration of economic questions. The government was pro-labor and opposed the predominance of foreign capital. Soon after coming to power, Grau abrogated the 1901 constitution, promulgated provisional statutes to govern Cuba, and called for a constitutional convention with elections subsequently set for April 1, 1934. He also demanded the abrogation of the Platt Amendment, which was subsequently abrogated on May 29, 1934. Taking immediate action to eliminate Machado's followers from government positions, Grau appointed commissioners to "purge" government offices. Because the dictatorship had utilized the machinery of the old political parties, Grau issued a decree dissolving them. The government also complied with one of the oldest demands of the university reform movement by granting the University of Havana autonomy from government control.

With the island facing a mounting wave of strikes and social unrest, Grau implemented a popular and reformist program. On September 20, he issued a decree establishing a maximum working day of eight hours. On November 7, the government issued a decree on labor organization that sought to Cubanize the labor movement and restrict communist and Spanish influences by limiting the role of foreign leaders. It required Cuban citizenship of all union officials, and all labor organizations were ordered to register with the Ministry of Labor. On the following day, Grau signed the Nationalization of Labor Decree, popularly known as the "50 Percent Law." This law required that at least half the total working force of all industrial, commercial, and agricultural enterprises be composed of native Cubans (except for managers and technicians, who could not be supplanted by natives), and that half the total payroll be allotted to Cubans. Although these two decrees gained much labor support for the government and diminished communist influence in the unions, they also alienated the many Spaniards and other foreign minority groups living on the island.

Grau's measures also aroused United States hostility. The United States viewed the unrest in Cuba with much concern. The overthrow of the United States-backed Céspedes regime was undoubtedly a defeat for President Roosevelt's policy toward Cuba in general and for Ambassador Sumner Welles's mediation efforts in particular. Grau's seizure of two United States-owned sugar mills that had been closed down because of labor troubles, and his temporary takeover of the Cuban Electric Company because of rate disputes and additional labor problems, increased Washington's apprehension.

The United States refusal to recognize Grau complicated the many problems facing him because Cuban political leaders considered United States recognition as a key factor for the existence of any Cuban government. The United States policy condemning the Grau regime encouraged opposition groups and rebellious purged army officers. Opposition was strongest from the communists, the displaced army officers, and the ABC. Student leader Eduardo (Eddie) Chibás bitterly complained that although the Directorio had never used terrorism against the ABC-backed Céspedes regime, the ABC used it to combat Grau's government. The ABC seemed unhappy over their inability to obtain a share of power and feared that the consolidation of the Grau regime might exclude them from future political participation.

Inner conflict in the government contributed to its instability. A faction led by student leader and Minister of Interior Antonio Guiteras advocated a continuation of the program of social reform. Strongly nationalistic and sincerely motivated, Guiteras initiated much of the regime's legislation, and many considered him the real brains behind Grau. Another faction, which was controlled by Batista and the army, wanted a conservative program that would bring about United States recognition. Grau seemed to have been caught in the middle of these conflicting forces. On November 6, 1933, the Directorio, feeling that its mandate had expired, declared itself dissolved, announcing, however, that its members would continue to support President Grau.

By January 1934, it became evident that the regime would soon collapse. Student support was rapidly waning, the military conspired to take power, and Washington refused to recognize a regime that threatened its vested interests in Cuba. In addition, industrial and commercial leaders opposed Grau's legislation. Fearing that the government's program would attract labor support, the communists violently attacked Grau. A national teachers' strike for better wages further aggravated the already unstable situation. On January 14, Army Chief Fulgencio Batista forced President Grau to resign. Two days later, Batista appointed Carlos Mendieta as Cuba's provisional president. Within five days after Mendieta's accession to power, the United States recognized Cuba's new government.

To the United States and to its ambassadors in Cuba—Sumner Welles and his successor, Jefferson Caffrey—Batista represented order and progress under friendly rule. Welles had been persistently hostile to Grau, distrusting his personality as well as his ideas and programs. He was fearful of the social and economic revolution that Grau was attempting to enact and the damage this might cause to United States interests in Cuba. Both Welles and Caffrey looked to Batista as the one leader capable of maintaining order while guaranteeing a friendly posture to the United States and its corporate interests in Cuba.

The Failure of Reformism, 1944–52

Despite its short duration, the revolutionary process of 1933 had a profound impact on subsequent Cuban developments and events. It gave university students a taste of power, catapulted them into the mainstream of politics, and created an awareness among the students and the population at large of the need, as well as the possibility, for rapid and drastic change. It also weakened foreign domination of the economy and opened new opportunities for several national sectors hitherto prevented from obtaining a bigger share of the national wealth because of Spanish and North American presence and control. Furthermore, the state's involvement in the management of the economy was accelerated, and new impetus given to the rise of organized labor. But the failure of the revolution also convinced many that it would be almost impossible to bring profound structural changes to Cuba while the country remained friendly toward the United States. For the more radical elements emerging out of the 1933 process, it became clear that only an anti-United States revolution that would destroy the Batista military could be successful in Cuba.

In the years following Grau's overthrow, the "generation of 1930" experienced the harsh facts of Cuba's power politics. The students thought that Machado's overthrow would signal the beginning of a new era of morality and change. They learned differently. Dominated by the army, Cuba's political life returned to the corruption and old ways of the past. To govern Cuba, Batista chose as allies many of the old politicians expelled from power with Machado. Opportunistic and unscrupulous individuals assumed important government positions, corruption continued, repression and terrorism flourished. The years of struggle and suffering seemed in vain.

Students felt disillusioned and frustrated. Most abandoned their earlier idealism and found comfort in professional and business ventures. Some departed for foreign lands, never to return. Others accepted radical ideologies such as communism or fascism. Several broke with their past and shared in the spoils of office. Desiring to continue fighting for their frustrated revolution, many joined the Cuban Revolutionary Party (PRC), which was organized in February 1934.

Taking their name from Martí's PRC of 1892, this group, also known as the Authentic Party, became the repository of revolutionary virtue. Former Directorio leaders joined the new party, and Grau, then living in exile in Mexico, was appointed president. The party's program called for economic and political nationalism, social justice, and civil liberties and emphasized the right of Cubans to share more fully in the country's economic resources. Although the party was silent on the question of peaceful or forceful methods of achieving power, Grau seemed at first to favor peaceful opposition to Mendieta and Batista.

In the years that followed, Batista and the army all but dominated Cuba's political life. Until 1940, when he officially assumed the chief-executive office, securing his election through a coalition of political parties that included the communists, Batista maintained tight political control, ruling through puppet presidents. In addition to Mendieta, these included José A. Barnet y Vinageras (president, 1935–36), Miguel Mariano Gómez y Arias (president, 1936), and Federico Laredo Bru (president, 1936–40). Desiring to win popular support and to rival the *auténticos* (members of the Authentic Party), Batista imitated his Mexican counterpart, General Lázaro Cárdenas (president, 1934–40), by sponsoring an impressive body of welfare legislation. Public administration, health, sanitation, education, and public works improved. Workers were allowed to unionize and organize the Cuban Workers Federation (Central de Trabajadores de Cuba—CTC). Legislation to provide pensions, insurance, limited working hours, and minimum wages largely satisfied the workers' demands.

Batista also made a serious effort to bring education and better living conditions to the countryside. Under his ambitious "civic-rural" program, numerous schools were built. Where teachers were lacking, he sent army personnel to fill their places. The Civic-Military Institute, which he established, provided for the housing and education of the orphans of workers, soldiers, and peasants. In 1936 he issued the Sugar Coordination Law, which protected the tenants of small sugar planta-

A view of the National Capitol (Capitolio Nacional)
Courtesy Danielle Hayes, United Nations
Development Programme

tions against eviction. Although Batista and his associates continued the practice of pocketing some of the funds earmarked for these projects, they nevertheless made a sincere attempt to improve the health and educational level of the rural population.

In the late 1930s, Batista called for the drafting of a new constitution. With elections for a constitutional convention and for a new president in sight, politics took a more normal course. Grau himself, aware that violence would not bring him to power, returned from exile and engaged in electoral practices, thus legitimizing the Batista-supported regimes.

When the convention convened in Havana in early 1940, Grau was chosen president of the assembly. Despite pressure from both right and left, work went smoothly, with Batista and Grau competing for popular support. But when Batista and former President Menocal signed a political pact that left oppositionist groups in a minority position in the assembly, Grau resigned. Nevertheless, there was an unusual degree of cooperation among the various political groups, and the constitution was completed and proclaimed that same year.

The constitution was in many respects the embodiment of the aspirations of the "generation of 1930." The president was to serve only one term of four years, although he might be reelected after eight years out of office. Many civil liberties and social welfare provisions were defined at great length. The state was to play a strong role in economic and social development. Workers were guaranteed paid vacations, minimum wages, and job tenure. Cuban nationals were to be favored over foreigners in the establishment of new industries. The University of Havana's autonomy received constitutional sanction in Article 53. The convention thus fulfilled one of the oldest demands of the students.

Batista was the first president elected under the new constitution. Supported by a coalition of political parties and by the communists, he defeated his old rival Grau. His administration coincided with World War II, during which Cuba collaborated closely with the United States, declaring war on the Axis powers in 1941. The United States, in turn, increased aid and trade relations with Cuba. It granted Batista credits for agricultural development and for public works in Havana. Batista allowed for the establishment of a variety of United States military facilities on Cuban territory, and in early 1941 he concluded a sugar deal with the United States authorizing the sale of the whole harvest at $.0265 per pound. Many Cubans complained that the low price represented an excessive sacrifice for Cubans. This burden, combined with a series of war taxes that Batista had earlier imposed and shortages of finished goods and some food, caused much unhappiness among the population.

Although Batista enjoyed wartime powers, his administration was short of dictatorial. He enjoyed the backing of the propertied classes, and he cultivated labor support. He also catered to the left, allowing the communists complete freedom of operation. After Germany attacked the Soviet Union in 1941, the Cuban communists ended their denunciation of the United States as an imperialist power and began defending President Roosevelt as a "great statesman" and the war against Germany as a "just war." In 1944 the communists changed the name of their party from Communist Revolutionary Union (Unión Revolucionaria Comunista—URC) to the People's Socialist Party (Partido Socialista Popular—PSP) and issued a mild political program that called for racial equality and women's rights. The program failed, however, to attack the United States or even to request agrarian reform or large-scale nationalization of foreign properties in Cuba.

At the end of World War II, as Grau and the *auténticos* came to power, the organized use of violence took on an unprecedented dimension. The relative calm of the war years suddenly ended, giving way to a violent and materialistic era. Urban violence reappeared, now with tragic proportions. Although part of the generation that emerged out of World War II retained a redemptionist fanaticism and a desire to fulfill the aspirations of "the frustrated revolution," a still larger part evidenced an insatiable appetite for power and wealth, and a determination to obtain both regardless of obstacles. Violence-prone refugees of the Spanish Civil War also extended their activism and rivalries to Cuba.

Elected to the presidency in 1944, Grau followed a conciliatory policy toward these groups and permitted their proliferation, in many instances placing their leaders on government payrolls. Fearing the power of these gangs and their troublemaking capabilities if employed against the government, Grau allowed them almost complete freedom of action. This situation continued under the presidency of Grau's protégé, Carlos Prío Socarrás (president, 1948–52). Elected in 1948, the former Directorio leader also avoided confronting his old friends and continued his predecessor's mild policies.

A system of nepotism, favoritism, and gangsterism predominated. Despite numerous accomplishments that included respect for human rights, freedom of the press, and a democratic climate, the *auténticos* failed to provide the country with an honest government or to diversify Cuba's one-crop economy. The reformist zeal evident during Grau's first administration had diminished considerably in the intervening decade. Grau himself seemed softened after years of exile and frustration. He faced, furthermore, determined opposition in Congress and from conservative elements that had joined his party. Not only Grau, but many of the old student leaders of the "generation of 1930," shared in the spoils of office. When confronted with the reality of Cuban politics, their early idealism and reformism gave way to materialism and opportunism.

For many, the *auténticos* had failed to fulfill the aspirations of the anti-Machado revolution, especially in the area of administrative honesty. Perhaps the Cubans expected too much too soon. The people still remembered the rapid reforms implemented during Grau's first administration and expected their continuation.

Grau's failure to bring honesty and order to Cuba's public life and the presidential aspirations of Eduardo Chibás, an *auténtico* congressman, produced a rift in the party. In 1947 Chibás and other *auténtico* leaders formed the Cuban People's Party (Partido del Pueblo Cubano—PPC), Orthodox (Ortodoxo) branch, also known as the Orthodox Party (Partido Ortodoxo). Led by Chibás, a former student leader of the generation of 1930, the PPC became the repository of the ideals of the "frustrated revolution" and the refuge of a new generation determined to transform those ideals into reality.

By 1950 the *ortodoxos* (PPC members) had become a formidable political force. Although the party lacked a well-defined platform, its nationalistic program of economic independence, political liberty, social justice, and honest government, and its insistence upon remaining free from political pacts, had won for it a considerable following, especially among University of Havana students. With the slogan *"vergüenza contra dinero"* (honor versus money), Chibás, now an elected senator, pounded on the consciences of the Cubans in his Sunday radio programs and sought to awaken their minds to the corruption of the *auténtico* administrations. Chibás monopolized the rhetoric of revolution, becoming the exponent of the frustrated old generation and the leader of a new generation bent on bringing morality and honesty to Cuban public life. It was he more than anyone else who, with his constant exhortations, calls for reform, and attacks on Cuba's political leadership, paved the way for the Revolution that followed.

One of those captivated by the Chibás mystique was Fidel Castro Ruz. As a student at the Jesuit Belén High School in Havana in the early 1940s, Castro fell under the particular influence of two of his teachers, who were admirers of Franco's Spain and his fascist Falangist ideology.

While studying law at the University of Havana in the late 1940s, Castro participated in the activities of student gangs and associated closely with violent leaders. He soon acquired a reputation for personal ambition, forcefulness, and fine oratory. Yet he never became a prominent student leader. On several occasions, he was defeated in student elections or prevented from winning by the nature of student politics.

Castro, as did many Cubans, followed Chibás with enthusiasm, regarding him as the only hope Cuba had of redeeming its political institutions and defending its sovereignty. Yet in one of the most bizarre episodes of Cuban political history, Chibás committed suicide in August 1951, at the end of his radio program. Chibás's death produced a feeling of shock and sadness among the masses. It also created a leadership vacuum, produced a rift in the Orthodox Party, and facilitated Batista's coup d'état of March 10, 1952.

By the time of Chibás's death, Cuba's political life was a sad spectacle. Although Carlos Prío Socorrás, elected president in 1948, had introduced a number of reforms and gangsterism had diminished within the University of Havana, his administration resembled that of his predecessor. Politics came to be regarded by the Cuban people with disrespect. To become a politician was to enter into an elite, a new class apart from the interests of the people. The elected politicians did not owe allegiance to their constituents, not even to their nation, but only to themselves and their unsatisfied appetites for power and fortune. Political figures, furthermore, were the objects of popular mockery. In particular, the image of the presidency was ridiculed and abused. Chibás's criticism, furthermore, helped to undermine not only the authority of the *auténticos*, destroying what little prestige they still enjoyed, but also the stability of Cuba's already fragile political institutions. The breakdown in morale, respect, and values was aggravated by Batista's interruption of constitutional government in 1952. What Cubans believed would never happen again—the return to military rule—became a reality.

Background to Revolution, 1952–59

Convinced that he could not win the election scheduled for June 1952, Batista overthrew President Carlos Prío's regime in a bloodless and masterfully executed coup d'état on March 10. The coup was almost entirely dependent on army backing and caught the Cuban population, as well as Prío and his followers, by surprise. Batista quickly consolidated his position by replacing dissenting army officers with his own loyal men, exiling or arresting key Prío supporters, and taking temporary control over the mass media. Prío himself sought asylum in the Mexican Embassy and later left the country.

The ease with which Batista took over underscored the weakness of Cuba's political institutions. The legislative branch was weak and permeated with corruption. Even the judiciary had lost prestige because of its subservient role to the executive branch. The *ortodoxos* were leaderless and had been largely ineffectual since Chibás's death. The *auténticos'* corruption and inability to bring profound structural changes to the Cuban economy had cost them a good deal of support and discredited them in the eyes of many Cubans. The failure of this democratic reformist party was perhaps the single most important factor contributing to the 1952 coup and the events that followed.

By then the importance and power of the business community had grown significantly, helped in part by the rapid economic growth experienced by the island in the 1940s. World War II had paralyzed sugar production in many areas of Europe and Asia, making possible the further expansion of Cuba's sugar industry. At the same time, the deterioration of international trade during the war years gave Cuba an extraordinary amount of foreign exchange that would otherwise have gone toward the purchase of agricultural and industrial import items. All of this served to accelerate the diversification process in Cuba's economic development. Domestic production flourished, and other new productive activities were established. This circumstance was put to good use by Cuban entrepreneurs, who began to occupy relatively important positions in the development of the island's economy.

Yet despite this progress, the Cuban economy suffered from certain structural weaknesses that prevented any sustained period of rapid economic growth. Chief among these was an excessive concentration on sugar production and foreign trade, a critical dependency on one major buyer-supplier, substantial unemployment and underemployment, and inequalities between urban and rural living standards.

Despite the apparent support of business, labor, and peasant groups, Batista failed to develop an active base of political backing. Political loyalties were often the result of intimidation or expediency and for that reason were often short-lived. Batista's actual political base was now narrower than in the 1930s. Even within the armed forces, and particularly in the middle and lower echelons of the officer corps, there were numerous disgruntled *ortodoxo* and *auténtico* officers who engaged in conspiratorial activities against the regime.

The imposition of strict censorship by the Batista regime silenced all criticism. Opposition leaders were either jailed or exiled. Repression increased. The voices that clamored for a peaceful solution to the interruption of Cuba's constitutional process were soon drowned by voices clamoring for violence. Cuba again was submerged in terrorism and violence, a violence that finally culminated in a major revolution.

Opposition developed from various sectors. Numerous *ortodoxos*, a faction of the Authentic Party under Grau, and most of Cuba's politicians peacefully opposed Batista, hoping for an honest election. Another faction of the *auténticos*, together with several Ortodoxo leaders, went underground and began plotting insurrectionary activities.

The active banner of rebellion, however, was to be carried by university students. Students laid aside their rivalries, directing all their efforts against the new regime. Militant anti-Batista student leaders emerged with effective political power, not only in the student community, but nationally as well. During the first three years of Batista's rule, student opposition was limited to sporadic riots, demonstrations, and protests. Although at the time these unorganized acts may have seemed unimportant, they did help awaken the minds of Cubans to the increasingly oppressive nature of Batista's regime and thus paved the way for the insurrection that followed.

A small faction within the *ortodoxos* advocated violence as the correct tactic to combat Batista. Fidel Castro belonged to this group. After receiving his law degree from the University of Havana in 1950, he joined the party and was nominated to run as an *ortodoxo* candidate to the House of Representatives in the aborted 1952 election. Batista's coup thwarted Castro's ambitions for a parliamentary career, and Castro began organizing a small group of followers for his ill-fated attack on the Moncada military barracks in Oriente Province on July 26, 1953.

Expecting army discipline to be low, Castro and his group planned a surprise attack to capture the Moncada barracks. The attack would coincide with a vigorous publicity campaign projecting the movement as an *ortodoxo* uprising supported by pro-*ortodoxo* army officers. Castro hoped for sufficient confusion to paralyze the army and thus prevent it from reacting against the rebels. Batista would then be forced to resign, and the *ortodoxos* would be catapulted into power with Castro as the party's undisputed leader. In reality, the party was not consulted, and its leaders were informed of Castro's plans only the day before the Moncada assault.

Castro's Moncada attack ended in disaster. The garrison's discipline was not relaxed, and the army fought back the attack. Some of the attackers failed even to enter the military barracks. Those who did were massacred. Castro himself escaped to the mountains, only to be captured and sentenced to prison.

In "History Will Absolve Me," his speech before the tribunal that sentenced him, Castro outlined his political program. He associated his movement with the ideals of Martí and Chibás and called for reforms that were within the mainstream of Cuba's political tradition. At no time during his struggle against Batista did Castro outline a program that departed from Cuba's political tradition. Although the most radical elements of the revolutionary leadership thought that Cuba needed major economic changes that would cure the ills of monoculture, unemployment and underemployment, and dependence, most of the oppositionist leaders to Batista wanted political changes. None of these groups offered a program along Marxist lines. The great majority of the Cuban people who supported the anti-Batista struggle were hoping for a return to the constitution of 1940, honesty in government, and an end to violence.

Cuba's small communist party, the PSP (People's Socialist Party), also opposed Batista, but through peaceful means. Since the 1930s, when it supported the Machado dictatorship, the party had lost prestige and membership and was a weak, ineffectual contender in the political process. Now, as a result of the international situation, particularly the pressure of the United States, the communists were unable to arrive at a modus vivendi with Batista. Not until very late in the anti-Batista struggle did the communists join the revolutionary forces, and even then their participation contributed little to the final overthrow of the regime.

The mock election of November 1954, from which Batista, running unopposed, emerged victorious, placed Cuba at a dangerous crossroads. The opposition wanted a new election, while Batista insisted on remaining in power until his new term expired in 1958. Government officials and oppositionist leaders met throughout 1955 in an attempt to find a compromise. The failure to reach an agreement forced the Cuban people reluctantly onto a road leading to civil war, chaos, and revolution.

The students reacted violently to the failure of political groups to find a peaceful solution. At the end of 1955, a series of riots shocked the country. On November 27, the FEU organized a ceremony to honor the memory of eight students shot by Spanish authorities in 1871. Rioting quickly spread to Havana. On April 21, a group of university students stoned a TV station where a government-sponsored youth program was being televised. Several participants were wounded. A police cordon was thrown around the grounds of the University of Havana, and, on the pretext of searching for hidden arms, government forces entered the university, demolishing the rector's office and destroying documents, scientific equipment, and furnishings. Batista replied to the moral indignation of university authorities and students by declaring that the autonomy of the university was limited to educational, administrative, and internal affairs; when subversive political elements were entrenched within the university, the government must enforce law and order.

Instead of seeking to discourage rebellion and demonstrations, particularly from university students, by moderation, the regime encouraged it by meeting terrorism with a counterterrorism that defeated its own ends. No better method could have been devised to increase the bitterness and opposition of the people. Each murder produced another martyr and new adherents to the struggle against Batista. By the end of 1955, the leaders of the FEU realized that the efforts of nonpartisan organizations to reconcile government and opposition were futile. They proposed the creation of an insurrectionary movement to lead the struggle against Batista. When the FEU proposal found little response among the electorally oriented politicians, the students formed their own clandestine organization—the Revolutionary Directorate.

While student riots and demonstrations were going on, other Cubans not connected with student activities were plotting to unseat Batista. A group known as Montecristi plotted with army officers to overthrow the regime, but Batista uncovered the conspiracy and arrested its principal instigators in April 1956. That same month, another group, belonging to Prío's Authentic Organization (Organización Auténtica), unsuccessfully attacked the Goicuría army barracks in Matanzas Province. From jail, Fidel Castro exhorted his supporters to organize and to cooperate with other groups.

In 1956 Castro was released from jail and traveled to the United States seeking funds for the revolutionary cause and organizing his followers into the Twenty-Sixth of July Movement (Movimiento 26 de Julio), an organization named after his ill-fated Moncada attack. In December 1956, Castro and a group of more than eighty young revolutionaries, including his brother Raúl and an Argentine physician, Ernesto "Che" Guevara, left from Mexico in the small yacht *Granma* and landed in Oriente Province. There, underground commando groups had attacked several military installations, touching off a wave of sabotage throughout the province. Terrorism flared, and bombs exploded. Underground cells derailed trains and sabotaged power lines, blacking out entire towns.

By the time that Fidel Castro landed on December 2, however, the uprising was well on its way to being crushed, and most of the leaders of Castro's Twenty-Sixth of July Movement were either dead or in jail. In response to the uprising, Batista suspended constitutional guarantees and established tighter censorship of news. The dreaded military police patrolled the streets of Havana day and night, rounding up suspected revolutionary elements. When Castro found that his actions were not supported by the general public, the army, or regular opposition parties, he and about a dozen survivors found refuge in the Sierra Maestra mountain range and from there began waging guerrilla warfare against the regime.

Despite the instability of the late 1930s, the fall of Machado had ushered in almost two decades of political freedom and constitutional government. The students and the Cuban people in general saw Batista's regime as only a temporary interruption of Cuba's democratic political development and as the consequence of Batista's own ambitions for power and Prío's corrupt rule rather than a symptom of more profound national problems.

The elimination of Batista's dictatorship became the panacea to cure all of Cuba's ills. This simplistic thinking served Fidel Castro's purposes well during his stay in the Sierra Maestra. Lacking a well-defined ideology, he proclaimed the overthrow of the regime as the nation's sole, overriding task, advocating only the most obvious popular reforms.

The Revolutionary Directorate, together with several *auténtico* leaders, planned to overthrow the government by assassi-

Fidel Castro flanked by Raúl Castro and Camilo Cienfuegos
at a Rebel Army camp in the Sierra Maestra
Courtesy Library of Congress

nating Batista. Student leaders reasoned that such fast, decisive action would cause the regime to crumble and prevent unnecessary loss of life in a possible civil war. On March 13, 1957, in one of the boldest actions of the anti-Batista rebellion, a group of forty men stormed the presidential palace in the center of Havana and almost succeeded in killing Batista.

Fidel Castro, from his hideout in the mountains, criticized the students' attack. In a taped interview shown in the United States in May, Castro called it "a useless waste of blood. The life of the dictator is of no importance. Here in the Sierra Maestra is where to fight." Throughout his stay in the mountains, Castro opposed a military coup, the assassination of Batista, or any other violent act by a group not directly under the control of his Twenty-Sixth of July Movement.

The defeat suffered at the presidential palace and the death of student leader José A. Echeverría, perhaps the most popular figure opposing Batista, during a simultaneous attack on a Havana radio station left the Revolutionary Directorate leaderless and disorganized. Almost a year went by before the organization recovered from the blow, and even then it never regained the prestige and importance that it had enjoyed prior to the palace assault. While the Revolutionary Directorate declined, Castro, unchallenged in the mountains, grew in prestige, strength, and following. He gained adherents in the cities and won to his side many discontented elements who, whatever differences they might have had with his Twenty-Sixth of July Movement, found no other insurrectionary organization to join.

Corroded by disaffection, corruption, and internal disputes, the army was unable to defeat the guerrillas during Batista's final year in power. This inability increased the guerrillas' prestige and contributed to the internal demoralization of the armed forces. The guerrillas had certain other advantages over the army. For years the peasantry in the Sierra Maestra had been terrified by Batista's Rural Guard (Guardia Rural), and they welcomed the protection and promises offered by Castro and his group. The knowledge of the terrain and the intelligence provided by these allies proved invaluable. In addition, the guerrillas operated in extremely mobile units in a vast and rugged terrain. The Cuban army was not trained in guerrilla tactics and also lacked the military leadership capable of carrying out this type of warfare against highly motivated guerrilla fighters. For many of the urban youth who joined Castro in the mountains, there was a sort of mystique in being a guerrilla, fighting for a just cause against an oppressive regime, and living in a rural environment. Finally, the guerrillas were supported by an urban network that supplied manpower, weapons, money, and other necessary aid.

Guerrilla warfare in the rural areas was accompanied by increased sabotage and terror in the cities. A large and loosely related urban resistance movement developed throughout the island. Underground cells of the Twenty-Sixth of July Movement, the closely allied Civic Resistance Movement (Movimiento Cívico Revolucionario—MCR), the Revolutionary Directorate, and the *auténticos* conducted bombings, sabotage, and kidnappings, as well as distributed propaganda. These actions undermined the foundations of the government and helped to create the atmosphere of civil war.

This urban underground developed into the backbone of the anti-Batista struggle. It was the work of the urban underground more than anything else that brought about the downfall of the regime. The action of these groups provoked Batista and his repressive forces into such extreme retaliatory measures that the Cuban population became almost totally alienated from the regime.

United States policy also contributed somewhat to the growing demoralization within the military. Although the United States had supported the Batista regime, by the fall of 1957 the United States government began holding up shipments of weapons and munitions. An arms embargo was publicly announced in March 1958. Although these arms shipments were small and from Batista's point of view not decisive in the struggle against Castro, they did represent a sign of continuous backing for his administration. Thus, when the embargo was declared, many Cubans saw it as a change in Washington's policy, indicating disapproval and withdrawal of support for the regime. United States actions were undoubtedly a strong blow to the declining morale of the Batista regime and of the armed forces in particular.

The regime was further weakened when several institutions and sectors of Cuban society began a progressive withdrawal of their support. The church, professional and business groups, and the press exerted pressure on the government to allow a peaceful solution. At first they advocated free elections with absolute guarantees for all political parties, but the rigged election of November 1958, in which Batista's hand-picked candidate, Andrés Rivero Agüero, won the presidency for a new four-year term, convinced many that violence was the only means of eliminating Batista's rule. The army's refusal at the end of 1958 to continue fighting dealt the final blow to a crumbling regime.

The Cuban Revolution, 1959–

Fidel Castro Takes Charge

When Batista and his closest allies escaped to the Dominican Republic in the early hours of January 1, 1959, power lay in the streets. Of the several groups that fought the Batista regime, the Twenty-Sixth of July Movement had an almost undisputed claim to fill the vacuum left by the dictator. Castro's charisma and his revolutionary prestige made him, in the eyes of the Cuban people, the logical occupant of Batista's vacant chair; he was the man of the hour, the new messiah. The other insurrectionary organizations lacked the mystique, the widespread support, and the organized cadres of Castro's movement.

Castro had unquestionable qualities of leadership. Endowed with an extraordinary gift of oratory and an exceptional memory, he would speak extemporaneously for hours. Like Martí had done years earlier, Castro lectured the Cubans on the evils of their society and the need for profound and rapid changes. The overwhelming majority of the Cubans accepted his leadership enthusiastically. The atmosphere of gloom that had prevailed during the Batista era was now converted into euphoria and hope for the future. Even those who had failed to participate in the anti-Batista struggle fervently joined the revolutionary ranks with a feeling of guilt for their past behavior.

During the first few weeks in power, Castro assumed no official position except commander of the armed forces. His handpicked president, former Judge Manuel Urrutia, organized a government, appointing a civilian cabinet composed mainly of prominent anti-Batista political figures. Urrutia then proceeded to tear down Batista's governmental structure.

It soon became clear, however, that real power lay with Fidel and his youthful Rebel Army officers. In public addresses, Castro announced major public policies without consultation with the Urrutia cabinet and complained of the slowness of reforms. In mid-February, Prime Minister José Miró Cardona resigned in favor of Castro, and by October Castro had forced Urrutia to resign and had replaced him with Oswaldo Dorticós

Four Batista men (among seventy-one executed the next day) on summary trial on Sunday, January 11, 1959, with Rebel Army members in the audience
Courtesy National Imagery and Mapping Agency, Washington

Torrado (president, 1959–76), an obscure lawyer and former communist party member.

Fidel Castro's formal assumption of power initiated a period of increased radicalization. Some of Batista's more prominent military and civilian leaders were immediately and publicly brought to trial before revolutionary tribunals, and the proceedings were televised; hundreds were executed summarily. Faced with mounting criticism, the regime ended these public trials but continued them in private, while also confiscating property of Batista supporters or collaborators.

On May 17, 1959, the first Agrarian Reform Law was passed. It required expropriation of farm lands larger than 404 hectares and forbade land ownership by foreigners. The law, together with a sharp reduction in urban rents, marked the beginning of the rapid confiscatory phase of the Revolution, which lasted until the formal establishment of the socialist economy in April 1961, when Castro proclaimed that the Revolution was socialist. The revolutionary leadership aimed at agricultural diversification and industrialization, thus hoping to lessen dependence upon sugar. They also sought to weaken United States economic presence and influence in Cuba by confiscating foreign and domestic enterprises. Natural resources, utility companies, the credit system, and most large and medium industries fell into the hands of the government. As a result of these actions and the Agrarian Reform Law, the upper classes were wiped out, and middle-class families lost most of their income-producing property. Many emigrated, particularly to the United States, or were absorbed into the larger proletariat created by the Revolution. A gradual takeover of the mass communication media and the educational system also took place, and both became powerful tools of the state apparatus. In addition, the government initiated a program of low-income housing and a massive literacy campaign, which, according to official claims, has wiped out the 30 percent illiteracy rate that existed prior to the Revolution.

New equal educational and employment opportunities offered to women had the effect of undermining the family, one of the most important conservers of the old order. Relations between husband and wife were undermined, and the family largely lost control of the children. Large numbers of children attended free boarding schools and saw their parents for only short periods of time during the year. There was, therefore, not only frequent separation of husband and wife because of the work demands of the Revolution, but also separation of parents from children (see The Family Institution, ch. 2). The regime systematically encouraged these developments, perhaps aware that the only way to develop Cuba's new socialist man was through the destruction of culture-transmitting institutions, such as the family and the church. During the 1960s, the Castro government sharply curtailed the power and influence of the church (see The Roman Catholic Church, ch. 2).

In February 1960, the regime created a Central Planning Board (Junta Central de Planificación—Juceplan) to plan and direct the country's economic development. For the most part, the board adopted the organizational models followed by East European countries and transformed Cuba's private enterprise system into a centralized state-controlled economy. The transformation resulted in disorganization, bureaucratic chaos, inefficiency, and growing shortages. Agricultural production declined sharply, partly as a result of neglect and Castro's plan for industrialization, and by 1961 food rationing was introduced for the first time in Cuba's history.

The growing radicalization of the regime was accompanied by the destruction of possible opposition and by the growth in influence of the PSP. Political parties were not permitted to function, with the exception of the communist PSP, which later merged with Castro's own Twenty-Sixth of July Movement and adopted the party's original name, the PCC. Abetted by Castro, communists progressively occupied important positions in the government, gaining in prestige and influence. As a result, former Castro allies became disenchanted with the Revolution, believing that Castro had betrayed the ideals that he espoused while in the mountains.

Evidently, Castro saw significant advantages in using the PSP. The party provided the trained, disciplined, and organized cadres that Castro's movement lacked. But more importantly, the party had Moscow's ear, and therefore could serve as the bridge for any possible Cuban-Soviet rapprochement. Castro knew well that as he developed an anti-American revolution and insisted on remaining in power, a conflict with the United States would ensue. Only the protective umbrella of the Soviet Union could defend him against possible United States pressures or attack. No other power, Castro reasoned, could or would confront the United States over Cuba.

Ideologically, Fidel Castro was far from being a Marxist. Although strongly influenced by Falangist and fascist ideas while a high school student, and by Marxist ideas while at the University of Havana, Castro embraced none of these ideologies and was instead more a product of the Martí-Chibás tradition, although he broke with it in several fundamental respects. Whereas Martí and Chibás had envisioned reforms in a democratic framework in a nation politically and economically independent of the United States, they both advocated friendly relations with the "northern colossus." Castro did not. He had been anti-United States since his student days, when he distributed anti-United States propaganda in Bogotá, Colombia, in 1948. Perhaps because of his anti-North Americanism, and particularly his conviction that a major revolution with himself in absolute control could not be undertaken within Cuba's political framework and in harmony with the United States, Castro broke with the Martí-Chibás tradition.

Initially, the United States, which recognized the Castro government on January 7, 1959, followed a "wait and see" policy. The Dwight D. Eisenhower administration seemed to have been caught by surprise over events in Cuba and failed to grasp the magnitude of the changes going on or the nature of the leader sponsoring those changes. Differences arose between those who, believing that Castro was a Marxist, advocated a hard line toward Cuba and those who counseled patience with him.

Although tensions arose in connection with the public trials and executions of Batista supporters, serious differences did not emerge until after the Agrarian Reform Law had been promulgated. The United States protested, to no avail, the expropriations of United States properties without compensation that were initiated under the law. Agricultural expropriations were followed by additional expropriations of foreign investments, notably in the mining and petroleum industry. Complicating the relations between the two countries were arrests of United States citizens, Castro's refusal to meet with United States Ambassador Philip W. Bonsal in late 1959, and the sabotage and raids carried out against the Castro government by Cuban exiles operating from United States territory.

Fidel Castro, Che Guevara, and Raúl Castro believed that the political, social, and economic conditions that had produced their Revolution in Cuba existed in other parts of Latin America and that revolutions would occur throughout the continent. From 1960 onward, Cuban agents and diplomatic representatives established contact with revolutionary groups in the area and began distributing propaganda and aid. Several Cuban diplomats were expelled for interfering in the internal affairs of the countries to which they were accredited. As tensions mounted between the United States and Cuba, Fidel Castro's assertion of the international character of his Revolution increased, as did his involvement in promoting violence in Latin America. By July 1960, Castro was boasting that he would convert "the cordillera of the Andes into the Sierra Maestra of Latin America," and money, propaganda, men, and weapons began to flow from Havana in increasing quantities to foment the "antiimperialist" revolution.

The radicalization of the Revolution and the deterioration of relations with the United States grew apace with Cuban-Soviet rapprochement. During the February 4–13, 1960, visit to Havana of Soviet Deputy Premier Anastas Mikoyan, Cuba

*Cuban government officials, including Ernesto "Che" Guevara,
Raúl Castro, Fidel Castro, and President Osvaldo Dorticós
Torrado, lead the May Day parade, May 1, 1961.
Courtesy National Imagery and Mapping Agency, Washington*

signed a major commercial agreement with the Soviet Union.
The agreement provided that Cuba would receive, among
other products, Soviet oil in exchange for sugar. Formal diplomatic relations between the two countries were established on
May 8, 1960. That April and May, the Cuban government
nationalized major foreign businesses, including the transportation, banking, communications, and educational systems and
the media. On June 28, the Castro regime confiscated United
States-owned oil refineries without compensation. On July 26,
Castro issued the "Declaration of Havana," claiming Cuba's
right to export revolution and calling for Soviet support.
Nationalization of United States- and other foreign-owned
property in Cuba began on August 6. And on October 13, the
Castro government expropriated most Cuban-owned businesses. In October the United States announced an embargo
on most exports to Cuba, and when Castro restricted the staff
of the United States embassy to eleven persons, the United

States, on January 3, 1961, severed diplomatic relations and withdrew its ambassador.

By then the United States had embarked on a more aggressive policy toward the Castro regime. Groups of Cuban exiles were being trained, under the supervision of United States officials, in Central American camps for an attack on Cuba. The internal situation on the island then seemed propitious for an attempt to overthrow the Cuban regime. Although Castro still counted on significant popular support, that support had progressively decreased. His own Twenty-Sixth of July Movement was badly split on the issue of communism. Also, a substantial urban guerrilla movement existed throughout the island, composed of former Castro allies, Batista supporters, Catholic groups, and other elements that had been affected by the Revolution, and significant unrest was evident within the armed forces.

The Bay of Pigs Invasion of April 17–19, 1961, was a tragedy of errors. Although the Cuban government did not know the date or the exact place where the exile forces would land, the fact that an invasion was in the offing was known both within and outside of Cuba. The weapons and ammunition that were to be used by the invading force were all placed in one ship, which was sunk the first day of the invasion. The site for the invasion was sparsely populated, surrounded by swamps, and offered little access to nearby mountains, where guerrilla operations could be carried out if the invasion failed. The invading forces could, therefore, all but discount any help from the nearby population.

At the last minute, a confused and indecisive President John F. Kennedy canceled some of the air raids by Cuban exiles that were intended to cripple Castro's air force. Perhaps trying to reassert his authority over the Central Intelligence Agency (CIA)-sponsored invasion, to stymie possible world reaction, or to appease the Soviets, Kennedy ordered no further United States involvement.

The failure of the invasion and the brutal repression that followed smashed the entire Cuban underground. On the first day of the invasion, the regime arrested thousands of real and suspected oppositionists. The resistance never recovered from that blow. His regime strengthened and consolidated, Fidel Castro emerged victorious and boasted of having defeated a "Yankee-sponsored invasion." The disillusionment and frustration caused by the Bay of Pigs disaster among anti-Castro forces, both inside and out of Cuba, prevented the growth of significant organized opposition. Meanwhile, United States prestige in Latin America and throughout the world sank to a low point.

Following the Bay of Pigs fiasco, the United States turned to other methods of dealing with Fidel Castro. It pursued a vigorous, although only partially successful, policy to isolate the Cuban regime and strangle it economically. The nation pressured its allies throughout the world to reduce their commerce with Cuba. In the Organization of American States (OAS—see Glossary), the United States forced the expulsion of Cuba by a slim majority in January 1962, and several countries broke diplomatic relations with the Castro regime at this time. In 1964, after Castro had increased subversive activities in Latin America and had moved fully into the socialist camp, the OAS voted to suspend trade and diplomatic relations with Cuba; except for Mexico, all countries that had not already done so severed relations.

The single most important event accelerating Soviet military involvement in Cuba was the Bay of Pigs fiasco. The failure of the United States to act decisively against Castro gave the Soviets some illusions about United States determination and interest in Cuba. The Kremlin leaders now perceived that further economic and even military involvement in Cuba would not entail any danger to the Soviet Union itself and would not seriously jeopardize United States-Soviet relations. This view was further reinforced by President Kennedy's apologetic attitude concerning the Bay of Pigs invasion and his generally weak performance during his summit meeting with Soviet Premier Nikita Khrushchev in Vienna in June 1961.

The Soviets moved swiftly. New trade and cultural agreements were signed, and increased economic and technical aid was sent to Cuba. By mid-1962 the Soviets had embarked on a dangerous gamble by surreptitiously introducing nuclear missiles and bombers into the island. Through these actions, Khrushchev and the Kremlin leadership hoped to alter the balance of power and force the United States to accept a settlement of the German issue. A secondary and perhaps less important motivation was to extend to Cuba the Soviet nuclear umbrella and thus protect Castro from any further hostile actions by the United States.

On October 22, 1962, President Kennedy publicly reacted to the Soviet challenge, instituting a naval blockade of the island

and demanding the withdrawal of all offensive weapons from Cuba. For the next several days, the world teetered on the brink of nuclear holocaust.

Finally, after a hectic exchange of correspondence, Khrushchev agreed to remove the missiles and bombers, and to allow unsupervised inspection of the removal in exchange for the United States' pledge not to invade Cuba. Although Castro refused to allow a United Nations inspection, the missiles and bombers were removed under United States aerial surveillance, and the crisis ended. The United States has never publicly acknowledged that it pledged not to invade Cuba, but subsequent United States policies indicate that a United States-Soviet understanding was reached over Cuba that included a United States "hands off" policy toward the island.

The missile crisis had a significant impact on the countries involved. Although it led to a thaw in United States-Soviet relations, it significantly strained Cuban-Soviet relations. Castro was not consulted throughout the negotiations between Kennedy and Khrushchev, and the unilateral Soviet withdrawal of the missiles and bombers wounded Castro's pride and prestige. It was a humiliating experience for the Cuban leader, who was relegated throughout the crisis to a mere pawn on the chessboard of international politics. Castro defiantly rejected the United States-Soviet understanding and publicly questioned Soviet willingness and determination to defend the Revolution.

After the missile crisis, Fidel Castro increased contacts with communist China, exploiting the Sino-Soviet dispute and proclaiming his intention of remaining neutral and maintaining fraternal relations with all socialist states. Cuba also signed various trade and cultural agreements with Beijing, and Castro grew increasingly friendly toward the Chinese, praising their more militant revolutionary posture. He also defied the Soviets, as he joined the Chinese in refusing to sign the Nuclear Test Ban Treaty (1963). All of this maneuvering somewhat increased Castro's leverage with the Soviets and gained him more assistance.

The Chinese honeymoon was short-lived, however. In 1966 Fidel Castro blasted the Chinese for reducing rice shipments to Cuba below the quantities that Castro alleged had been agreed on between the two countries. He described Mao Tse-tung's ideological statements as lightweight, called for the creation of a "council of elders" to prevent aged leaders from "putting

MISSILE SHELTER TENT

TRACKED PRIME MOVERS

OXIDIZER TANK TRAILERS

NK TRAILERS

A medium-range ballistic missile site in San Cristóbal, Pinar del Río
Province, on October 23, 1962
The Soviet cargo vessel **Anosov,** *carrying eight missile transporters*
with canvas-covered missiles, departs Cuba on November 7, 1962.
Courtesy National Imagery and Mapping Agency, Washington

their whims into effect when senility has taken hold of them," and threatened to handle Chinese diplomats the same way "we handle the American Embassy." By then Castro had also become disappointed with China's attitude toward Vietnam and by its propaganda efforts to sway Cubans to its side in the Sino-Soviet conflict. Castro's insistence on absolute control of the revolutionary movement in Latin America and his awareness of China's limitations in supplying Cuba's economic needs were further key factors in the cooling of the friendship between the two nations. Subsequently, relations became more cordial, but never reached the closeness achieved before 1966 (see Foreign Relations, ch. 4).

Revolutionary Adventurism and Institutionalization

Revolutionary Adventurism

The principal area of Soviet-Cuban conflict in the early 1960s was Fidel Castro's revolutionary ventures in Latin America, beginning with his attempt in 1963 to subvert and overthrow the Venezuelan government and his guerrilla operations in Guatemala and Bolivia. Castro's attempts at revolution all ended in disaster, however. His failures weakened his leverage with the Soviets, increased Soviet influence with Cuba, and forced him to look inward to improve his faltering economy.

In the early 1970s, Castro's speeches played down the notion of Latin American revolution; Castro had come to recognize that there were "different roads to power." Although not completely renouncing his original goal of exporting his own brand of communism, he became more selective in furnishing Cuban support.

The overthrow of the Salvador Allende Gossens regime in Chile in September 1973, however, marked a turning point for the Cuban-inspired revolutionary struggle in Latin America. The Cuban leadership examined its strategy and tactics in the area and concluded that the way to power in Latin America was not through ballots but through bullets. Beginning in the mid-1970s, Castro increased his support to select groups, particularly in Central America, providing them with propaganda material, training, advisers, financial help, and ultimately weapons. An acceleration of the revolutionary armed struggle in the area followed.

The acceleration coincided with the United States debacle in Vietnam and the Watergate scandal. The inability of United

States administrations to respond swiftly and decisively to conditions in Central America, as well as in other parts of the world, and to the Soviet-Cuban challenge in Africa, emboldened the Cuban leader. More than 40,000 Cuban troops, supported by Soviet equipment, were transferred to Africa in order to bring to power communist regimes in Angola and Ethiopia.

Encouraged by Cuban-Soviet victories in Angola and Ethiopia, the Castro regime focused its attention on the rapidly deteriorating conditions in Nicaragua. Cuba, together with Panama and Venezuela, increased support to the Sandinista National Liberation Front (Frente Sandinista de Liberación Nacional—FSLN), the principal guerrilla group opposing the Anastasio Somoza regime. In July 1979, Somoza fled and the FSLN rode victorious into Managua.

The Sandinista victory in Nicaragua stands as an imposing monument to Cuban strategy and ambitions in the hemisphere. The overthrow of Somoza gave the Castro line its most important boost in two decades. It vindicated, although belatedly, Castro's ideological insistence on violence and guerrilla warfare as the correct strategy to attain power in Latin America. Castro's long-held belief that the political, social, and economic conditions that had produced the Revolution in Cuba existed or could be created in other parts of Latin America, and that revolution would occur throughout the continent, seemed at last justified.

From that time on, the tempo of Cuban-supported violence accelerated in Central America. Aided by an extensive network of intelligence, military forces, and sophisticated propaganda machinery, the Cuban government increased its support to various groups in the area. In cooperation with Sandinista leaders, Cuba aided insurgent groups in El Salvador, Guatemala, and Colombia. Castro's commitment to revolutionary violence had been reinforced once again, showing convincingly that the Cuban leadership was willing to seize opportunities and take risks to expand its influence and power.

Cuban-Soviet Rapprochement

By the late 1960s, the Cuban economy was plagued by low productivity, mismanagement, poor planning, and shortages of almost every item (see Structure of the Economy, ch. 3). Structural shortcomings seemed more entrenched than ever. The ills of the past were still there, with renewed vengeance. Long-term trade agreements with the Soviets were perpetuating Cuba's role as a sugar producer, forcing the country to abandon indefinitely any plans for significant diversification and industrialization. Trade continued with one large industrialized nation, whose commercial policies reminded Castro of those pursued by Cuba's previous trading partner, the United States. Cuba's foreign debt also reached alarming proportions without significant improvements in the island's ability to save foreign exchange. The unemployment of the pre-Castro era gave way to a new type of unemployment in the form of poor labor productivity, absenteeism, and an ineffective and overstaffed bureaucracy. In response to the situation, the regime resorted to coercive methods to ensure a labor supply for critical agricultural tasks. The living standard of Cubans also deteriorated, as high capital accumulation was given first priority over consumer goods.

In its second decade, the Cuban Revolution faced critical problems. Internally, mounting economic difficulties inspired a new frenzy of planning activity and greater regimentation in the hope of stimulating productivity. One result was the expanded influence of the military in society, and its increasingly important role in both economic and political life. The party, which had remained weak and ineffective throughout the 1960s, was enlarged and strengthened its efforts to spread its influence throughout society. Meanwhile, the regime continued to pursue its aim of transforming Cuba in accordance with a new set of values and with the ultimate end of creating a new socialist citizen. Externally, the Cuban leadership attempted to break out of its isolation in Latin America, became selective in its support of revolutionary movements in the area, moved even closer to the Soviet Union, increased its influence on the Nonaligned Movement (see Glossary), and embarked on a series of successful military interventions, primarily on the African continent.

Although past Cuban-Soviet relations had been punctuated by frequent instances of Castro's insubordination and attempts to assert his independence, in mid-1968 relations entered a period of close collaboration and friendliness. A turning point occurred in August 1968, when Castro supported the Soviet invasion of Czechoslovakia, a response dictated primarily by political and economic considerations.

In the early 1970s, Soviet military and economic aid increased substantially, and Cuba moved closer to the Soviet

*Soviet rocket-launch vehicles in the fourth anniversary parade
in Havana on January 2, 1963
Courtesy National Imagery and Mapping Agency, Washington*

Union, becoming in 1972 a member of the Council for Mutual
Economic Assistance (CMEA; also known as Comecon—see
Glossary). The result was greater direct Soviet influence on the
island. During this period, Soviet technicians became extensively involved in managerial and planning activities at the
national level. The total number of Soviet military and technical advisers increased considerably, and numerous economic
advisers arrived. Of special significance were long-term agreements between Cuba and the Soviet Union that geared the
Cuban economy to the Soviet economic plans. A new Inter-
Governmental Coordinating Committee was also established,
giving the Kremlin considerable leverage over Cuban developments.

Institutionalization

In an attempt to increase economic efficiency and in line
with Soviet objectives, the PCC was expanded and strengthened in the 1970s. The aim was greater party conformity to the
needs of a socialist society, with principal emphasis on a higher

level of ideological training and the acquisition of specialized knowledge by party members.

During the early period, the party remained small, disorganized, and relegated to a secondary position vis-à-vis the military. It lacked a clear and defined role. Internal leadership and coordination remained poor, and meetings were few and of questionable value. Evidently, Castro saw little need for a well-developed party structure, which would have reduced or at least rivaled his style of *personalista* (personalism—see Glossary) leadership. Conflict between old-guard communists and Fidelistas also created tension and prevented the development of a strong organization. Competition from the military or the bureaucracy took the best talents away from the party. These cadres saw better opportunities for advancement in those other sectors than in a party riddled with factionalism and not warmly supported by the *líder máximo* (maximum leader).

The decade of the 1970s was one of expansion and consolidation for the party. During the first half of the decade, membership expanded from some 55,000 in 1969 to 202,807 at the time of the First Party Congress in 1975. During the second half, the rapid rate of expansion slowed down somewhat. By the time of the Second Party Congress in 1980, there were fewer than 400,000 members and candidates. At the Third Party Congress (1986), Castro disclosed that full members and candidates numbered 482,000.

The First Party Congress was a watershed in legitimizing the position of the party as the guiding and controlling force in society. It reassured the Soviet Union of Cuba's loyalty and friendship, extolling the Soviets' continuous military and economic aid to the Cuban Revolution, and rehabilitated old-guard communists, some of whom had been mistrusted and persecuted by the Castroites. The Congress also expanded the party's Central Committee from ninety-one to 112 members, increased the Political Bureau from eight to thirteen members, and maintained the Secretariat at eleven members, with Fidel Castro and Raúl Castro as first and second secretaries, respectively.

In his report to the Congress in 1975, Fidel Castro attempted to reconcile the adoption of Soviet-style institutions on the island with a renewed emphasis on nationalism and on the historical roots of the Cuban Revolution. He emphasized that Cuban socialism was the culmination of a struggle against Spanish colonialism and United States neocolonial involvement in Cuban affairs. With total disregard for Martí's ideas, Castro linked the Cuban independence leader with Lenin in order to justify Cuba's move into the communist camp. The Congress adopted a Five-Year Plan, calling for closer economic integration with the Soviet Union and an economic system modeled on other socialist states. The approval of the party's platform stressing "Marxist-Leninist principles and the leading role of the party" was further evidence of the impact of Soviet-style orthodoxy on the island.

Of paramount importance was the adoption of Cuba's first socialist constitution, which was approved by a 97.7 percent majority in a popular referendum in early 1976. Modeled on other communist constitutions, the Cuban document recognizes the party as "the highest leading force in state and society" and defines the function of mass organizations, such as the Committee for the Defense of the Revolution (Comité de Defensa de la Revolución—CDR) and the Federation of Cuban Women (Federación de Mujeres Cubanas—FMC). It divided the island into fourteen new provinces instead of the six old ones.

The Unchanging Revolution, 1980–89

In the early 1980s, the Cuban Revolution reached a critical stage in its development. Persistent structural and managerial problems in the economy, low prices for Cuba's export products, and an inability to break away from economic dependence on the Soviet bloc forced a reexamination of basic goals. Because production in most key sectors had fallen short of expected targets, emphasis was placed on increased planning with more modest goals. The regime adopted Soviet economic methods, decreased emphasis on moral incentives, and attempted to create more efficient economic organizations. In the process, the Cubans suffered more austerity, with greater rationing of food and consumer goods, and, therefore, harder times. Life became increasingly more difficult: people faced long lines to obtain the most basic goods, the public transportation system was collapsing, and the education and health systems were deteriorating rapidly. In desperation, many Cubans fled the country, preferring to risk dying in the Straits of Florida on flimsy rafts rather than live in Castro's Cuba.

The establishment of a Soviet-type, centrally planned economy burdened Cuba with a vast and cumbersome bureaucracy that stifled innovation, productivity, and efficiency. The island continued its heavy reliance on sugar for development of the domestic economy and for foreign trade, and made little attempt to achieve agricultural diversification or industrialization. At the same time, Cuba relied on the Soviets for massive infusions of aid to meet minimal investment and consumption needs and depended almost entirely on Soviet oil exports for energy requirements.

Popular expectations of rapid economic improvement were replaced by pessimism. There were signs of decreasing enthusiasm among Cuba's labor force and increasing signs of weariness with constant revolutionary exhortations. Underemployment was rampant, and labor productivity was at a low point. Absenteeism from the job place became common. Cubans stole from state enterprises and fed an already growing black market for food and goods. Graft and corruption became widespread as Cuban citizens rejected socialist morality and laws and struggled to survive on a daily basis.

Yet this is only one side of the picture. It is in the nature of totalitarian regimes that the key question relates not to economics per se, but rather to the effects of economic factors upon the levers of political and social control. In an effort to increase productivity and forestall any further decline in revolutionary momentum, the regime increased the militarization and regimentation of society and institutionalized its rule by expanding the role and influence of the party throughout society. This progressive institutionalization contributed to the further stabilization of the system, while reducing its vulnerability to threats of external subversion and internal revolt. From an institutional standpoint, the regime appeared equipped to withstand the difficult years ahead. Fidel Castro was still dominant. He remained "the Revolution" and "the maximum leader." The evidence seemed to indicate that significant segments of the Cuban people continued to be attracted by his personalized style of government. Some regarded him as a protection against the state structures, resembling a traveling ombudsman ready to change or challenge policies of which he was the author. His lengthy speeches before huge throngs served both as a pedagogical device and as an instantaneous plebiscite. Despite some friction within the military after the United States invasion of Grenada in 1983 embarrassed the Cubans, Castro maintained absolute control of his government, with no other public figure in a position to challenge his undisputed authority.

The political elite's values, policy goals, and organizational interests were driven to reinforce Fidel Castro's political inclinations and policy preferences. The hard foreign policy objectives of this group were maintaining Cuba's independence from, and opposition to, the United States; actively supporting revolutionary movements in Latin America; promoting national liberation and socialism in the developing world; acquiring influence and supportive allies among the developing world states; and securing maximum military, economic, and political commitments from the Soviet Union.

In foreign affairs, the Cuban Revolution achieved significant successes. In the late 1970s, Fidel Castro emerged as the leader of the Nonaligned Movement. There he espoused four important themes for the future that became the cornerstone of Cuba's policy toward the developing world: support for violent revolutions; anticolonialism; an end to white supremacy in Africa; and reduction of dependency on Western economies. These policies coincided with Soviet objectives and produced a convergence of Soviet and Cuban actions in the developing world. Castro's willingness to commit his Soviet-equipped, well-trained armed forces on the African continent gained for Cuba much respect and admiration, but also created some fear among African leaders.

The Cuban leadership saw its support for revolution as an integral and critical part of Cuba's foreign policy. Helping leftist insurgents throughout the world was a revolutionary commitment, ensuring that these allies would come to Cuba's aid in times of need. But more important, worldwide revolution directed against the United States, the principal enemy of the Cuban Revolution, was used to divert United States attention and resources, and perhaps to restrain its policies and actions against the island. The ultimate goal was to ensure the survival of the Cuban Revolution and its leadership, the most important objective of Cuba's foreign policy.

Armed struggle was fundamental to Fidel Castro's mystique as well as to the image that he projected onto the larger world stage, where he was determined to play a prominent role. Other revolutionary leaders might shed, in time, doctrinaire excesses in favor of the pragmatic pursuit of comfortable rule. Yet there is truly nothing in Castro's personal makeup to suggest that he would forsake the global floodlights and renounce his "internationalist" commitments.

Perhaps the Sandinista victory in Nicaragua and the establishment, albeit temporarily, of a Marxist regime in Grenada were Cuba's most important revolutionary achievements in the Western hemisphere. Although the overthrow of the Somoza regime in Nicaragua was as much the result of internal opposition as of external aid, Cuba claimed a joint effort with Venezuela and Panama in bringing down the Somoza dynasty. For Cuba, Nicaragua exemplified the vindication of the Cuban line, which had been emphasizing for years the need for violence and particularly guerrilla warfare to attain power in Latin America.

The Sandinista victory gave new life to revolutionary violence in Central America, much of it supported by Cuba. Yet Cuba's support for insurgent groups in the area, particularly in El Salvador and Guatemala, was channeled increasingly through Nicaragua. Using Nicaragua or other third countries facilitated the flow of weapons, propaganda, and aid, while making the task of detection and resistance that much harder. Cuba also denied supporting revolutionary groups, thus weakening United States credibility and influence, while at the same time facilitating relations with more conservative governments in Latin America. Castro's willingness to come to the aid of the Argentine military regime during the Falklands War (1982) was a further indication of Cuba's pragmatic and opportunistic foreign policy. Throughout these maneuvers in Cuba's foreign policy, Castro remained closely tied to the Soviet Union. Although there were frictions between Castro and the Kremlin, the latter's influence and presence in Cuba were far more extensive than ever before. At the same time, solidarity with the Soviet Union remained a vital element of Cuba's foreign policy. Cuba's policies and actions in the international arena operated in the larger framework of Soviet objectives. Castro continued to pursue his own policies only as long as they did not clash with those of the Soviets.

Uncomfortable as he felt in the embrace of the Russian bear, Castro's options were limited. Although relations with China improved from their nadir in 1967, the Chinese seemed unable or unwilling to take Cuba on as an expensive client. Beijing decried Castro's support of Moscow's policies as "revisionist," and the Chinese still remembered his denunciations of Mao in the late 1960s with bitterness and anger.

Increased commercial ties with Canada, Western Europe, and Japan beckoned as a healthy development from Cuba's standpoint. Yet the ability of these countries to absorb the island's sugar exports was limited, and Havana had scant cash reserves with which to purchase European and Japanese goods. Cuba's heavy economic commitment to the Soviet Union and the East European countries was an additional deterrent to a broadening of its trading partners, and United States pressures on Western allies tended to limit their willingness to trade with Cuba.

To be sure, all of this could have enhanced the desire of the Castro regime to reduce its reliance on the Soviet Union and to reach some accommodation with the United States. Rapprochement with the United States could have led to a loosening of the embargo and even access to an important neighboring market, if the United States were willing to buy Cuban sugar. It could have bolstered Cuba's immediate security position and provided Castro with leverage in his dealings with the Soviet Union. United States recognition would have meant an important psychological victory for Castro. In Latin America, it would have been interpreted as a defeat for "Yankee imperialism" and as an acceptance of the Castro regime as a permanent, albeit irritating, phenomenon in the Caribbean.

Cuban moves toward accommodation with the United States would have posed some major problems for the Kremlin. The Soviets were not averse to some amelioration in Cuban-United States tensions, especially if the result was to reduce Cuba's heavy demands for Soviet aid. The Kremlin was fearful, however, that ties with the West could foster a desire for increasing independence by other Soviet bloc members and lead to progressive internal liberalization, as the results of the West German efforts to establish diplomatic and trade relations with Eastern Europe showed. Although Cuba was not as critical to the Soviet Union as was Eastern Europe, a resumption of Cuba's relations with the United States and a significant weakening in Soviet-Cuban ties would have been seen as leading to the eventual subverting of the Revolution and the renunciation of membership in the "socialist camp." Moscow viewed Cuba's possible defection as a blow to its prestige and as damaging to the Soviet power posture vis-à-vis the United States.

Rapprochement with the United States would also have been fraught with danger and uncertainties for the Cuban leadership. It would have required a loosening of Cuba's military ties with the Soviet Union, the abandonment of visible support for violent revolutions in Latin America, and the withdrawal of

Cuban troops from Africa and other parts of the world. These were conditions that Castro was not willing to accept. He perceived them as an attempt by the United States to isolate Cuba and strengthen anti-Castro forces within Cuba, thus posing a threat to the stability of his regime. Castro, therefore, was not able or willing to offer meaningful concessions that would be indispensable for United States-Cuban rapprochement. Negotiations proceeded, however, and ad hoc agreements were struck on some issues such as skyjacking and the Mariel Boatlift, which brought 125,000 Cuban refugees to the United States in 1980.

Cuban-Soviet relations, for their part, also were beset with serious irritants. Moscow's claim to leadership of the "socialist bloc" and its interference in Cuba's internal affairs have clashed with the forces of Cuban nationalism. Given Castro's personality and past policies, his suspicion, if not dislike, of the Soviets, and his desire to play a leading role in world affairs, he remained an unstable and unpredictable Soviet ally. Yet in the 1980s, Castro had no choice but to follow the Soviet lead, while attempting to emerge from his isolation in Latin America and improve Cuba's faltering economy.

By the 1990s, Cuba's international relations revolved around seven main goals: the survival of the Castro Revolution; the internationalization of Castro's personal prestige and charisma, with a resulting increase in power and influence; the maintenance, until the collapse of communism, of a close alliance with the Soviet Union and its interests throughout the world; the preservation of an anti-United States posture in an attempt to weaken United States power and influence worldwide; the acquisition of influence and supportive allies among developing world states; the development of a "new international economic order"; and the continuous support of "movements of national liberation" in Asia, Africa, the Middle East, and Latin America. The image of a nonaligned Cuba was repeatedly tarnished, however, by Castro's close partnership with the Soviets. His stature suffered as a result of his failure to condemn the Soviet invasion of Afghanistan in December 1979 and to rally Latin American leaders to repudiate their foreign debt.

The Cuban government has helped a broad range of "progressive forces," terrorist groups, and religious fanatics opposing the United States. Since the 1970s, however, the regime has been increasingly willing, despite its Marxist rhetoric, to establish ties with conservative Latin American states. Clearly, ideology is not the sole factor shaping Cuba's external behavior. Cuban interest in developing such relations has been motivated by a desire to foster Cuban and, in the past, Soviet objectives, and to undermine United States interests in the area.

Despite perestroika (restructuring) and glasnost (political opening) in the Soviet Union and differences with Mikhail Gorbachev, Castro remained a close Soviet ally until the end of communism in 1991. Since the late 1960s, the relations between Havana and Moscow had taken the form of a progressively closer alliance. The incorporation of Cuba into the Soviet camp was evident not only in economic terms (Cuba was a member of Comecon and was heavily dependent on Soviet economic and military aid and trade) but also was clearly manifested in its model of government and its international behavior. Undoubtedly, Cuba was subservient in most cases to Soviet interests, but Havana had considerable leverage with Moscow, as well as some freedom to act and react in external affairs (especially in the Caribbean and Latin America in general).

Problems and Prospects in the Post-Soviet Era

In the 1990s, Castro faced some of the old problems that had plagued the Cuban Revolution in the past, as well as new and critical challenges. Internally, there was growing evidence of disillusionment with the party's and Castro's exhortations. Absenteeism and youth apathy were increasing. Castro seemed to be losing the battle to create a new generation devoted to the party and to the Revolution. Despite more than forty years of education and indoctrination, the new socialist man was nowhere to be found. The loss of this generation represented, perhaps, the greatest challenge for the continuity of the Revolution.

Economically, the Revolution was extremely weak. Persistent structural problems, low prices for Cuba's export products, and the inability to obtain aid from the Soviet Union forced yet another reexamination of basic goals. The deepening economic crisis, aggravated by the collapse of communism not only in the Soviet Union, but also in Eastern Europe, produced a new frenzy of planning activity and greater regimentation, in the hope of stimulating productivity. Rejecting perestroika and glasnost, Castro returned to the failed path of the past, insisting that the Cubans should work harder, sacrifice more, and expect less in the years ahead. Among the populace, pessimism and cynicism replaced revolutionary fervor.

Mild overtures from Castro toward the United States and Cuba's deepening economic crisis encouraged those in the United States who believed it was time for a rapprochement with Cuba. In 1989 Castro tried and executed three high-ranking officers of the Ministry of Interior and Division General Arnaldo Ochoa Sánchez, former commander of Cuban troops in Africa, accusing them of drug trafficking. The execution seemed more connected with the elimination of a potential rival than with drugs. Denying his or his brother's involvement with drugs, Castro called on the United States for cooperation in fighting the drug trade. As he had in the past, Castro was willing to negotiate and to cooperate with the United States on specific issues.

Mired in economic crisis and without the support of his former benefactor, Castro braced for the difficult times ahead. Yet he was unwilling to budge and change the Marxist course he had set for his Revolution four decades earlier.

Fearful that economic change could lead to political change, he rejected both. He remained committed to the cornerstones of his policies—a command economy, violent revolution, anti-North Americanism, "internationalism," and personal rule. Although his support for violent revolution and "internationalism"z was quite limited, Castro was unwilling to modify or abandon the five cornerstones of his policies.

*   *   *

The study of Cuban history from colonial times to the present has produced a wealth of scholarly works both in Cuba and abroad. Multivolume histories and general histories of the island include Charles E. Chapman's *A History of the Cuban Republic*, Ramiro Guerra y Sánchez et alia's *Historia de la nación cubana*, Willis F. Johnson's *The History of Cuba*, Wyatt MacGaffey and Clifford R. Barnett's *Cuba*, Levi Marrero's *Cuba*, Louis A. Pérez's *Cuba*, Fernando Portuondo del Prado's *Historia de Cuba*, Jaime Suchlicki's *Cuba: From Columbus to Castro*, and Hugh Thomas's *Cuba: The Pursuit of Freedom*.

The era of Spanish domination has produced an extensive and varied literature, including Gerardo Brown Castillo's *Cuba colonial*, José M. Carbonell y Rivero's eighteen-volume *Evolución de la cultura cubana*, Richard B. Gray's *José Martí: Cuban Patriot*,

Pedro José Guitera's *Historia de la Isla de Cuba*, Kenneth T. Kiple's *Blacks in Colonial Cuba*, Allan J. Kuethe's *Cuba, 1753–1815*, Manuel Moreno Fraginals's *The Sugarmill*, Medardo Vitier's *Las ideas en Cuba*, and Irene A. Wright's *The Early History of Cuba, 1492–1586*. The institution of slavery and the role of blacks in Cuba have been revisited in numerous studies, especially since the Castro Revolution, in such works as Arthur F. Corwin's *Spain and the Abolition of Slavery in Cuba, 1817–1886* and Franklin W. Knight's *Slave Society in Cuba During the Nineteenth Century*.

The independence struggle and United States intervention are controversial subjects and have produced a vast literature. Since the Revolution, numerous studies have been published in Cuba highlighting the role of certain leaders in the wars, particularly Antonio Maceo, a mulatto general, and Martí, the father of Cuban independence. The José Martí National Library's *Anuario del Centro de Estudios Martianos* is the best guide to the extensive literature on Martí. Other useful sources include José Franco's three-volume *Antonio Maceo*, Herminio Portell-Vilá's *Historia de la Guerra de Cuba y los Estados Unidos contra España*, Julius Pratt's *Expansionists of 1898*, and Miguel A. Varona Guerrero's *La Guerra de Independencia de Cuba*.

The prerevolutionary period that lasted from 1902 until 1959 produced an incisive and critical literature that examined the problems of nationhood and the development of the new nation. A few of the useful books include Luis E. Aguilar's *Cuba, 1933: Prologue to Revolution*; Raymond L. Buell's *Problems of the New Cuba: Report of the Commission on Cuban Affairs*; Russel H. Fitzgibbon's *Cuba and the United States, 1900–1935*; Ramiro Guerra y Sánchez, José M. Cabrera, Juan J. Remos, and Emeterio S. Santovenia's *Historia de la nación cubana*; Allan Reed Millett's *The Politics of Intervention: The Military Occupation of Cuba, 1906–1909*; Lowry Nelson's *Rural Cuba*; Louis A. Pérez's *Army Politics in Cuba, 1898–1958*; Robert F. Smith's *Background to Revolution: The Development of Modern Cuba*; Suchlicki's *University Students and Revolution in Cuba, 1920–1968*; Francis Adams Truslow's *A Report on Cuba*; and Medardo Vitier's *Las ideas en Cuba*.

The Cuban Revolution generated a vast literature that focused originally on the causes of the Revolution, the nature of the leadership, and United States policy. Later on, studies addressed the nature of Castroism, Castro's alliance with the Soviets, Castro's internationalism, and the failings of Cuba's economic model. A few of the useful books include those by Juan M. del Aguila's *Cuba: Dilemmas of a Revolution*; James G. Blight's and David A. Welch's *On the Brink: Americans and Soviets Reexamine the Cuban Missile Crisis*; Jorge I. Domínguez's *Cuba: Order and Revolution*; Theodore Draper's *Castroism: Theory and Practice*; Raymond W. Duncan's *The Soviet Union and Cuba: Interests and Influence*; Richard R. Fagen's *The Transformation of Political Culture in Cuba*; Pamela Falk's *Cuban Foreign Policy*; Carlos Franqui's *Diary of the Cuban Revolution*; Georgie Anne Geyer's *Guerrilla Prince: The Untold Story of Fidel Castro*; Edward González's *Cuba Under Castro: The Limits of Charisma*; Maurice Halperin's *The Rise and Decline of Fidel Castro*; *Cuban Communism*, edited by Irving L. Horowitz and Suchlicki; Haynes Johnson's *The Bay of Pigs*; *Revolutionary Change in Cuba*, edited by Carmelo Mesa-Lago; Carlos Alberto Montaner's *Fidel Castro and the Cuban Revolution*; Andres Oppenheimer's *Castro's Final Hour*; Thomas G. Paterson's *Contesting Castro*; Marifeli Pérez-Stable's *The Cuban Revolution*; Elizabeth Stone's *Women and the Cuban Revolution*; three volumes edited by Suchlicki: *Cuba, Castro, and Revolution*, *Cuba in a Changing World*, and *The Cuban Military Under Castro*; Szulc's *Fidel: A Critical Portrait*; and Peter Wyden's *Bay of Pigs: The Untold Story*. (For further information and complete citations, see Bibliography.)

Chapter 2. The Society and Its Environment

A view of the smoke-covered Havana skyline and the seaside highway (el Malecón), 1996
Courtesy National Imagery and Mapping Agency, Washington

CUBA CONFRONTS DAUNTING social issues in its fifth decade of socialist rule, despite having a fairly well-educated and healthy population and low fertility and mortality rates. Many of the widely praised social achievements of the 1970s and 1980s—in health, education, and social security—are no longer sustainable given the absence of Soviet subsidies and the poor performance of the economy. The health sector, severely battered by the economic crisis of the "special period in peacetime" (*período especial en tiempo de paz*; hereafter Special Period—see Glossary), and with some indicators suggesting worsening standards, lacks even the most elementary medical inputs and no longer delivers the services Cubans had come to expect. It is also burdened by a bloated staff of physicians, nurses, and other health personnel far too numerous for the country's needs. Similar difficulties are plaguing the education sector, where even pencils and notebooks are scarce. Cuba has far more teachers than it can use productively, its educational infrastructure is crumbling, and its study programs are poorly attuned to the needs of a country urgently needing to restructure its economy and become integrated into the world economy (see Performance of the Economy, ch. 3).

To make matters worse, the financial resources needed to maintain the generous safety net developed since Fidel Castro Ruz (president, 1976–) seized power in 1959 are simply not available. Pensions for early retirement and extensive unemployment programs—crucial national entitlements—are taxing the country's finances, while providing only miserly benefits. A rapidly aging population is adding to the onerous cost of these programs. Regardless of developments in the economy, low birth rates ensure that problems associated with the elderly population will intensify as the number of working-age Cubans relative to the elderly continues to decline. On the positive side, Cuba can count on a relatively well-trained work force and the fact that the number of children relative to the working-age population continues to decline further. (The relative decline in the number of children counterbalances the increasing dependency ratio as the proportion of elderly in the total population rises.) Under the proper economic incentives system, Cuban workers have the potential to become highly productive.

Cuba must also address worrisome environmental trends. Concern is most warranted in the agricultural sector, where widespread adoption of capital-intensive (see Glossary) methods, such as chemical inputs and mechanization; grandiose but often poorly conceived infrastructure development plans, such as dams and irrigation projects; and central planning (see Glossary) may have compromised the sustainable use of some of the country's soils. Cuba, however, is one of the few developing countries that has managed to reverse a long-term deforestation trend, although this achievement may now be threatened by the country's current inability to import lumber and cooking fuels.

Because of the Special Period, economic and social initiatives have been implemented that are reversing a long-term commitment to maintaining the national income distribution within a narrow band. The free circulation of the dollar, the assigning of priority to foreign tourism, and policies designed to increase emigrant remittances are having a regressive effect on income distribution. Not all Cubans have ready access to dollars; most of those who do either have family members residing abroad or are employed in, or derive some benefit from, the tourism sector. Because relatively few black Cubans have emigrated, this particular social group suffers the brunt of the perverse income-distribution effects of remittances. So do those Cuban families, who, regardless of race, have no immediate relatives abroad, or whose wage earners are employed in state enterprises or in social sectors, such as health, in which the government has proscribed self-employment. The increasing number of visits by emigrants further contributes to the growing income differential trend and serves to highlight social disparities. In response to these conditions, social ills less visible in Cuba before the Special Period—such as prostitution, begging, and property and violent crimes—are on the rise.

Mass organizations, although still a dominant feature of social life in Cuba, have lost much of their influence because of general apathy and disillusionment with Cuba's state of affairs. A religious revival is underway; many Cubans seem to want to fill a spiritual void. Participating in religious ceremonies, an activity no longer stigmatized, has become an important social safety valve inasmuch as doing so permits citizens to show discontent without fear of government retribution. Pope John Paul II's visit in January 1998 gave added legitimacy to religion as a valid component of Cuban life (see Religion and the State, ch. 4).

Physical and Natural Setting

Principal Geographic Features

The Cuban archipelago—two main islands plus 3,715 small and large keys and inlets—has a total land surface of 110,860 square kilometers. It is nine times as large as Jamaica and twelve times the size of Puerto Rico. The westernmost of the Greater Antilles island chain, the Cuban archipelago is strategically located in the Atlantic Ocean, just below the Tropic of Cancer at geographic coordinates 21°30'N, 80°00'W, safeguarding the entrances to the Gulf of Mexico to the west and the Caribbean Sea to the south. Cuba lies seventy-seven kilometers west of Haiti, 140 kilometers north of Jamaica, 150 kilometers south of Key West, and 210 kilometers east of Mexico's Yucatán Peninsula.

Cuba proper is a long and elongated island that accounts for 94.67 percent of the country's land area, or 104,945 square kilometers. The island is 1,250 kilometers in length from east to west and averages about 100 kilometers in width. Isla de la Juventud (formerly Isla de Pinos), the second largest land mass, located southwest of Cuba in the Golfo de Batabanó, has an area of 2,200 square kilometers, or 1.98 percent of the country's total. The remaining keys and inlets cover 3.35 percent of the national territory, or 3,715 square kilometers. The small keys and inlets are primarily clustered in five subarchipelagos, two of which are off the northern coast. The Archipiélago de los Colorados (with about sixty keys and inlets) is off Pinar del Río Province; and the Archipiélago de Sabana and the Archipiélago de Camagüey (with about 400 keys and inlets) run along the northern center of the island. The most important archipelagos on the southern coast are the Archipiélago de los Canarreos, which encompasses Isla de la Juventud and 300 other keys and inlets; the Banco de los Jardines and Jardinillos keys, off the Zapata Swamp in central Cuba; and in eastern Cuba, in the Golfo de Guacanayabo, the Archipiélago de los Jardines de la Reina.

The Cuban coastline measures 5,746 kilometers. The north coast accounts for 3,209 kilometers, while the coastline of Isla de la Juventud has a length of 327 kilometers. Hundreds of kilometers of sandy beaches dot the Cuban archipelago, many still in their natural state. Fossilized coral formations occupy about half of Cuba's coastline, while living coral reefs are found in adjacent waters—often extending for hundreds of kilometers. The coral reef along Cuba's northern coast is second in length in the world only to Australia's Great Barrier Reef.

Many of Cuba's more than 200 bays, which have narrow entrances but ample inner areas, make some of the world's best harbors. Several of the country's many harbors, some with deep channels and horseshoe shapes, offer excellent protection from the fury of the seas. The most important harbors on the northern coast—from west to east—are Bahía Honda in Pinar del Río Province; Bahía de Cabañas, Bahía del Mariel, and Bahía de La Habana in La Habana Province; Bahía de Matanzas in Matanzas Province; Bahía de Nuevitas in Camagüey Province; Bahía de Puerto Padre in Las Tunas Province; and Puerto Gibara and Bahía de Nipe in Holguín Province. Major harbors on the southern coast—from east to west—are located at Bahía de Santiago in Santiago de Cuba Province and Cienfuegos in Cienfuegos Province. The only major deep-water ports are the bays of Cienfuegos, Havana, Mariel, Matanzas, Nipe, Nuevitas, and Santiago de Cuba. Although relatively small, Havana Bay (Bahía de La Habana) is the country's most heavily used harbor (see Transportation, ch. 3).

Topography and Drainage

Although it has three principal mountain ranges, the Cuban landscape is dominated by plains that cover approximately two-thirds of the land surface and are, on average, 100 meters above sea level. The mountainous zones are isolated and separated by the extensive plains and flatlands. The elevation of the ranges is modest even by Caribbean standards. Only in eastern Cuba, in the provinces of Guantánamo, Santiago de Cuba, and Granma, do mountain peaks exceed 1,200 meters above sea level. Several mountain ranges are found there, including the Sierra Maestra (along the southern coast), famous for harboring Fidel Castro and his guerrillas between December 1956 and January 1959 (see Background to Revolution, 1952–59, ch. 1). Cuba's tallest peak, the Pico Real del Turquino, at 1,974 meters, is in the Sierra Maestra mountain chain (see fig. 2). Other important mountain chains in the northern section of this region are the Sierra de Nipe, Sierra de Nicaro, Sierra de Cristal, and Cuchillas de Toa. In central Cuba, to the south of the provinces of Cienfuegos and Sancti Spíritus, is the Sierra de

Escambray chain. The tallest mountain in this chain, in the Sierra de Trinidad, is the Pico San Juan (also known as Pico La Cuca), at 1,156 meters. The third mountain range is in Pinar del Río Province in western Cuba. With a modest elevation, the Cordillera de Guaniguanico includes the Sierra de los Órganos and the Sierra del Rosario. The Pan de Guajaibón, at 692 meters, is the highest peak in this region.

In between these mountain ranges are flatlands and coastal plains, many rich in clay. Some of Cuba's richest soils are found in the central provinces, whereas some of the poorest are in the eastern regions of the country, as well as in portions of Pinar del Río, the westernmost province. Poor drainage is a serious problem in about 37 percent (or 4 million hectares) of the country's territory, with about 1 million hectares suffering from some degree of salinization. The latter problem is more severe in coastal areas exposed to seawater intrusions. According to a soil-quality typology developed with Soviet assistance, of the 6.6 million hectares (or 60.6 percent of the national land surface) of agricultural soils, approximately 12 percent (some 800,000 hectares) consists of highly productive deep and permeable soils. A further 2.3 million hectares (35 percent) are lightly waterlogged soils, which can become productive if adequately drained. The productive potential of the remaining agricultural land is modest, with approximately 22 percent deemed to be marginal for agriculture. Many of the latter soils are easily eroded and prone to salinization.

In 1996, according to official Cuban statistics, 6,614,500 hectares, or 60 percent of the total land area (11 million hectares), were used for agriculture, whether under permanent crops (2,767,100 hectares) or temporary crops (994.5 million hectares). Of the remaining noncultivated land, 21 percent (or 2,311,000 hectares) was in pastures or fallow, and 25.7 percent (or 2,831,600 hectares) was forested. Human settlements accounted for 6.3 percent (or 694,000 hectares). Approximately 537,000 hectares, or 4.9 percent of the land surface, were classified as "unusable."

Cuba has 632 hydrographic basins measuring more than five square kilometers, the most important being the Cauto, Zaza, and Sagua la Grande. Although the country has numerous rivers and streams, they tend to be short because of Cuba's narrow and elongated shape. The beds of many watercourses dry out for months at a time, except during the rainy season. Most rivers run from the central spine of the island to either the northern or the southern coast. The average length of the country's major rivers is ninety-three kilometers. The Cauto, which flows from the eastern mountains to the southern coast, is the country's longest, at 370 kilometers. Also among Cuba's longest rivers are several Cauto tributaries, including the Saldo (126 kilometers), the Contramestre (ninety-six kilometers), the Bayamo (eighty-nine kilometers), and the Cautillo (eighty-four kilometers). After the Cauto, the next two longest rivers are in central Cuba. The Sagua la Grande, with a northerly flow and a length of 163 kilometers, is the country's second longest, followed by the southern-flowing Zaza (155 kilometers). The Almendares, the best-known watercourse in the capital city of Havana (La Habana; hereafter, Havana), is only fifty-two kilometers long.

Natural lagoons and other still-water bodies are small and few in number. Laguna de la Leche (6,700 hectares) and Laguna de Barbacoa (1,900 hectares) are the most prominent saltwater lagoons; the two most important freshwater lakes are the Ariguanabo and Laguna del Tesoro, each with a surface area of approximately 900 hectares. Since the 1960s, a considerable number of man-made reservoirs (*embalses*) have been built; they numbered nearly 200 large dams and 800 minidams by the early 1990s. Natural and artificial water bodies account for about 3 percent of the country's land surface, or some 330,000 hectares.

Climate and Precipitation

Cuba's tropical climate is warm and humid. Annual mean temperatures vary within a narrow range of 24°C to 27°C, but average 25°C. Annual monthly mean temperatures in different regions of the country fluctuate between 4.8°C and 6.8°C. January, the coldest month, has an average temperature of 22.5°C, and August, the warmest month, has an average temperature of 27.8°C. Average monthly temperatures in Havana range from 27°C in July and August to 22°C in January and February; the annual average is 24.5°C. Fluctuations in regional temperatures are primarily determined by elevation, although the Caribbean Sea's moderating influence is also an important factor. The maximum temperature ever recorded was 40°C. At the other extreme, temperatures as low as 1°C to 2°C have been noted on the country's highest mountain peak. During the dry season, temperatures moderate somewhat, especially in the west, as alternate cold and warm fronts dominated by the

The Río Yumurí, Guantánamo Province, as it enters the ocean
Courtesy National Imagery and Mapping Agency, Washington
The dry southeast coast
Courtesy Danielle Hayes, United Nations Development Programme

arrival of dry Arctic masses descend on Cuba and collide with warm southern winds. The average relative humidity is 81 percent.

On average, Cuba receives about 1,400 millimeters of rainfall a year, although the amount of rainfall from year to year can vary greatly. Two well-established dry and rainy seasons characterize Cuba's climate. During the dry season, from December to April, the country receives, on average, between thirty-two and ninety-nine millimeters of rainfall a month. Because of the alternating pattern of cold and warm fronts, Cuba is prone to receive considerable amounts of rainfall even during the dry season.

The rainy season runs from May through November, during which the amount of rainfall increases to between 200 and 260 millimeters per month. Annual and seasonal variations in rainfall amount are influenced by the frequency and severity of hurricanes. Because of its tropical location, Cuba is hit periodically by different kinds of storms, especially hurricanes, some with winds of more than 200 kilometers an hour and heavy rains of up to 300 millimeters in a twenty-four-hour period. Hurricane season lasts from July to November. September and October are the months of the most frequent storms.

Throughout the island, precipitation levels increase from the coast to inland locations because the volume of precipitation is influenced by elevation. As a general rule, the drier areas are on the southern coast. The Moa-Toa-Baracoa region in northeastern Cuba receives the most rainfall (an annual average of 3,000 millimeters), whereas the least amount of rain falls in the semidesert cactus-scrub belt of Guantánamo Province (600 millimeters), a region on the southern coast just below this mountain range.

Environmental Trends

Cuba's environmental record over the last forty years is mixed. The country has avoided some ecological calamities, such as beach erosion, that have left deep scars in other Caribbean and Central American neighboring countries, while managing to partially reverse others, such as deforestation. There is mounting evidence, however, that some of the economic development policies pursued under socialist rule, mostly when the country was the recipient of Soviet subsidies, may have exacerbated certain environmental problems, most of all in agriculture. Agricultural development was predicated on the large-scale use of mechanical and chemical inputs that, when poorly managed, particularly in tropical countries, can damage natural ecosystems. The widespread use of fuel-inefficient vehicles and industrial equipment imported from the former socialist world and excessive reliance on subsidized, cheap imported fuel also has had adverse environmental consequences.

Economic Policy and Regulatory Environment

Until recently, the regulatory framework for environmental protection in Cuba, as in most other countries, was weak and poorly articulated. Although some environmental regulations had been implemented before the socialist revolution, they were largely ignored and seldom enforced. In most respects, this situation did not change appreciably after 1959, although the 1976 constitution, amended in 1992, incorporates the modern notion of sustainable development (see Glossary) and makes explicit the right of the state and its citizens to protect the environment. Cuba enacted a comprehensive environmental law (Law 33) in 1981.

Decree-Law 118 was adopted in 1990. It allowed various agencies to establish a system to protect the environment called the National Commission for Environmental Protection and Conservation of Natural Resources (Comisión Nacional para la Protección del Medio Ambiente y la Conservación de los Recursos Naturales—Comarna). The system was chartered initially in 1977. Led by a scientific council composed of representatives of numerous national ministries and agencies, Comarna was empowered to chart environmental policies, study the causes of water and agricultural pollution, and assist with the development of plans to protect the environment and conserve natural resources. The agency was also tasked with reviewing the development plans of other government agencies and with suggesting measures to minimize adverse environmental impacts. Comarna, however, reportedly was dissolved in 1994 and its functions transferred to the new Ministry of Science, Technology, and the Environment.

In 1994, in the midst of a major economic crisis and following the 1992 Earth Summit (Eco–92) in Rio de Janeiro, Brazil, a new Ministry of Science, Technology, and the Environment was created as part of a major reorganization of the national administrative apparatus. Its tasks include ensuring compliance with environmental law, conducting environmental impact assessments, making recommendations based on the assessment findings, assisting with the further development of a body of national environmental legislation, and forging closer links between scientific knowledge and environmental management. Cuba's current policy of making tourism a principal engine of national economic growth has given urgency to these tasks.

In July 1997, a new environmental law approved by the National Assembly supplanted Decree-Law 118. A year later, the Forestry Law (Law 85) was approved. The intent of this law is to promote the sustainable development and effective protection of forest resources. In addition, Cuba has ratified most international environmental conventions. Enforcement of environmental laws has not kept pace, however, with the regulatory framework. The problem largely lies with the broad nature of regulations, the weakness of regulatory institutions, and the inability of these institutions to enforce their authority over other economic sectors that had been expected to regulate themselves and had been granted much discretion within the dictates of a command economy. The underlying but faulty ideological assumption is that in a socialist economy (devoid of the profit motive) state agents would by definition protect the environment. A highly centralized and regimented economic decision-making approach has also been a leading cause of Cuba's environmental deterioration over the last several decades.

Land Use

Socialist policies substantially altered land-use patterns in Cuba. The most notable change was an expansion in cultivated land at the expense of pastures, and a sizable increase in the amount of forested land. The former was achieved by bringing under the plow formerly nonagricultural land that prior to 1959 had been held in reserve by large sugar mills or because it was agriculturally marginal. Forest growth was achieved through an aggressive reforestation program. Urban land use changed as well through policies designed to slow down the demographic growth of Havana and promote the growth of secondary cities and towns. Another factor was the creation of approximately 335 new towns in agricultural regions.

The establishment of new rural communities was associated with the implementation of an agricultural development model dependent on the establishment of large-scale state farms and agricultural cooperatives. The new communities were to facilitate capital-intensive agriculture by concentrating dispersed rural populations, thus allowing the unimpeded use of agricultural tractors and combines in large and contiguous fields. They also facilitated the provision of social and educational services to families living in close proximity to each other. Incentives and disincentives were used to encourage small private landowners to settle in these communities. Those willing to cede their farms to the state and relocate to these communities had access to modern housing and social services; those refusing to do so were provided with only limited access to agricultural inputs. In some instances during the 1960s, peasants were forcibly relocated to new communities to deny a base of support to armed guerrilla bands opposing the government (the best known instance is that of the Escambray mountain population relocated to Pinar del Río Province in western Cuba). By 1987 Cuba was one of the socialist countries with the highest concentration of agricultural land in state farms (73 percent) and collective farms (12.5 percent), with the former averaging 14,260 hectares, or seven times larger than the average prerevolutionary latifundio (see Glossary).

The agricultural land concentration trend began to be reversed in the early 1990s, when, in an attempt to cope with the economic consequences of the Special Period, policies were implemented to provide more economic incentives to the peasantry to increase agricultural production, but, thus far, with only limited success. A new type of agricultural cooperative was introduced, the Basic Units of Cooperative Production (Unidades Básicas de Producción Cooperativa—UBPC; see Agricultural Cooperatives, ch. 3). Members of these cooperatives do not own the land. Instead, they are granted use of the soil for indefinite time periods and limited control over what they produce, although the UBPCs continue to be tightly regulated by the state. By 1994, 2,643 UBPCs, occupying 3 million hectares, had been established throughout Cuba. With an average size of 1,133 hectares, they were eleven times smaller than former state farms. Other measures introduced to increase agricultural production have also contributed to the reversal in land concentration. For example, several thousand families have been provided with small individual farms to produce tobacco, coffee, and dairy products.

Agriculture

Between 1945 (the date of the last and only prerevolutionary agricultural census) and 1989, the country's agricultural land area increased by 1.3 million hectares, from 2 million to 3.3 million hectares. Two-thirds of the additional cultivated land was devoted to sugarcane; the amount of land planted with other priority crops, such as citrus and rice, also rose significantly. The emphasis on sugar production (and citrus) was consistent with Cuba's assigned role within the Council for Mutual Economic Assistance (Comecon—see Glossary), the socialist trading bloc, as primarily a producer of agricultural commodities. In turn, these commodities were exchanged for other agricultural and industrial supplies, as well as oil and other fuels, in commercial terms highly advantageous to Cuba. According to *Anuario Estadístico de Cuba*, the actual amount of agricultural land being used by tenancy totaled 6,614,600 hectares in 1997.

In 1999, the term "desertification" began to be used for the first time in official circles to refer to the deterioration of soils in several regions of the country. In southern Pinar del Río Province, independent sources (that is, nongovernmental) have alleged that desertification (caused by erosion and salinization) is expanding by 11 kilometers a year. A January 2000 report by Agencia Ambiental Cubana, a leading independent environmental group, whose leader, Eudel Cepero Varela, went into exile in 1999, describes the deterioration of Cuban soils as an "environmental catastrophe."

As a result of excessive use of Soviet agricultural inputs, inadequate management of irrigation, costly improvements of soils ill-suited for agriculture, and poor soil conservation practices within the context of a command economy, the environmental situation in Cuba's agricultural sector appears to have deteriorated. Several soil degradation problems have attracted considerable attention. These include soil compaction (as a result of excessive use of heavy farm equipment) in many areas, salinization in others, and a plethora of other problems. Although not yet fully documented, there is evidence suggesting that in some regions of the country soils are chemically contaminated because of poorly regulated pesticide use. In the early 1990s, according to official figures, 4.2 million hectares were eroded to one degree or another, 1.6 million hectares had been damaged by compaction, 780,000 hectares were affected by salinization, 2.7 million hectares were poorly drained, and the productive potential of 1.1 million hectares had been reduced by acidification. The Cauto basin, which covers 301,700 hectares and is inhabited by about half a million people, has suffered serious ecological damage, partly as a result of some of these agricultural practices and partly as a result of deforestation.

As Cuba became a principal supplier of agricultural commodities to the Soviet bloc, it became increasingly reliant on food imports from the former socialist countries. Cuba has had difficulties in feeding its population since the 1960s, despite major agricultural investments. Food supplies, as well as most other consumer goods, have been tightly rationed for decades, although the most vulnerable social groups, such as children, pregnant women, and the elderly, are eligible for special allocations. The end of European socialism and Soviet subsidies made evident the extent to which Cuba had become dependent on subsidized food imports to feed its population. Without guaranteed export markets and subsidized inputs, agricultural production collapsed. In 1995 the country managed to produce only 3.3 million tons of sugar, 60 percent less than in 1990, the peak production year since 1970 (see Agriculture, ch. 3). The 1998 harvest was even smaller; Cuba managed to produce only 3.2 million tons of sugar during 1998. The trend was reversed in 1999 and 2000, when 3.8 and 4.1 million tons, respectively, were produced. Between 1989 and 1993, beef and milk production, as well as the output of eggs and poultry, also fell dramatically, as feed grain imports declined by 72 percent. Equally significant declines, often exceeding 60 percent, occurred in the production of rice, citrus, and fruits. Nutritional standards suffered accordingly.

In an attempt to arrest the declining agricultural production trend, the government has revived traditional agricultural practices neglected for decades. These practices include substituting beasts of burden for mechanized agricultural equipment, increasing reliance on organic fertilizers and biological pest controls, and assigning additional land to the production of food crops. The attempt to become more food self-sufficient also relies on shifting surplus urban labor to the countryside, encouraging city and town dwellers to plant urban gardens and raise pigs and chickens for home consumption, and reauthorizing peasant markets (allowed briefly during the 1980s, but outlawed in 1986). The success of these polices has been limited, with no end in sight for food-supply and nutrition problems.

Water Policies

By the 1980s, ambitious agricultural development plans and

population growth had led to a major increase in water demand. In response, the socialist government, with extensive Soviet technical and financial assistance, embarked on a major water-resources development program, which included construction of numerous dams and more extensive utilization of the country's underground water stores. As a result of the dam construction program of the microbrigades (see Glossary), the country's stored water capacity increased from 48 million cubic meters in 1959 to 7 billion cubic meters in 1987, or by a factor of 150. The increase in capacity was accompanied by the development of a large-scale irrigation infrastructure that in 1989 included 500 kilometers of master distribution channels, fifty electric pumping stations, irrigation channels to serve more than 1 million hectares of agricultural land, and other facilities. The dam construction program has continued despite the economic difficulties of the Special Period.

By 1989, some 900,000 hectares, or 13.3 percent of the agricultural land, was irrigated, a considerable increase over the amount of land irrigated in prerevolutionary Cuba (estimated at 160,000 hectares in 1958). Efforts to increase the irrigated land area were unfortunately not accompanied by corresponding measures to increase the drainage infrastructure, a development linked, as in other countries, with the salinization of some of the country's soils. By 2001 the number of hectares irrigated had likely declined as a result of the abandonment of marginal agricultural land, the dearth of investment resources, and poor maintenance of the irrigation infrastructure.

The increase in water demand came in response to policy initiatives that mandated either providing secondary cities and newly created urban communities in the countryside with water-distribution systems, or improving their existing system. The upkeep of the aging water infrastructure of metropolitan Havana was, meanwhile, largely neglected. In 1992, according to official statistics, 83 percent of the urban population and 78 percent of the rural population were provided with drinking water. The number of sewerage lines and other sanitary services also increased rapidly in the 1970s and 1980s as efforts were made to promote the development of urban areas beyond Havana (by 1992, 100 percent and 39 percent of the urban and rural population, respectively, were served). There has been, however, a rapid deterioration of water-distribution systems in both rural and urban sectors as a result of poor infrastructure maintenance. The waste of much water has been attributed to poor record keeping and the policy of not charging users according to consumption. State enterprises did not begin to pay for water consumption in order to promote conservation and efficient resource use until the 1980s. And the government did not introduce water meters and urban residential consumption charges until the early 1990s.

The dam construction program, with its associated natural water flow disruptions and excessive aquifer water withdrawal rates, has been linked with salinization of coastal aquifers and sea-water intrusions. These problems are reported to be most acute along Cuba's southwestern coast, where inland sea water intrudes as much as two to fifteen kilometers. In 1985 the government began to address this problem by building a 100-kilometer underground dike to prevent sea-water intrusions and trap fresh water inland. The South Dike (Dique Sur), which, if completed, will run from Majana in western La Habana Province to Batabanó in the south-central part of the province, has a width of seven meters and is between two and four meters deep. It is not known yet whether or not the dike will accomplish its objectives, although concern has been expressed about potentially severe adverse environmental consequences.

Forestry

Cuba and Costa Rica are the only two Caribbean Basin countries to have achieved the rare accomplishment of reversing a long-term deforestation trend. In 1992, according to official figures, 18.2 percent of Cuba's national territory (approximately 2 million hectares) was forested, as compared with 14 percent in 1959. Two-thirds of the forested areas are set aside as protected areas, and one-third is used for harvesting timber. The increase in forest cover was achieved through a reforestation program, whereby more than 2.5 billion trees were planted between 1960 and 1990; by better management of timber harvesting; and by the expansion of the country's national park system. Article 10 of the 1959 Reforestation Law created nine new national parks (Ciénaga de Lanier, Cuchillas de Toa, Escambray, Gran Piedra, Guanacabibes, Laguna del Tesoro, Los Órganos, Sierra de Cubitas, and Sierra Maestra). Cuba also has the Sierra de Cristal National Park, as well as a number of municipal parks. In support of the reforestation and forest-management strategy, Cuba managed to train an important cadre of forestry professionals during the last several decades. The availability of these professional foresters was crucial in overcoming early meager results and mistakes, such as excessive reliance on a few, poorly adapted tree species. There is limited evidence from accounts in the official press suggesting that forest resources may be under increasing pressure because of a shortage of cooking fuels and because more and more domestic lumber is being used to build a rapidly growing tourism infrastructure.

Mining

Strip-mining has caused major environmental damage in the Sierra de Nipe mountain range of northeastern Cuba, where the country's most abundant nickel reserves are found. With close to 20 percent of the world's exploitable nickel resources, Cuba has been an important producer since the 1940s. The United States government, as part of its World War II effort, developed the processing plant at Nicaro. Construction of a second nickel processing plant began in Moa Bay in 1953, but it did not become operational until 1961. Two other plants were built in the 1970s at Punta Gorda and Las Camariocas. The environmental damage arising from strip-mining and compounded by inadequate reclamation efforts is further aggravated by the discharge of processing by-products into bodies of water (12,000 cubic meters a day of light and heavy metals) and the atmosphere, inasmuch as processing plants also release vast amounts of sulphur compounds into the air (see Mining, ch. 3).

Urban and Industrial Pollution

Sugar mills are highly polluting because they release liquid waste products—such as molasses, filter mud, and bagasse composts, that is, composted stalks and leaves of sugarcane—into streams and rivers and can severely damage coastal ecosystems. During the 1970s and 1980s, with Cuba's emphasis on increasing sugar production, the volume of these discharges rose. As a result, there have been reports of collapsed fisheries, destroyed clam beds, and contaminated shrimp farms. Some corrective measures, such as monitoring discharge rates, have been discussed, but with unknown results.

Other major sources of air pollution are fuel-inefficient industrial plants, in particular cement plants, and transportation equipment acquired from the former socialist bloc. Of six cement plants operating in Cuba in the late 1980s, the two that relied on the least environmentally friendly dry manufacturing process—at Mariel and Artemisa—were heavy air and water polluters. Other heavy polluters are the country's two largest fertilizer production plants, located in Cienfuegos and Nuevitas, and several chemical and metalworking plants in Havana and other large cities. In addition, Cuba's old Soviet-designed vehicles lack pollution-control devices, and thus release significant amounts of air contaminants.

Inadequate and poorly maintained sewerage systems are also a problem and are responsible for the extensive pollution of many streams and harbors. Havana Bay, for example, is notorious for its contamination: the United Nations Development Programme (UNDP—see Glossary) designated Havana Bay as one of the ten most polluted harbors in the world. Pollutants tend to accumulate in Havana Bay because of its shape, which prevents water from circulating rapidly in and out of the bay. The lack of circulation is a serious problem because 300 tons of organic matter and forty tons of oil and oil products flow each day into the bay, which is relatively shallow and only 3.7 kilometers in length by 4.6 kilometers in width.

Environmental Consequences of the Special Period, 1990–2000

The end of Soviet subsidies and of a preferential trade relationship with the former socialist bloc that ushered in the Special Period had profound consequences for Cuba's environmental situation. As a result of the ensuing deep economic contraction, environmentally damaging agricultural practices had to be curtailed, and industrial pollution declined. The Special Period's austerity measures and the economic slowdown adversely affected every economic sector. Without guaranteed overseas markets and foreign inputs bartered for Cuban goods or supplied on credit, agricultural production plummeted. Between 1980 and 1992, fertilizer imports declined by 80 percent and those of herbicides by 62 percent. The contraction in fuel imports was equally severe, declining by 53 percent. Machinery imports, including spare parts, were reduced to a minimum. Under these conditions, the input-intensive agricultural model was largely replaced and/or complemented— according to agricultural priorities, crops, and so forth—by traditional practices, such as the use of beasts of burden, hand harvesting, and the application of agricultural byproducts, such as organic fertilizers. To the extent that the inputs used in capital-intensive agriculture had adverse environmental impacts, these impacts were reduced by the unavailability of those inputs. The same occurred in the urban industrial and transportation sectors where as of the end of 2000 heavily polluting factories were idle and thousands of bicycles had replaced fuel-inefficient Hungarian buses and Soviet trucks.

On the negative side, the Special Period's emergency economic program rests on the accelerated development of several priority sectors. Foremost is tourism, a sector that had been largely neglected by the international tourist trade prior to 1990. Cuba is currently embarked on an all-out effort to increase the number of hotel beds and tourist resorts to accommodate a growing number of visitors. In 1996 more than 1 million foreign tourists visited Cuba, as compared with 340,000 in 1990 (see table 10, Appendix). About 1.7 million tourists visited Cuba in 1999. Crash infrastructure development programs were instituted in previously undisturbed coastal regions and offshore keys and inlets. In some of these resort areas, particularly in Cuba's northern coast, such as the area around Varadero and the northern keys of Ciego de Ávila Province, environmental preservation standards appear to have been neglected. Other priority sectors, such as oil exploration and mining, are also potentially threatening to the environment. Several large oil multinationals have been granted exploration rights, so far with limited success. Much of the effort has been geared to offshore drilling, often in areas adjacent to national tourist resort areas, such as Varadero. Increases in oil output have been achieved, but mostly of sulfur-rich heavy oils that are being used in lieu of imports of lighter oils to fuel the country's electric plants. The heavy oils, when burnt, emit large quantities of air pollutants. In the Moa Bay region, pollution levels have increased in tandem with nickel production.

Demography

Population

In 2000 Cuba had 11.2 million people. Annual population growth rates in the late 1990s were low—less than 0.4 percent a year, down from 0.67 in 1995—and projected to decline further by the twenty-first century (see table 2, Appendix). Population size is likely to stabilize or to actually begin to contract by the early years of the twenty-first century, given the country's low growth rate and continued emigration. Current demographic projections assume that population size is unlikely to

Bicycle traffic on a street in Guantánamo, 1996
A view of the city of Guantánamo, 1996
Courtesy National Imagery and Mapping Agency, Washington

reach 12 million people. According to the United Nations' low-variant projection, Cuba's population will peak at about 11.5 million people by about the year 2015 and begin to decline in absolute size thereafter.

With a population density of 101 inhabitants per square kilometer in 2000, the country is primarily urban, with 78 percent of the population residing in cities and towns. By far the largest city is Havana; it had 2,204,333 inhabitants in 1996. The second largest city is Santiago de Cuba, which had 405,000 inhabitants in 1989. The four next largest cities, with their 1989 populations, are Camagüey (283,000), Holguín (228,000), Guantánamo (200,000), and Santa Clara (194,000). Cities and towns dot the national landscape. An agglomeration of as few as 500 people is defined as urban, as long as it meets several minimum requirements, such as having a public electric-power network, paved roads, and so forth.

Cuba's demographic trajectory has been distinctive and, in many regards, different from that of other Latin American and Caribbean countries. The demographic transition (to low birth and death rates) began earlier and is more advanced than in most countries in the region. Further, international migration has played a major role in the country's demographic history. Cuba's indigenous population was decimated during the first centuries of colonial domination by epidemics and forced labor, or was largely absorbed through *mestizaje* (see Glossary) into the general population. In the nineteenth century, more than 560,000 African slaves reached Cuban shores, as did 120,000 Chinese indentured workers, a few hundred Mexican-origin contract workers, hundreds of thousands of Spanish immigrants, and other Spanish and European settlers seeking safehaven in the last (together with Puerto Rico) and "most faithful" Spanish colony in the Western Hemisphere. European settlers included Spaniards from the former Spanish colonies in South America and French planters from Haiti.

Another major immigration surge followed during the first three decades of the twentieth century, when some 700,000 people settled in Cuba, most of Spanish and other European origins. This episode also included sizable immigration flows from Haiti and Jamaica, as well as smaller ones from Mexico, the Dominican Republic, and other Latin American and Caribbean countries.

Demographic Transition

Cuba began its demographic transition (a gradual shift from high to low birth and death rates) in the late nineteenth century, well before other Caribbean countries began theirs. Cuba's mortality started to decline as a result of the basic public health and sanitary measures, such as mosquito eradication, that began to be implemented during the United States occupation following the end of the Spanish-American War (1895–98), when the country had 1.6 million people. As a result of these measures, the incidence and severity of many infectious diseases—such as yellow fever, malaria, and smallpox—were reduced significantly. A Cuban physician, Dr. Carlos Juan Finlay, was the first to hypothesize in 1881 that yellow fever was transmitted by the aedes aegypti mosquito; his theory helped physicians throughout the world to conquer this tropical disease. Over the next several decades, mortality rates declined further as a result of the continued application of public health measures, economic growth, and the introduction of medical measures since the 1930s. By 1960 life expectancy at birth (for both sexes combined) had reached sixty-four years.

Fertility rates began to decline in the 1920s. Factors likely to have influenced the fertility decline were the country's relatively early modernization, the large influx of European immigrants, and perhaps most of all a severe economic depression. The latter was caused by a sharp contraction in demand for sugar in international markets that preceded and was later magnified by the Great Depression of the 1930s. By 1958 the Cuban birth rate stood at twenty-six births per 1,000, with the average woman having 3.6 children during her reproductive lifetime. This fertility level is comparable with that of Canada and the United States at the time, and lower than in several European countries. In Latin America, only Argentina and Uruguay had attained comparable fertility levels by the mid-twentieth century.

Life expectancy at birth (for both sexes combined) in 2000 was seventy-five years (seventy-four for males and seventy-seven for females). The infant mortality rate had declined to 6.5 infant deaths per 1,000 live births, placing Cuba among the twenty-five countries in the world with the lowest rate in this health indicator. Some of the mortality improvements responded to public health policies instituted in Cuba since 1959, such as egalitarian access to heath care services, emphasis on primary health care, and the widespread application of medical and public health advances. An additional three indicators in 1997 were at their lowest historical levels: under five-year-olds' mortality (9.3 per 1,000 live births), maternal mortality (2.2 per 10,000), and low weight at birth (6.9 per 100). The trend toward a reduction in infant mortality actually started well before 1959. Similar developments in public health led to comparable trends in other countries that shared Cuba's general mortality profile in the early 1960s (for example, Costa Rica, Chile, and Jamaica), as well as in countries with far less favorable mortality indices (for example, Mexico and Colombia) at the time. For a number of reasons, Cuba's achievements have drawn far more attention than those of these countries.

The post-1959 fertility trend was first characterized by an abrupt increase during the 1960s, with the birth rate rising from twenty-six births per 1,000 in 1958, to thirty-six in 1963, followed by a rapid decline in the early 1970s. In 1999 the birth rate stood at 12.5 births per thousand population, the lowest in the Western Hemisphere except for Barbados and Canada. Between 1970 and 1978, the total fertility rate declined by nearly half, from 3.7 to 1.9 children. The latter level is below that needed in the long term to assure the continued replacement of the population through natural increase (the difference between the birth and death rate), or approximately 2.1 births per woman at Cuba's current mortality level. In the 1990s, the total fertility rate declined even further, dropping, according to a press report in *Granma*, the official newspaper, to below 1.5 in 1999. Fertility fluctuations have been associated with numerous factors related to changing socioeconomic conditions in Cuba, including increased female educational attainment and labor force participation rates. Other important considerations are contraceptive availability and induced abortion. Cuba's abortion rate (abortions per 1,000 women fifteen to forty-four years of age) in 1989 was 56.5, a rate exceeded only by former socialist bloc countries, and twice as high as in the United States. About seven abortions per ten deliveries were practiced in Cuba in 1995. In 1995, 2.6 percent of women of reproductive age reported an abortion, representing some 80,000 cases. The continued fertility decline during the 1990s may be in response to difficult economic conditions, including shortages of basic necessities. Only about two dozen, mostly developed countries in the world—including Austria, Germany, Greece, Italy, Portugal, and Spain—in the late 1990s had total fertility rates at or below Cuba's.

Since 1959 emigration has been a primary determinant of Cuba's demographic evolution and its relatively slow population growth rate. Approximately 800,000 persons emigrated from Cuba between 1959 and 1980, primarily for political reasons or their unhappiness with socioeconomic conditions. Three emigration waves dominated this period. Some 215,000 people, mostly drawn from the country's economic and professional elite, left between 1959 and 1962—the period of the most dramatic political and economic changes. A second emigration surge followed during the "freedom flights" of 1966–73, when 344,000 people departed. The third largest outflow and the biggest in a single year was in 1980, as 125,000 Cubans went to the United States through the Mariel Boatlift and others found their way to other countries. After a decade of only modest emigration, the number of people leaving the country began to increase again in the early 1990s. Many departed the country illegally in makeshift rafts. Another 50,000 tried to leave during the 1990–94 period, but were prevented from doing so by Cuban authorities, according to Fidel Castro. The rafter (*balsero*) outflow came to an end when the United States and Cuba entered into a migration accord in 1994. Under the United States-Cuba Migration Agreement, the United States assigned to Cuba a minimum quota of 20,000 legal permanent residence permits a year and modified the practice of granting preferential treatment to Cuban migrants. Cubans currently intercepted by the United States Coast Guard at sea (those referred to as "wet feet") are repatriated, while those who manage to reach United States soil (those referred to as "dry feet") are allowed to take advantage of the Cuban Adjustment Act and remain in the United States. Because of renewed immigration, the number of people of Cuban birth residing in the United States increased from 737,000 in 1990 to 913,000 in 1997 (net of deaths).

Fluctuations in fertility and emigration have contributed to the evolution of an irregular and deeply indented age-sex population pyramid (see fig. 3). The aging of the 1960s baby boomers is apparent, as is their childbearing during the 1980s. Also of note is the much smaller size of the 1990s birth cohort. The country's current median age (thirty-three years) is relatively high and projected to increase further (to thirty-nine years) by the year 2010 (comparable United States figures are thirty-four and thirty-seven). In contrast, in 1995 the median age for Latin America and the Caribbean was twenty-four, ris-

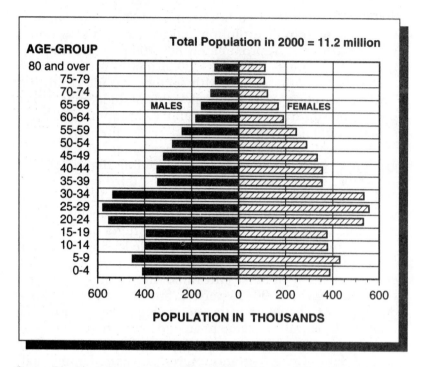

Source: Based on information from Oficina Nacional de Estadísticas, Centro de
Estudios de Población y Desarrollo. *Estudios y datos sobre la población cubana,*
Havana, May 1997, Table 2, IX; Department of Economic and Social Affairs,
Population Division, *The Sex and Age Distribution of the World Populations: The
1996 Revision,* New York, 1997, 307; and information from the United States
Bureau of the Census.

Figure 3. Population Distribution by Age-Group and Sex

ing to twenty-seven years by 2010. A high and rising median age
translates into a relatively old age structure. Whereas in 2000,
9.6 percent of the Cuban population was sixty-five years of age
or older, by 2010 this figure will increase to 12.5 percent, a
value comparable with that projected for the United States and
much higher than for Latin America and the Caribbean as a
whole. By the end of 2000, 1.5 million Cuban citizens, or 13
percent of Cuba's approximately 11 million people (mid-2000
figures), were sixty years old or older. By 2010 Cuba will have
more than 2 million citizens over sixty, a figure that will represent 18 percent of the total projected population.

Migration

Aside from emigration and continued fertility decline, another important demographic development during the 1990s was the resurgence of internal migration from rural areas and smaller cities to Havana and, to a lesser extent, to other large cities (see table 3, Appendix). This resurgence marks a departure from earlier trends because a major objective of urban policies over the last four decades has been containing Havana's demographic growth. During this period, infrastructural investments in the city were reduced and redirected to other parts of the country. As economic conditions worsened and living conditions were perceived to be better in Havana than in other parts of the country, internal migrants began to move to the capital. Between 1993 and 1996, 100,000 migrants settled in Havana. The migrants have compounded problems in a city already suffering from a crumbling infrastructure and a severe housing shortage. This situation prompted the authorities in May 1997 to issue Decree 217, requiring that prospective migrants to Havana must first secure a resident's permit from the municipal authorities, a measure intended to manage the city's growth. Resumption of large-scale emigration, a process that has always disproportionately involved Havana residents, should help ease demographic pressures on the city.

Racial Composition

The 1981 Cuban census, following practices akin to those used in United States censuses, classified 66 percent of the population as "white" and 34.0 percent as "nonwhite," the latter including black (12.0 percent), mulatto or mestizo (21.9 percent), and Asian (0.1 percent) (see table 4, Appendix). The reliability of these figures, like those from earlier twentieth-century censuses, has been called into question; most analysts have concluded that the nonwhite share of the population is much higher than suggested by the censuses.

There is no broad consensus, however, regarding the "true" race distribution, although there is demographic evidence suggesting that since the 1959 Revolution the nonwhite share of the population has increased significantly. The socialist government has handled the race statistics issue very gingerly. This development, as in other countries with ethnic, religious, or racial cleavages, is not entirely surprising given the country's troubled history of slavery and race relations. Race data collected during the 1970 census were never released, and even those available from the 1981 census are very limited. Several explanations have been offered for the unwillingness of the government to make these statistics public. One interpretation is that by not releasing the race statistics the revolutionary authorities have attempted to minimize racial distinctions formerly permeating Cuban society. The Revolution presumably did away with all racial distinctions. A more skeptical explanation is that by withholding the data, the socialist government can conceal remaining socioeconomic race differentials avowedly eradicated under the more equitable social and economic policies pursued over several decades. Yet a third and more cynical explanation is that by not releasing the data, the government withholds from a still racist white population the fact that since the Revolution Cuba has become a majority nonwhite country.

Some analysts have noted that Cuban censuses have always inflated, for a variety of reasons, the share of the "white" population, while underestimating that of others—blacks and mulattos in particular. The broader and most generally accepted reason is that in a historically stratified society of African-origin black slaves and dominant Spanish-origin whites, being regarded as "white" conferred privileges and opportunities denied to "nonwhites." Also, as in other countries (for example, in the Caribbean, Brazil, and the United States) cultural mores that evolved over centuries of slavery gave rise to racist attitudes that assign more positive valuations to notions of "whiteness" as opposed to "blackness." "Passing" from one race to another (for example, from black to mulatto, mulatto to white, or Asian to white) can occur because the designation of race, while primarily dependent on physical attributes, also involves cultural, social, and economic yardsticks. In the Cuban and Caribbean context, contrary to the situation in other societies (for example, the United States), being regarded as "white" does not necessarily preclude some degree of racial intermingling, something that has been occurring in the country for centuries.

The issue of population distribution by race categories is made even more complex when consideration is given to how the race of any given individual is determined (and by whom). While enumerators in the 1931 and 1943 censuses asked respondents to assign themselves a race category, in the 1953 and 1981 censuses enumerators determined the race of respondents on the basis of their observations. Between 1943 and 1953, the shift from self-reports to enumerator designations may have contributed to declines of 1 percent and 2 percent, respectively, in the mulatto and white populations, with a corresponding 3 percent increase in the number of those classified as black.

These shifts suggest that enumerators were more prone to classify individuals as nonwhite than were the respondents themselves. Enumerators in 1981, the year of the most recent census, assigned racial categories according to the "concept commonly understood by the population, although [the categories] may not necessarily reflect races or colors" (when in doubt, the enumerators were also instructed to ask respondents about the racial categories to which those not present in the households during the count belonged).

In general, however, the evolution of the population's race distribution tracks well with known demographic trends, including immigration and emigration, although other factors (for example, differential completeness of enumeration by race, emigration rates by race, fluctuations in fertility by race, and infant mortality rates by race) may cloud these trends. For example, between 1899 and 1931, when Cuba received hundreds of thousands of Spanish immigrants, the share of the population classified as white increased from 67 percent to 72 percent. Between 1931 and 1943, in contrast, when Cuban authorities deported thousands of Haitian and Jamaican immigrant workers, the black and mulatto share declined from 27 percent to 25 percent. Race distribution changes between 1953 (the year of the last population census before the 1959 Revolution) and 1981 are particularly consistent with well-established fertility, nuptiality, and emigration trends. The percent of the population classified as white declined from 73 percent in 1953 to 66 percent in 1981, whereas the share of mulattos rose from 14 percent to 22 percent (while the black percentage remained almost the same).

The dominance of white emigration from Cuba since 1959, particularly during the first fifteen years after the Revolution, is well established; some estimates suggest that more than 90 percent of those leaving socialist Cuba during this period were white. Later emigration has included a more representative cross-section of Cuba's racial composition, but the vast majority of the emigrants continue to be classified as white. Thus, emigration alone accounts for a major share of the decline in the white population between 1953 and 1981. Perhaps an even more important factor explaining the growth of the nonwhite population is differential fertility. At the time of the Revolution, nonwhite Cubans had birth rates considerably higher than white Cubans. Further, higher proportions of the former were concentrated in the provinces with the highest fertility rates (primarily in easternmost Cuba), whereas most white emigrants were from Ciudad de La Habana Province, the country's region with the lowest fertility. In addition, during the last four decades and partly because of more equitable social, educational, and employment policies, social barriers to cross-race sexual and marital unions have weakened, thus leading to an increase in the number of interracial births, another factor behind the increase in the mulatto population.

According to figures from the 1981 census, the provinces with the highest percentages of whites are Sancti Spíritus (84 percent of the population classified as white), Villa Clara (82 percent), and Ciego de Ávila (81 percent), all in central Cuba, plus La Habana Province (82 percent), the province that surrounds the country's capital. Guantánamo (74 percent nonwhite), Santiago de Cuba (70 percent), and Granma (57 percent), in eastern Cuba, are the country's provinces with the highest nonwhite percentages, followed by the capital, Ciudad de La Habana Province (37 percent).

In summary, there is consensus in the academic literature that censuses in Cuba have generally overestimated the share of the population classified as "white," while underestimating the percent of the nonwhite population, specifically its mulatto component. It is also generally accepted that since 1959 the share of the Cuban population classified as white has declined for several demographic reasons, namely differential fertility, selective emigration, and an increase in the number of interracial births. The actual extent of the bias is as difficult to establish as it is to define unambiguous criteria with which to define the concept of "race," although some observers claim that Cuba has become primarily a nonwhite country.

Prerevolutionary Society

Since 1959 there has been scholarly debate regarding the nature of prerevolutionary Cuban society. The conclusion reached by a majority of analysts is that by developing-country standards, Cuba was fairly modernized; others assume that the country was mired in social and economic backwardness. The first view has more merit, although in some respects Cuba was a dichotomous society: an undetermined minority of the population enjoyed high living standards, but most were poor and some quite poor. Estimates of prerevolutionary income distribution validate this assessment. The richest 40 percent of the population received close to 80 percent of total income, and the poorest 40 percent only 10 percent. Urban Cuba, particularly Havana, was home to the elite and most of the country's social and cultural amenities. Consumption patterns for the country's middle and upper classes were deeply influenced by United States geographic proximity and cultural practices.

Prerevolutionary Cuba's urban educational levels were well above national norms. According to the 1953 population census, the last before the Revolution, one out of every four Cubans above age ten (24 percent) could not read and write. In La Habana Province, site of the capital city, in contrast only 9 percent were illiterate, whereas in Oriente, the country's most educationally backward province, the figure was 35 percent. The better educational institutions, including the nation's leading university, were also in Havana.

Comparable patterns characterized other demographic and social indicators. Access to health and sanitary facilities, as well as to other social amenities, was determined by degree of urbanization. Regional variations were also present; the country's central provinces were generally more developed than the provinces of Pinar del Río and Oriente, at both extremes of the country. In urban areas, according to 1953 census data, 42 percent of dwellings had toilets (86 percent in urban La Habana Province), as compared with 8 percent in rural areas. The same could be said about the regional distribution of physicians and medical facilities. Nutritional standards were generally adequate: in the mid-1950s, the typical Cuban consumed, according to a national survey, more calories (2,740 calories) than daily requirements (2,460 calories). Many rural children, however, suffered from infantile protein malnutrition and avitaminosis, although the incidence of anemia among school-age children was modest.

The hierarchical nature of prerevolutionary Cuban society was profoundly affected by the cyclical nature of economic activity and by the pervasive legacy of slavery. The annual economic cycle was dominated by the sugar harvest (*la zafra*), which coincided with the coffee harvest and the peak period of foreign tourist arrivals (late December through March). Unemployment, a pervasive problem in prerevolutionary Cuba, normally fluctuated in unison with the seasonal cycle, from a low of 10 percent during the early months of the year, to more than 20 percent during the summer months. High levels of urbanization and the limited prevalence of subsistence agriculture meant that many of the country's poorest families derived their annual income solely from seasonal agricultural wage labor. Blacks and mulattos were disproportionately represented among the chronically unemployed.

Social Mobility and Income Distribution

Profound transformations of Cuba's social and income distribution structures accompanied Fidel Castro's Revolution. The country's old elite abruptly lost its privileged position as members of a younger generation assumed political power and began to institute radical social and economic policies, ranging from agrarian reform, beginning with the promulgation of the first Law of Agrarian Reform on May 17, 1959, to the eventual elimination of most forms of private property. Large-scale emigration of formerly privileged social classes accompanied the transformation of Cuban society. Their departure, together with the nationalization of private property, the growth of the state bureaucracy, the country's militarization, the gradual implementation of populist policies, such as crash rural development programs to reduce unemployment, and a rapidly expanding educational system, completely reshaped Cuba's social structure. In its place emerged an egalitarian and austere society with a state-dominated economy. Prior income and salary differentials were reduced substantially by state ownership, the almost complete elimination of private employment (other than for a limited number of small farmers), narrow salary scales, and a full employment policy.

By the early 1970s, income differentials had been reduced substantially. According to one estimate, the national income flowing to the richest 40 percent of the population had declined to 60 percent, increasing to 20 percent for the bottom 40 percent. Abject poverty was eliminated, thanks to guaranteed employment, a comprehensive social safety net (universal disability, as well as pension and survivor coverage), and free access to education and health services. Low average levels of material consumption remained a concern; access to nonessential and "luxury" (by revolutionary Cuba's standards) items

A street vendor selling churros (fritters) in Havana, 1999
Courtesy Maria M. Alonso

continued to be determined largely by political affiliation and real or apparent ideological fervor, as in other communist societies. Members of the Communist Party of Cuba (Partido Comunista de Cuba—PCC), "vanguard" workers, and participants in "internationalist" missions (internationalism—see Glossary) were rewarded through the preferential allocation of housing and consumer goods.

Within the strictures of a socialist state, educational attainment became the most significant path to social mobility, aside from ideological commitment. The elimination of social and regional differentials in access to educational opportunities played a vital role in this respect, as average educational achievement levels increased rapidly between the 1960s and the 1980s. The number of secondary school and university graduates mushroomed, the former increasing from 76,961 in the 1975–76 academic year to 317,598 in 1988–89, and the latter from 5,894 in 1975–76 to 33,199 in 1988–89 (see Education, this ch.). Equal educational and employment opportunities were extended to women, a development that also engendered social mobility by reducing traditional gender-based labor force barriers. The same approach was used to help erode race discrimination. Race and gender discrimination, however, like homophobia, continues to linger in Cuban culture, although discriminatory practices are legally banned. On the negative side, access to technical and professional education is severely restricted for those who do not share the socialist ideology, are overtly homosexual, or, until recently, for those who were willing to profess religious beliefs in an officially atheistic state.

Mass Organizations and Socialization

Mass organizations have served important social functions in Cuba since the early 1960s. As in former communist states such as the Soviet Union, mass organizations have been used to inculcate socialist values and to mobilize the population in support of the state. Mass organizations have also been entrusted with security, educational, and public health functions. Although in principle voluntary in nature—except for military service—mass organization membership since the 1960s has been a prerequisite for full participation in the country's political, economic, and social life. Nonmembership is viewed as deviant and leads to ostracism by signifying either a refusal to accept or actual opposition to the prevailing political and social order. Those refusing to join mass organizations pay a dear price by being prevented from pursuing higher education or engaging in certain occupations, as well as by forfeiting material rewards. Given their enormous membership (in some instances in the millions), it is far from simple to determine what motivates individuals to join mass organizations. Social, political, and educational pressures are a major factor. Membership may be motivated as much by conviction as by the desire to avoid the penalties inherent in failing to join.

Article 7 of the 1976 constitution recognizes, protects, and promotes the establishment of mass organizations. In practice, however, Article 61 severely curtails the actions of the various mass organizations by stating explicitly that "none of the freedoms that are recognized for citizens may be exercised contrary to what is established in the constitution and the law, or contrary to the decision of the Cuban people to build socialism and communism. Violation of this principle is punishable by law."

Among the better known and largest Cuban mass organizations are the Committee for the Defense of the Revolution (Comité de Defensa de la Revolución—CDR), Federation of

Cuban Women (Federación de Mujeres Cubanas—FMC), Cuban Workers Federation (Central de Trabajadores de Cuba—CTC), National Association of Small Farmers (Asociación Nacional de Agricultores Pequeños—ANAP), Youth Labor Army (Ejército Juvenil de Trabajo—EJT), and Union of Young Communists (Unión de Jóvenes Comunistas—UJC). There are also several student organizations, such as the Federation of University Students (Federación Estudiantil Universitaria—FEU) and the Federation of Secondary School Students (Federación de Estudiantes de la Enseñanza Media—FEEM).

Some of these organizations, however, were actually established before the Revolution. For example, the CTC and the FEU were autonomous trade and student organizations, with their own political agendas. Although the FEU actively opposed the Fulgencio Batista y Zaldívar dictatorship (1940–44, 1952–59), the CTC leadership connived with it. Under socialist rule, these historical organizations were transformed and became agents of social and political control.

During the 1990s, some of the mass organizations were redefined in name by being labeled as nongovernmental organizations (NGOs), despite their official origins and orientation. This redefinition arose from the government's desire to replace some former Soviet subsidies with Western financing in order to conduct activities, such as self-employment training, generally sponsored by NGOs in other countries. Among the mass organizations currently labeled as NGOs are the FMC and ANAP.

Committee for the Defense of the Revolution

The best-known Cuban mass organization, the Committee for the Defense of the Revolution (CDR), was established on September 28, 1960. A CDR unit was set up on each square block throughout all urban areas, and equivalent counterparts were located in rural areas. By 1985 there were an estimated 6.1 million members of CDRs, or about 80 percent of Cuba's adult population. Using a pyramidal organization, the CDRs continue to operate at the city-block level and are jurisdictionally connected to the smallest administrative units of the National Revolutionary Police (Policía Nacional Revolucionaria—PNR).

Originally established to "defend the Revolution" by preventing counterrevolutionary activities and monitoring neighborhood developments, the mission of the CDRs gradually expanded. By the late 1960s, aside from their monitoring mission, the CDRs had a major impact on the average citizen's life through their functions of revolutionary socialization and social control. The block-to-block CDRs are ubiquitous. They mobilize the population and ensure that the citizens under their purview attend mass rallies and participate in government-sponsored "voluntary" activities, such as the collection of bottles and other recyclable materials, blood donation drives, or educational programs. Neighborhood CDRs maintain detailed records on a person's whereabouts, family and work history, involvement in political activities, and overall revolutionary moral character. They also assist in ensuring compliance with compulsory military service. CDR approval must be obtained when requesting a change of residence; the CDRs are charged with registering the family food ration card when people move from one retail distribution location to another. CDR endorsements are also required for students applying for membership in the UJC (Union of Young Communists) or seeking university admission. In the late 1990s, however, participation in CDRs was much more perfunctory than in the past.

Women's and Youth Organizations

Another well-known Cuban mass organization, founded on August 23, 1960, is the Federation of Cuban Women (FMC). The FMC's founder, Vilma Espín Guillois, a Rebel Army coordinator during the 1950s and the wife of Vice President Raúl Castro Ruz, has been its only president. Espín noted that the FMC was established to facilitate the entry of women into the labor force and to help them become educationally, politically, and socially involved with the Revolution. The FMC has been active in efforts to combat illiteracy, in projects to improve educational and labor market skills of poorly educated and peasant women, and in programs to reduce family burdens of working women, such as the establishment of day-care centers. By the mid-1970s, 80 percent of Cuban women fourteen years of age and older, or about 2.3 million women, were FMC members (*federadas*).

Several foreign observers have noted that although the FMC has made major contributions to raising the educational and labor market skills of Cuban women, it did so through a different prism than women's organizations in developed Western countries. Whereas the women's movement in these developed countries has sought to drastically modify traditional female role perceptions, most roles assigned to Cuban women under socialism follow traditional gender attitudes. This is not to say that gender roles have not changed, but that changes have occurred from a "feminine" rather than from a "feminist" perspective.

The FMC, although nonvigilant in nature, has been instrumental in increasing female participation in neighborhood CDRs and other mass organizations, and in mobilizing its members in support of government initiatives. Many of Cuba's public health and educational initiatives have relied on the mobilization of FMC human resources. FMC members have supported mass vaccination campaigns, promoted maternal-child health educational programs sponsored by the national health ministry, and participated in numerous adult education programs. The FMC has also assisted with the task of integrating women into the Revolutionary Armed Forces (Fuerzas Armadas Revolucionarias—FAR). The FMC, however, has come to be seen in many respects as a bureaucratized and unrepresentative entity.

The government relies on youth and student mass organizations to instill socialist and collective values. The process begins at FMC day-care centers called Children's Clubs (Círculos Infantiles) and continues as children join the Pioneers Union, that is, the Organization of José Martí Pioneers (Organización de Pioneros José Martí—OPJM), which was established in April 1961. All children in Cuba belong to the OPJM. In his July 1983 speech, Fidel Castro noted that "many Pioneers must be trained to become cadres or combatants of the Revolutionary Armed Forces, or of the militia ...." As they advance through the educational system, youth socialization continues through the Federation of Secondary School Students (FEEM) and the Federation of University Students (FEU). Youth political education culminates in the Union of Young Communists (UJC), a selective organization with membership in the hundreds of thousands, rather than the millions.

Other Mass Organizations

Most workers belong to the Cuban Workers Federation (CTC). As in other socialist countries, the CTC is not an independent organization representing the interests of the workers. Rather, it is a transmission belt for government and party commands to workers. CTC functions have varied over time but have included providing a forum for leadership and workers' dialogues, garnering worker support to accomplish production goals, enforcing labor discipline, and managing the distribution of material and other rewards. At local assembly meetings, production issues and matters related to labor discipline are reviewed, and government policies discussed. During the Special Period, for instance, assembly meetings across the nation were convened to discuss emergency measures being introduced to cope with the economic crisis and related labor adjustment policies. These policies included reallocating workers from one work site to another, closing numerous production facilities, and implementing transitory financial compensation mechanisms for dislocated workers. Another important function of the CTC is maintaining individual worker file records detailing an individual's labor history, including skills, training, voluntary labor, absences, merits, and demerits (partly based on work discipline and political criteria). The CTC also supports government efforts regarding voluntary labor and mass mobilizations.

The National Association of Small Farmers (ANAP), created in May 1961, was established with the goal of integrating small farmers into the revolutionary process and convincing them to voluntarily join collective farms. Small farmers were provided with such incentives as centrally located modern housing, electricity, schools, and medical services, as well as mechanized equipment and other agricultural inputs, if they agreed to farm their fields collectively. By the mid-1980s, collective farms numbered close to 1,500 and were, by Cuban standards, relatively autonomous and productive. During the Special Period, a new form of agricultural cooperative was created as former state farm employees were granted land in usufruct. Members of the latter group, called Basic Units of Cooperative Production (UBPCs—see Agricultural Cooperatives, ch. 3), however, are not ANAP members but rather are affiliated with a CTC workers' union, the National Trade Union of Agricultural and Forestry Workers (Sindicato Nacional de Trabajadores Agrícolas y Forestales—SNTAF).

The Military

Military service, of course, has also acted as a socialization agent since mandatory male military service began in 1963. Under the 1973 Law of Compulsory Military Service, draftees receive a heavy dose of ideological instruction. Other military institutional mechanisms that are used to attempt to socialize male youths not deemed fit for regular service—whether for ideological orientation, social attitudes, or poor academic preparation—have included the notorious Military Units in Support of Production (Unidades Militares de Ayuda a la Producción—UMAPs). The intent of the UMAPs' forced labor camps, while they were operational in the 1963–65 period, was to punish and modify the behavior of "antisocial" individuals, including religious believers and homosexuals. In more recent years, many draftees have been made to serve in the EJT (Youth Labor Army). These militarized but poorly trained units perform primarily economic tasks, such as sugarcane harvesting and construction work.

The Family Institution

The saga of Elián González (see Foreign Relations, ch. 4) and the intense emotions it generated within the Cuban-American community can be explained when placed within the context of the major changes that the family institution has experienced in Cuba over the last four decades. These changes, which in part reflect global forces that have influenced family structures in most countries, were also influenced by political and social developments arising from the ideological underpinnings of the 1959 Revolution and some of the policies pursued by the Castro government. Some of the leading trends involved in this historical evolution were changing female roles; a more intrusive state agenda in the upbringing and education of children; ideological cleavages that fractured the Cuban nation, and within it, many of its families; and large-scale, permanent emigration that over time contributed to the corrosion of family bonds.

The global revolution in women's roles, arising from commonly recognized major changes in educational, labor force, and reproductive functions, has been echoed in Cuban society. It has been manifested, as in other countries, by higher levels of female educational attainment and labor force participation. Extensive use of contraception and induced abortion have led to low childbearing and high divorce rates. High divorce rates have contributed to the weakening of traditional family bonds. Men and women have opted to exit unsatisfactory marital relations, thereby giving rise to less permanent and more unstable family arrangements, which, in turn, have led to an increase in the number of children residing with only one biological parent, blended families, and so forth.

The Castro regime's Marxist orientation accentuated this trend by assigning a prominent political role to educational— some may say, indoctrination—policies that directly and indirectly weaken parental rights over child-rearing practices by imposing the ideological views of a monolithic and all-powerful state. Article 3 of the Code of the Child and Youth (Law No. 16 of June 28, 1978), states, for example, that "The communist formation of the young generation is a valued aspiration of the state, the family, the teachers, the political organizations, and the mass organizations that act in order to foster in the youth the ideological values of communism." Article 8 goes even further as it reads that the society and the state "work for the efficient protection of youth against all influences contrary to their communist formation." Implied in these articles is the overriding power of the state upon universally recognized parental rights to choose for their children the values and type of education they wish. Further contributing to the weakening of parental oversight is the requirement that most children eleven years of age and over provide thirty to forty-five days of "voluntary" farm labor during their school vacations and the separation of students from their families while enrolled and residing at boarding schools (see Education, this ch.).

Another factor that in many instances severely contributed to the weakening of the Cuban family was the deep political cleavage that accompanied the revolutionary process, particularly during the 1960s, as Cuban families fractured along ideological lines. As members of many families were imprisoned or chose what eventually became a permanent exile option, others enthusiastically embraced the revolutionary banner. These divisions within families left deep scars that were accentuated by permanent emigration—and for many years, by the government prohibition against émigré family visits—and an informal yet not so subtle government policy of discouraging party militants and government sympathizers from maintaining family contacts with their relatives abroad. These policies only began to be eased under President Jimmy Carter's administration, when family visits on a significant scale were first authorized. In fact, many observers feel that the 1980 Mariel Boatlift was a direct result of family visits as many disaffected Cubans were deeply influenced by contacts with Cuban-American visitors and the perceptions of their experiences abroad.

Visits by Cuban-Americans became more numerous during the 1990s. Several developments contributed to the growing number of visitors, not least of which was the Cuban government's decision to ease, if not encourage, family contacts. This policy, to some extent forced on the government by the economic difficulties associated with the Special Period, was partly intended to facilitate the transfer of emigrants' financial resources to their Cuban families. Foreign remittances had become an important source of foreign exchange. The generosity of the Cuban-American community and the resilience of family bonds were also at play because in response to the economic crisis and often despite long years without any contact, remittances had begun to flow. Family visits followed shortly thereafter. Also contributing to the rise in the number of visitors was the resurgence of large-scale emigration following the rafter (*balsero*) outflow of the early 1990s, and regularized legal emigration following the 1994 United States-Cuba Migration accord. Many of the most recent emigrants have close relatives in Cuba, and their antagonism to the Havana regime is more muted. Thus they are less reticent about periodically visiting the island nation. The United States government has contributed, as well, to the more frequent family contacts by issuing more temporary visas, particularly to the elderly, for Cubans to visit their relatives here.

Despite increasing family ties, it is rare indeed today, as it has been for the last four decades, for a recent or long-time Cuban emigrant to resettle in the country of birth. On a permanent basis, families are reunited only abroad. Not even the elderly retire in their home country, as so often happens with emigrant communities from other national origins.

Religion

Cuba is usually characterized as a country in which religion is not a powerful social force. Such views are based on estimates of membership in formal religious institutions and on assessments of the impact of institutionalized religion in Cuban history, both before and after the 1959 Revolution. Although nearly 90 percent of the population was nominally Roman Catholic in prerevolutionary Cuba, the number of practicing Roman Catholics was probably less than 10 percent. Other estimates suggest that about half of all Cubans were agnostic, that slightly more than 40 percent were Christian, and that less than 2 percent practiced Afro-Cuban religions. Membership in other religions, including Judaism, was limited. Religiosity estimates may be considerably higher, however, if due credit is given to the cultural relevance of informal religions, particularly of syncretic Afro-Cuban rites (including *espiritismo* and *santería*), which historically were minimized. Another issue to consider is the resurgence of the Roman Catholic Church and many Protestant denominations in the 1990s, a development perhaps explained by the government's more tolerant attitude and the despair gripping many Cubans. Open expression of religious faith, further, offers one of the few relatively safe channels of expressing dissatisfaction with the government's policies.

The Roman Catholic Church

Several historical factors contributed to the relative weakness of the Roman Catholic Church in prerevolutionary Cuba. The church had long been viewed as conservative and as serving the country's political elite. During the country's wars of independence (1868–78 and 1895–98) in the late nineteenth century, the church was aligned with Spain, the colonial power. The church's local hierarchy and most priests were Spanish; many chose to return to the Iberian peninsula following the colonial army's defeat in the Spanish-American War (1895–98). After independence, the church gradually regained some of its prestige and influence through its educational and charitable deeds, and by ministering to hundreds of thousands of Spanish immigrants who settled in Cuba during the first three decades of the century. By the late 1950s, however, only about a third of all Roman Catholic priests and nuns were Cuban-born; the church was still relying heavily on Spanish-born priests and nuns, as well as other foreign missionaries. The church was present mostly in urban areas, where it enrolled more than 60,000 students in 212 schools and managed hospitals and orphanages. The schools, among the finest in the country, were run by various orders—such as the Jesuits, Christian Brothers, Dominicans, and Ursuline Sisters—and catered primarily to the educational needs of the country's middle and upper classes. The church also ran Villanueva University (Universidad de Villanueva). Although most Cubans were baptized, few, even in the cities, attended mass regularly. The church was notably absent from rural Cuba, where only a handful of priests were assigned and few peasants ever went to church.

Church-state relations deteriorated rapidly in the early 1960s because of the radicalization of Fidel Castro's government and its growing alignment with the Soviet Union, and also because

*The Belén Church and Convent in Old Havana
Courtesy Danielle Hayes, United Nations
Development Programme*

of historical antagonisms between the Roman Catholic Church and communism. Even though many Roman Catholics remained sympathetic to the goals of the Revolution, increasing emigration by the upper and middle classes and the departure of many priests and nuns eroded the church's base of support. Following the failed United States-sponsored Bay of Pigs invasion in April 1961 and growing social tensions, the government nationalized all private schools, including church-affiliated schools. The government's absolute control of the mass media and its decision to erase religious holidays from the national calendar also curtailed the power of the church. Shortly thereafter, in September 1961, the government deported 130 priests, bringing the total number left in the country to about 200, from about 800 three years earlier. Many of the more than 2,000 nuns in the country in 1960 departed as well. Cuba officially became an atheistic state in 1962.

The next decades saw a gradual easing of tensions between the government and the Roman Catholic Church. Several factors accounted for the rapprochement. Rome and the national hierarchy came to terms with the strength of the socialist government and accepted that pastoral functions had to be conducted within the new sociopolitical context. In 1969 Cuban bishops also denounced the United States economic embargo against Cuba. Underlying currents behind these developments were the flowering of liberation theology (see Glossary) in Latin America in the 1970s and 1980s and a growing awareness of doctrinal affinity in some social goals between Christianity and socialism. By the mid-1980s, government/church cooperation was evident in some respects, such as the upkeep of churches and church training of selected social services government personnel.

In practice, however, and until the 1980s, those openly professing a religious faith had to continue to contend with social and political penalties. Whereas Article 54 of the 1976 constitution provides for freedom of religion, those professing their faith publicly were effectively discriminated against. Believers were barred from membership in Cuba's elite organizations, such as the UJC and the PCC, and thus prevented from gaining access to university education and high-level government positions. Other restrictions, such as the inability to hold meetings in public places or to evangelize through the mass media, continued as barriers to the church's activities through the 1980s. Although official attitudes had become less restrictive by 2000, the government continues to tightly regulate public displays of faith.

Afro-Christian Rites

Afro-Christian rites, deeply ingrained in Cuba's cultural ethos, are one of the leading vehicles through which many Cubans of all races, but primarily black and mulatto, manifest religious faith. An important African cultural legacy, the Afro-Cuban religions constitute a syncretism between Roman Catholic and African beliefs that evolved over time as slaves pretended to accept a faith being forced on them by slaveholders. Combining elements of several religious traditions, the Afro-Cuban rites, like similar rites in Brazil and other former slaveholding societies, juxtapose Roman Catholic saints with African deities. African deities are known by their African as well as by their Roman Catholic names and are depicted as they would be in the Roman Catholic Church tradition. For example, the Virgin Mary, in one of its Afro-Cuban versions, is known as

Obatalá. This superficiality in appearance conceals the strength of underlying African beliefs and rituals, while not masking the syncretic relationship between the two religious traditions.

Afro-Cuban religions, while informal and poorly institutionalized, are divided into three main rites (*reglas*), all of West African origin. The Lucumí rite, or *santería* (see Glossary) of Yoruba origin, is widely practiced in Nigeria. Of Bantu origin, the Congo rite arose along the Congo River all the way to the Kalahari Desert. The third rite, practiced by the male Abakuá society, and also of Nigerian origin, is best known by the name given to its followers, Ñáñigos. These rites combine monotheistic and polytheistic elements, mysterious and supernatural powers associated with living organisms and nonliving natural objects, the belief that spirits reside in these organisms and natural objects, and complex rituals. The rites also assign important roles to magic, music, and dance. *Espiritismo*, a less Africanized practice, implies the ability to communicate with the dead, often through a chosen few who possess the ability to do so.

Tension has always existed between the Roman Catholic Church and Afro-Cuban rites, partly because the former recognizes the popular strength of the latter, and also because of the church's inability to come to terms with many features of Afro-Cuban religions unacceptable to Rome. Thus, there has always been ambivalence, the church embracing the Afro-Cuban faithful entering a church to pray, yet maintaining considerable distance between the formal church hierarchy and the very informal Afro-Cuban priestly class. A tribute to the strength of Afro-Cuban rites in the national culture is the relative tolerance shown toward these rites by the socialist government, a predisposition enhanced by the lower-class origins of most adherents to these religious beliefs.

Other Religions

The Protestant Church had a very limited presence in Cuba until the early years of the twentieth century. This situation changed during the United States' first Cuban occupation (1898–1902), when several denominations—Baptists, Congregationalists, Episcopalians, Methodists, and Presbyterians—established footholds in the country with the financial support of United States-based mother churches. As did the Roman Catholic Church, Protestant churches emphasized education and limited evangelization activities to urban areas. In the Revolution's early days, there were as many as 100,000 Protestants grouped in forty denominations. The government, however, nationalized the Protestant schools, and many Protestants emigrated because of disagreement with the Revolution.

Gradually, Protestant denominations, as had the Roman Catholic Church, sought to come to terms with the new political status quo. Because they were less structured, the Protestant denominations were regarded by the government as effective counterbalances to the more organized Roman Catholic Church. Nevertheless, some denominations, for example, Jehovah's Witnesses and Seventh Day Adventists, that have opposed such socialist dictates as pledging allegiance to national symbols have been at times harshly persecuted.

Although Jews were barred from settling in the Spanish colonial empire, their presence in Cuba dates to the days of the island's discovery and the arrival of Jews who were nominally Roman Catholic. The prerevolutionary Cuban colony was diverse in origin and included both Sephardic and Ashkenazic Jews. The Jewish population peaked in 1959, when it reached about 15,000. Between the 1920s and 1940s, Cuba was an important transit point for Jews seeking permanent settlement in the United States. Most Jews left after the Revolution; in 1990 only about 300 Jewish families remained. Buddhist and Muslim influence in Cuba is very slight. Few traces remain today of the legacies of the thousands of Chinese and Arab emigrants to Cuba. The former arrived mostly as indentured workers during the late nineteenth century, and the latter as independent migrants during the first three decades of the twentieth century.

Religion in the Special Period

Church/state relations have continued to improve during the Special Period. The ban barring religious believers from membership in the PCC was lifted in 1991, and in 1992 the constitution was amended to make Cuba a secular rather than an atheistic state. The church's reception of these measures was guarded but generally positive. The 1990s saw a notable increase in church attendance, and the church continued to seek additional freedoms from the government.

The difficult church-government dialogue has highlighted common points of view, for example, condemnation of the United States economic embargo, but has been punctuated by open disagreements. During his visit to Cuba in January 1998, Pope John Paul II articulated some of these disagreements. Cuba's bishops have also expressed their views in pastoral letters. In one pastoral letter in particular, issued on September 8, 1993, and entitled "El amor todo lo espera" ("Love Hopes All Things"), the bishops called for national reconciliation among all Cubans, including those abroad, and openly called into question Cuba's one-party system (see Religion and the State, ch. 4).

Despite these tensions, the government has been allowing more public religious ceremonies. It has also granted in principle entry permits to several hundred foreign priests and nuns and has allowed the church to expand its humanitarian services, such as direct distribution of foreign donations of medications. In addition, by inviting the pope to visit, the government tacitly recognized the Roman Catholic Church's importance as an independent national institution. The PCC's Political Bureau made a major gesture when it announced in *Granma* on December 1, 1998, that henceforth December 25 would be considered a national holiday "for Christians and non-Christians, believers and nonbelievers."

The more positive official attitude toward religion has benefitted Protestant churches, too, inasmuch as they have been allowed to expand their humanitarian activities in response to the country's economic crisis. Afro-Cuban rites are also being practiced more openly. Some observers have suggested that the government is encouraging public displays of these beliefs to enhance the country's international tourist appeal. Selective repression of religious acts deemed to be contrary to official interests continues, however, as does the occasional criticism by the official press of some sectors of the Roman Catholic Church. In addition, in May 1995, eighty-six Pentecostal churches were closed in Camagüey Province. Five years later, *Granma* accused some members of the Church hierarchy of "conspiracy" following the celebration of several public events that were cosponsored by the Religious Civic Training Center (Centro de Formación Cívico Religiosa) of Pinar del Río, a lay religious organization, and visitors from a Polish official delegation.

Social Consequences of the Papal Visit of January 1998

During his January 1998 trip to Cuba, the details of which had been carefully negotiated between Rome and Havana,

Pope John Paul II celebrated four large-scale open masses in the cities of Camagüey, Havana, Santa Clara, and Santiago de Cuba. These masses, attended by hundreds of thousands and broadcast on national television, were the first large-scale public events since the early days of the Revolution that were not officially organized. Although the open-air masses were a welcome departure from totalitarian control, it is not clear what long-term consequences will follow from the pope's visit.

Massive outward professions of religious faith in a Cuba confronting economic and ideological difficulties suggest several interpretations. The official interpretation is that the massive outpouring arose out of curiosity and its encouragement by the authorities. A second and more plausible interpretation is that Cubans saw the pope's visit as an opportunity to safely demonstrate unhappiness without fear of government retribution. A complementary interpretation is that Cuba is experiencing a renaissance of religious faith as many Cubans seek spiritual alternatives to fill the ideological void left by the collapse of Marxism-Leninism. Finally, in Cuba's economy of scarcity, organized religion has become an increasingly important source of hard-to-get products, such as food and medications. The Roman Catholic Church has been a distributor of foreign food and medical donations, for example. Thus, the popular outpouring may signal that Cubans are beginning to consider alternatives to the socialist state, and that religion may offer a path through which desired changes can be achieved. The greater freedom and economic clout of the Roman Catholic Church and other religious institutions, together with the pope's visit, will inevitably contribute to the undermining of the ideological, social, political, and economic power of the Cuban totalitarian state. So will embracing December 25 as a national holiday, although public religious manifestations continue to be highly regimented by the authorities.

Health

Revolutionary Cuba is proud of and constantly proclaims its achievements in the health sector. These claims are validated by the government's release of copious volumes of statistical data with some regularity (such as the *Anuario Estadístico* of the Ministry of Public Health) and by its calling attention to the success of domestic programs designed to reduce infectious diseases, promote maternal and child health, and develop a modern biotechnology industry. Cuba is also proud of the

Health workers at the health unit for Battalion 2721 in San José
de las Lajas, La Habana Province, 1998
Courtesy National Imagery and Mapping Agency, Washington

"internationalist" public health assistance programs that it launched in Africa and other developing regions (often in support of Soviet-assisted internationalist ventures, as in Angola and Nicaragua), the many foreign physicians it has trained at home, and the medical services it offers in Havana hospitals to fee-paying foreign patients. In 2000 the latter service was expanded when Cuba began to offer medical services to selected patients from Venezuela in exchange for oil under an agreement negotiated between President Fidel Castro and President Hugo Chávez Frías. These achievements are partially rooted in the relatively advanced medical system inherited by the socialist government and in the priority accorded by the authorities to the health sector since the earliest days of the Revolution. In fact, since 1978 President Castro has often boasted about his intent to make Cuba a world "medical power" capable of challenging the United States in many public health areas.

In prerevolutionary Cuba, public hospitals, private physicians, and mutualist welfare associations provided medical services. The latter, the equivalent of modern-day prepaid medical plans, were established in Cuba by Spanish immigrants, although the mutualist model was later adopted by labor unions, professional groups, and private medical practitioners. By 1958 mutualist associations served about half of Havana's population, as well as 350,000 members in other cities of the country. Although relatively extensive by developing country standards of the 1950s, the national health network was primarily urban-based. It consisted of thirty hospitals and dispensaries administered by the Ministry of Health and Social Assistance plus fourteen other hospitals and sixty dispensaries managed by autonomous public entities, such as the National Tuberculosis Council (Consejo Nacional de Tuberculosis). The primacy of the country's capital was reflected in the national distribution of hospital beds: 62 percent of all hospital beds were in La Habana Province in 1958. Access to health care for the poorest segments of the population, particularly in the countryside, and for blacks and mulattos was mostly limited to public facilities.

Redressing these inequities in health care access was at the heart of the populist agenda of the Revolution. The early public health reforms were based on four pillars: increasing emphasis on preventive medicine, improving overall sanitary standards, addressing the nutritional needs of disadvantaged social groups, and increasing reliance on public health education. Another important component was expanding the national health and hospital infrastructure and equalizing access to health care facilities throughout the country, most of all in rural areas. Rural medical facilities, capable of providing only the most essential services, began to be built in the early 1960s. Fifty-six rural hospitals and numerous rural medical posts were operating by 1975. At the same time, the government aggressively began to expand training programs for physicians and other health personnel needed to staff these facilities. Physician training became a priority inasmuch as approximately half of the prerevolutionary stock of medical doctors, dissatisfied with the radicalization of the Revolution, emigrated. By the late 1960s, the private practice of medicine had largely been banned; only a few older physicians were still being allowed to see private patients.

The Ministry of Public Health administers a hierarchical and regional system of public health facilities and hospitals, whereby the most routine needs of patients are attended to at the local level; referrals are made to increasingly specialized facilities as the need arises. Each province has a hierarchical structure of medical facilities capable of providing all types of care, except for the most specialized and costly. The latter are available only in selected Havana hospitals. Municipalities within each province are divided into basic health units, or health areas, which act as service areas for polyclinics (*policlínicos*) or the traditional basic primary health care facilities. These units provide preventive and curative services in internal medicine, pediatrics, obstetrics and gynecology, and dentistry, as well as elementary sanitary and psychological services. The next three levels—municipal, provincial, and national—are responsible for increasingly specialized hospital and other services.

The polyclinics began to be supplemented by "family doctors" in 1984. The intent of the Family Doctor Program is to monitor the health of all Cubans by assigning physician-nurse teams to groups of 120 to 150 families. These teams play a frontline preventive-medicine role and intervene the moment an incipient medical condition is identified. Each family group, ranging in size from 600 to 700 individuals, is provided with locally based medical dispensaries equipped to provide essential preventive services. To be familiar with the communities they serve, physician-nurse teams and their families must reside there, often in apartments built at or in close proximity to the dispensaries. The health teams must also provide health and nutrition education, as well as organize adult exercise classes. Family Doctor teams must be available at all times, pay home calls to patients unable to visit dispensaries, and provide services to the elderly and chronically ill. Family doctors must also monitor patient treatment and serve as patients' advocates when hospitalizations are required. In 1993 about half of the Family Doctor teams were deployed in urban areas.

In 1997 Cuba had 339,943 health personnel, including 62,624 physicians and dentists, of which 28,855, or 46 percent, were family doctors. The total also included 81,333 nurses and more than 56,342 mid-level technicians. The ratio of population to physicians in 1997 was 214, one of the lowest in the world, down from 1,393 in 1970. In a May 1998 speech, Fidel Castro noted that Cuba has a doctor for every 176 inhabitants.

141

As a point of comparison, Cuba has physician-to-population ratios 2.5 and two times higher than Canada and the United States, respectively, two of the countries that spend the most in health care costs. In contrast, the Cuban nurses to physicians ratio of 1.3 is about two-thirds lower than in these two countries.

Physicians are trained in twenty-three medical schools, ten of which are located in Havana, and four dentistry schools. The 1993 graduating class consisted of 4,780 doctors, with an additional 20,801 students enrolled that year in medical school. Interestingly, the 4,781 students in the sixth (and last) year of medical training was nearly double the number (2,608) enrolled in the first year. The dramatic enrollment decline indicates that the educational authorities are concerned about a physician surplus created by medical school admission policies (which became more selective in the 1990s), declining population growth, and lessened demand for Cuban "internationalist" physicians since the end of the Cold War. The number of medical graduates drastically declined in 1996, when they totaled only 3,418, a decline of 28.5 percent in relation to 1993.

The health infrastructure in 1997 included 283 hospitals, 440 Polyclinics, 161 medical posts, 220 maternity homes, 168 dental clinics, and other facilities. Forty-eight hospitals are in Havana, and sixty-four are in rural areas. Other facilities included 196 nursing homes for the elderly (sixty-three of which provide only day services) and twenty-seven homes for the disabled. The total number of hospital beds in 1997, including military hospitals, reached 66,195, up from 51,244 in 1975. The number of social assistance beds has been doubled since 1975 to at least 14,201.

Cuba's contemporary health profile resembles that of developed nations. Most causes of death are degenerative in nature, for example, cancer and diseases of the heart and cardiovascular system. Infectious diseases account for only a small share of all deaths. The general outlines of this mortality pattern preceded the Revolution, however; by the 1950s, cardiovascular diseases and cancer already were the leading causes of death.

In 1996 the five leading causes of death were diseases of the heart (with a death rate of 206 deaths per 100,000 population), malignant tumors (137 deaths per 100,000 population), cerebrovascular disease (72 deaths per 100,000 population), accidents (51 deaths per 100,000 population), and influenza and pneumonia (40 deaths per 100,000 population). Deaths from these five causes accounted for 70.1 percent of all deaths in 1996. The death rate from infectious and parasitic diseases was low (53 deaths per 100,000 population), representing only 7.4 percent of all deaths.

The first individuals identified as human immunodeficiency virus (HIV)-positive were found in Cuba in 1986. Through an aggressive prevention program that has included close monitoring of cases, large-scale screening, and extensive education programs as well as the controversial practice of isolating infected patients by forcibly interning them in sanatoriums, the health authorities succeeded in minimizing the number of cases. By 1999 only 2,155 cases had been diagnosed as HIV positive, 811 of which were known to have developed full-blown acquired immunodeficiency syndrome (AIDS). Some of the most controversial practices of the National AIDS Program have been somewhat relaxed; for example, patients considered to pose low risks of infecting others are being allowed to receive treatment on an outpatient basis. At the close of 1995, about a fourth of HIV-positive cases were enrolled in the outpatient program. Vigilance continues to be strict because there is concern that, with the combination of a rising tide of foreign tourists and the reappearance of prostitution, the disease is becoming more widespread.

As part of its overall health development strategy, and in keeping with Fidel Castro's wishes of making Cuba a world medical power, major investments have been made since the early 1980s to develop a national biotechnology industry. In addition to acquiring foreign technology, the government has devoted much attention to training abroad the Cuban scientists currently staffing the Center for Genetic Engineering and Biotechnology (Centro de Ingeniería Genética y Biotecnología—CIGB) and other research facilities. Cuba has produced some biotechnology health products for domestic use and exported small quantities to developing countries and the former socialist world. Inadequate marketing capabilities and quality-control problems hamper Cuba's ability to sell biotechnology products abroad, but attempts along these lines continue to be made through joint-venture agreements with firms from Canada and other countries. Some observers have voiced concerns that the major biotechnology investments are also related to a desire to develop the capacity to produce biological weapons.

Despite the country's emphasis on preventive medicine, Cuba's public health approach was and continues to be hospital- and physician-intensive. This public-health approach places a heavy financial burden on the nation not only by being physician-intensive but also by emphasizing other costly medical inputs. These include obtaining the latest medical equipment and consistently exceeding internationally recommended medical norms as regards, for example, the number of recommended prenatal visits and the constant monitoring of healthy people by family doctors. Cuba was able to bear these excessive costs as long as its economy was cushioned by Soviet subsidies. Without subsidies, the unsustainable character of the national public health approach became apparent: equipment and medicine shortages currently hamper the effectiveness of the Cuban health system (see Social Consequences of the Special Period, this ch.). These high costs explain why many other developing countries were unwilling to emulate Cuba's public health model, despite its many well-publicized achievements during the 1970s and 1980s. In the late 1990s, the provision of quality health care services deteriorated to such an extent that commonly prescribed medications were often not available and patients, when hospitalized, were often asked to bring their own bed sheets, towels, and other personal supplies. The government has even been forced to accept medical donations from abroad that are distributed through the Roman Catholic Church and other charities. In addition, Cubans residing abroad provide an unknown, but very substantial, number of the medications consumed.

Education

Another priority of Cuba's revolutionary leadership was education. As a result, the country's educational profile was quantitatively transformed. Although Cuba was a relatively well-educated country by developing country standards in the 1950s, many shortcomings confronted the sector. Among these were limited educational opportunities. Access to formal schooling depended on one's social class, urban residence, and race. Data from the 1953 census reveal that nearly one of every four Cubans ten years of age and older was illiterate. Only half of primary school-age children and only one in ten of secondary school-age children attended school. The country's public universities enrolled 20,000 students, but relatively few pursued careers in fields relevant to the country's development, such as agriculture and engineering. Despite much concern about the nation's education situation, the general sense was that standards were deteriorating and not enough was being done to improve the country's educational system. An extensive network of private schools made up for some public-sector deficiencies. In 1958 Cuba had 1,300 secular and religious private schools and four private universities.

The educational reforms begun in 1959 were designed to make educational opportunities more accessible and to increase the literacy rate. Between 1959 and 1961, at least 1,100 new schools were built. Crash programs to train new teachers were initiated. Volunteers in the 1961 literacy campaign taught 1 million students, with varying success. On July 6, 1961, the government promulgated the Law on the Nationalization of Education, by which all private education was nationalized, and all schools were placed under the Ministry of Education.

Since 1959 the increase in the number of teachers and school enrollments has been dramatic. Primary school enrollments rose from 811,000 to 1.7 million between the 1958–59 and 1970–71 academic years. A few years later, secondary school enrollments reflected primary school attendance gains, increasing from 88,000 students in 1958–59 to 1.2 million students in 1985–86. University enrollments rose just as markedly, from 26,000 in 1965–66 to 269,000 in 1985–86, when they peaked. Vocational and adult education programs were also expanded. Most previous regional educational differentials were erased, although school attainment rates were still somewhat higher in urban than in rural areas. By the late 1980s, more than three-quarters of the population had at least completed primary education, and 20 percent had some technical training. In 1995 Cuba reported an adult literacy rate of 95.7 percent. By the late 1990s, there were eighteen teachers per 1,000 population, and the country had 12,223 schools, including 9,481 primary schools, 1,891 secondary schools, and thirty-two higher education institutions. These achievements must be placed in the context of similar policies pursued in other countries that had comparable successes during the second half of the twentieth century. Literacy rates in countries like Argentina, Chile, Costa Rica, Paraguay, and Uruguay are at levels similar to that of Cuba.

Cuba has developed a comprehensive national educational system that includes the Children's Clubs and preprimary education, primary education schools (first to sixth grades), and secondary education (seventh to ninth grades). After basic secondary education, students are tracked into preuniversity education (tenth to twelfth grades) or vocational/technical training. Secondary education includes, as well, the training of kindergarten, preprimary, primary, and secondary education teachers. Adult education programs are available for peasants at the primary (Educación Obrera Campesina), secondary (Secundaria Obrera Campesina), and university (Facultad Obrera Campesina) levels. Adults can also attend language schools. Students thirteen to sixteen years of age with poor scholastic records can enroll in remedial schools providing vocational training. Schools also cater to the needs of handicapped children and young adults. At the apex of the educational system are thirty-five centers for higher education under the aegis of the Ministry of Education, the Ministry of Higher Education, and other government entities, including the military.

In the 1995–96 academic year, student enrollment in primary, secondary, and higher education was, respectively, 933,000, 639,000, and 111,000. Declines in primary and secondary school enrollments in 1995–96, as compared with earlier years, such as the 1970s, resulted from a contraction in the number of school-age children because of low birth rates. University enrollment declines, on the other hand, were caused by deliberate state policies formulated in the 1990s to reduce the number of university graduates, to the benefit of vocational training. This policy was guided by the conclusion that Cuba had a surplus of university graduates but lacked a sufficient supply of trained technicians, especially in the agricultural sector. In the mid-1990s, 60 percent of students completing primary education were enrolled in vocational and technical training, while the remaining 40 percent were channeled into pre-university schools, in effect reversing the previous distribution of students.

One of the most commented on features of Cuban education is its emphasis on combining work and study. The objective of this practice, begun in the 1960s, was to create a "new man" with strong work habits. The practice was also designed to erase social distinctions between physical and intellectual work, as well as between urban and rural lifestyles. Through the Schools in the Countryside (Escuelas al Campo) and, since the 1970s, the Basic Secondary Schools in the Countryside (Escuelas Secundarias Básicas en el Campo) programs, many

Cuban children have attended coeducational boarding schools that combine formal schooling with agricultural, industrial, or manufacturing work. By working, the students presumably help finance their own education. Another important objective of the work-study program is the ideological preparation of the nation's youth. While separated from their parents and living in boarding schools, they are exposed to socialist ideological messages. In the 1989–90 academic year, of the 728,000 students enrolled in basic secondary and preuniversity education, 27 percent and 63 percent, respectively, were attending schools in the countryside. Parents have objected to the schools-in-the-countryside concept, alleging, among other things, that such schools adversely affect the parent-child relationship, that parents have difficulty visiting their offspring, and that the schools provide poor living conditions. By isolating children from their parents for long periods of time, the state obviously gains the upper hand in its attempt to inculcate political and other values that may be at odds with parental preferences, a practice that has been commonplace in totalitarian societies. This concern was at the heart of the Cuban-American community's objection to the return of Elián González to Cuba.

Ideological criteria have had a very important role in educational policies, particularly regarding university enrollments. In order to enroll, university applicants not only must submit preuniversity transcripts and provide evidence of passing an entrance examination, but also must pass a test designed to evaluate the applicant's ideological commitment to revolutionary principles. Representatives from one of the country's mass organizations must also submit a report vouching for the applicant's ideological standing. Admission to academic fields considered politically and ideologically sensitive, such as political science and economics, is dependent on ideological criteria. Such screening is not applied so consistently to fields such as the natural sciences, however. Before the late 1980s, professing a religious belief disqualified an applicant from admission.

At all levels of the educational system, the ideological content of formal education is considerable. In recent years, this content has been revised in response to changes in political and economic circumstances. For example, since the collapse of the Soviet Union the teaching of Marxist philosophy and economics has been downplayed. The emphasis is now placed on Cuba's historical nationalistic roots and the teaching of market economics and modern managerial principles. Educational content in the social and political realms, however, largely continues to reflect the Revolution's ideological perspectives to the exclusion of all others.

During the 1970s and 1980s, Cuba hosted large numbers of international students (at all school levels) from African and Latin American countries closely aligned with Cuba during the Cold War. Many of the students on scholarships financed by the Cuban government—mostly from Angola, Ethiopia, Mozambique, Namibia, and Nicaragua—were boarded in schools in the countryside established for them on Isla de la Juventud. National student groups were kept together in schools assigned to them, where they were instructed by Cuban teachers, although teachers from the students' own countries taught language, history, and cultural studies. These programs were obviously loaded with a heavy ideological content. As many as 22,000 foreign students attended Cuban schools in 1986. With the end of the Cold War and Cuba's financial crisis of the 1990s, most of the foreign-student programs were phased out, although Cuba still provides university training to foreign students. In the 1989–90 academic year, more than 4,000 foreign students were enrolled in Cuban universities, while more than 6,000 Cubans attended Soviet and East European universities.

In 1999 Cuba announced that it would considerably expand physician training for foreigners in the country through the establishment in Havana of the Latin American Medical University (Universidad Latinoamericana de Medicina); the university was to have an initial enrollment of 1,000 scholarship students from Guatemala, Honduras, and Nicaragua. The impetus for the establishment of this medical education institution, at a time when Cuba could hardly afford it, was the emergency caused in Central America by Hurricane Mitch in late 1998. During the recovery, Cuba provided emergency medical brigades to the countries in need, in addition to offering medical educational opportunities to aspiring physicians from these and other countries. Aside from being a generous humanitarian gesture, the assistance gave Cuba an opportunity to gain influence with these countries as it sought closer political and economic ties with formerly hostile neighbors. The geographical reach of the new medical training institution has been further expanded and now enrolls students from many other countries. To allay concern about ideological indoctrination, the Cuban government has even stated its willingness to minimize discussions of political perspectives at this university. The

As many as 300 passengers crowd into Havana's large-capacity public buses called camelos *(camels).*
Courtesy Maria M. Alonso

quality of the medical education being imparted at the facility, however, is questionable given that many of the admitted students have deficient backgrounds and need remedial crash courses on basic sciences and other disciplines. In private, many Cubans question the reasonableness of this initiative at a time when Cuba faces so many unmet domestic economic needs.

Social Consequences of the Special Period

In social terms, the consequences of the Special Period have been monumental. Severe problems have crippled the formerly vaunted Cuban health and educational systems. Massive labor force realignment measures offer convincing testimony of Cuba's extreme reliance on Soviet subsidies and how ineffectively they were utilized. Because of the economic crisis, social ills presumably eradicated in the 1960s, such as prostitution, have reemerged. Explosive growth in foreign tourism and emigrant remittances are inexorably altering Cuba's socialist social fabric.

Health and Education

Health and education, the social sectors much praised for

their achievements under Fidel Castro's rule, have been severely affected by the economic austerity of the Special Period. Cuban hospitals and other public health facilities are experiencing chronic and severe shortages of medicines and other basic supplies. The government has authorized Catholic Relief Services (Caritas), which is the Roman Catholic Church's humanitarian arm, and other religious and humanitarian organizations to import and distribute medical donations because they cannot be found in government pharmacies. Food shortages have been blamed for serious nutritional problems. Daily caloric and protein intake declined drastically after 1990. Vitamin B–12 deficits among Cubans also led to a serious outbreak of optic neuropathy that was responsible for the temporary blindness of 50,000 people in 1991–93; the outbreak was arrested by the emergency nationwide distribution of vitamin supplements. In addition, the proportion of newborns with low birth weights began to rise in the early 1990s, as did the number of underweight pregnant women. Mortality rates have also risen among elderly nursing-home residents.

As domestic health care standards deteriorated, Cuba was promoting medical services for paying foreign patients at the country's leading medical institutions. This practice has led to charges that the medical needs of Cuban patients are being sacrificed ("medical apartheid") for the benefit of foreigners. The government responds that the foreign currency earned by treating foreign patients benefits all Cubans because the earnings are used to buy medical supplies abroad. That health standards have not deteriorated even further is thanks to the importance accorded the sector and the extensive health care infrastructure, including medical personnel, developed in earlier decades.

Since the onset of the Special Period in the early 1990s, the educational system, like other sectors of the economy, has suffered from severe funding cutbacks. Thousands of teachers are reported to have left their posts for employment in other better-paying sectors, such as tourism, where dollars can be earned. This trend has led to expressions of alarm over a likely and growing teacher shortage. However, the number of teachers trained in Cuba is so large and the decline in the number of students (because of declining birth rates) so significant, that this concern seems groundless. Although no schools have been shut down, schools are poorly maintained, and educational supplies are scarce. In addition, some educational facilities have been abandoned or converted to other uses because of the declining number of students. The government has also taken steps to reduce university enrollments.

The Social Safety Net

The extensive and generous social safety net developed by socialist Cuba is currently incapable of providing the protection for which it was designed: government financial resources have contracted dramatically. Left to its own domestic resources, Cuba can no longer afford to extend extremely liberal social and economic benefits. These include, aside from full employment, generous social entitlements, such as early retirement (at age sixty for men, and fifty-five for women) and a broad array of partially or wholly subsidized social services, such as meals in government-owned cafeterias and public transportation. An extreme example of such entitlements was described by the Cuban Workers Federation (Central de Trabajadores de Cuba—CTC) in 1996, when it announced that 38 percent of all workers managed to obtain a disability certificate in 1995 entitling them to retire and receive a pension. Many of these "retirees" are known to then engage in informal sector economic activities or to seek employment in state enterprises other than the one from which they retired. Demographic trends further aggravate the erosion of the safety net. As was indicated earlier, Cuba's population is aging rapidly, and as the number of elderly increases, the demands placed on the social safety net grow apace.

Employment Policies

Cuba's employment situation is at the crux of the economic crisis. According to United Nations Economic Commission for Latin America and the Caribbean (ECLAC—see Glossary) estimates, in 1996 Cuba had an equivalent unemployment rate (combined unemployment and underemployment (see Glossary) rates) of 34 percent, which translates into the need to create 1 million new jobs. The government has responded to the crisis by expanding unemployment benefits, shifting urban labor to the countryside, and reassigning and re-training surplus workers. Because the government lacks sufficient financial resources, these adjustment mechanisms have been unable to prevent a brutal contraction in real income for the average Cuban worker (see Labor, ch. 3).

151

Remittances and Closer Bonds with the Émigré Community

The economic crisis has intensified and in many cases reawakened family bonds severed by decades of emigration. The émigré community has responded generously to the plea for assistance received from relatives in Cuba, even when families had not been in contact for many years. Cuban families abroad are remitting hundreds of millions of dollars (up to US$500 million annually, although ECLAC claims the figure may be as high as US$800 million) in assistance, including food and medicines. To facilitate the inflow of remittances, previous restrictive measures imposed by the Cuban government have been lifted. These measures extend to the easing of visa procedures as a means to encourage emigrant visits. Among the most decisive measure was the 1993 decision to decriminalize the holding of United States dollars and to authorize the free circulation of United States currency.

Closer ties between Cubans at home and abroad have important social implications. They chip away at the ideological and political cleavages separating Cuban families, and thereby lead to the questioning of the official stigmatization of those who left for ideological or material reasons. Second, and perhaps most important, remittance inflows have substantially modified the country's pattern of income distribution and granted a measure of economic freedom to families formerly totally dependent on the state. The latter fact has curbed the power of the state, particularly given the fact that a few dollars are the peso equivalent of the average monthly salary. The regressive effects of remittances are substantial given that not all families have access to them. Families without close relatives abroad are excluded, including those belonging to social categories underrepresented in the emigration stream, such as Cubans of African descent (see Attracting Foreign Investment and Remittances, ch. 3).

Tourism

In response to government policies to promote international tourism, millions of foreign tourists have traveled to Cuba since the early 1990s. If current trends persist, the annual number of foreign tourists visiting Cuba will rise to as many as 2 million annually—more than 1.6 million tourists visited in 1999—by the beginning of the twenty-first century, as compared with 270,000 in 1989 (see Tourism, ch. 3). This development, together with the dollarization of the domestic economy, will further accelerate a process of social change in a country that up to the late 1980s was largely, although not completely, isolated from outside influences. This impact is already evident in numerous ways.

The arrival of hundreds of thousands of foreign tourists has led to charges of "tourism apartheid," or the discrimination to which Cubans without dollars are subjected by not being able to pay for services available only in tourist facilities, such as hotels and nightclubs. Like foreign remittances, tourism also contributes to increases in income differentials. Workers in the foreign tourist sector have access to dollars (in tips and other compensation) and other goods not available to workers in other economic sectors. Foreign tourists, through their life-styles and behaviors, such as consumerism, provide alternative role models at variance with those of socialism. They also provide a conduit for news from the outside world. The culture of service in the tourism sector, essential if the industry is to prosper, to some extent is inimical to egalitarian socialist principles. With hundreds of thousands of foreign visitors present, it is no longer wise for the government to openly suppress social and political dissent. Tourism, by contributing to a more relaxed social environment, will force the government, albeit reluctantly, to tolerate alternative behaviors that challenge conformist socialist norms.

Tourism and the poverty associated with the economic crisis have contributed to the resurgence of several social ills that had presumably been eradicated under socialism. Prostitution is endemic, particularly in tourist areas, and until recently the government has been unable or unwilling to stop it, despite some high-visibility attempts to do so. Many prostitutes are young, well-educated women (and men) who practice the ancient trade to feed families or purchase expensive (by Cuban standards) and coveted foreign goods in dollar-only stores. Sexually suggestive advertisements in Europe and South America lure tourists seeking amorous adventures while enjoying affordable vacation packages. In early 1999, the authorities took drastic measures to remove prostitutes from the streets of Havana and from important tourist resorts. The measures included the institutionalization of repeat offenders, forcing young prostitutes from the interior of the country to return to their places of origin, and reeducation plans. To what extent these policies will be effective, however, remains to be seen because the economic conditions behind prostitution have not changed, nor are they likely to change in the near future.

Petty crime, as well as a rising trend of violent crime, much of it targeting foreign visitors, is a cause of concern (see Crime and Punishment, ch. 5). Drug use is on the increase as well, although its incidence is still low. The allegiance of the people to the socialist state is gravely compromised by these developments. They are indicative of the implosion of the implicit cradle-to-grave social bargain promised and delivered by the once-subsidized socialist government.

Outlook

Any reasonable observer must forecast that profound social changes are in store for Cuba. Four decades of social engineering designed to create a society populated by men and women schooled in Marxist-Leninist principles and committed to internationalist solidarity were rattled by the disintegration of the communist world. The austere social environment created by the Revolution, including many of its social welfare institutions, managed to function relatively well as long as Cuba's inefficient economy was sheltered from outside shocks, and costly health, education, and safety-net programs could be sustained with external financial transfers. In this context, the educational system and highly structured mass organizations conveyed ideological messages whose credibility was enhanced by socialist Cuba's ability to construct an equitable, if totalitarian, society. These social achievements had an important symbolic value in legitimizing socialist Cuba's policies, even providing a veneer of justification for its totalitarian excesses. Repressing competing worldviews, whether in the political, economic, social, or religious realms, was feasible in a totalitarian state that controlled practically all aspects of the country's life. Outside influences were contained in a Cuba only partially open to the outside world; the permanent exile option, often employed on a massive scale, was used to rid the country of those citizens most unhappy with government policies.

The context is vastly different today. Whether the leadership wants it or not, Cuba must open to the world. Foreign values and influences are coming into Cuba in the form of international tourism; with the tourists come the demonstration effects of consumer societies and a growing appetite for material well-being, as well as more tolerant social and political attitudes. As this happens and as the distribution of income becomes more unequal, socioeconomic differentials can only increase and alternative ideological viewpoints become more widespread. Past ideological messages are as irrelevant today as they are impractical. The socialist government is no longer able to deliver on its social-compact promises of equity and universal access to quality social services. It is difficult to predict the long-term consequences of these developments. The Cuban people show many signs of restlessness, ideological exhaustion, and the search for viable individual alternatives. The only thing certain is that social relations and Cuba's social fabric in the early twenty-first century will be vastly different from those dreamed of and partially achieved by the revolutionary leadership in the 1970s and 1980s.

*   *   *

The literature on Cuba is vast and growing, in Spanish as well as in English and other languages. Much of it touches on the country's social history and contemporary social conditions up to the early 1990s. Among the most comprehensive and authoritative references is the journal *Cuban Studies/Estudios Cubanos*, published since 1970 by the University of Pittsburgh Press. Also replete with information is *Cuba in Transition* (available on the Internet at http://www.ascecuba.org), the proceedings of the annual meeting of the Association for the Study of the Cuban Economy, published since 1991. Aside from books on specific topics published by university and academic presses, edited collections (with varying ideological tinges) are available. They focus on different facets of Cuban affairs, dating back to the 1960s, and cover developments since the early 1990s. Of particular note are the ten editions of *Cuban Communism*, a comprehensive compilation of essays culled from many sources and edited by Irving Louis Horowitz.

Many of the excellent studies conducted over the years about Cuba's social situation do not capture the reality of the country since the early 1990s given the drastic changes that have occurred. But important sources that could be consulted on the evolution of different facets of social life in Cuba include Juan Clark's *Mito y realidad,* Julie Feinsilver's *Healing the Masses*, and Julie Marie Bunck's *Fidel Castro and the Quest for a Revolutionary Culture in Cuba.* One noted source dealing with contemporary Cuba, but with a major emphasis on economics, is *La economía cubana: Reformas estructurales y desempeño en los noventa,* a study sponsored by the Economic Commission for Latin America and the Caribbean (ECLAC) and published in 1997 by the Fondo de Cultura Económica in Mexico City.

Among major American newspapers, the most extensive Cuban coverage is provided by the *Miami Herald,* in particular by its Spanish-language version, *El Nuevo Herald.* Excellent but more sporadic coverage can also be found in other major national newspapers, such as the *New York Times* and the *Washington Post,* both (like the *Miami Herald* and other newspapers) accessible through the Internet. Internet readers have at their reach a wealth of additional information on Cuba that can be located in various Web pages and associated links. Selected web pages range from those of Florida-produced *Cuba Free Press* and *Cuba Press,* which offer accounts of daily life provided by independent, and often persecuted, journalists in Cuba, to English-language versions of official Cuban newspapers, such as the daily *Granma,* Cuba's most important newspaper, and the weekly *Granma International* [Havana]. Equally important sources of news on Cuba are the various international news agencies, such as the Associated Press and Cuba's own official news agency, Prensa Latina. These news agencies can also be accessed through the Internet. (For further information and complete citations, see Bibliography.)

Chapter 3. The Economy

Havana's main train station, 1999
Courtesy Maria M. Alonso

NEARLY FOUR DECADES SINCE the triumph of the Revolution of 1959, the Cuban economy remains based on agriculture, notwithstanding the rhetoric of Cuba's government. Sugar remains the mainstay of the economy, the largest employer, and the main generator of net export revenues (see Key Economic Sectors, this ch.). The tourism industry grew rapidly in the 1990s, however, spurred by foreign investment in the form of joint ventures. By the late 1990s, gross revenue generated by tourism had surpassed that earned by sugar. Net revenues generated by tourism are only about one-third of gross revenue, however, reflecting the high import content of activities of this industry.

Cuba remains nominally a centrally planned economy (see Glossary), and the Cuban government controls the bulk of the productive resources of the nation. By the 1980s, however, some economic activities for private gain existed. Such activities included agriculture (private farmers owned a small portion of the island's agricultural land); the sale of some personal services; and, for a period in the early 1980s, farmers' markets and artisan markets. In addition, black market (see Glossary) operations were illegally conducted outside of state control. Other illegal activities with economic consequences included unauthorized use of government resources and corruption.

During the 1990s, Cuba faced perhaps its most serious economic crisis of the twentieth century. The crisis was triggered by the breakup of economic and trade relations with East European countries and the Soviet Union as these countries abandoned socialism and began their transition to market economies. The results have been devastating for Cuba and for the Cuban people: a contraction in national product of one-third to one-half between 1989 and 1993, a fall in exports by 79 percent and imports by 75 percent, a tripling of the budget deficit, and sharp declines in the standard of living of the population. The economic crisis of the 1990s, and the austerity measures put in place to try to overcome it, are referred to by the Cuban government as the "special period in peacetime" (*período especial en tiempo de paz*; hereafter Special Period—see Glossary).

In the summer of 1993, faced with a badly deteriorating economic picture, the Cuban government began to take steps to liberalize certain areas of the economy, attract foreign investment by offering tax holidays and other incentives to foreign investors, and attain some measure of macroeconomic stabilization. The pace of reforms slowed down in 1995, although the National Assembly of People's Power (Asamblea Nacional del Poder Popular—ANPP; hereafter, National Assembly) passed a tax code and Foreign Investment Decree-Law 77 that year. Law 77 clarifies the concept of private property and provides a legal basis for transferring state property to joint ventures established with foreign partners. Law 77 also authorizes 100 percent foreign ownership of investments, simplifies the screening of foreign investment, and explicitly allows foreign investment in real estate.

In 1996 the National Assembly passed legislation to create free-trade zones and in 1997 a bill to reform the banking system. Far from being a well-articulated set of reforms to liberalize the Cuban economy and make it more efficient and productive, the reforms were opportunistic measures to ease the economic crisis and maintain the Cuban government and the Communist Party of Cuba (Partido Comunista de Cuba—PCC) in political control. Modest positive economic growth during 1994–98 arrested the economic deterioration experienced over the first half of the 1990s, but did not result in a significant improvement in the standard of living of the population.

Several of the reform measures implemented in the 1990s stimulated economic activity outside of the control of the state. These reform measures included the decriminalization of the holding and use of foreign currencies, the breakup of state farms and their reinstitution as cooperatives, the authorization of self-employment, the reestablishment of agricultural and artisan markets, the decentralization of foreign trade, and the creation of semiautonomous corporations. By 1998 about one-quarter of the Cuban labor force was engaged in activities outside of the state sector, compared with about 5 percent in 1989.

Attraction of foreign investment was one of the bright spots of the Cuban economy in the 1990s, although the levels of incoming investment were very small in comparison with the foreign support that was lost as a result of the change in economic and trade relations with the former Soviet Union and the socialist countries of Eastern Europe. The impact on investment of the Helms-Burton Act (see Glossary), adopted by the United States in 1996, is difficult to ascertain given the secrecy with which the Cuban government deals with foreign investment information.

Cuba has had great difficulties in borrowing funds in international markets since it suspended service on its convertible currency (see Glossary) on July 1, 1986. As a result, the island has had to rely on short-term loans at very high interest rates. At the end of 1998, Cuba's convertible currency debt amounted to more than US$11.2 billion. In addition, Cuba has a substantial debt with the former Soviet Union (this debt has been assumed by Russia) and with East European nations denominated in rubles. Very little is known about the magnitude of this debt or the exchange rate at which it is to be converted to either pesos or dollars for purposes of repayment.

In the second half of the 1990s, foreign remittances—the funds that Cuban individuals and families receive from relatives and friends living abroad—became the lifeline of the external sector of the Cuban economy. The Cuban government adopted policies that facilitate the use of remittances by Cuban citizens and encourage relatives and friends abroad to increase remittance levels. These policies include permitting Cuban citizens to hold foreign currencies, establish stores where such currencies can be used, and set up a system of exchange houses to facilitate conversion into domestic currency. According to Cuban official sources, foreign remittances amounted to 820 million pesos in 1998 (for value of the peso—see Glossary).

Performance of the Economy

Background

Buffered by economic assistance from the Soviet Union and other socialist countries, the Cuban economy showed positive economic growth in the 1970s and 1980s. According to official statistics, the global social product (GSP—see Glossary), a broad, Soviet-style measure of the economy under Cuba's Material Product System (MPS—see Glossary), grew at an average annual rate of 7.5 percent during the first half of the 1970s and 3.5 percent during the second half. In 1972 Cuba became a member of the Council for Mutual Economic Assistance (CMEA; also known as Comecon—see Glossary), the organization that promoted and guided trade and economic cooperation among the socialist countries. In that same year, Cuba and the Soviet Union formalized a system of preferential prices—

that is, higher than world market prices—for Cuban sugar exports that would result in very large price subsidies for the island throughout the 1970s and 1980s.

In the first half of the 1980s, socialist Cuba recorded its strongest economic performance, with GSP growing at an average annual rate of 7.2 percent. Economic growth slowed during the second half of the 1980s, when GSP growth rates of 1.2 percent in 1986, -3.9 percent in 1987, 2.2 percent in 1988, and 1.1 percent in 1989 were recorded. During this period, Cuba was engaged in the "rectification process of errors and negative tendencies" (*proceso de rectificación de errores y tendencias negativas*—see Glossary) and began to face a tightening of its economic relations with the Soviet Union under former president Mikhail Gorbachev's policy of economic and governmental reform (perestroika).

In late September 1990, Fidel Castro Ruz (president, 1976–) announced that the country had entered a Special Period. He likened the economic situation—sharply reduced levels of imports of fuel, food, raw materials, machinery, and spare parts—to what would have ensued from the imposition of an air and naval blockade in a war situation. Surviving this Special Period would require emergency measures similar to those called for in a war setting. Indeed, in the 1990s Cuba has faced its most serious economic crisis in the twentieth century.

The events that triggered Cuba's economic crisis are undoubtedly related to the shift in trade and economic relations with the former socialist countries that began in 1989 as these economic partners abandoned central planning and began their transition toward market economies. In the late 1980s, East European countries and the former Soviet Union purchased 85 percent of Cuba's exports, provided a like share of imports, and were the main source of the island's development financing. The disappearance of the socialist regimes in Eastern Europe and the former Soviet Union, and these countries' demand that henceforth trade relations be conducted using convertible currencies and following normal commercial practices, meant that the economic support that the socialist community had given Cuba for nearly three decades vanished almost overnight.

External sector shocks triggered the economic crisis of the 1990s, but they alone are not responsible for its occurrence, severity, or length. The underlying causes of the crisis are the well-known inefficiencies of centrally planned economies, compounded by distortions created by massive inflows of resources from the socialist bloc and the leadership's refusal to undertake the necessary political and economic reforms.

The Economic Crisis of the 1990s

Official information on the performance of the Cuban economy during the 1990s remains scanty. The official statistical yearbook, *Anuario estadístico,* which was published annually during the 1970s and 1980s, ceased publication with the issue for 1989 and did not appear again until the issue for 1996, under the auspices of the newly formed National Statistical Office (Oficina Nacional de Estadísticas—ONE). Beginning in August 1995, the Cuban National Bank (Banco Nacional de Cuba—BNC) and its successor, the Cuban Central Bank (Banco Central de Cuba—BCC), have published annual reports on the performance of the Cuban economy that include some statistical information. The national product statistics in the BNC, BCC, and ONE reports follow the System of National Accounts (SNA—see Glossary), a different methodology than was used by socialist Cuba through the early 1990s, thereby making long-term comparisons impossible.

In mid-1997, the Economic Commission for Latin America and the Caribbean (ECLAC—see Glossary) of the United Nations released a comprehensive study of the Cuban economy prepared with the cooperation of the Cuban government. A statistical annex to this report—reportedly based on information provided by Cuban government statistical agencies—provides economic data not published directly by the Cuban authorities. Using information contained in the BNC, BCC, ONE, and ECLAC reports, analysts may be able to gauge the depth and breadth of the economic crisis of the 1990s.

National Product

After falling freely since 1989—by 3 percent in 1990, 11 percent in 1991, 12 percent in 1992, and 15 percent in 1993—the Cuban economy apparently hit bottom around mid-1994. The gross domestic product (GDP—see Glossary) at constant prices of 1981 was about 12.8 billion pesos in 1993, 35 percent lower than in 1989 (see Table 5, Appendix).

According to official statistics, the GDP grew by 0.7 percent in 1994, 2.5 percent in 1995, 7.8 percent in 1996, 2.5 percent in 1997, and 1.2 percent in 1998. As had been the practice in the 1990s, Cuba has not provided detailed statistics to support reported growth rates. Experts on the Cuban economy have raised fundamental questions about the reliability of Cuban economic statistics for 1996 and, by extension, about those for other years and more broadly about the Cuban system of national accounts. If the official statistics are taken at face value, the cumulative GDP growth rate over the 1993–98 period is about 16 percent, compared with a contraction of 35 percent between 1989 and 1993.

Foreign Trade

Cuban merchandise exports in 1993 amounted to less than 1.2 billion pesos, 79 percent lower than the nearly 5.4 billion pesos recorded in 1989 (see Foreign Economic Relations, this ch.; table 6, Appendix). Over the same period, merchandise imports fell from 8.1 billion pesos to slightly more than 2.0 billion pesos, or by 75 percent. Exports began to recover in 1994, rising to about 1.3 billion pesos in 1994, 1.5 billion pesos in 1995, and 1.9 billion pesos in 1996, then falling to 1.8 billion pesos in 1997 and 1.4 billion pesos in 1998. Meanwhile, imports were 2.0 billion pesos in 1994, 2.9 billion pesos in 1995, 3.6 billion pesos in 1996, 4.0 billion pesos in 1997, and 4.2 billion pesos in 1998. In 1998 exports and imports were still substantially lower than in 1989, by 73 percent and 49 percent, respectively.

State Budget

During the crisis, the nation's budget deficit nearly tripled, deteriorating from 1.4 billion pesos in 1989 to nearly 5.1 billion pesos in 1993 (see table 7, Appendix). In 1993 the budget deficit amounted to more than 30 percent of the GDP. Shortages of consumer products in the state distribution system, coupled with low (officially set) prices for basic consumption goods, the lack of a tax system, and government policies of continuing to pay a portion (60 percent) of salaries to idle workers, led to a sharp rise of monetary balances in the hands of the population. These balances grew from about 4 billion pesos in 1989 to 11.4 billion pesos in 1993.

The government's budget deficit fell to the pre-crisis level of -1.6 billion pesos in 1994, -766 million pesos in 1995, -570 million pesos in 1996, -459 million pesos in 1997, and -560 million pesos in 1998. Meanwhile, monetary balances in the hands of the population declined to 9.9 billion pesos in 1994 and 9.3 billion pesos in 1995, but rose again in 1996 to 9.5 billion pesos and reached 9.7 billion pesos in 1998.

Performance of Economic Sectors

The economic crisis affected nearly all sectors of the economy. As discussed above, GDP fell by 35 percent during 1989–93, according to official statistics. However, the performance of several key sectors of the economy was significantly worse: output of the construction sector fell by 71.4 percent, agriculture by 51.9 percent, transportation by 45.8 percent, commerce by 43.0 percent, and manufacturing by 36.5 percent. The downturn of the construction industry was attributed to a sharp contraction in domestic investment and shortages of construction materials; nonsugar agriculture was adversely affected by the lack of imported inputs—for example, fertilizers, pesticides, and spare parts for machinery—and of manpower to cultivate the land and harvest crops. Sugar production, still the mainstay of the economy and the most significant source of export revenue in the early 1990s, fell from 7.3 million tons in 1989 to 4.1 million tons in 1993, or by 43.8 percent, contributing to the decline in the output of the manufacturing sector. Nickel production declined by 35.2 percent. By 1995, however, the manufacturing sector had increased its share of GDP by 2 percent, to 27 percent (see fig. 4).

Two bright spots for the Cuban economy during the gloomy 1989–93 period were the oil and tourism industries. Domestic oil production for the first time exceeded 1 million tons in 1993. Between 1989 and 1993, the number of international tourists visiting the island jumped from 300,000 to 546,000 persons, and gross income from tourism increased more than fourfold (from 166 to 720 million pesos).

Population consumption of food, consumer durables (see Glossary), and nondurables, such as vegetables, dropped sharply in the early 1990s, with rationing reinstated for a wide range of staple food, personal hygiene, and clothing items. Moreover, monthly rationing allowances were trimmed back so that the typical household could satisfy only about two weeks of its consumption needs through the rationing system. The cutbacks forced most consumers to turn to more expensive alternatives—especially the very active black market—and affected, in particular, consumption levels of pensioners. Electricity shortages and blackouts became commonplace, and public transportation was cut back sharply. The availability and quality

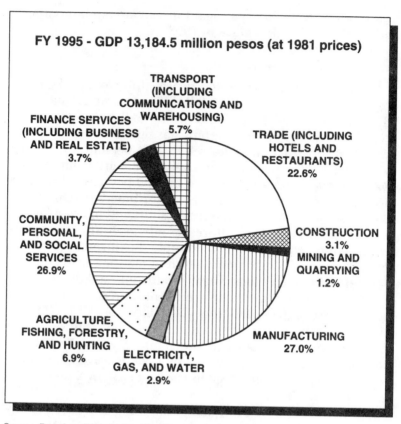

FY 1995 - GDP 13,184.5 million pesos (at 1981 prices)

Source: Based on information from Banco Nacional de Cuba, *Informe económico 1995*, Havana, August 1995, Appendix A.

Figure 4. Gross Domestic Product (GDP) by Sector, 1995

of public health and education services, two of the most lauded accomplishments of Fidel Castro's government, also declined severely.

Economic Reforms

Far from an articulated and comprehensive blueprint to transform the economic system into a market-oriented one, the reform measures taken to date represent a survival strategy—modest, opportunistic measures that seek to allow the government and the PCC to cope with the economic crisis and remain in power. In the summer of 1993, Cuba took steps to liberalize certain areas of the domestic economy and to attract foreign resources. A second set of initiatives, including stabilization measures, was implemented in May 1994 together with a sweeping law, Decree-Law 149, against "improper enrichment."

In mid-1995, however, Fidel Castro vowed not to abandon Cuba's socialist principles and Marxist-Leninist convictions. Subsequently, the pace of change slowed down as the government postponed implementation of enterprise-restructuring measures that would inevitably have resulted in the shutdown of inefficient plants and increased unemployment.

In March 1996, Raúl Castro Ruz, the minister of defense and vice president, strongly criticized some of the economic changes that had been implemented. He lashed out at foreign influences associated with the international tourism industry and the wealth acquired by individuals engaged in legal forms of self-employment, and called for renewed ideological vigor in defense of communism. Raúl Castro's broadside squelched an incipient domestic dialogue on reforms centered on the work of several Cuban economists.

Stabilizing the Economy

Cuba's macroeconomic situation in the early 1990s was dismal. The country had a very large government budget deficit, very high levels of repressed inflation (manifested through physical shortages and rampant black markets), and large cash balances in the hands of the population. To address these problems, Cuba took a number of actions to introduce fiscal discipline, including reducing government expenditures, increasing revenues, and reforming the tax system.

Meeting in early May 1994, the National Assembly adopted a resolution calling for strict discipline in the implementation of the budget law and for reductions in expenditures and increases in revenues at all levels of government. On the expenditures side, the National Assembly directed the executive to take concrete steps to reduce subsidies to loss-making enterprises, stimulate personal savings, increase revenue collection through increases in prices of nonessential goods and some services, and develop a comprehensive tax system that would be equitable, foster production and work effort, and raise sufficient revenue to balance the state budget. A reorganization of the central state administration reduced the number of entities from fifty to thirty-two, eliminating altogether 984 organizational units, such as departments, sections, and directorates, and reducing personnel and administrative expenses.

On the revenue side, the Executive Committee of the Council of Ministers decreed increases in the prices of cigarettes and alcoholic beverages, gasoline, electricity, and public transportation, and in the rates for sending mail and telegrams; eliminated subsidies to workplace cafeterias; and imposed a charge for services formerly provided free, such as school lunches, some medications, and attendance at sports and cultural events. Assessing fees on self-employed workers is a new source of government revenue.

The results of the implementation of austerity measures in 1994–95 were sharp reductions in the budget deficit and in the amount of currency in circulation. All areas of government expenditure were subject to cuts, particularly subsidies to enterprises. The budget deficit in 1994 was 1.6 billion pesos, 50 percent lower than the projected deficit of 3.2 billion pesos. For 1995 the budget deficit was anticipated at 1 billion pesos, but the actual deficit was 766 million pesos, and it was 570 million pesos in 1996, 459 million pesos in 1997, and 560 million pesos in 1998. The budget deficit as a share of GDP was 39.5 percent in 1993, 12.6 percent in 1994, 5.8 percent in 1995, 4.0 percent in 1996, 3.1 percent in 1997, and 3.8 percent in 1998.

Currency in circulation fell from 11.0 billion pesos at the end of 1993 to 9.9 billion pesos at the end of 1994, or by 10 percent, as a result of increased savings and price increases. Cash holdings were 9.5 billion pesos in 1995, 9.4 billion pesos in 1997, and 9.7 billion pesos in 1998.

In August 1994, the National Assembly approved a new and very broad tax code, to be implemented gradually beginning in October 1994. The new system levies taxes on the income of enterprises, including joint ventures with foreign investors, as well as on the value of assets owned; earned income; sales; consumption of products, such as cigarettes, alcoholic beverages, domestic electric appliances, and other luxury goods; public services, such as electricity, water and sewer, telephone, telegrams, transportation, restaurants, and lodging; real estate holdings; gasoline- or draft animal-powered transportation vehicles; transfer of property, including inheritances; public documents issued; payrolls; and use of natural resources. The law also provides for employer contributions to social security, user fees on roads (tolls) and airport services, and charges for advertising of products or services. Implementation of the law has been gradual, with personal income taxes, user fees on air-

A pedicab and its driver in Havana
A knife sharpener plying his trade on a Havana street
Courtesy Danielle Hayes, United Nations Development Programme

port services, and charges on advertising becoming effective in October 1994 and the rest since 1995.

Stimulating Production

Cuba took some tentative steps to liberalize selected sectors of the economy to stimulate production. The most significant such steps were those related to the liberalization of self-employment, agricultural production and sales, and the decentralization of foreign trade. Concern about the possibility that economic liberalization measures would bring about the enrichment of some individuals prompted the adoption, in March 1994, of Decree-Law 149 (effective that May) to facilitate the prosecution of "profiteers."

In September 1993, the Cuban government authorized self-employment in more than 100 occupations, primarily those related to transportation, home repair, and personal services. It took this long overdue measure in order to legitimize a booming black market for personal services and handicraft production and to absorb the large number of workers unemployed and underemployed because of the idling of their workplaces.

169

However, under Decree-Law 186, restrictions on self-employment remain quite severe. Professionals with a university degree cannot become self-employed in the occupation for which they were trained; moreover, physicians, dentists, teachers, professors, and researchers are not allowed to engage in self-employment because education and public health services continue to be supplied by the state. Even with regard to the occupations where self-employment is allowed, restrictions apply: the self-employed have to request a license, cannot hire others, have to pay fees and taxes to the government, and are limited on how they sell the goods or service they produce. In October 1993, the state expanded the list of occupations amenable to self-employment by twenty occupations. In June 1995, it designated additional occupations for self-employment, bringing the number of authorized occupations to 140; in July 1995, the Ministry of Labor authorized university graduates to become self-employed, provided the occupations they performed differed from those for which they were trained—for example, an engineer could be self-employed as a messenger or a taxi driver.

Shortly after self-employment was authorized, there was an explosion of home restaurants—commonly called *paladares* (see Glossary)—set up pursuant to the provisions of the law that authorized self-employment related to food preparation. Most of the home restaurants were modest operations and provided relatively simple staple foods, but some were fancy and charged high prices. The government first banned home restaurants, arguing that they were inconsistent with the authorized forms of self-employment, but in 1995 it reversed course and explicitly authorized them, provided they sat twelve or fewer customers and complied with a stiff schedule of monthly fees. At the end of 1995, approximately 208,000 workers had been authorized to engage in self-employment, less than 5 percent of the economically active population of 4.5 million workers and about one-fifth of the estimated 1 million workers who would be subject to dismissals in an overall rationalization of state enterprises.

New fees and taxes—pursuant to the 1994 tax code—began to be charged to the self-employed effective February 1, 1996. Fees paid by self-employed taxi drivers jumped from 100 to 400 pesos per month, manicurists from 60 to 100 pesos, hair dressers from 90 to 200 pesos, and *paladares* charging prices in domestic currency (pesos) to 800 pesos per month. The new progressive income tax system levied taxes of 10 percent on annual incomes up to 2,400 pesos and 50 percent on annual incomes exceeding 60,000 pesos. By January 1998, the number of self-employed had fallen to about 160,000, from about 209,000 in March 1996, and reportedly has continued to fall.

In September 1993, the Council of State approved breaking up state farms into a new form of agricultural cooperatives, the Basic Units of Cooperative Production (Unidades Básicas de Producción Cooperativa—UBPC). The UBPCs have the use of the land they work for an indefinite period of time, own the output they produce, have the ability to sell their output to the state through the state procurement system or through other means, have the authority to contract and pay for the technical and material resources they use, have their own bank accounts and buy necessary inputs on credit, and are able to elect their own management, which must report to its members periodically. The UBPCs also have to pay taxes. The rationale for the policy change was that the shift from state farms to cooperatives would give workers greater incentives to increase production with the least expenditure of material resources.

In essence, the UBPCs operate as production cooperatives within each state farm, breaking up the larger estates and creating smaller units that compete with one another. Workers of former state farms shift from being wage workers in the employ of the state to being cooperative members, with their earnings connected to the profitability of their units. Cooperatives are able, within some constraints, to make decisions regarding how they use their land. They are permitted to set aside some land for growing agricultural products and raise livestock to meet their own consumption needs.

In early May 1994, the Council of State adopted a broad statute that would allow confiscation of assets and income of individuals who had obtained them through "improper enrichment" (*enriquecimiento indebido*). This law grants the government sweeping powers to confiscate cash, goods, and assets of individuals found guilty of "profiteering" and provides for retroactive application of sanctions against this offense. Seizures ordered by the Office of the National Prosecutor in "improper enrichment" cases are not appealable.

In late September 1994, Cuba authorized agricultural markets (*agros*—see Glossary), locations at which producers of selected agricultural products can sell a portion of their output at prices set by demand and supply. Before an agricultural producer—private farmer, cooperative member, or even state enterprise—can sell his or her output in the new markets, sales obligations to the state procurement system (*acopio*—see Glossary) must be met. Participants in the agricultural markets would also have to pay a fee to participate and a tax on sales conducted. In most respects, the agricultural markets authorized in September 1994 are similar to the farmers' free markets (*mercados libres campesinos*) that were in operation during 1980–86 and scuttled during rectification.

In October 1994, following on the establishment of agricultural markets, the Cuban government announced that it would also allow the free sale of a wide range of consumer products through a network of artisan and manufactured products markets. The new markets could be used by artisans to sell handicrafts and also by the government to dispose of inventories of manufactured goods and surplus products made by state enterprises. These markets resemble very closely the artisan markets that were in operation during 1980–86 and eliminated during rectification.

Prior to the 1990s, Cuban foreign trade was a state monopoly, based on Article 18 of the socialist constitution of 1976, which decrees that "foreign trade is the exclusive function of the state." Cuban foreign trade institutions mirrored those of the Soviet Union and East European socialist nations: exports were conducted by specialized enterprises of the Ministry of Foreign Trade; imports were primarily the responsibility of the State Committee for Technical and Material Supply (Comité Estatal de Abastecimiento Técnico-Material—CEATM).

Among the reforms to the constitution implemented in 1992 was a reformulation of Article 18 that eliminated the state monopoly over the conduct of foreign trade, and shifted the role of the state to directing and controlling foreign trade. Cuba has created various foreign trade corporations that operate largely independently of the state. Examples are Acemex, S.A., a private shipping company registered in Liechtenstein; Diplomatic Corps Service Company (Empresa para Prestación de Servicios al Cuerpo Diplomático—Cubalse), which imports consumer goods for the diplomatic corps and foreign technicians residing in Cuba and exports beverages, tobacco, leather goods, and foodstuffs; Havana Tourism Company (Havanatur); International Tourism and Trade Corporation (Corporación de Turismo y Comercio Internacional—Cubanacán), a tourist agency; the military-owned tourism company Gaviota; the Pan-

An artisan market on Cathedral Plaza (La Plaza de la Catedral) in Havana, 1997

The Agricultural Market (Mercado Agropecuario) in Havana, 1997 Courtesy Mark P. Sullivan

ama-based Import-Export Company (Compañía Importadora-Exportadora—Cimex); Union of Caribbean Construction Enterprises (Unión de Empresas de Construcción del Caribe—Uneca); and International Financial Bank (Banco Financiero Internacional—BFI), a commercial bank that promotes Cuban exports and banking relations. Cuba has also experimented with the establishment of quasi-private companies called *sociedades anónimas* (S.A.), stock companies controlled by government loyalists. Cuba's *sociedades anónimas* have considerable autonomy from the state. Many organizations that produce goods and services are also permitted to import and export, with many working on the basis of self-financing arrangements using convertible currency.

The slight economic recovery registered in 1994 was reportedly fed by sharp growth in the manufacturing sector (7.6 percent) and in the electricity industry (4.4 percent). Cuba reported a growth rate of 2.5 percent for 1995, 7.8 percent for 1996, 2.5 percent for 1997, and 1.2 percent for 1998. Unfortunately, the requisite data and information on methodology to confirm aggregate growth trends are not available. Data on detailed physical output data, product prices adjusted for inflation, and the relative importance of each product within a sector and within the economy at large are also not available. The fragmentary data that are available raise some questions. For example, the recovery of the manufacturing sector suggested by the official statistics is incongruent with the poor performance of the sugar industry, a principal component of that sector. With the exception of nickel—where foreign investment has played a key role—manufactured products showed output in 1998 below the level reached in 1989.

Agricultural production continued to decline despite the breakup of state farms and creation of the UBPCs. By the end of 1994, the state had distributed the bulk of agricultural land to the UBPCs, retaining only 25 percent. Unable to obtain necessary inputs, the UBPCs struggled to adjust to their new independent status after being part of large enterprises and accustomed to extensive use of mechanization, fertilizers, and pesticides; most of the 1,500 sugarcane UBPCs were unprofitable in 1994.

Overall, the agricultural sector has continued to perform poorly. By 1997 production of tubers, plantains, corn, and beans had reached or exceeded 1989 levels, but other agricultural products, such as vegetables, rice, citrus, other fruits, tobacco, eggs, and milk were still below the level reached in 1989 (see table 8, Appendix).

The agricultural markets reportedly got off to a good start, quickly increasing the amount and variety of produce available to the public, although at very high prices. According to a 1998 Cuban survey, the origin of produce sold through the farmers' free markets was as follows: private farmers, 60 percent of meats and 50 percent of all other products; state sector, 39 percent and 51 percent, respectively; and cooperatives (including the UBPCs), 0.2 percent and 8.3 percent, respectively. Prices in farmers' markets continue to be very high and unaffordable to the average Cuban consumer. The average monthly salary of workers in the state sector was 203 pesos in 1998 and 1997, and 200 pesos in 1996. Meanwhile, prices in agricultural markets in La Habana (hereafter, Havana) in August 1998 were 4.50 pesos for a pound of rice, 10 to 12 pesos for a pound of beans, 2 pesos for one egg, and 23 to 25 pesos for a pound of pork.

Attracting Foreign Investment and Remittances

To ease severe external-sector pressures, Cuba has taken a number of steps to reform its foreign sector. Cuba's main interest has been to attract foreign resources—primarily in the form of remittances and foreign investment—that can help reactivate its economy.

In the summer of 1993, Cuba decriminalized the holding and use of convertible currency (mostly United States dollars) by Cuban citizens. The government also created special stores at which Cuban citizens holding convertible currencies can shop and obtain items that are not available to Cubans holding pesos. In addition, the government liberalized travel to the island by relatives and friends of Cuban citizens. The intent of the measures was to stimulate convertible currency remittances to Cuban citizens from family and friends living abroad, mostly in the United States, and to reduce the importance of a very active convertible currency black market.

Other complementary steps have been taken to accommodate the needs of citizens holding convertible currencies. In September 1995, the BNC for the first time began to accept from the population deposits denominated in convertible currency and offered to pay interest on such savings also in convertible currency. And in mid-October 1995, the government created Exchange Houses (Casas de Cambio—Cadeca), at which Cuban citizens can buy and sell foreign currencies at rates close to those prevailing in the black market.

In December 1994, Cuba announced the creation of a new currency, the convertible peso (peso *convertible*—see Glossary), that would gradually replace the United States dollar and other foreign currencies within the island. The convertible peso, valued at par with the United States dollar, would eventually be the currency used in the tourism sector and in outlets authorized since mid-1993 to sell goods for foreign currencies. Incentive payments to workers of certain key industries that generate hard currency—for example, tourism, oil extraction and tobacco—are now made in convertible pesos rather than in foreign currencies, as had been the practice.

Cuba first passed legislation allowing foreign investment on the island—mostly in the form of joint ventures—in February 1982. This innovation generated very little interest among Western investors until the 1990s, when Cuba began an aggressive campaign to attract foreign capital. In 1992 the National Assembly passed a number of amendments to the 1976 constitution clarifying the concept of private property and providing a legal basis for transferring state property to joint ventures with foreign partners.

One of the areas in which Cuba has been particularly active in seeking foreign investment has been mining. In December 1994, the National Assembly passed a new Mining Law, which became effective in January 1995, aimed at encouraging foreign investment in exploration and production of oil and minerals. In the 1990s, mining has received a boost from foreign joint ventures, primarily with Canadian investors (see Mining, this ch.).

To institutionalize the "irreversibility" of the opening to foreign investment, in September 1995 the National Assembly adopted Foreign Investment Law 77, which codifies the de facto rules under which joint ventures had been operating and introduces some changes to the legal framework for foreign investment. The law guarantees that investors in Cuba will be protected from expropriation, except for "public utility or social interest"; will be able to sell shares of investment to the state or to a third party, depending on the initial agreement; and will be able to fully transfer profits abroad. The new law for the first time permits 100-percent foreign ownership of investments, up from the 49 percent allowed by the earlier statute. Similarly, the new law simplifies the screening of foreign investment practiced by Cuba, explicitly allows foreign investments in real estate, and authorizes the establishment of free-trade zones. However, the 1995 Foreign Investment Law does not change regulations that ban joint ventures from directly hiring Cuban citizens as employees. Such hiring continues to be carried out by an entity of the Cuban government with power to select, hire, and fire employees, powers that individual joint ventures do not have.

Complementing the September 1995 Foreign Investment Law, the Council of State passed legislation in June 1996 creating export-processing zones, that is, free-trade zones and industrial parks (*zonas francas y parques industriales*). Investors settling in the free-trade zones are subject to a special and more beneficial regime regarding customs, banking, taxes, labor, migration, public order, and foreign trade. Specifically, investments in free-trade zones are exempt from tariffs (see Glossary) and other levies on imports and are also exempt from taxes for a twelve-year period. Regulations establishing an official registry of export-processing zone operators and investors and issuing special customs regulations applicable to foreign investments locating in the zones were issued in October 1996.

Since 1960, when the private banks were nationalized, the BNC has operated as both a central bank (see Glossary) and a commercial bank, arranging short- and long-term credits, financing investments and operations with other countries, and acting as a clearing and payments center. Under a centrally planned system, the BNC's main function was financing the implementation of the national economic plan as reflected in the national budget. In 1984 the BFI was created to operate solely with convertible currencies and to support the activities of foreign investors.

In response to the perception by foreign investors that the financial sector was not sufficiently developed, Cuba has taken a number of steps to allow more choice. In 1994 Cuba granted a license to ING Bank of Holland to operate on the island, the first foreign bank to be so permitted since 1960. In 1995 similar licenses were issued to the General Society of France (Société Générale de France) and to the Sabadell Bank (Banco Sabadell) of Spain. Other foreign banks have also been allowed to establish representative offices in Cuba. Moreover, in order to expand the number of financial services available to foreign investors and semiautonomous enterprises, the BNC created the New Banking Group (Grupo Nueva Banca—GNB), a holding company, to supervise the operations of Cuba's reformed financial sector. The network of new financial institutions under the GNB's supervision includes, in addition to the already mentioned Cadeca and BFI, the Agro-Industrial and Commercial Bank (Banco Agro-Industrial y Comercial), which provides commercial banking services to farmers and cooperatives; the International Bank of Commerce (Banco Internacional de Comercio S.A.—BICSA), a merchant bank that, like the BFI, provides trade finance to Cuban institutions and arranges financing transactions with overseas lenders; the Investment Bank (Banco de Inversiones), which provides medium- and long-term development finance; the Metropolitan Bank (Banco Metropolitano), which caters to diplomats and other private customers; the National Financier (Financiera Nacional—FINSA), an export-import bank that provides short-term finance for Cuban enterprises; and the People's Savings Bank (Banco Popular de Ahorro), which provides retail banking.

In May 1997, the Council of State finally passed long-expected legislation to reform the banking system. Decree-Law 172 established the BCC (Cuban Central Bank) as an autonomous and independent entity and assigned to it the traditional central banking functions. The BNC, which, as mentioned above, had performed central and commercial banking functions since 1960, continued to operate, but its role was relegated to commercial banking. Decree-Law 173, also passed in May 1997, set out the legal framework for registration and operation of commercial banks and financial institutions under the supervision of the BCC.

As a result of its dollarization policies, Cuba de facto adopted a dual currency system that has introduced severe inequalities on the island. Citizens with access to foreign currency (dollars)—because they receive remittances from family or friends abroad, tips in the tourism sector, or bonuses paid by the government in hard currency to stimulate production of exportables—have access to goods and services not available to those citizens without it. In the second half of the 1990s, remittances became a very significant source of foreign currency to Cuba (see Foreign Economic Relations, this ch.).

According to government officials, 231 joint ventures had been created as of the end of May 1995. By the end of 1998, the number of joint ventures had increased to 345. There are no reliable statistics on the amount of foreign investment that has actually flowed into the Cuban economy. Cuban government officials have used the figure of about US$2.1 billion for the 1985–95 period, a figure that may overstate actual investment. Although small when compared with the volume of resources that flowed into Cuba from the former Soviet Union and Eastern Europe, incoming foreign investment has had a salutary effect on the island's economy: it has eased somewhat Cuba's very severe shortage of international financing, provided access to new technology, financed imports of raw materials and equipment that have kept workers at their jobs, and created markets for exports that otherwise would not have been available to domestic entities.

Structure of the Economy

Background

Since the early 1960s, Cuba's official economy has been organized along the lines of the socialist, centrally planned model. In addition to central economic planning, some of the elements of this model, common to the former Soviet Union and other centrally planned economies, are as follows: government control over the bulk of the economic resources of the country, especially major industries, foreign trade, banking, and usually commerce and land; and state regulation and subordination of a highly circumscribed private sector.

With the collapse of economic and commercial relations with the former Soviet Union and East European socialist countries, application of the central planning model in Cuba began to break down. Institutions created to support central planning and economic and trade relations with socialist countries, such as the Central Planning Board (Junta Central de Planificación—Juceplan), became obsolete and began to undergo a process of transformation and adjustment to the new economic reality. Additional space has been created for the nonstate sector through the expansion of the number of occupations suitable for self-employment, the conversion of state farms into cooperatives, and the reinstatement of farmers' markets.

At a rhetorical level, economic policies pursued by Cuba's socialist government have supported industrialization and diversification of the economy away from sugar. The reality is that Cuba continues to be primarily an agricultural country, and sugar remains the mainstay of the economy, its largest employer, and primary net generator of export revenue.

Cuba's specialization in sugar and other basic commodities was formalized through its participation in the CMEA (Council for Mutual Economic Assistance), within which the island was assigned the role of supplier of raw materials to other members of that organization.

In the 1990s, Cuba focused its efforts on reviving its sugar industry, increasing nonsugar agricultural production, and stimulating development of its tourism and biotechnology industries. The record so far has been mixed, with the sugar industry continuing to perform poorly and food production also lagging behind. The tourism industry has been the focus of a significant number of joint ventures with foreign enterprises and has become a major contributor to economic activity, particularly the generation of convertible currency.

Key Economic Sectors

Agriculture

In 1997 Cuba had 6,686,700 hectares of agricultural land, of which 3,701,400 hectares were cultivated. However, the cultivated land suffers from various degrees of soil degradation (see Topography and Drainage, ch. 2). In 1997 the state directly controlled 24.4 percent of the agricultural land and the nonstate sector, 75.6 percent. The nonstate sector includes the newly formed UBPCs, the former state farms converted to cooperatives. The UBPCs alone accounted for 47.0 percent of cultivated land. In addition to sugarcane, state enterprises and UBPCs specialize in the production of rice, citrus, coffee, and tobacco, as well as livestock. In addition to UBPCs, nonstate actors include Agricultural-Livestock Cooperatives (Cooperativas de Producción Agropecuaria—CPA), Credit and Services Cooperatives (Cooperativas de Créditos y Servicios—CCS), and individual farmers.

A large portion of the nation's industrial capacity and agricultural lands are devoted to sugar production. During the 1975–87 period, the sugar industry was the largest recipient of investment resources, averaging about 20 percent of manufacturing investment. Similarly, investments in sugar agriculture took about one-third of overall agricultural investment during this same period.

By the mid-1990s, Cuba's sugar industrial complex comprised 156 sugar mills; seventeen refineries; more than fifty plants producing derivatives, such as pulp and paper made

A fertile farming valley near Havana
Courtesy Suzanne Petrie
Sugarcane workers in Camagüey Province
Courtesy Danielle Hayes, United Nations Development Programme

from bagasse (that is, stalks and leaves that remain after sugarcane is ground for sugar production), bagasse boards, ethanol, rum, yeast, and wax; electric-power generation plants; mechanical shops that produce parts for the sugar industrial facilities and manage their maintenance; an extensive internal transportation network; and eight export shipping terminals capable of handling sugar in bulk. Although many of the sugar mills date from the 1920s, most of them have been thoroughly overhauled.

A large sugar industry such as Cuba's requires prodigious volumes of cane as inputs into the industrial process. Assuming an industrial yield of 11 percent—roughly the average yield obtained in Cuba in 1950–80—means that the agricultural sector must deliver 100 tons of sugarcane to mills to produce eleven tons of raw sugar. The timely delivery of such large amounts of sugarcane to mills requires very close coordination between agricultural and industrial sectors: the sugarcane must both be ground at a time when its sucrose content is highest and enter the mills in a steady flow to avoid costly (in terms of energy consumption) shutdowns.

Socialist Cuba has experimented with different forms of organization to manage the sugar process. Three of these organizational methods have included totally separate agricultural and industrial enterprises controlled by different ministries, joint management of agricultural and industrial activities under a single Ministry of the Sugar Industry, and agroindustrial complexes, where both sets of activities are coordinated by one management team. However, these organizational changes have not been able to resolve the agricultural bottlenecks that have plagued the Cuban sugar industry.

In 1989 nearly 2.0 million hectares were devoted to sugarcane cultivation, with the state sector accounting for more than 1.9 million hectares and the nonstate sector for less than 100,000 hectares. That is, 53 percent of cultivated land in that year was devoted to sugarcane production. It is also clear from the above data that sugarcane production was skewed toward the state sector, with the nonstate sector controlling less than 5 percent of sugarcane lands. In 1997, 1.8 million hectares, or 48 percent of cultivated land, was devoted to sugarcane production.

Implementation of the 1959 Agrarian Reform Law and subsequent confiscatory laws with respect to the sugar industry resulted in the expropriation of large amounts of land controlled by sugar mills. These lands were first organized as cooperatives and in 1962 converted into state farms. In state farms, agricultural workers were essentially wage earners, with no involvement in management decisions. Sugarcane state farms were unwieldy and notorious for their low productivity and failure to meet production targets. In part to try to improve their management and performance, state farms were broken up and converted into smaller UBPCs in September 1993.

Cuba has made significant gains in harvesting its sugarcane crop through mechanical means. Cutting and loading sugarcane by hand is exhausting and dangerous work. Cuba's socialist government has made a sustained effort to mechanize these tasks and has been largely successful, thereby freeing a significant number of workers to participate in other economic activities. By the end of the 1980s, about 70 percent of harvested sugarcane was cut by mechanical harvesters, and almost 100 percent was loaded mechanically (generally using front loaders). Although mechanization of the harvest has eliminated the problem of shortages of cane cutters, it has created new problems, such as increased extraneous matter entering sugar mills (which lowers yield and often results in equipment breakdowns) and higher demand for fuel and spare parts for the equipment.

Consistent with its plan to expand sugar production to about 11 million tons per year by 1990 and 13 to 14 million tons per year by 2000, in the 1980s Cuba began to build new sugar-grinding capacity. At least seven new mills (of a planned fifteen) were built, each capable of producing about 100,000 tons of sugar in a 150-day *zafra* (harvest). However, production fell behind schedule during the late 1980s, averaging about 7.5 million tons per annum during 1985–89. Then the crisis of the 1990s took a heavier toll on the industry. At first, production fell gradually, from 8.1 million tons in 1989 to 8.0 in 1990, 7.6 in 1991, and 7.0 in 1992, but then fell precipitously to 4.1 in 1993, 3.9 in 1994, and 3.3 in 1995 (the lowest output in fifty years). Production recovered somewhat in 1996, when 4.4 million tons were produced, but slumped again to 4.2 million tons in 1997 and 3.2 million tons in 1998 (see table 9, Appendix).

In addition to sugarcane, Cuba produces a broad range of other agricultural products, among them roots and tubers, vegetables, grains, beans, citrus, plantain and bananas, tropical fruits, coffee, tobacco, livestock, and forest products. No statistics on the relative importance of each of these products (in terms of value) within the nonsugar agricultural sector are available. Other important segments of the nonsugar agriculture sector in terms of land area devoted to cultivation in 1997 are rice (6.1 percent of total area); pastures (9.9 percent); coffee (3.8 percent); beans, bananas, and plantains (3.3 percent); and citrus (2.5 percent). Most of the output of the nonsugar agricultural sector is consumed domestically, but some products—for example, tobacco and citrus—are significant generators of export revenue.

The cattle-raising industry, seriously affected by the collapse of trade with the former Soviet bloc, has suffered from prolonged neglect. Its problems began after 1959 when government experts, relying on genetics and artificial insemination, introduced a radical change into the composition of the herd, which previously consisted primarily of Cebú and Criollo breeds. The new breeds produce more milk but are less resistant to the tropical climate and require greater attention and expenditures. By the beginning of the 1970s, the national herd declined by one-quarter, and by 1997 there were only 0.42 head of cattle per capita, close to the lowest figure on record in the twentieth century.

Cuba's agriculture relies heavily on the use of imported inputs and of mechanized equipment. Shortages of imported fertilizers, herbicides, pesticides, fuels, and spare parts for equipment have taken a heavy toll on agricultural production. Nonsugar producers have been seriously affected. Output of key agricultural products was lower in 1993 than in 1989: tubers by 17 percent, vegetables by 36 percent, grains by 61 percent, beans by 38 percent, citrus by 22 percent, eggs by 46 percent, and milk by 66 percent. At the same time that production slumped, sharp reductions in food imports gave rise to severe food shortages. The government responded by instituting an ambitious food production program that had as its objective securing increases in the output of staple foods and becoming self-sufficient in food production. Although the food program has failed to achieve most of its objectives, by 1997 food production had improved in nearly all categories over 1993, although production levels of many commodities remained below levels in 1989. To increase the domestic rice yield, the government in 1996, for the first time in decades, began to encourage the planting of small rice pads (known officially as "popular rice") by individual farms. This practice, which was widespread before 1959, was almost eradicated in subsequent years.

In accordance with the national *acopio* procurement system instituted in 1962 and covering all agricultural products, non-state producers are required to sell certain volumes of their output to the state. Statistics on the contribution by nonstate producers to *acopio* in 1980 provide insights into the range of agricultural commodities produced in the nonstate sector. Thus, the latter producers contributed 6.5 percent of the rice, 57.9 percent of the papayas, and 87.7 percent of the green peppers procured by the state, suggesting that the nonstate sector specialized in fruits and vegetables. The breakup of state farms and the creation of the UBPCs in September 1993 have expanded considerably the role of the nonstate agricultural sector. By 1997 the 1,567 UBPCs controlled 3 million hectares of land (37 percent of Cuba's state and private land not dedicated to sugarcane) and employed almost 122,000 workers, 114,000 of whom are members and the rest contracted laborers.

Manufacturing

In 1986, the most recent year for which these data are available, Cuba's manufacturing sector consisted of 827 enterprises, employing 726,000 workers. The size of the enterprises varied significantly, with twenty-six having more than 4,000 workers each, nineteen between 3,001 and 4,000 workers, ninety-three between 2,001 and 3,000 workers, 190 between 1,001 and 2,000 workers, and 499 up to 1,000 workers. Industries with the largest number of enterprises manufactured nonelectrical machinery (150 enterprises), sugar (148 enterprises), and foodstuffs (145 enterprises). The majority (nineteen out of twenty-six) of the largest manufacturing plants, that is, those employing more than 4,000 workers, were part of the sugar industry; other industries having plants with more than 4,000 workers were textiles (three), mining and nonferrous metallurgy (one), apparel (one), fishing (one), and beverages and tobacco (one).

In addition to the sugar and nickel mining industries, the most significant contributors to national product in 1989 within the manufacturing sector were the following industries: beverages and tobacco, foodstuffs, nonelectrical machinery, chemical, electricity generation, and construction materials. Enterprises producing beverages and foodstuffs are under the control of the Ministry of Foodstuffs Industry. Among the most important products of this industry are dairy products, processed meats and fruits, beverages and liquors (including rum and beer), and bakery products. The nonelectrical machinery industry produces a range of outputs, from transportation equipment for the railroads to consumer products such as metal pots and pans; however, it is also heavily geared to supplying and servicing the sugar industry, including producing Soviet-designed KTP mechanical harvesters and equipment for sugar mills. The chemical industry specializes in the production of fertilizers and rubber and plastic products. Cement production dominates the construction materials industry.

During the economic crisis, the manufacturing sector was affected severely. Over the 1989–93 period, production fell as follows: steel, down 69 percent; cotton yarn, 85 percent; textiles, 77 percent; pasta, 75 percent; lard, 99 percent; powdered milk, 75 percent; cement, 74 percent; crushed stone, 85 percent; and cement blocks, 74 percent. Although production of most manufactured products improved in the second half of the 1990s, production levels in 1998 of key manufactured products were below 1989 levels, with the exception of nickel, oxygen gas, canned meats, and soft drinks.

Mining

Metal commodities produced in Cuba include chromite, cobalt, copper, crude steel, and nickel (see fig. 5). Other nonfuel industrial mineral products include cement, gypsum, lime, ammonia, salt, silica sand, and sulfur. Nickel is the most important metal to the Cuban economy and the export sector. In 1998 Cuba was the eighth leading producer of nickel in the world, producing about 4 percent of total primary nickel production. Cuba's nickel reserves, among the largest in the world, are concentrated in the northeastern region of the country, around the town of Moa in Holguín Province, and consist primarily of laterites in which nickel is mixed with other metals such as iron, chrome, and cobalt. The Moa-Baracoa massif is not only the site of the country's largest reserves of nickel and cobalt, but also of considerable deposits of chromite.

In the 1990s, Cuba's nickel-processing industry consisted of three plants: the Comandante René Ramos Latour plant, located in Nicaro, which began operations in 1943 and produces nickel oxide; the Comandante Pedro Soto Alba plant, located in Moa Bay, which began operations in 1959 and pro-

duces nickel and cobalt sulfides; and the Comandante Ernesto "Che" Guevara plant, located in Punta Gorda, which began operations in 1988 and produces nickel oxide. Construction of a fourth plant at Las Camariocas, which was being carried out with financial assistance from the CMEA countries, has been suspended until new forms of foreign financing are found.

As a result of the economic crisis of the 1990s, nickel production fell steadily from approximately 47,000 tons (mineral content) in 1989 to approximately 27,000 tons (mineral content) in 1994, or by 43 percent, mainly because of maintenance problems and energy shortages. Production bounced back in 1995, when nearly 43,000 tons (mineral content) were produced. A significant factor in the recovery of the nickel industry has been influxes of capital and technology and export markets provided by foreign investors. In 1994 Sherritt International, a Canadian company, entered into a fifty-fifty joint venture arrangement with Cuba's General Nickel Company (Compañía General del Níquel). The joint venture agreement included mineral concessions; the operation of the nickel-production facility Comandante Pedro Soto Alba at Moa Bay and a nickel refinery in Fort Saskatchewan, Alberta, Canada, owned by Sherritt; and a joint enterprise to market the products produced by the joint venture. Other reported foreign investments in the nickel industry include a credit from a Dutch bank to modernize facilities and an agreement between the Western Mining Company of Australia and the Cuban Commercial Caribbean Nickel Company to assess and develop mineral deposits in the Pinares de Mayarí area.

Joint ventures with foreign investors have also been active in exploration and production of copper, silver, gold, and other minerals. Cuba's state mining agency, Geominera, has entered into joint venture agreements with a number of Canadian companies: Joutel Resources Limited, Republic Goldfields, Miramar Mining Corporation, Caribgold Resources, Homer Goldmines, and Macdonald Mines Exploration. Cuba has granted concessions to the foreign companies to explore for silver, gold, and copper in specific areas of the country. The joint ventures have also taken over the exploitation of existing mining operations, injecting capital to purchase equipment and fund operating expenses.

Energy

Cuba has traditionally relied on imports to meet its energy requirements. The island is not well endowed with energy resources: coal is not found in commercial quantities; hydro-electric resources are limited by rivers that have low heads, carry relatively small quantities of water, and are subject to uneven flow during the year; and oil and natural gas deposits discovered to date are woefully inadequate to meet demand. Biomass (in the form of bagasse) is an important energy source for the sugar industry. However, the use of bagasse by the economy at large is constrained by its bulkiness, its low caloric value, and its demand by the sugar industry and several factories, which use bagasse as a raw material for producing building and consumer products. In 1988 Cuba met 70 percent of its energy requirements with liquid fuels (crude oil, light oil products, and heavy oil products), about 29 percent with biomass, and the remaining 1 percent with other energy sources such as coal, coke, and hydroelectricity.

In the 1990s, Cuba relied on oil to generate more than 80 percent of its electricity. Cuba's electricity generation industry had a combined generation capacity of 4.33 gigawatt hours in 1997 and 15.274 billion kilowatt hours in 1998. With the exception of several small hydroelectric plants with a combined capacity of 55.4 megawatt hours, the remaining power plants were fueled with oil, oil products, and natural gas. Cuba's electricity consumption in 1998 totaled 14.205 billion kilowatt hours.

Cuba began an ambitious nuclear power program in the early 1980s, with the objective of meeting up to one-fifth of electricity demand through nuclear power. The first nuclear reactor, being built with technology and financial assistance from the Soviet Union at Juraguá, on Cuba's southern coast, has been delayed because of lack of financial resources, and it is now questionable whether the project will ever be completed.

Oil has been produced in Cuba commercially since 1915, but domestic production has traditionally provided only a small fraction of consumption. Domestic oil production's share of apparent consumption (domestic production plus imports minus exports) has been estimated at about 1 to 3 percent in the 1960s and 1970s and 6 to 9 percent in the 1980s. Despite this increase, domestically produced oil still accounted for less than one-fifth of the depressed oil consumption level of about

5 million tons in the first half of the 1990s. Apparent consumption of oil and oil products was in the range of 10 to 12 million tons per annum in the late 1980s. Domestically produced oil (mostly heavy crude) rose from 0.67 million tons in 1990 to nearly 1.7 million tons by 1998.

Oil exploration (onshore and offshore) and production have been a priority in the 1990s, mainly through partnerships with foreign companies. In 1994 at least eleven foreign companies were involved in oil exploration and production in Cuban territory, both on land and offshore; eleven others were working in oil production services. Firms from Britain, France, Canada, Germany, and Sweden were operating eighteen of thirty-three oil fields in the nation. Almost 90 percent of Cuba's still limited oil production is concentrated in an extensive line of coastal territory running north of Havana and Matanzas provinces, and in the area between Sancti Spíritus and Ciego de Ávila provinces.

As a result of the 1992 reorganization of Cuba's petroleum industry, a new state enterprise, Cubapetroleum (Cubapetróleo—Cupet), was established, under the Ministry of Basic Industries, with responsibility for the entire petroleum sector: exploration, drilling, and refining and distribution. Another entity, Commercial Cupet (Comercial Cupet), is in charge of negotiating with foreign companies.

Production partnership agreements appear to be risk contracts, where the foreign entity typically undertakes the investment risk and shares the oil that may be produced with the domestic partner. As a result of foreign participation, oil production has been one of the few economic activities not severely affected by the economic crisis. Crude oil production dipped from around 700,000 tons in 1989–90 to 527,000 tons in 1991, but recovered to 882,000 tons in 1992 and for the first time exceeded 1 million tons in 1994, when 1,107,600 tons were produced. Oil production was roughly 1.5 million tons in 1995–97 and 1.7 million tons in 1998.

The Soviet Union was Cuba's primary source of energy (primarily oil and oil products) imports from 1960 to 1990. Domestic energy demand rose rapidly through the end of the 1980s, with imports from the Soviet Union increasing as well. In the 1960s, Cuba imported 4 to 6 million tons of Soviet oil and oil products per annum; in 1985–88 Cuban oil imports exceeded 13 million tons per annum. Not all of the imported Soviet oil was consumed domestically. During the 1980s, Cuba reexported significant quantities of Soviet oil to the world market to generate convertible currencies; as many as 3.6 to 3.7 million tons of Soviet oil were reexported in 1985–86.

Oil imports from the Soviet Union were disrupted beginning in 1990. In August 1990, the Cuban government announced the imposition of mandatory energy conservation measures to address a 2-million-ton shortfall in Soviet deliveries of oil and oil products. The shift in pricing of Soviet (and subsequently Russian) oil exports to convertible currency forced Cuba to cut imports drastically. It is estimated that Cuba's oil and oil products imports in the second half of the 1990s are in the range of 5 to 7 million tons per annum; even with higher domestic oil output, domestic production was about 20 percent of apparent consumption.

Cuba relies on three refineries—located in Cabaiguán, Havana, and Santiago de Cuba—to process domestic and imported crude oil into a range of derivatives demanded by Cuban industries, agriculture, the transportation sector, and consumers. A fourth refinery, at Cienfuegos, with a capacity of 3 million tons of crude per year, is still only partially completed. The others date from the 1950s and were expropriated in 1960 from the international oil companies (Esso, Texaco, and Royal-Dutch Shell) that operated on the island prior to the revolutionary takeover of 1959. In the late 1980s, Cuba completed an oil import facility at the port of Matanzas and a pipeline linking it with the new Cienfuegos refinery.

Transportation

A relatively small and densely populated country that relies heavily on foreign trade, Cuba has a well-developed transportation infrastructure. By 1997 Cuba had an estimated 60,858 kilometers of highways, including 29,820 kilometers of paved roads and 31,038 kilometers of unpaved roads. The country's railroads total 4,807 kilometers of standard gauge. The highways, railroads, and air and maritime transportation services provide access to almost every location on the island (see fig. 6). Cuba also has an infrastructure of ports, airports, and warehouses to support extensive foreign trade.

For many years, the main highway was the Central Highway, mostly a two-lane highway running for 1,200 kilometers from Pinar del Río in the west to Santiago de Cuba in the east. In the late 1970s, construction began on a new eight-lane National Expressway (commonly known as "Ocho Vías," or Eight

Lanes), which now reportedly runs the length of Cuba, from Pinar del Río in the west to Santiago de Cuba in the east. Private ownership of vehicles is very low. Passenger transportation within the island depends heavily on public buses and trucks. Cuba's stock of passenger cars and commercial vehicles in 1988 was 241,300 units, of which 208,400 (86.4 percent) were commercial vehicles. In 1985 Cuba had thirty-eight motor vehicles per 1,000 population, a rate much lower than for developed countries (United States, 717; Canada, 567; Australia, 532; Germany, 451) and also for the more highly developed Latin American countries (Argentina, 175; Brazil, 88; Chile, 73; Mexico, 94; Uruguay, 117; Venezuela, 117).

Land transportation has been severely affected by the economic crisis. Lack of spare parts for the bus and truck fleet has reduced significantly the number of vehicles in operation. (Hungary and the former Soviet Union scrapped production of some of these vehicles and spare parts.) Moreover, fuel shortages have forced cutbacks in the number of routes and their frequency. Transportation bottlenecks have affected labor productivity because workers are unable to get to their jobs on time or have to spend an inordinately long period of time in reporting to their jobs.

Railroad transportation has been neglected since 1959 in favor of truck transport, despite being much more energy efficient than truck transport, particularly in transporting sugarcane. Cuba's poorly maintained railroad system consists of one main axis running the length of the island, connecting all of the major urban centers, economic zones, and ports, either directly or through branches. A bit more than one-third of the railroads carry both passengers and freight, with the rest dedicated to the transport of sugarcane. A major reconstruction of the central railroad line began in the late 1970s; equipment was updated with diesel locomotives manufactured in the Soviet Union and Czechoslovakia. Railroad transportation has also been affected by shortages of fuel and spare parts during the Special Period; the four daily trips from Havana to Santiago de Cuba have been reduced to one a day, and frequent equipment breakdowns have made the system largely unreliable.

Cuba has eleven main ports capable of handling general export and import cargoes. The most important of these are Antilla, Cienfuegos, Havana, Mariel, Matanzas, Nuevitas, and Santiago de Cuba (see Principal Geographic Features, ch. 2). The major deep-water ports are the bays of Cienfuegos,

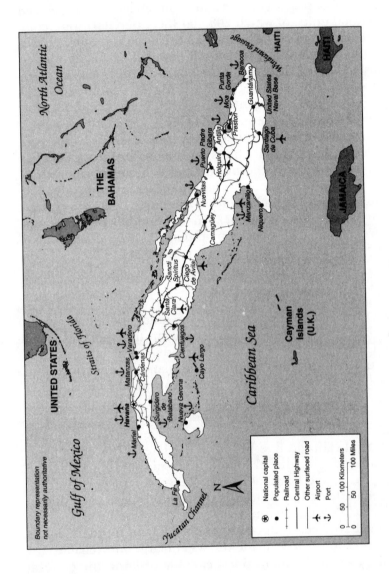

Figure 6. Transportation System, 1999

Havana, Mariel, Matanzas, Nipe, Nuevitas, and Santiago de Cuba.

Havana is by far the most important port. In addition, Cuba has eight bulk sugar loading terminals, one supertanker terminal at Matanzas, and several other smaller import facilities, as well as specialized port facilities for the fishing fleet. Number one in sugar export, the port of Cienfuegos is capable of handling one-third of Cuba's sugar production through its bulk sugar terminal. Its pier for handling oil and oil byproducts allows the berthing of ships up to 50,000 tons.

In part because of the fast-growing tourism industry, Cuba has made considerable investments in upgrading and expanding its airport infrastructure. Ten of the seventeen civilian airports can now handle international flights, and nine of them are linked to the nine largest tourist resorts. Of Cuba's 170 airports in 1999, seventy-seven were paved and ninety-three unpaved. Cuba's main international airports include Camagüey, Ciego de Ávila, Cienfuegos, Havana, Matanzas, Santiago de Cuba, and Varadero. In May 1997, Cuba began a US$70 million, seven-month modernization project at its two most important airports, those in Havana and Varadero, as a result of an agreement between the Cuban Airport Services Enterprise (Empresa Cubana de Aeropuertos S.A.—ECASA) and the British company, Airport Planning Development (APD). Inaugurated in mid-1998, the José Martí International Airport's new terminal expands the Havana airport's capacity to 3 million people per year. The main national airports that handle primarily domestic flights include Baracoa, Bayamo, Cayo Largo, Guantánamo, Holguín, Manzanillo, Moa, Nicaro, Nueva Gerona, and Santa Clara. The Consolidated Cuban Aviation Company (Empresa Consolidada Cubana de Aviación—Cubana), Cuba's flag carrier, moves 45 percent of international tourism into Cuba and manages all seventeen civilian airports.

Telecommunications

Cuba's telecommunications infrastructure improved in the late 1990s as a result of government efforts to increase the availability of telephones throughout the island and the participation of foreign investors. Telephone density remains low by global standards, approximately between 4.5 and 5.5 telephones per 100 inhabitants, and is below the telephone density of neighboring Caribbean countries. Approximately 45 percent of Cuba's telephone lines serve residents within Havana's metropolitan area.

The island's national infrastructure supports national and international telecommunications services utilizing wired and wireless facilities. The majority of the infrastructure dates to the period before the 1959 revolution and uses technology that has surpassed its life cycle multiple times. Newer facilities were installed during the 1990s with the assistance of foreign telecommunications services partners.

Cuba's first private investment participation in the telecommunications industry began in 1991, when a joint venture was formed between Empresa de Telecomunicaciones de Cuba, S.A. (ETECSA), the state-owned telecommunications company, and Teléfonos Internacionales de México, S.A. (TIMSA), creating Teléfonos Celulares de Cuba, S.A, (Cubacel). Cubacel became a provider of cellular telephone service within the city of Havana and the tourist corridor connecting Havana and Varadero. In 1998 a Canadian company, Sherritt International Corporation, acquired 37 percent of Cubacel for US$38.2 million. This acquisition gave Sherritt twenty-year rights for the 800 Megahertz (MHz) bands for provisioning of analog and digital telecommunications services. The target industry sectors are tourism, diplomatic corps, joint ventures, and government; most of the current 5,500 to 7,000 subscribers come from these sectors. A second wireless cellular system is planned.

In June 1994, Cuba announced a joint venture between ETECSA and Grupo Domos Internacional, a holding group based in Monterey, Mexico, wherein Grupo Domos would own 49 percent of the island's telephone infrastructure. Planned investments of approximately US$700 million by Grupo Domos in the development and upgrade of the telephone infrastructure ran aground because of the group's financial difficulties associated with Mexico's economic recession of 1995. Domos subsequently sold its participation in the joint venture to Italy's largest telecommunications concern, STET International Netherlands N.V. In 1997 the United States approved a private agreement between STET and the International Telephone and Telegraph (ITT) company, the owner of Cuba's telephone system prior to the revolution, wherein STET agreed to pay approximately US$25 million to ITT for the right to use its telephone system and avoid sanctions under the Helms-Burton Act.

Estimates of required investment for upgrading Cuba's national infrastructure range from US$900 million for the national telephone infrastructure to approximately US$2.5 billion for upgrading the full complement of voice, data, and video communications infrastructure. These estimates support a plan to increase the national telephone density from its present levels to approximately eleven per 100 inhabitants, while increasing the density to fifteen per 100 inhabitants in the city of Havana. To attain a density of nine per 100 by the year 2004 would require the installation of approximately 100,000 telephones per year. New telephone line installation has been programmed at approximately 70,000 per year, with an increased emphasis on the installation of public telephones throughout the island. An additional 8,000 coin- and card-operated public telephones (CCOPT) were planned for installation during 2000, with a planned deployment of an additional 52,000 public telephones by the year 2004.

The bulk of the conversion to digital facilities by 2000 occurred within the city of Havana consistent with the plan to increase telephone density in areas that promise a higher return on investment. As part of the infrastructure improvement effort, approximately 11,200 lines were assigned for award by municipal governments to residential users.

Future development and deployment of Cuba's telecommunications infrastructure will be limited by per capita disposable income. The latter is a primary factor that has slowed the deployment of telephone service into the population mainstream. CCOPTs have served to fill this economic void. United States foreign policy is having and will have an impact on the development and growth rate of Cuba's telecommunications infrastructure because foreign investors have been careful not to violate United States law.

Cuba receives hard-currency revenue from its international long-distance services. Approximately 70 percent of Cuba's international calls are made to or from the United States, connecting the island to the large Cuban-American community living in the United States. Annual revenue from United States-Cuba long-distance services ranges from US$50 million to US$70 million for Cuba and approximately US$60 million to US$80 million for United States-based carriers that provide such service.

Cuba's government has realized the importance of the development of a telecommunications infrastructure in support of its economic development efforts and has prioritized the development of limited high bandwidth facilities, including Internet access for the diplomatic corps, joint ventures, and the government, education, tourism and financial sectors. Although limited, this development has allowed sectors such as banking to provide and support basic services such as automatic teller machines (ATMs). Chinese interests have created an additional force within the telecommunications industry, including the manufacture of telecommunications hardware for internal use and export. Cuba's telecommunications system naturally also includes television and radio. In 1997 Cuba had fifty-eight television broadcast stations and 2.64 million televisions. Cuban radio became a more dynamic mass medium in the late 1990s. The number of radio broadcast stations in 1998 totaled 169 AM, fifty-five FM, and one shortwave. The country had 3.9 million radios in 1997.

Tourism

After shunning international tourism in the 1960s on the grounds that it represented foreign exploitation and behavior that was inconsistent with a socialist society, Cuba created the National Institute of Tourism (Instituto Nacional de Turismo—Intur) in the mid-1970s and began to encourage international tourism. In the 1980s, international tourism was recognized as a potentially important source of revenue for the island, but it became apparent that after more than two decades of neglect, the tourism infrastructure had deteriorated to the point that Cuba was incapable of competing with other tourist destinations. Cuba created two semiautonomous corporations—Cubanacán in 1987 and Grupo Gaviota in 1989—to enlist foreign participation in the international tourism industry. The emphasis has been on building a physical infrastructure for the industry and improving the quality of services so as to be able to compete in the international tourism market.

Tourism is the sector of the economy that first began to attract foreign investment, with the first joint venture established in 1988. Particularly active in joint venturing in the tourism industry have been investors from Canada, Germany, Mexico, the Netherlands, and Spain. In many instances, the joint ventures are actually closer to management contracts: the foreign partner assumes management of a tourism facility, obtaining a flow of tourists from its home market, and ensuring

A performer at the Tropicana nightclub in Havana, 1999 Courtesy Maria M. Alonso

The neocolonial Hotel Nacional, Havana's most opulent hotel, overlooks the Port of Havana. Courtesy Phillips Bourns

that the quality of the tourism services meets international standards.

The Cuban tourism industry has thrived in the 1990s. This growth is reflected in the increasing capacity to accommodate tourists; the stock of hotel rooms increased from about 32,000 in 1991 to about 41,000 in 1997 (see table 10, Appendix). Meanwhile, the stock of hotel rooms suitable for international tourism more than doubled between 1990 and 1996, from 12,900 to 26,900 rooms, evidence that new construction is aimed at the international tourism market and that some of the stock of hotel rooms have been upgraded to meet higher international standards.

The number of foreign visitors nearly tripled, going from 340,000 in 1990 to nearly 1.2 million in 1997. Gross revenue from international tourism in 1997 has been estimated at 1,543 million pesos. About a third is estimated to be net revenue.

With regard to efficiency indicators, the occupancy rate of hotel rooms overall was nearly 70 percent in 1991; it fell to about 60 percent in subsequent years. For hotel rooms suitable for international tourism, the occupancy rate increased from about 40 percent in the early 1990s to more than 50 percent in 1995–96. However, the average length of stay of foreign visitors declined from 8.7 days in 1990–91 to 7.3 days in 1996.

Income per visitor per day increased steadily over the 1990–96 period, from US$82.50 in 1990 to US$187.80 in 1996. According to an industry expert, Cuba continues to be regarded as an inexpensive "package" destination, reflecting the initial tourism strategy of quickly penetrating source markets by offering low, all-inclusive packages. Moreover, the ability to increase prices is hindered by the lack of quality of products and services in other associated industries: food and beverage operations, retail facilities, recreation and entertainment activities, and other tourism infrastructure.

Labor

The 1981 population census, the last such census conducted on the island, revealed that 52.3 percent of the population fifteen years of age and over was economically active (that is, employed or looking for work, excluding retirees, students, those unable to work, and persons who were primarily homemakers). With respect to gender, 71.5 percent of males and 32.8 percent of females fifteen years of age and over were economically active.

Labor statistics published by the Cuban government through the 1980s were scanty and tended to focus on employment in the state sector. This emphasis on state-sector employment reflected both the very small role of the nonstate sector in the economy and the full employment policy of the government. Cuban economist José Luis Rodríguez has estimated that in 1988 the Cuban state controlled all of the industrial, construction, retail trade, wholesale and foreign trade, banking, and education sectors, almost all of the transportation sector, and 92 percent of the agricultural sector. The full employment policy pursued by the government resulted in bloated payrolls of state enterprises, very low open unemployment rates—for example, a reported 1.3 percent in the 1970 census of population and 3.4 percent in the 1981 census—but very high rates of underemployment (see Glossary).

Since 1962, wages of Cuban workers have been set on the basis of a uniform, nationwide wage scale for various categories of jobs. Prior to a wage reform carried out in 1981 to stem the flight of workers from the agricultural sector, average earnings of agricultural workers were substantially below those of other sectors of the economy. They were, for example, about 20 percent below the overall average for all workers in 1975 and 14 percent in 1980. After 1981 the gap between wages of agricultural and nonagricultural workers was closed. By 1988–89, average monthly earnings of agricultural workers were at, or near, the average for workers in the productive sphere and higher than the average earnings of workers in certain sectors within the productive sphere, such as commerce and communications.

In 1989 average monthly earnings of Cuban workers in each of the main economic sectors, in pesos per month, were culture and arts, 223; science and technology, 217; transportation, 211; administration, 201; construction, 201; public health, social security and tourism, 195; education, 191; finance and insurance, 190; agriculture, 186; industry, 186; forestry, 184; communications, 176; community and personal services, 164; and commerce, 163. Within the industrial sector, average monthly earnings ranged from 237 pesos per month for workers in electricity production and distribution to 141 pesos per month for workers in the apparel industry.

Statistics released by Cuba to ECLAC (Economic Commission for Latin America and the Caribbean) permit an examination of the labor market in the 1990s. In 1989, the year just prior to the beginning of the economic crisis, 92.1 percent of the economically active population was reported as being employed and 7.9 percent as unemployed. Of those employed, 80.1 percent held jobs as state civilian employees, 13.8 percent held other state jobs, and 5.3 percent held nonstate jobs, such as cooperative members, private farmers, and self-employed or salaried workers. With regard to the unemployed, four-fifths had lost their jobs and were seeking a new one, while one-fifth were new entrants into the labor force seeking a first job.

During the 1990s, the economically active population actually declined, from 4.7 million persons in 1989 to 4.5 million persons in 1995, recovering to 4.6 million in 1996 (see table 11, Appendix). The decline in the economically active population is attributable to several factors, among them declining fertility, the shift of some persons from the formal to the informal economy, early retirement, and emigration. Employment also fell during the 1990s; in 1996 total employment was nearly 3 percent below the corresponding level in 1989.

State-sector employment in 1989 was roughly 4.1 million workers, of whom 3.5 million were civilian employees and 600,000 were classified as other state employees. During the 1990s, state-sector employment fell sharply, reflecting the severe dislocations suffered by state enterprises and sharp reductions in the size of the armed forces. By 1996 overall state employment was roughly 3.2 million workers, 22 percent lower than in 1989. State civilian employment was 24 percent lower in 1997 than in 1990; particularly significant were reductions in state employment in agriculture and related activities (77 percent) because of the creation of UBPCs and in manufacturing (18 percent) (see table 12, Appendix).

The sharp reductions in economic activity of the 1990s are not reflected in the open unemployment statistics because of explicit government policies to shield workers from the impact of the economic crisis and the rapid growth of employment in the nonstate sector. However, severe reductions in imports of fuels, raw materials, and spare parts have significantly reduced economic activity and labor demand. In September 1990, for example, President Castro announced that several recently completed investments would remain idle, among them a nickel production plant and an oil refinery, and that an existing nickel-producing plant would cease to operate because of lack of fuel. In mid-October 1990, the Ministry of Light Industry reported that 321 factories under its control were operating at the rate of twenty-four hours per week and that twenty-six others had been shut down altogether. In 1992 the State Committee on Labor and Social Security (Comité Estatal de Trabajo y Seguridad Social—CETSS) reported that 155,000 workers had lost their jobs as a result of the lack of imported inputs. Finally, in May 1993 about 60 percent of Cuba's factories were reportedly idle because of shortages of fuels, raw materials, and spare parts. Yet the number of workers who had lost their jobs and were seeking new employment peaked at nearly 300,000 workers in 1989 and fell to fewer than 215,000 workers in 1992–93.

The Fourth Congress of the PCC, held in October 1991, addressed the problem of worker dislocations and adopted new rules as part of its resolution on economic development. The document assures a basic income for every family or worker and maintains the right of each citizen to work. In those cases where it is not possible to keep someone working, the worker will retain the right to the post and will receive a percentage of his or her salary, according to current legislation."

In July 1990, in anticipation of the worst in economic dislocations, the CETSS adopted rules to facilitate the transfer of dislocated workers (*trabajadores disponibles*) from one workplace to another. The rules identified agriculture as the employer of last resort, that is, a sector of the economy that could absorb additional workers from other sectors. The rules also retained the existing system of payments to dislocated workers, which ranged from one month to a maximum of one year depending on the length of service in the job (payments for a full year were available only to workers with job tenure of more than ten years) and calculated on the basis of a declining wage replacement formula of 100 percent for the first month, 70 percent for the second month, and 50 percent for subsequent months.

In November 1990, as the economic situation deteriorated and it became increasingly clear that the nature and depth of the dislocations could not be addressed by shifting workers from one workplace to another, the CETSS issued new rules to deal with the problem of redundant or surplus workers (*trabajadores sobrantes*). The new rules made it easier to reassign workers to other workplaces or occupations and modified the compensation system to recognize the long-term duration of the dislocations. Thus, time limits on payment of compensation were removed, and the wage replacement percentages were readjusted to 100 percent for the first month and 60 percent for each subsequent month. While receiving these benefits, workers maintained an association with their workplaces—even if their workplaces were shut down—and therefore were not considered unemployed.

At the same time that state-sector employment was shrinking, employment in the nonstate sector was growing at a very fast pace: nonstate-sector employment increased more than four-fold, from about 230,000 in 1989 to more than 1 million in 1996, absorbing a large portion of workers shed by the state sector. It should be noted, however, that the growth of employment in the nonstate sector does not uniformly represent net job creation because structural shifts have occurred that affect the distribution of employment between the state and nonstate sectors. The most significant shift is with regard to the agricultural sector, where the creation of the UBPCs added approximately 240,000 workers to the nonstate sector in 1994; these workers were formerly employees of state farms and were counted as employees of the state sector. Similarly, it is not clear that increases in the category of "salaried workers" actually represent new job creation because they may reflect the shift of some state enterprises to joint ventures with foreign investors or to *sociedades anónimas* (stock companies) operating outside of the state sector.

The only available statistics regarding the distribution of employment by economic activity are for employees of the state civilian sector. Although these statistics were a good proxy for overall employment during the time period when the state controlled the bulk of economic activities, they are less so now because of structural changes that have occurred, and therefore must be examined with much caution.

In 1990 the manufacturing sector accounted for about 19 percent of state civilian employment, while the percentage for the agriculture, hunting, forestry, and fishing sectors totaled 22 percent. Other significant economic activities in terms of employment were commerce, restaurants, and hotels (12 percent); and construction (nearly 9 percent). Employment in manufacturing, construction, commerce, restaurants, and hotels declined during the 1990s, consistent with reports that these areas of economic activity were particularly hard hit by shortages of imports.

Employment in agriculture, hunting, forestry, and fishing rose in the early 1990s, consistent with information suggesting

A 1950s-era North American automobile (una máquina)
still in use in Havana, 1997
Courtesy Mark P. Sullivan

that workers dislocated from manufacturing, construction, and other activities were being reassigned to agricultural activities. The sharp drop in agricultural employment in 1994 did not necessarily reflect a reversal of this trend but rather the shift of a large number of state workers to the nonstate sector upon the creation of the UBPCs.

The Second Economy

The term *second economy* originates from the literature on centrally planned economies. It has been used by scholars to comprise economic activities outside the first, official, or planned economy. Certain characteristics of centrally planned economies—overwhelming government ownership of the means of production, tautness or rigidity of central plans, and suppressed inflation—account for both the quantitative importance of the first economy and the pervasiveness of activities outside of it.

Cuba's first economy consists of economic activities under the control of the socialist state and subject to the central plan. Through the late 1980s, although the Cuban state controlled nearly all economic activities on the island, some economic activities for private gain were permitted to exist alongside the planned state economy. These second economy activities included agriculture, where private farmers controlled a portion of the land; the sale of certain personal services; and, for a period during the early 1980s, farmers' markets and artisan markets. Other economic activities outside of state control were those conducted illegally, such as black-market operations and unauthorized use of government resources.

There are no readily available measures or estimates of the magnitude of Cuba's second economy. However, an examination of official statistics on overall agricultural output, civilian employment, and the structure of the population's income suggests that private, legal economic activity in the 1980s probably accounted for about 6 percent of GSP (global social product), employed about 230,000 workers, or about 5 percent of civilian employment, and accounted for 5 to 6 percent of the population's income. It is even more difficult to estimate the value of illegal economic activities because participants in illegal economic activities place a high premium on the anonymity of their actions and deal almost exclusively with cash transactions in order to avoid audit trails that could reveal their activities.

As the bottom fell out of the first economy during the early 1990s, the second economy expanded to fill the gap. According to the Domestic Consumer Demand Institute (Instituto de la Demanda Interna—IDI), the value of black-market transactions rose from 17 percent of retail sales in 1990 to more than 60 percent in 1992 as money supply expanded and the availability of goods and services through the state distribution system contracted. Illegal forms of self-employment reportedly also increased during the early 1990s.

Several of the policy initiatives pursued in the 1990s have stimulated the second economy. These initiatives include the creation of the UBPCs, authorization of self-employment, stimulation of joint ventures with foreign investors, creation of agricultural and artisan markets, decriminalization of the use of convertible currencies, establishment of government-operated foreign currency Exchange Houses, decentralization of foreign trade activities, and formation of semiautonomous corporations. That the economic policies to overcome the economic crisis are centered on second-economy activities is a tacit admission that the first economy is no longer viable in an economic environment in which there are no trade subsidies or economic assistance from the former Soviet Union and Eastern Europe.

Foreign Economic Relations

Background, 1960–90

Beginning in the early 1960s, and through around 1990, Cuba's external sector was segmented into two parts: economic relations with the socialist world, conducted within the framework of the CMEA (Council for Mutual Economic Assistance), and economic relations with market economies, mainly West European nations, Canada, Japan, and some key developing countries. Economic relations with the socialist countries were by far the more significant quantitatively; relations with market economies, although quantitatively small, were strategically significant, however, because they afforded Cuba the possibility to import goods and services and obtain technology not available from the socialist nations.

Relations with Socialist Countries

Cuba's economic relations with the Soviet Union and socialist countries were based on a web of bilateral agreements covering merchandise trade, payments, credits, and technical assistance. During the 1961–69 period alone, Cuba concluded more than 400 bilateral agreements with socialist countries. To coordinate the burgeoning economic and scientific-technical assistance relationship, several government-to-government commissions were established in the 1960s and 1970s with the German Democratic Republic (East Germany) (in 1964), Bulgaria and Czechoslovakia (1965), Hungary (1966), Romania (1967), the Democratic People's Republic of Korea (North Korea) (1968), Poland (1969), and the Soviet Union (1970). Economic relations with socialist countries deepened after 1972, when Cuba became a member of the CMEA.

The bulk of Cuba's trade with socialist countries was conducted through bilateral balancing agreements—tantamount to barter arrangements—in which individual transactions were made and accounts settled, using either the currency of one of the partner countries or "transferable rubles." The latter was an artificial currency whose sole role was to serve as the unit of account in transactions among socialist countries. Because neither the currencies of socialist countries nor the "transferable ruble" could be freely converted or exchanged into "hard" currencies—for example, the United States dollar, Deutsche mark, and Japanese yen—to purchase goods and services in international markets, socialist nations made efforts to balance trade bilaterally each year. To the extent that trade was not balanced annually, the gap was covered by "soft" (transferable ruble) credits.

In the 1960s, the Soviet Union began to purchase Cuban sugar at prices that were fixed for several years (typically, five years). Because world market prices for sugar fluctuated—sometimes exceeding, but more often falling below the contracted price—the arrangement tended to favor Cuba. In December 1972, Cuba and the Soviet Union signed two agreements that formalized a system of preferential, that is, higher than world market, prices for Cuban nickel and sugar exports. The price of nickel was set for five-year intervals, but it was raised whenever the world market price exceeded this threshold by a substantial margin. In 1981–84, for example, Cuba greatly benefitted from Soviet concessionary prices for nickel imports, which were more than twice the world market price.

In the aftermath of very high world market prices for sugar in 1974 and 1975, the contract price for Cuban sugar exports to the Soviet Union and other CMEA nations was renegotiated and adjusted upward. In 1975 Cuba and the Soviet Union agreed to a mechanism whereby sugar export prices were adjusted annually, above a very high base price, in proportion to changes in the prices of a basket of commodities Cuba imported from the Soviet Union. As a result of this indexing arrangement, henceforth the price of Cuban sugar exports to the Soviet Union consistently exceeded the world market price by a considerable margin. Cuba also negotiated agreements with Bulgaria, Czechoslovakia, East Germany, Hungary, Poland, and Romania, all of which granted preferential prices to Cuban sugar exports. In addition, Cuba benefitted in the 1960s, 1970s, and the first half of the 1980s from pricing arrangements in intra-CMEA trade that held the price of oil below the world market price.

The Soviet Union became revolutionary Cuba's almost sole supplier of oil and oil products in 1960, on the heels of the Cuban government's takeover of the refineries operated by Western multinational oil companies. The price of Soviet oil exports, like the prices of other basic commodities traded by socialist countries among themselves, was fixed for a five-year period, purportedly to avoid fluctuations in capitalist world markets. Because of this arrangement, Cuba was spared the shock associated with the quadrupling of world oil market prices that occurred in 1973 and additional price increases in 1974. In 1975, however, the Soviet Union began to adjust prices of oil exports to its CMEA allies annually, based on a moving average of world market prices in the previous five years. Throughout the 1970s and early 1980s, as world oil market prices rose, Cuba benefitted from this arrangement. But as world oil market prices fell in the mid-1980s, the arrangement worked to Cuba's disadvantage, with the island paying prices in the late 1980s for Soviet oil that were above the world market price. Over the entire 1960–90 period, however, the oil price supply arrangements with the Soviet Union resulted in net gains for Cuba.

From 1962 to 1974, Cuba's merchandise trade turnover—the sum of merchandise exports and imports—averaged 24 percent of GSP; in 1985–89 it averaged 50 percent, evidencing greater openness of the economy and the greater influence of trade. Since the early 1960s, the Soviet Union and the other socialist countries had accounted for the bulk of Cuba's trade, far outstripping trade with capitalist countries and with developing countries. Over the 1983–89 period, the socialist country members of the CMEA (Bulgaria, Czechoslovakia, East Germany, Hungary, Poland, Romania, and the Soviet Union) absorbed 82.9 percent of Cuba's exports and accounted for 82.7 percent of Cuba's imports; other socialist countries (Albania, China, Mongolia, North Korea, Vietnam, and Yugoslavia) accounted for 3.9 percent of exports and 3.1 percent of imports; capitalist countries were responsible for 9.3 percent of exports and 9.9 percent of imports; and developing countries accounted for 6.8 percent of exports and 6.5 percent of imports.

Merchandise trade deficits set records in the 1980s, as Cuba's imports rose at a much faster rate than exports. The deficit rose from 660 million pesos in 1980 to 2.0 billion in 1985; in 1989 the deficit recorded an all-time record high when it reached more than 2.7 billion pesos. The percentage of the overall trade deficit incurred with the Soviet Union rose steadily in the second half of the 1980s, from about 50 percent in 1984–85 to more than 80 percent in 1988–89. These huge deficits in bilateral trade were routinely financed through transferable ruble credits underwritten by the Soviet Union.

The large trade deficits with the Soviet Union are the more remarkable given the very favorable terms of trade (see Glossary) for Cuba's main exports (sugar and nickel) and imports (oil). The socialist practice of fixing commodity prices for multiyear periods (typically the five-year period covered by a plan) eliminated the world market commodity price fluctuations. They also resulted in transfers from one country to the other (nonrepayable subsidies) whenever intra-CMEA prices diverged from world market prices.

Another oil trade arrangement between Cuba and the Soviet Union that benefitted Cuba was the latter country's ability to reexport Soviet oil to buyers willing to pay with convertible currency. In 1977 Cuba reexported more than 900,000 tons of oil obtained from the Soviet Union; the volume of reexported oil rose to 2 million tons in 1982 and peaked at 3.7 million tons in 1986. The significance of these exports for the Cuban economy should not be underestimated. In 1986 and 1987, oil reexports overtook sugar as Cuba's most significant convertible currency export earner, contributing 30 and 27 percent, respectively, of convertible currency earnings in those two years.

Economist Carmelo Mesa-Lago has estimated the magnitude of Soviet nonrepayable price subsidies to Cuba related to sugar, nickel, and oil trade on the basis of differences between the prices paid (in the case of sugar and nickel) or charged (in the case of oil) by the Soviet Union and world market prices. His estimates put overall Soviet nonrepayable price subsidies over the 1960–90 period at 39.4 billion pesos, of which 28.5 percent were granted during 1976–80, 40.0 percent during 1981–85, and 25.7 percent during 1986–90.

Relations with Capitalist Countries

Meanwhile, Cuban trade with developed market economies and with many developing countries was conducted following common commercial practices and using convertible currencies. Cuba earned convertible currencies through sale of its exports (especially sugar) and used such earnings to finance imports from convertible currency areas. On occasion, Western governments, financial institutions, or suppliers provided convertible currency credits to Cuba to finance imports; these interest-bearing credits were repayable in convertible currencies subject to a predetermined schedule. Because of currency inconvertibility, Cuba could not apply surpluses in trade with the socialist countries to offset deficits with developed market economies or to service debt with these nations.

In conclusion, Cuba's external accounts were segmented into nonconvertible or soft currency accounts that covered most of the country's commercial and financial relations with the socialist nations, and convertible currency accounts that applied to economic relations with the rest of the world. The nonconvertible currency accounts dominated: over the 1978–85 period, for example, Cuba sold 76 percent of its exports and purchased 83 percent of its imports using these currencies.

Even after the communist regimes in Eastern Europe had begun to disappear, Cuba continued to argue for maintaining the CMEA and the preferential relations it had enjoyed with socialist countries. At the January 1990 meeting of the CMEA, the Soviet Union proposed that, effective January 1, 1991, trade among member countries be conducted on the basis of market prices and convertible currencies. The Cuban representative took issue with the proposal, arguing that it would restore the "production anarchy" associated with markets and result in unfair terms of trade for developing countries within the CMEA (Cuba, Mongolia, and Vietnam), and calling for a continuation of preferential treatment for these countries. Not only were Cuba's arguments ignored, but a few months later the CMEA was dissolved. The CMEA's dissolution forced Cuba to adjust in a very short period of time to commercial relations based on world market prices and convertible currencies and eliminated the dichotomy in external sector accounts between nonconvertible and convertible currency accounts.

Foreign Trade and Finance

Currency

The official Cuban currency is the peso (for value of the peso—see Glossary). From 1914 to 1971, the peso was exchanged at par with the United States dollar, but since 1961 the Cuban currency has not been freely exchanged in international markets. The peso was linked to the pound sterling for trade purposes beginning in 1961. With the floating of the United States dollar in 1971, the value of the peso appreciated vis-à-vis the United States dollar through its link with the pound. The link with the pound was reportedly severed in 1974 by Cuban monetary authorities; beginning in 1976, the peso was placed on a controlled float, its value determined on the basis of the value of a basket of currencies that accounted for the bulk of Cuba's international transactions.

It is widely accepted that the official exchange rate of the peso vis-à-vis the United States dollar vastly overstates the purchasing power of the peso, but the precise extent of overvaluation has been difficult to establish. *Pick's Currency Yearbook* reported black-market Cuban peso exchange rates resulting from unauthorized dealings of foreign currency banknotes and/or unlicensed transfers abroad in the range of six to ten pesos for one United States dollar in 1970–72, about nine pesos for one United States dollar in 1973–76, and ten to fifteen pesos for one United States dollar in 1977–79. In the 1980s, the black-market rate was reported to be four to eight pesos for one United States dollar.

The value of the peso dropped precipitously in the 1990s as Cuban citizens expressed a very strong preference for holding United States dollars to obtain goods and services that were not available through the centrally planned first economy. In mid-1994 the peso reached probably its lowest point when it was exchanged at about 150 pesos for one United States dollar. In the second half of the 1990s, the unofficial exchange rate fluctuated in the range of twenty to twenty-two pesos for one United States dollar (twenty-two in 2000).

Cuban official statistics are invariably reported on the basis of domestic currency, that is, pesos. Given the large disparity between the official and unofficial exchange rate, it is difficult to determine which exchange rate to use to convert Cuban pesos data to a convertible currency, such as the United States dollar, for international comparisons and other purposes. Thus, much caution must be exercised in using statistics regarding the foreign sector that may have been converted to United States dollars or some other convertible currency.

Merchandise Trade

Cuban merchandise exports in 1993 amounted to slightly more than 1.1 billion pesos, 79 percent lower than the 5.4 billion recorded in 1989. Over the same period, merchandise imports fell from 8.1 billion to slightly more than 2.0 billion pesos, or by 75 percent. In 1994 exports recovered slightly, increasing by about 17 percent to about 1.3 billion, while imports fell by about 1 percent. In 1996 exports peaked at nearly 1.9 billion pesos, falling to 1.8 billion in 1997 and 1.4 billion in 1998. Meanwhile, imports grew steadily, to 4.1 billion pesos in 1997 and 4.2 billion in 1998.

Prior to the changes in international economic relations that occurred in the 1990s, Cuba routinely ran a very large merchandise trade deficit, financed mainly by bilateral credits from the Soviet Union. The disappearance of the Soviet Union as a source of trade financing meant that Cuba had to reduce its imports drastically to bring them closer to exports. Lacking financing from the former Soviet Union, Cuba saw its trade deficit fall sharply in 1992, to 535 million pesos, but grow thereafter to about 950 million pesos in 1993, 970 million pesos in 1994, 1.5 billion pesos in 1995, 1.8 billion pesos in 1996, 2.2 billion pesos in 1997, and nearly 2.8 billion pesos in 1998. The 1998 trade deficit was five-fold its level in 1992.

Russia occupied first place among destinations of Cuban merchandise exports in 1997, taking about 17 percent of Cuba's exports. Other top destinations of Cuban exports in 1997 (in descending order) were Canada, Spain, Egypt, China, Japan, Iran, Germany, Belgium, Italy, the Dominican Republic, and the United Kingdom.

Spain was Cuba's largest supplier of merchandise imports in 1997, providing 12 percent of imports. Other significant suppliers of merchandise imports to Cuba in 1997 (in descending order) were Venezuela, Mexico, Netherlands Antilles, Canada, France, China, Italy, and Vietnam.

With regard to the composition of merchandise exports, sugar and related products remain the most significant exports. Sugar and related products accounted for more than 50 percent of the value of Cuban merchandise exports in the first half of the 1990s, falling below this mark for the first time in 1997 (47 percent). According to statistics of the International Sugar Organization, Russia remained the top importer of Cuban sugar, accounting for 41 percent of the quantity of exports in 1997, with Egypt, China, Iran, and Japan also significant purchasers of Cuban sugar. Products of the mining industry, especially nickel, were the second most significant category of merchandise exports. Canada and the Netherlands purchased almost all such exports.

Fuels continue to be Cuba's most significant merchandise import, accounting for 33 to 35 percent of the total value of imports in the early 1990s and about 25 percent in 1997. Russia continues to be a principal supplier of Cuba's fuels, but Latin American countries—Venezuela, Mexico, and the Netherlands

Antilles—also provided significant amounts of fuels during some years in the 1990s. The Cuban leadership slashed imports of machinery, semifinished goods, raw materials, and consumer goods to be able to finance imports of fuels and foods: in 1993, imports of machinery amounted to 13 percent of their level in 1989, raw materials 15 percent, consumer goods 22 percent, and semifinished goods 26 percent. In 1995–97, imports in all four of these categories rose, contributing to the significant expansion of the merchandise trade deficit that occurred between 1994 and 1997.

Development Assistance

Socialist countries were the source of nearly all of the development finance received by revolutionary Cuba. No systematic data exist on development assistance to Cuba, but scattered information suggests that aid was substantial. Originating primarily from the Soviet Union, the aid covered a wide range of economic activities and took mostly the form of loans repayable at very low interest rates.

According to Cuban sources, during the 1981–85 period the Soviet Union provided the island with 1.8 billion rubles in development assistance (mostly loans), while East European socialist countries granted about 1 billion rubles and the CMEA another 1 billion rubles in multilateral assistance. Up through 1986, the Soviet Union had assisted Cuba in completing 360 development projects, and 289 others were in progress. Enterprises built with Soviet assistance were responsible for 15 percent of gross industrial output, 100 percent of the nation's output of steel plates, 90 percent of its steel products, 50 percent of mixed fertilizers, 70 percent of nitrogen fertilizers, 70 percent of electricity, 50 percent of products of the metalworking industry, 100 percent of the repair of Soviet vehicles, and 65 percent of textiles.

Economist Carmelo Mesa-Lago has estimated that the Soviet Union provided resources to Cuba amounting to more than US$65 billion during the 1960–90 period; about 67 percent of this total was extended in the 1980s. Approximately 40 percent of the flow of resources (about US$25.7 billion) took the form of repayable loans—credits to finance trade deficits (27 percent) and development credits (13 percent). As indicated above, about 60 percent (US$39.4 billion) was in the form of nonrepayable price subsidies.

Debt

Cuba has not officially released information on its debt with the former Soviet Union and East European socialist countries. According to Nikolay Ivanovich Ryzhkov, the then-Soviet prime minister, Cuba's debt to the Soviet Union on November 1, 1989, amounted to 15.49 billion transferable rubles; Cuba was the largest debtor country to the Soviet Union, accounting for 18.1 percent of outstanding debt. Cuba reportedly also had outstanding debt of more than 1 billion rubles with Bulgaria, Czechoslovakia, and Hungary and a debt of 2 billion East German marks with East Germany in 1989.

Mesa-Lago has estimated Cuba's overall debt to the Soviet Union and Eastern Europe in 1989 at nearly US$27 billion (using the official exchange rate of one ruble equals US$1.58) and at US$30.2 billion in 1990 (using the official exchange rate of one ruble equals US$1.78). Because the value of the ruble vis-à-vis the United States dollar fell sharply in the 1990s, so has the value of the Cuban debt in United States dollar terms. No information is available on the currency in which the Cuban debt to the former Soviet Union and Eastern Europe is to be valued or to be repaid.

In 1969 Cuba's convertible currency debt was small, amounting to US$291 million; it grew rapidly in the 1970s, reaching more than US$1.3 billion in 1975 and nearly US$3.3 billion in 1979 as Cuba borrowed heavily from commercial banks flush with "petrodollars" and official lenders willing to back sales of machinery and equipment to the island. In 1982 a sharp reduction in short-term loans and deposits prompted Cuba to seek to reschedule its convertible currency debt due in 1982–85. Cuba succeeded in getting some short-term relief, but a sharp deterioration in the balance of payments (see Glossary) in 1985 led to Cuba's decision to suspend payment on convertible currency effective July 1, 1986. The unpaid debt and accrued service payments amounted to nearly US$6.1 billion in 1987, US$6.5 billion in 1988, and US$6.2 billion in 1989.

Cuba suspended service on its convertible currency debt effective July 1, 1986. Although this action had a favorable impact on the balance of payments because service payments were avoided, it seriously impaired Cuba's ability to turn to foreign markets to obtain new long-term credits. As a result, since the mid-1980s Cuba has had to rely primarily on short-term debt at very high interest rates. Loans amounted to US$473 million in 1995. Convertible currency capital flows into the island during the 1960–90 period consisted primarily of loans from private and public institutions and supplier credits as Cuba effectively banned foreign investment.

Outstanding debt grew from nearly US$8.8 billion in 1993 to about US$9.1 billion in 1994, US$10.5 billion in 1995, and US$11.2 billion in 1998 (see table 13, Appendix). The fact that the outstanding debt grew does not mean that Cuba actually obtained fresh loans: the year-to-year value of the outstanding debt is affected by several factors, among them the accumulation of unpaid interest and relative changes in the value of currencies in which the debt was contracted.

Balance of Payments

Socialist Cuba began to publish balance of payments statistics in the 1990s. During the 1980s, Cuba did publish balance of payments statistics for its convertible currency accounts, in a series of reports that were issued beginning in 1982 by the BNC (Cuban National Bank) to support renegotiation of the convertible currency debt held by Western creditors. These partial balance of payments statistics are of very limited value because convertible currency transactions accounted for only a small share of overall economic activity in Cuba during the 1980s. The lack of comprehensive balance of payments statistics means that there are no data on important components of the external sector, such as overall trade in services, transfers, and capital flows.

The shift in Cuban external economic relations in the 1990s to the use of convertible currencies did away with the dichotomy in external accounts, eliminating the soft currency accounts. The BNC and its successor, the BCC, have published balance of payments statistics (in pesos, at the official rate of one peso equals US$1) for 1993–98 purporting to cover the totality of external economic relations (see table 14, Appendix).

Cuba ran surpluses in services trade every year during the 1993–98 period; the surpluses were quite sizable, particularly after 1994. The favorable balance in the services export account presumably reflects the performance of the international tourism industry. As discussed above, foreign investment has played an important role in the development of this industry.

Income generated by tourism rose by 535 percent between 1990 and 1997; it first exceeded the US$1 billion mark in 1995

Taxis and buses waiting for tourists in downtown Havana
Courtesy Suzanne Petrie

and reached more than US$1.5 billion in 1997. Tourism surpassed nickel to become the second largest source of revenue in 1991 and overtook sugar exports in 1994. It should be noted, however, that these income figures refer to gross income and include the value of imported goods and services consumed by visitors; the foreign exchange cost of capital investment; payments that leave Cuba in the form of profits, interest payments, royalties, management fees, payments to foreign travel agents and so on; the cost of advertising and promoting travel to Cuba; the overseas cost of training service personnel; and aviation receipts from its airlines and airport fees.

A better measure of tourism's contribution to the balance of payments would be net receipts, that is, gross receipts minus the associated convertible-currency imports and other expenditures. For the Cuban tourism industry, net receipts are a fraction of gross income: in the range of 30 to 38 percent, according to studies conducted by the Ministry of Tourism, and about 33 percent according to Françoise Simon, an expert in international tourism. Reports on the performance of the Cuban tourism industry often do not distinguish between gross and net receipts, with Cuban officials tending to report only gross receipts, which are, of course, larger.

Transfers

In the balance of payments methodology, transfers are flows of resources from one economy to another for which there is no quid pro quo. Transfers could be official—for example, foreign grants or aid in kind for which no repayment is required—or private remittances from persons who have emigrated to relatives or friends who have remained at home. According to ECLAC (Economic Commission for Latin America and the Caribbean), net transfers were negative in 1989–90, meaning that resources actually flowed out of the Cuban economy in those two years in the form of transfers; they turned positive beginning in 1991, however, and boomed thereafter. According to Cuban official statistics, transfers were US$263 million in 1993, US$646 million in 1995, and US$820 million in 1998. Transfers have been Cuba's most significant source of convertible currency since 1996, exceeding gross revenue from sugar or nickel and *net* revenues from tourism.

According to ECLAC, transfers received by Cuba are predominantly private and take the form of cash remittances from residents of the United States to persons in Cuba. The primary motivation for private remittances to Cuba appears to be the desire on the part of emigrants to ease the economic hardships being experienced by relatives and friends on the island during the Special Period. The ECLAC private remittance estimates should be used with caution, as they seem to be derived as a residual from the balance of payments rather than through direct measurement.

Investment

Balance of payments statistics report that direct investment on the island amounted to US$54 million in 1993, US$563 million in 1994, US$4.7 million in 1995, US$82 million in 1996, US$442 million in 1997, and US$207 million in 1998. These statistics are significant for at least two reasons: First, they are the first official statistics on actual investment flows reported by the Cuban government. And second, they suggest lower investment flows than had been reported by Cuban officials and are found in Cuban investment promotional literature.

Cuban officials have cited the threat of possible action by the United States government against potential or actual investors as justification for the secrecy with which they treat investment data. The rationale behind the policy of "minimum reporting," as articulated by Vice President Carlos Lage Dávila, is "the pressure which everyone who comes to invest in Cuba is subjected to by the United States." Although this may be so, it is also possible that the lack of transparency in reporting foreign investment information may be a deliberate act to influence the investment climate by giving the impression that larger investments have occurred, or are under negotiation, than is actually the case.

Cuban officials have reported flows of foreign investment that appear too optimistic in the light of other information and the balance of payments data mentioned above. For example, in October 1991, Julio García Oliveras, chairman of the Cuban Chamber of Commerce, reported that negotiations were ongoing with investors representing investments of US$1.2 billion. Carlos Lage stated in November 1994 that by the end of 1994 joint ventures would have provided Cuba with US$1.5 billion in investment. By the end of 1995, according to official sources, foreign investment had reached more than US$2.1 billion.

Official estimates of foreign investment probably overstate actual equity capital flows into the island for several reasons. First, multiyear disbursements may be involved. Second, some investments may be contingent on performance. Third, some investments may take the form of assets rather than fresh investments. Fourth, some of the investments may be management contracts, production partnership agreements (particularly in mining and oil exploration), or debt-equity swaps, where funds invested are minimal. And fifth, others may actually be supplier contracts rather than equity investments. At best, the figures reported by Cuban government officials might represent the intentions of foreign investors, but they significantly overstate actual capital that has flowed onto the island. Thus, according to the United States-Cuba Trade and Economic Council (see Glossary), investments amounting to nearly US$6.1 billion had been "announced" through March 1999. However, the volume "committed or delivered" was a more modest US$1.8 billion, or 29.5 percent of the announced amount.

Although legislation authorizing the creation of joint ventures was enacted in 1982, only three joint ventures were established during the 1982–90 period (see table 15, Appendix). Foreign investment activity increased in 1992–94, with thirty-three joint ventures established in 1992, sixty in 1993, and seventy-four in 1994, but slowed in 1995, when thirty-one joint ventures were created. In all, Cuban government statistics indicate that 212 joint ventures with foreign investors had been established through the end of 1995; Spanish investors were responsible for the largest number of joint ventures (forty-seven, or 22 percent) followed by Canada (twenty-six, or 12 percent), Italy (seventeen, or 8 percent), and France and Mexico (thirteen, or 6 percent each). The largest concentration of joint ventures was in the industrial sector (fifty-six, or 26 percent), followed by tourism (thirty-four, or 16 percent), mining (twenty-eight, or 13 percent), and the oil sector (twenty-five, or 12 percent) (see table 16, Appendix).

Title III of the Cuban Liberty and Democratic Solidarity Act (the Helms-Burton Act), enacted by the United States in 1996, gives United States citizens who hold valid claims a right of action in United States courts against those who knowingly "traffic" in their confiscated Cuban properties. Title IV allows the exclusion of these violators of United States property claims and their immediate families from the United States. Canada, Mexico, and the European Union (see Glossary) have vigorously protested the enactment of the Helms-Burton Act, claiming that it impinges on their sovereignty and that its extraterritorial reach is inconsistent with international obligations of the World Trade Organization (WTO—see Glossary) and the North American Free Trade Agreement (NAFTA—see Glossary).

According to Ibrahim Ferradaz, the then minister of foreign investment and economic cooperation, 260 joint ventures with foreign capital had been established on the island by the end of 1996 in thirty-four sectors of the economy. This number showed an increase of forty-eight joint ventures or 23 percent over the 212 joint ventures at the end of 1995. During the first half of 1997, according to Ferradaz, more joint venture deals were consummated than during a like period in 1996, and 140 new projects were under active consideration. Ferradaz stated that the impact of the Helms-Burton Act on foreign investment in Cuba was "difficult to estimate," noting that some foreign investors had "become fearful [of Helms-Burton] and called off their projects." More recent data indicates that there were 345 joint ventures by the end of 1998. The main sources of foreign capital, as measured by the number of joint ventures, were Spain (seventy joint ventures), Canada (sixty-six), Italy (fifty-two), the United Kingdom (fifteen) and France (fourteen). The main recipients of foreign investment, again as measured by the number of joint ventures, were mining, oil and heavy industry (eighty-eight joint ventures), tourism (fifty-eight), light industry (thirty), food processing (twenty-four) and agriculture (seventeen).

Cuba's first two export processing zones, created pursuant to Decree-Law 165 of 1996, opened in May 1997 in Berroa and Wajay, near the city of Havana. These zones were followed by another export processing zone in the port of Mariel.

Economic Outlook

At the dawn of the twenty-first century, the prospects for the economy of socialist Cuba appear bleak. Although the economic free fall experienced at the beginning of the decade has been arrested since about 1994, there is no end in sight for the Special Period. Growth rates recorded since then have been quite modest and do not come close to offsetting the large drop in economic activity. At the current rates of growth, it will take more than ten years for the Cuban economy to return to 1989 levels.

The foreign sector, critical to the performance of the Cuban economy, has improved its performance during the second half of the 1990s, but the level of foreign resources attracted into the country is still very small in comparison with the subsidies and financial assistance from the Soviet Union and other socialist countries to which Cuba had grown accustomed. Cuba has very limited access to foreign financial markets, and it is not a member of the international financial institutions that could assist it in overcoming balance of payments difficulties. Cuba has played but a marginal role in the process of economic integration of the Western Hemisphere, a situation that is not likely to change until Cuba and the United States normalize diplomatic and economic relations. Foreign investment is having a positive impact on the economy; in addition to providing foreign resources, it also transfers technology and provides additional markets for Cuban exports. However, its magnitude is too small to overcome the scarcity of foreign exchange. In the next few years, the external sector is likely to perform as it has since the mid-1990s, providing just enough foreign resources to allow the economy to continue to operate at very low levels of capacity and efficiency.

The process of economic reforms that began in 1993 slowed down after the economy reached bottom and began to recover in 1994. Since then, there have been no significant policy departures. Critical reforms, such as the liberalization of prices, enterprise reform, privatization, and the creation of factor markets, have been put on hold indefinitely because the government fears that their implementation would weaken its political stranglehold on the Cuban nation. Unless Cuba sheds its statist model entirely, adopts a free-market economy consistent with the principles of the international trading system, and changes its political system to allow some space for alternatives outside of the PCC, the economy is likely to continue to stagnate, to the detriment of the standard of living of the Cuban people.

*   *   *

Detailed information on the performance of the Cuban economy in the 1990s is limited and often inconsistent. In the late 1990s, Cuba published the first statistical yearbooks since 1989, the *Estadístico, 1996* and *Anuario estadístico, 1997*. These two volumes begin to fill the statistical gap since *Anuario estadístico de Cuba 1989*, which contains statistical information through 1989 (1988 in some instances). Reports by the National Bank of Cuba (BNC) and its successor the Cuban Central Bank (BCC) released since the mid-1990s—*Economic Report 1994* and *Informe económico 1997*—contain some useful data. In 1997 the United Nations' ECLAC published a massive volume titled *La economía cubana: Reformas estructurales y desempeño en los noventa* with nearly seventy tables prepared from information made available by the BNC, the Ministry of Finance and Prices, the ONE (National Statistical Office), and other instrumentalities of the Cuban government. Since the early 1990s, the United States Central Intelligence Agency has been preparing estimates of Cuban merchandise foreign trade based on information from Cuba's trading partners; its latest issue, *Cuba: Handbook of Trade Statistics, 1998* is the best source of information on Cuban foreign trade.

The most solid analysis of Cuba's economic policies and reforms during the 1990s is Carmelo Mesa-Lago's *Are Economic Reforms Propelling Cuba to the Market?* A Cuban perspective on economic reforms, including reform proposals that the Cuban government has been unwilling to undertake, is *Cuba: La restructuración de la economía: Una contribución al debate* by Julio Carranza Valdés, Luis Gutiérrez Urdaneta, and Pedro Monreal González. Another important source of analysis on the Cuban economy is the proceedings series of the Association for the Study of the Cuban Economy titled *Cuba in Transition,* which have appeared annually beginning in 1990 (for the series, see http://www.lanic.utexas.edu/la/cb/cuba/asce/index.html). (For further information and complete citations, see Bibliography.)

Chapter 4. Government and Politics

The National Capitol (El Capitolio Nacional), the seat of government until 1959, now houses the Cuban Academy of Sciences (Academia de Ciencias de Cuba) and the National Library of Science and Technology (Biblioteca Nacional de Ciencia y Tecnología).
Courtesy Mark P. Sullivan

SUDDENLY, DRAMATICALLY, ALMOST unexpectedly, the Cold War came to an end in Europe, and the world changed. Communist governments tumbled throughout Central and Eastern Europe in 1989, and, by the end of 1991, the Soviet Union itself collapsed. Constitutional governments, increasingly democratic, emerged in the 1990s in much of Central and Eastern Europe.

For Fidel Castro Ruz (president, 1976–) and his associates in the Cuban government and the Communist Party of Cuba (Partido Comunista de Cuba—PCC), these results were a catastrophe. As a result of a trade protocol signed in Moscow in late December 1990, Soviet economic subsidies to Cuba ended as of January 1, 1991. Bilateral trade between Cuba and the Soviet Union would henceforth be conducted at world market prices. Whereas in the past Cuba had dealt with only sixty-two Soviet agencies and enterprises, the trade protocol abolished the central management of trade relations and required Cuba to develop commercial relations with some 25,000 Soviet firms. The Russian government, successor to the Soviet Union, retained similar policies: trade with Cuba would be conducted on a commercial basis presuming no "special relationship" between Russia and Cuba. Stunned and inexperienced, Cuban government officials at first had great difficulty coping with these changes. And, bereft of economic subsidies, Cuba's economy collapsed (see The Economic Crisis of the 1990s, ch. 3).

Cuba also lost the political and military protection provided by the Soviet Union that it had enjoyed since 1960. Cuban leaders, consequently, felt nakedly vulnerable facing the United States. The United States government, for its part, increased its pressure on the Cuban government in the 1990s to force it to change or, preferably, to fall.

Cuba was unable to pay on its own for the costs of its worldwide activist foreign policy. Absent Soviet backing, the Cuban government risked United States retaliation for overseas military expeditions. Consequently, Cuban foreign policy retreated across the board. In September 1989, Cuba completed the repatriation of its troops from Ethiopia. In March 1990, all Cuban military personnel in Nicaragua were brought home. In May 1991, Cuba's last troops were repatriated from Angola. Also in 1990 and 1991, Cuba brought back its troops and military advisers from various other countries. Cuba's global military deployments ended nearly instantaneously as the Cold War was winding down in Europe and as Cuba was rapidly losing Soviet political, economic, and military backing. Cuba had become once again only a Caribbean island archipelago—no longer an aspirant to major-power status astride the world stage.

Born bristling in radicalism, Cuban state socialism changed in the 1990s. In 1960 the government expropriated all foreign firms. In 1989 it launched a campaign to attract private foreign direct investment once again (see Economic Reforms, ch. 3). In May 1990, President Castro inaugurated the first of many foreign-owned hotels on Cuba's premier tourist beach at Varadero. He announced that Cuba would henceforth seek foreign investment to develop its economy. These policies would soon be endorsed by the PCC's executive organ, the Political Bureau (Buró Político). These changes had implications well beyond their economic significance. In reversing the regime's founding policies, President Castro and his comrades signaled that they could no longer govern Cuba as they had and as they would still prefer. Other modest market-oriented economic policy reforms further communicated to the population the state's retreat from orthodox bureaucratic socialism (see Economic Reforms, ch. 3). Cuban leaders were compelled to change by a world suddenly averse to their brand of bureaucratic socialism.

The capacity of the Cuban state weakened at home as well. This weakening was in part a consequence of the leadership's unexpected inability to govern as had been their practice. Citizens who witnessed Fidel Castro's reluctant retreat from the policies he still cherished and had long implemented felt newly free to begin to take their lives into their own hands. An illegal economy or black market (see Glossary) boomed in Cuba in the early 1990s (see The Second Economy, ch. 3). The government could no longer prevent it, nor could it assure an acceptable standard of living to the population. The grip of the state loosened gradually in various aspects of social life. Religious activity revived (see Religion in the Special Period, 1990–97, ch. 2), and intellectual life became more independent in some respects. Human rights and political opposition activists undertook bolder actions, and their groups became more likely to endure.

The story of Cuban politics in the 1990s, therefore, has three principal strands. First, government and PCC leaders have sought to retain enough political support to continue to govern, adapting policies, streamlining organizations, and replacing personnel to make their survival more likely. Particularly significant have been a major replacement of the political leadership just below the very top of the regime and a substantial downsizing of the armed forces (see Ministry of the Revolutionary Armed Forces, ch. 5). Second, a slow political transition has gotten underway, unloved by the rulers but constructed by Cuban citizens who, step by step, have edged away from the control that the state and the PCC had held over Cuban life for the preceding decades. Third, internationally, the Cuban government has designed a strategy to resist United States pressures and to fashion a new network of international relations for the only surviving communist regime outside East Asia. Cuban leaders have gained support in Europe, Latin America, the Middle East, Canada, and East Asia from governments that object to United States attempts to force them to follow United States policy toward Cuba. This "negative" international coalition in opposition to United States policy is a key to the Cuban regime's capacity to survive seemingly against all odds years after the Soviet Union crashed.

Institutional Structure

Cuba features a formidable array of state, government, and partisan entities. Some have endured for nearly forty years, and all have lasted for at least two decades. And yet, in the 1990s as in earlier decades, these formal institutions manifest only one of the two "faces of power" in Cuba. Officeholders in state, government, and PCC organs and in the mass organizations often have less power than it would seem from a description of their formal rights and duties.

The other "face of power" in Cuba is intensely personal. It derives its clout from the Revolution in the 1950s and from "revolutionary accomplishments" in the years that followed. A key feature of these "accomplishments" is that they appeared to require heroic deeds and leaders who succeeded in reaching an impossible dream. Fidel Castro epitomizes this source of power. His towering role in Cuban politics at times has allowed him to override institutional rules and constraints to veto some policies and enact others. Other men (and some, but not very many, women) have also acquired significant public standing as a result of their heroic deeds over the years, but most of them died during the revolution of the 1950s and in the 1960s. Fidel Castro's capacity to make policies happen, or to stop their implementation, and his unmatched capacity to pick and choose officials to whom he delegates extraordinary powers shape the capacity of these institutions to function.

The Constitution

The Fourth Congress of the PCC met in October 1991 to review the debris from the collapse of the communist world in Europe and its impact on Cuba. One of its decisions was to revise Cuba's constitution of 1976. The leadership closely controlled the process of constitutional revision, and PCC and National Assembly committees carried out the task. Although the text was open to discussion by Cubans through the country's official mass organizations and other means, no plebiscite was held to approve the substantially revised text. The PCC and the National Assembly approved the new constitutional text in July 1992.

The new constitution signaled Cuba's changed circumstances and, especially, a more tolerant approach to certain differences within society. Unlike the old constitution, the text of the new constitution makes no reference to the Soviet Union, a country that had ceased to exist. The normative chapters of the constitution seek to embrace all Cubans, not just those ideologically committed to Marxism-Leninism. Its preamble and opening chapters invoke the mantle of nationalism in an attempt to cover all Cubans. The new Article 1 (unlike its predecessor) refers to José Martí and affirms that the socialist state seeks to serve all and the good of all. The PCC remains enshrined in Article 5 as the single party, still Marxist-Leninist, but now also a follower of José Martí. Whereas the old Article 54 proclaimed that the state based its actions on and advocated a "scientific materialist conception of the universe," while also guaranteeing freedom of conscience and worship, the new Article 55 omits all reference to scientific materialism and simply seeks to guarantee freedom of religion. In these and other symbolically significant ways, the 1992 constitution seeks to include all Cubans ready to pledge their allegiance and otherwise attempts to marginalize none.

The 1992 constitution retroactively legitimizes the changed property regime inaugurated with the search to lure foreign investment that started in 1989 and was made public in 1990.

The 1976 constitution had authorized only state property, except for what individuals were authorized to own directly. The 1992 constitution limits state ownership to the "fundamental" means of production (Article 14). Article 15 goes further, however. It opens by seemingly prohibiting the privatization of most enterprises and other forms of economic activities, but it goes on to authorize the privatization of every property, provided such transfer of ownership is approved by the Executive Committee (Comité Ejecutivo) of the Council of Ministers (Consejo de Ministros).

The ideological and property regime shifts of the 1992 constitution made the political regime more inclusive and, especially, more tolerant of religious belief, behavior, and organizations. They signaled as well a much greater emphasis in public discourse on Cuban nationalism rather than on the canonical texts of Marxism, Leninism, socialism, or communism. The changes in the property regime, of course, accelerated the process of private foreign direct investment.

The 1992 constitution remains deeply authoritarian, however. The PCC remains the only legal political party. The bill of rights is as riddled with exceptions as it was in the 1976 constitution. The new Article 53 is identical to its predecessor in recognizing freedom of expression, but only so long as it conforms to the "goals of a socialist society." All mass media must remain in state hands. And the article also enables the government to further regulate whatever residual freedoms remain. Other articles recognize the privacy of the home and of personal correspondence, unless, of course, the law states otherwise. Finally, Article 62 (like its predecessor) prohibits the use of any of these freedoms "against the existence and purposes of the socialist state." Indeed, in one important respect the 1992 constitution is more authoritarian than its predecessor. The new Article 67 empowers the president of the Council of State (Fidel Castro) on his own authority to declare a state of emergency and to modify the exercise of rights or the obligations embedded in the constitution.

National Assembly of People's Power

The 1992 constitution also institutes some modest changes in the design of the organs of the state (see fig. 7). The 1992 constitution, like its predecessor, vests all formal legislative powers (including the powers of amending the constitution) in the National Assembly of People's Power (Asamblea Nacional

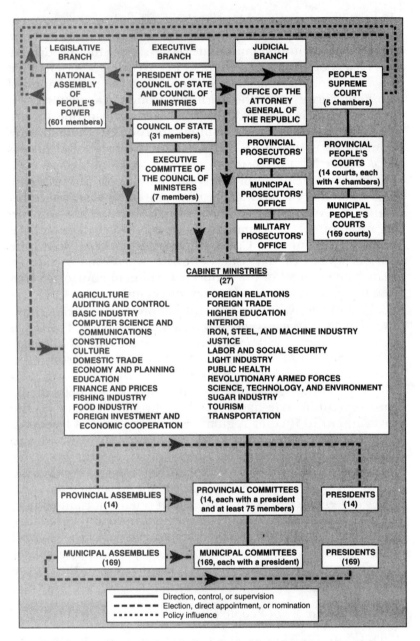

Source: Based on information from Roberto Segre, Mario Coyula, and Joseph L.
Scarpaci, *Havana: Two Faces of the Antillean Metropolis*, New York: 1997, 178; and
Jorge I. Domínguez.

Figure 7. Central Administrative Structure, 2001

del Poder Popular—ANPP; hereafter, National Assembly). The National Assembly has the formal powers, among others, to declare war in the event of military aggression; make peace; enact or modify legislation; approve the budget and the national economic plan; elect the members of the Council of State (Consejo de Estado), including its president; and elect the members of the Supreme Court (Tribunal Supremo Popular). (The Supreme Court cannot judge the constitutionality of National Assembly decisions.) National Assembly leaders also generally oversee the rule-making activities and electoral processes of the provincial assemblies and municipal assemblies.

Despite all of its functions, the National Assembly is not a powerful institution. For the most part, it ratifies decisions made prior to its meetings; it typically votes unanimously or nearly unanimously to endorse government bills. Deputies have other full-time jobs, and the National Assembly characteristically meets only twice a year, three times at most. Each time it usually meets for two or three days. Founded in 1976, the National Assembly became, in the 1990s, simultaneously marginally less institutionalized but also more effective. Institutionalization declined because officials at times failed to observe their own rules. For example, National Assembly elections should have been held in 1991 but were postponed until February 1993 in order to defer the electoral process well past the shock of the collapse of the Soviet Union and other communist regimes. And, at times in the 1990s, National Assembly sessions were canceled or deferred arbitrarily instead of meeting at their normal times.

The National Assembly became more effective, however, under the leadership of Ricardo Alarcón de Quesada, who became its president in March 1993. Alarcón reinvigorated the National Assembly's working commissions, which aid the National Assembly and the Council of State in carrying out their functions. Alarcón urged the commissions to audit the operation of state agencies, ask questions, and write reports. The National Assembly's debate in its standing commissions has at times forced the executive branch to amend, reconsider, or delay the submission of bills for formal approval. Among the most vigorously debated bills was the Law on Foreign Investment, finally approved after much delay and several drafts in September 1995. Alarcón has also urged deputies to remain in closer touch with the voters and to campaign actively for office as if they were contested. In these respects, the National Assembly's political efficacy has risen, and so has Alarcón's political star.

National Assembly deputies are elected for five-year terms. In 1998 the new National Assembly had 601 members. The 1992 constitution mandates that the deputies be elected directly by the people, in contrast to the previous system, in which the provincial assemblies elected the deputies. However, the Electoral Law of 1992 requires that the number of candidates equal the number of posts to be filled. The old Electoral Law required that a provincial assembly (Asamblea Provincial) be given a choice of nominees somewhat larger than the number of posts to be filled. Thus, the change in national electoral procedures had the appearance of democratization while embodying a reduction in effective choice. The election of deputies through the provincial assemblies had fostered some competition within the elite; the 1992 changes reduced the level of open political contestation.

Candidates for National Assembly deputy, candidates for membership in the Council of State, and candidates for National Assembly president, vice president, and secretary originate with a National Commission for Candidacies. This commission is constituted of appointees designated by the officially sponsored mass organizations. These mass organizations are the Cuban Workers Federation (Central de Trabajadores de Cuba—CTC), the Federation of Cuban Women (Federación de Mujeres Cubanas—FMC), the Committee for the Defense of the Revolution (Comité de Defensa de la Revolución—CDR), the National Association of Small Farmers (Asociación Nacional de Agricultores Pequeños—ANAP), the Federation of University Students, and the Federation of Secondary School Students (Federación de Estudiantes de la Enseñanza Media—FEEM) (see Mass Organizations, this ch.). The CTC representative chairs the commission. The commission, which consults various national, provincial, and municipal leaders, proposes a list of precandidates (with a number of precandidates equal to no fewer than twice the number to be elected) to a similarly constituted commission at the municipal level. The latter commission formally nominates the candidates for deputy. Those nominated for candidacy are almost certain to be elected because the final list of candidates equals the number of posts to be filled.

After the 1993 national elections, reelected incumbents constituted only 17 percent of the new National Assembly. This figure was not the result of voter discontent (all the incumbents who stood for reelection were reelected), but of a prior elite decision not to renominate most incumbents. In contrast, after the 1998 national elections, reelected incumbents constituted 35 percent of the new National Assembly. (Average age in the National Assembly rose from forty-three to forty-five from one election to the next.) In general, this pattern of sweeping personnel change in the early 1990s but somewhat greater continuity in the late 1990s reflected the top leadership's greater confidence that it had removed the "dead wood" and identified a good political team to ensure the continuation of the political regime. A similar pattern would be evident in the composition of the PCC's Central Committee (Comité Central) (see Political Bureau and Central Committee, this ch.).

The proportion of female members of the National Assembly rose from 23 to 28 percent from the 1993 to the 1998 elections. In addition, 78 percent of the deputies were university graduates in 1998 (versus 75 percent in 1993). The number of deputies on active duty in the Revolutionary Armed Forces (Fuerzas Armadas Revolucionarias—FAR) or in the Ministry of Interior remained the same (thirty-five deputies). The number of high PCC officials dropped substantially, however, from 24 percent to 11 percent in part as a result of the downsizing of the PCC's Central Committee in 1997.

Council of State

The Council of State is elected by the National Assembly and is empowered to make all decisions on behalf of the National Assembly when the latter is not in session, which is most of the time. Among other powers, the Council of State can appoint and remove ministers, ambassadors, and other high officials, issue decrees with the force of law, declare war or make peace, ratify treaties, and suspend or revoke the decisions by all provincial or local governments. In effect, the Council of State, not the National Assembly, is the routine, constitutionally authoritative collective decision maker.

The president of the Council of State, who under the constitution is also president of the Council of Ministers, is the chief of state. These functions had been performed by different individuals before the adoption of the 1976 constitution, as had been the norm in communist countries. Since 1976, these posts have been held by Fidel Castro, who, in taking on these functions, adopted a pattern of presidentialism familiar to Latin Americans.

The six vice presidents of the Council of State are among Cuba's most important politicians. The first vice president is General of the Army Raúl Castro Ruz, minister of the FAR and Fidel Castro's formally designated successor. The other vice presidents are Commander of the Revolution Juan Almeida Bosque, who has long played a role in maintaining discipline and morale in the military and the PCC; Army Corps General Abelardo Colomé Ibarra, minister of interior and decorated hero of the republic of Cuba for his role in Cuba's wars in Africa; Carlos Lage Dávila, secretary of the Executive Committee of the Council of Ministers and, in effect, chief operating officer for the Cuban economy; José Ramón Machado Ventura, long-time secretary of organization of the PCC's Central Committee; and Estéban Lazo Hernández, first secretary of the PCC in Havana City Province (Ciudad de La Habana Province).

The Council of State has thirty-one members, including its president, vice presidents, and secretary, all of whom were reelected in 1998. Its membership had been relatively stable from the mid-1970s to the early 1990s. Six leaders—the Castro brothers, Almeida, Armando Hart Dávalos, Machado, and Pedro Miret Prieto—have been members of the Council of State since its establishment in 1977 and were reelected again in 1998. In 1998, however, there was a major overhaul of the council's membership, the only top leadership organ to be reorganized so thoroughly in the late 1990s. Only seventeen of the thirty-one members of the 1993 Council of State were reelected in 1998; only two of the departing fourteen members had died. On balance, there were three fewer ministers in the 1998 Council of State, two fewer generals, and none of the three members of the old council without significant political responsibilities. However, three local government officials joined the Council, as did two intellectuals. Some of the rotation was intended to retain the representation of a political role that had passed from one individual to another. By tradition, the heads of the most important mass organizations belong to the Council of State. The number of women in the Council of State was the same in 1993 and in 1998: five women, one more than in the first Council of State chosen in 1976. There are six Afro-Cubans in the 1998 Council of State (the non-white share of Cuba's population was one-third in the 1981 census). In general, the slight changes in membership led away

Fidel Castro Ruz in the early 1980s
Courtesy Ministry of Foreign Relations

from those with administrative responsibilities and toward those with political responsibilities, paying little attention to concerns for gender or racial representation.

Council of Ministers

The Council of Ministers is the highest executive and administrative organ. The constitution empowers it to issue regulations to administer laws and decrees and to authorize exceptions to state ownership of the means of production. It responds to the National Assembly and to the Council of State. Ministers are formally chosen by the National Assembly on the recommendation of the president of the Council of State, but they can be changed as well by the Council of State, on its president's recommendation.

Ministers are replaced one by one, or in small numbers. There has never been a wholesale replacement of the Council of Ministers; there is no provision for such National Assembly action in the constitution. In the 1990s, the National Assembly began to ask for more information from ministers about the work of their agencies, but ministers are, in practice, principally responsible to the Executive Committee of the Council of Ministers and to President Castro. On April 21, 1994, the Cuban government adopted a drastic reorganization and simplification of its administrative structure, reducing the number of ministries to twenty-seven and abolishing, combining, or downsizing another sixteen major agencies of the national government. In 2000, the Council of Ministers included a president (Fidel Castro), a first vice president (Raúl Castro), a secretary (Carlos Lage), four vice presidents, a minister of government, twenty-six ministers, the president of the central bank, and the directors of four cabinet-level institutes.

Courts

The Supreme Court of Cuba is organized into five chambers: criminal, civil and administrative, labor, state security, and military. The members of the Supreme Court are nominated by the minister of justice and confirmed by the National Assembly, with two exceptions. First, the Supreme Court's president and vice president are nominated by the president of the Council of State (Fidel Castro); second, the members of the military chamber are nominated jointly by the ministers of justice and the FAR (the latter minister is Raúl Castro). The minister of justice exercises administrative control over all the courts, including the Supreme Court; the Ministry of Justice thus has full authority over budget, payroll, and personnel.

The Supreme Court and all the courts are subordinate to the National Assembly and the Council of State (Article 121). The Supreme Court has no authority to declare a law unconstitutional. The courts are formally much less independent, therefore, than in other political systems. Judges are appointed for a term, not for life, and they can be removed from office if proper cause is shown. As a result of these measures, the courts show considerable deference to executive authority and are marked by political timidity.

There are also provincial courts in each province. These courts have four chambers, the same as for the Supreme Court except for the military chamber. The provincial courts exercise jurisdiction over crimes for which punishment will not exceed eight years; thus, about three-quarters of all crimes fall within its realm.

There are municipal courts in each municipality. They serve as trial courts at the lowest level, and they have jurisdiction over minor crimes that typically carry a penalty of imprisonment for less than one year or small fines. They are also the courts of first instance in civil and labor cases. Municipal courts are not divided into chambers, but trials are always held before a panel of three judges.

All of Cuba's courts have both professional and lay judges. Each of the chambers of the Supreme Court, for example, has professional and lay judges, as is also the case at the provincial and municipal levels. The reliance on lay judges reflects a political judgment that decisions in courts belong to the people, and that ordinary citizens with relatively little training are appropriate judges nonetheless. (In United States jurisprudence, the role of juries bears some resemblance to this Cuban procedure.) Professional judges are selected through a competitive examination administered by the Ministry of Justice. About half of Cuba's judges are members of the PCC, with a higher proportion of PCC members in the Supreme Court.

The role of the Cuban courts is quite similar to that in other countries. The courts are key institutions in law enforcement. In Cuba they also seek to educate the population about their rights and obligations. The Supreme Court, as an appellate court, is responsible for ensuring uniformity in the application of law throughout the country; the Supreme Court revokes lower-court decisions that are contrary to law or precedent.

Cuban courts are unusual in one respect: they are very harsh in their treatment of the political opposition. Cubans can be jailed for speaking ill of their rulers or for organizing groups to contest political power. The number of political prisoners has declined from the very high levels of the 1960s, but it remains characteristically in the hundreds. In the 1990s, the Cuban government often released some political prisoners at the request of visiting foreign dignitaries. For example, in 1998, many political and common prisoners were released on the occasion of Pope John Paul II's visit to Cuba that January. Nonetheless, the existing rules to protect "state security" make it probable that the overall number of political prisoners remains the same: some are freed, but others are arrested.

The Office of the State Prosecutor (Fiscalía General de la República) is subordinate to the National Assembly, which formally elects the prosecutor (Fiscal General de la República), and the Council of State. The prosecutor has wide latitude to review the past conduct and prospective actions of all organs of state power. The prosecutor has specific oversight over all law enforcement, with a rank equal to a Supreme Court justice. The prosecutor is directly responsible for cases of treason or corruption.

Provincial and Local Government

Cuba has fourteen provinces. From west to east, they are: Pinar del Río, La Habana, Ciudad de La Habana, Matanzas, Villa Clara, Cienfuegos, Sancti Spíritus, Ciego de Ávila, Camagüey, Las Tunas, Granma, Holguín, Santiago de Cuba, and Guantánamo. The Isla de la Juventud (Isle of Youth), the Cuban archipelago's second-largest island, is a special municipality. The entire national territory is subdivided into 169 municipalities.

Each province is formally governed by a provincial assembly and each municipality by a municipal assembly (Asamblea Municipal). The respective assemblies elect municipal committees. The president of a provincial assembly's provincial committee functions as a provincial governor; the president of a municipal assembly's municipal committee functions as mayor. Provincial assembly delegates serve for five years; municipal assembly delegates serve for two and one-half years. Provincial assemblies must have no fewer than seventy-five members, although some are larger because of a province's greater population.

The Provincial Commission for Candidacies, constituted in the same manner as the National Commission, proposes precandidates for provincial assembly delegates to the Municipal Commission for Candidacies. The list of precandidates equals no fewer than twice the number of posts to be filled. The Municipal Commission formally nominates the candidates for delegates. As at the national level, the number of candidates for provincial delegate equals the number of seats to be filled. Voters have no choice among candidates for provincial delegates, just as they have no choice among candidates in the vote for national deputies. (The Provincial Commission also nominates the candidates for provincial assembly president, vice president, and secretary.)

The Municipal Commission for Candidacies is constituted in the same way as its national and provincial counterparts. Formally, it nominates candidates for municipal assembly president and vice president. The Municipal Commission also formally sorts out the precandidacies for provincial delegate and national deputy, and presents the respective lists to the municipal assembly for final nomination. As a practical matter, the political process that leads to these nominations is controlled carefully from national headquarters. Nonetheless, because the number of precandidates is twice the number of

*Restored and unrestored homes
in Old Havana
Courtesy Suzanne Petrie*

*A cobblestone side street in Old
Havana
Courtesy Suzanne Petrie*

eventual nominations and posts, there is some significant competition among insiders for these symbolically important posts.

The elections for municipal assembly are different, however. Nominations come from assemblies of neighbors held at the precinct level. For each post, there must be at least two candidates, and there may be more. To be elected, a candidate must receive more than half the valid votes cast. Because of multiple candidacies, runoff elections between the top two contenders from the first round are common in many municipalities. In the municipal elections in spring 2000, for example, 5.7 percent of these municipal posts were filled in the second round. Overall, approximately half of the incumbent municipal assembly members were reelected in these elections.

Research by Cuban scholars shows that many voters are often unaware whether candidates for municipal assembly delegate are members of the PCC. Membership in the PCC serves typically neither as an asset nor as a liability in local elections, although, in fact, most elected officials are party members. The main motivations for voters are whether local candidates have a reputation for honesty, good neighborliness, and humane sensibilities. Cubans vote for their friends and neighbors for local office in ways not unlike voters do in United States local elections. Thus, it is noteworthy that many of these are, indeed, PCC members; the party members seem to be held in high regard even if the PCC as an institution is not an object of popular affection.

Municipal governments provide social services and run retail trade enterprises, as well as restaurants and cafeterias, at the local level. They also build residential housing. They have no control over provincial and national enterprises that have offices or subsidiaries in the municipality, but they can at times develop collaborative relations with the larger state firms for the benefit of the community. Through their relations with local governments, large national state enterprises, in effect, have local "charitable" activities that are somewhat similar to the practices of large firms in other countries.

The main limitation on the scope of municipal government is the principle of double subordination. That is, local firms and agencies supposedly owned and operated by the municipality must still meet the standards for quality of performance and personnel set at the national level. In practice, this principle has greatly limited the municipality's actual discretionary powers; there are few significant policies they can change on their own.

In 1988 the government authorized the creation of People's Councils (Consejos Populares) to expedite the administration of services at the local level. There are several People's Councils within each municipality. Each People's Council includes the municipal delegates elected within a given territory as well as representatives from the mass organizations and state institutions operating within that locality. People's Councils became, in effect, one more layer in Cuba's administrative structure; they did not materially change the efficacy of the delivery of services or the quality of political representation.

Cuba's provinces face significant problems in carrying out their tasks. From 1986 to 1996, the percentage of nationwide budget expenditures disbursed at the provincial and municipal levels fell from 35 percent to 27 percent. For the most part, this drop was accounted for by the collapse of subnational government entrepreneurial and investment expenditures, while local governments attempted to sustain their funding of basic services. In 1996 every provincial government ran a deficit (although Havana's budget was nearly balanced). The size of the deficit of the provincial governments of Ciego de Ávila, Las Tunas, Matanzas, Pinar del Río, Sancti Spíritus, Santiago de Cuba, and Villa Clara was equal to more than half of the revenues of these provinces. The size of the deficit of the provincial governments of Granma and Guantánamo was larger than the revenues of these provinces.

National and Local Elections

Elections for the National Assembly are held in multimember districts. Voters have three choices: they can vote for the single official slate; they can vote for some of the candidates on the official slate (but never for opposition party candidates); or they can cast a blank ballot. To be elected, a candidate has to receive more than half of the valid votes cast. No candidate failed to be elected in the 1993 and 1998 National Assembly elections. The government, the PCC, and the mass organizations campaign vigorously to increase voting turnout, and, in particular, they urge citizens to vote for the entire single official slate. Thus, one measure of lawful dissent is the percentage of Cubans who vote for something other than the single slate (see Table 17, Appendix).

In the 1998 National Assembly elections, the overall results were slightly more favorable to the government than in 1993, reflecting the trend toward economic stabilization and recovery during the intervening years. In 1998, 89.7 percent of the voters cast their ballots for the single slate, and only 5 percent of the voters voided their ballots or voted blank. The results were also more favorable to the government in La Habana Province, where the single slate received 88.4 percent of the votes cast and the percentage of null or blank ballots fell to 7 percent. These results necessarily imply, however, that the single slate performed less well in some of the other provinces.

Comparative inter-provincial data, available for the 1993 National Assembly election and the 1997 and 2000 municipal elections, show a fairly consistent geographic distribution of dissent (see Table 18, Appendix). Voiding one's ballot or voting blank are the only two means of expressing displeasure with the political system at the municipal level, so the percentage of voters who choose them is somewhat larger than in national elections. At the National Assembly level, there is the additional option of not voting for the entire official slate. In all three elections, the largest proportion of dissenters was found in the western provinces (Pinar del Río, Ciudad de La Habana, La Habana, Matanzas, Villa Clara, and the special municipality of Isla de la Juventud, or Isle of Youth). And in all three elections, the smallest proportion of dissenters was evident in four eastern provinces: Las Tunas, Granma, Santiago de Cuba, and Guantánamo. The overall trend toward a decline in voting null or blank was evident in both National Assembly and municipal elections in the 1990s.

Cuba's Electoral Law of 1992 treated national, provincial, and municipal elections differently with regard to campaigning. Up until 1992, there was no campaigning at all for any post. At the municipal level, the "campaign" was limited to the posting of the photographs and biographies of the candidates in public places. These biographies were prepared and posted by the public authorities and could include derogatory comments about the candidates. At the provincial and national levels, provincial delegates and national deputies were chosen by the municipal assemblies. Their names were made known only after they were so chosen.

The 1992 Electoral Law did not change the procedures for municipal elections. For provincial and national elections, as already noted, one change enacted in 1992 was direct popular election—a change rendered nearly meaningless because there was no choice among candidates in the 1993 and 1998 National Assembly and provincial assembly elections.

Another change was the posting of photographs and biographies of provincial and national candidates in public places and encouraging candidates to meet voters and answer questions. Thus, since 1992, the Electoral Law has featured multi-candidate single-party elections with no effective campaigning at the municipal level and entirely uncompetitive rules but some campaigning at the provincial and national levels.

At all levels, the political regime sharply constrained the freedom of political association. Cubans were not free to associate in a political party other than the PCC to contest elections. Candidates for office in different provinces and municipalities on the official slate could not even associate into formally constituted "factions." The public authorities and the PCC retained the right to shape associational patterns at all levels.

Communist Party of Cuba

Fourth and Fifth Party Congresses

In October 1991, the Fourth Congress of the PCC met to assess the wreckage of international communism. The Soviet Union was on the verge of disintegration, and the Soviet Communist Party was rapidly losing its hold on power. The Fourth Congress declared that the collapse of the Soviet Union and the communist regimes of Europe was a "political disaster" that stemmed from avoidable mistakes, which the PCC would avoid. One consequence, according to the Fourth Congress, was the establishment of a "unipolar world" in which United States military power reigned. And one manifestation of that power was the Gulf War on Iraq, which was designed to intimidate any government daring to differ with the United States.

Thus, the Fourth Congress took heart that Cuba had been invited to the first Summit of Iberoamerican heads of government, held in Guadalajara, Mexico, months earlier, and hoped that Latin American countries would join to advance their common interests. It hailed the world's remaining communist governments, all of them in East Asia. But it reached out generally to governments everywhere in search of support. It underlined the repatriation of Cuban troops from African soil and Cuba's disposition to work within the United Nations system. It clearly sought to avoid needless trouble.

At home, the Fourth Congress affirmed its conviction that Marxism-Leninism remained its guide to the future, but it noted—for the first time in the history of these documents—that this ideology "should not be applied dogmatically." Moreover, the PCC would apply these principles taking into account Cuba's new circumstances. The Fourth Congress recognized that "the world has changed. Today the enemies of the people feel stronger than ever." But it stated its conviction that a greater strength is the "will to independence, freedom, and development of every people. The duty of every revolutionary continues to be to make the Revolution, and to defend it." Thus, the Fourth Congress proclaimed that it would make no concessions, for concessions are the path to ruin. Defiant still, Fidel Castro's government was not ready to fold.

And yet, the Fourth Congress understood that it had to adjust to the changed international circumstances. One adjustment has already been mentioned: the full repatriation of Cuban troops, mainly from Africa but also from other countries, which was completed by the time the Fourth Congress met. A more regime-changing adjustment was the reorientation of economic policy. The Fourth Congress set its own priority clearly: "The supreme objective [is] to save the Homeland, the Revolution, and Socialism." The Fourth Congress endorsed the continued use of traditional instruments, such as mass mobilizations, to produce food or address other tasks; these measures had typically been inefficient in their use of resources and often ineffective in terms of reaching their objectives, however.

In Cuba's newly dire circumstances, the Fourth Congress understood that it had to authorize changes in economic policy. It endorsed the development of an international tourism industry as a new engine of growth that, by the late 1990s, had become a crucial earner of foreign exchange (see Key Economic Sectors, ch. 3). The Fourth Congress authorized a slight liberalization of self-employment, especially in services, even though clear preference was expressed for centralization of ownership, management, and planning; such liberalization of self-employment would be implemented two years later.

More dramatically, the Fourth Congress authorized retroactively a new policy on foreign direct investment. In so doing, the Fourth Congress departed from a foundational decision at the origins of revolutionary rule in Cuba, namely, the expropriation of all foreign firms. The Fourth Congress affirmed that foreign investment should be not just tolerated but "promoted" and that considerable flexibility should govern its terms of entry.

An important social and political change had also been authorized by the PCC's Political Bureau prior to the Fourth Congress and simply ratified by it. In the "Call to the Fourth Congress," the party pledged "sincere communication with . . . members of various religious denominations who share our life and endorse our program . . . although some aspects of their ideology may differ from ours." At the Fourth Congress, PCC Statutes were changed to permit religious believers to join its ranks provided they otherwise supported the party's program.

Despite these significant changes, the main thrust of the Fourth Party Congress was to resist widespread political change. In December 1991, Carlos Aldana Escalante, PCC secretary for ideology and for international relations and Fidel Castro's principal political agent in the late 1980s and early 1990s, addressed the National Assembly. Aldana had been the only top PCC leader who had ever implied in public that he thought well of "reform communism" in Central and Eastern Europe and the Soviet Union in the 1980s. Aldana rectified his views. He denounced those who still advocated the implementation in Cuba of reforms akin to those blamed for the collapse of communist regimes in Europe. Despite his adoption of this harder line, Aldana, too, was dismissed from office for various reasons in September 1992.

In October 1997, the Fifth Congress of the PCC convened, to the general relief of its members. They had survived. Their political regime had endured. Cuba had succeeded in resisting the sharper onslaught of United States policies during the 1990s. The Cuban economy had nosedived in the early years of the decade as a consequence of the ending of Soviet subsidies and the disruption of Cuban international trade, but the economy's decline had stopped in 1994, and a modest economic recovery had begun. Cuba was the only extant communist regime outside East Asia. The forecasts of many in Washington and Miami that the Cuban regime would tumble like other communist regimes had proved off the mark. From the perspective of the leadership of the PCC, Cuba's survival was a stunning triumph.

Nonetheless, there was a cloud hovering over the party. Fidel Castro had disappeared from public view during the preceding summer months. Now he looked gaunt, having lost much weight in the interim. As if seeking to reassure the 1,500 delegates to the Fifth Congress that he was still in fine shape, Castro spoke for six hours and forty minutes. He recalled the difficult days of the early 1990s and detailed the significance of their success in overcoming those problems. The PCC, he believed, had made "acceptable concessions" in its preferred policies in order to survive. As he had said so many times during the early 1990s, Castro emphasized that he did not like the policies that he and the government and the party had been compelled to authorize, in particular the large-scale development of the tourism industry and the welcome to foreign investment. But these policies were necessary to obtain capital, technology, and access to markets, and they had already proven successful, he said.

Castro noted new sources of concern. Market-oriented policies had generated new inequalities. Crime had increased. And some of the newly preferred strategies for development, such as Basic Units of Cooperative Production (Unidades Básicas de Producción Cooperativa—UBPC), which are semi-private agricultural cooperatives, were not working well. But he praised the party's resourcefulness in overcoming the "setbacks, bitterness, and deceptions" associated with the collapse of the Soviet Union. The PCC had rallied to the defense of the regime, said Castro, and it had prevailed.

The principal debate at the Fifth Congress centered on the new economic policy of the 1990s. Successful though it had been in rescuing the Cuban economy from further catastrophes, it was very different from the preferences of many Fifth Congress delegates for a centralized command economy. Vice President Carlos Lage, the political architect of the economic reforms, admitted that prices in those food markets and restaurants where demand and supply were allowed to play freely were often well above the purchasing power of Cuban workers. But he resisted suggestions for renewed state intervention in these markets, arguing instead for further incentives to increase production. Lage warned that renewed statism would stimulate criminality and the black market. Lage also resisted a generalized salary increase; the nation could not afford it. He preached the virtues of efficiency, balanced budgets, and control of inflation. Fortunately for Lage, he was publicly backed by Fidel Castro. Castro acknowledged the problems and reiterated his dislike of these "painful remedies," but argued that current economic policies were sound.

The Fifth Congress's resolution on the economy reflected the prevailing balance of power. The Fifth Congress took note that the United States should be expected to continue its "economic war" on Cuba. Consequently, Cuba would continue to face an adverse international economic and financial environment. Therefore, the "key objective of economic policy is efficiency," provided, to be sure, that all of the changes already adopted or about to be introduced "would always be directed to preserve the socialist essence of the Revolution."

The Fifth Congress stood firm on political changes. Perhaps its aversion to change is best summarized in the title of the political resolution approved by the Fifth Congress: "The Party of Unity, Democracy, and the Human Rights That We Defend." The closing phrase of the title implied that there were some human rights that this party chose not to defend.

Political Bureau and Central Committee

Political Bureau

The PCC's Political Bureau is the party's leading decision-making institution, and Cuba's most important decision-making entity (see fig. 8). The Political Bureau meets regularly to discuss the nation's key issues. Membership on the Political Bureau best identifies Cuba's most powerful leaders. Political Bureau members typically have responsibilities in other spheres of public life as heads of key provinces, military commands, mass organizations, or major PCC posts. Three leaders have led the Political Bureau since 1965—Fidel Castro, first secretary of the PCC; Raúl Castro, second secretary of the party; and Juan Almeida, chief of the party's disciplinary commission.

From 1965 through 1980, no member was ever dropped from the Political Bureau, although its membership expanded from eight in 1965 to thirteen in 1975 and sixteen in 1980. By the time of the Third Party Congress (1986), death and voluntary and involuntary retirements had led to a six-member reduction (37 percent) from the Political Bureau's 1980 membership; meanwhile, four new members joined the bureau in 1986, leaving its membership at fourteen members.

The Fourth Party Congress (1991) witnessed the most dramatic change in membership in the Political Bureau since its founding. The Congress wanted to promote a younger and more dynamic leadership. Six of the members (43 percent) left the bureau during the Congress. Because the Political Bureau's

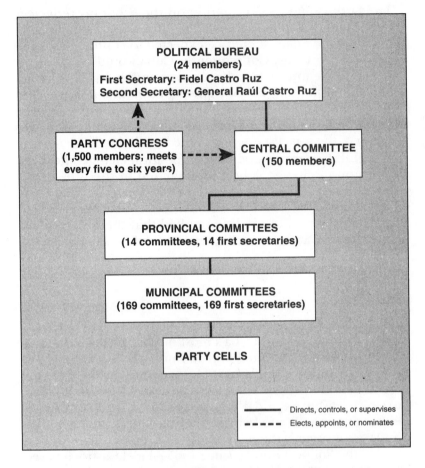

Source: Based on information from Jorge I. Domínguez; and Raimundo López, "Prela Report on PCC Membership, Percentages," October 8, 1997.

Figure 8. Organization of the Communist Party of Cuba (Partido Comunista de Cuba—PCC), 2001

size had expanded to twenty-five members, seventeen of its 1991 members (68 percent) were new—unprecedented since the party's founding in 1965. The Fifth Party Congress (1997) dropped nine members (36 percent) of the Political Bureau and added only eight new members. Thus, the Fifth Party Congress's Political Bureau (twenty-four members) suffered from less volatility than had its predecessor, as would be expected from a leadership that felt more politically secure.

By the conclusion of the Fifth Congress, only the Castro brothers and Almeida had served continuously on the Political Bureau since 1965, and only José Ramón Machado, party organization secretary, had been a member since 1975. The next two longest-serving members, both since 1986, were Army Corps General Abelardo Colomé Ibarra, minister of interior, and Esteban Lazo, who had served at various times as party provincial secretary in Matanzas, Santiago de Cuba, and Ciudad de La Habana Province.

In sum, only six of the twenty-four members of the 1997 Political Bureau had been members of Cuba's top decision-making organ before the collapse of the Berlin Wall in 1989. Cuba's top leadership, therefore, has already undergone an important transition at the levels just below the Castro brothers and their closest associates. Most Political Bureau members in the 1990s are themselves the product of a transition that took place under the communist political system. They do not count on Soviet subsidies. They do not count on external military support. They do not expect to be engaged in military or other foreign expeditions. They are much readier to experiment at home with various economic policy changes. They are younger. The median birth year of the 1997 Political Bureau was 1943; six were born after the assault on the Moncada barracks on July 26, 1953. They expect to have a political future in Cuba regardless of the name of the nation's president or the form of its political regime. The transition among Cuba's political elite is already underway.

In 1991 three women belonged to the twenty-five-member Political Bureau; that number dropped to two in 1997. In 1991 four military officers on active duty belonged to the Political Bureau; that number rose to five in 1997. In 1991 five of the provincial first secretaries belonged to the Political Bureau; that number rose to six in 1997. The post of provincial first secretary is perhaps Cuba's most challenging position, for all subnational responsibilities fall on the persons occupying these posts. Not surprisingly, three of the five provincial first secretaries from 1991 were dropped from the Political Bureau to be replaced by others. In the judgment of their superiors, the dismissed first secretaries were poor managers.

In contrast to previous decades, in 1991 Carlos Lage, secretary of the Executive Committee of the Council of Ministers, was the only civilian minister on the Political Bureau. The PCC leadership clearly understood that its problem in 1991 was eminently political: how to survive the collapse of European communism and retain the support, or at least the forbearance, of the Cuban people. By 1997 three of the Political Bureau members first chosen at the previous party congress had switched jobs to become government ministers: Alfredo Jordán Morales, minister of agriculture; Abel Prieto Jiménez, minister of culture; and Roberto Robaina González, minister of foreign relations. They were joined by Marcos Portal León, minister of basic industries. Division General Ulises Rosales del Toro became minister of the sugar industry, although he remained formally on active military duty. In 1997, with six out of twenty-four Political Bureau members serving also as members of the cabinet (along with FAR Minister General Raúl Castro, Interior Minister Army Corps General Abelardo Colomé, and President Fidel Castro), the PCC leadership signaled a higher priority for improving the tasks of governance and in particular the economy's performance.

Central Committee

The PCC's Central Committee, a much larger group than the Political Bureau, is made up of many key leaders from intermediate levels of responsibility. The Central Committee met infrequently in the late 1960s; for the most part, it convened only in times of crisis. The committee met more regularly in the 1970s and 1980s; the original party statutes called for a meeting of the Central Committee Plenum approximately every six months to enable the Central Committee to have an impact on major decisions. The party statutes in place since the 1997 party congress stipulate a plenum meeting at least once a year.

The history of membership on the Central Committee resembles that of the Political Bureau. The 1975 First Party Congress reelected 77 percent of the 100 founding members of the 1965 Central Committee. The 1980 Second Party Congress reelected 79 percent of the 1975 full members still active in 1980; the size of the committee had expanded to 148 in 1980. The 1986 Third Party Congress reelected 61 percent. The lower rate of continuity in 1986 parallels what was happening at the Political Bureau. The size of the Central Committee remained stable at 146.

In 1991 the Fourth Party Congress removed half of the members of the old Central Committee, and it expanded the size of the new Central Committee to 225. Consequently, only 32 percent of the new Central Committee members had served on the previous committee. Not only was the rate of continuity the lowest since the Central Committee had been founded, but the proportion of newcomers was the highest since the PCC's founding.

The Fifth Party Congress stabilized membership on the Central Committee just as it had done for the Political Bureau. The expansion of the size of the Central Committee in 1991 had been a temporary experiment that the Fifth Party Congress reversed in 1997. The size of the Central Committee shrank to 150 members, and 56 percent of the members of the 1991 Central Committee were dismissed. The 1997 Central Committee's veterans from 1991 constituted, however, two-thirds of the membership of the new Central Committee, and accordingly the new body was far more experienced than its predecessor.

The oversized and inexperienced Central Committee in place between 1991 and 1997 was the least important Central Committee since the late 1960s. Then, as in most of the 1990s, the Central Committee met rarely—in the 1990s less often than expected from the party statutes. Moreover, although the party statutes mandate a PCC congress every five years, the Fourth Party Congress met nearly six years after its predecessor. The Fifth Congress met a full year late. In general, the Central Committee's excessive size, inexperience, and infrequency of meetings in the 1990s marked a process of party de-institutionalization that the Fifth Congress sought to reverse, hence the reduction in size and the renewed premium on experience. One result of these processes, however, was to install and sustain a Central Committee that was younger than its predecessors in the 1970s and 1980s. The Political Bureau and the Central Committee finished the century with a young and energetic leadership, steeled in Cuba's troubled life in the 1990s, ready for political competition with any challenger.

The Central Committee chosen at the Fifth Party Congress has an additional characteristic: 36 percent of its members have posts only in the PCC and its youth wing, the Union of Young Communists (Unión de Jóvenes Comunistas—UJC). This Central Committee is full of municipal party first secretaries, not just first secretaries at the level of provinces or on the staff of national party headquarters. This Central Committee represents the party elite better than its predecessors. It is much less a mere assembly of those who have performed meritorious service in various spheres of life. It is no longer broadly representative of Cuban society and institutions. Its members seek to rule.

Party Organization, Membership, and Role

Formally, the PCC is governed by its party congresses. These adopt the party's statutes and its programs, and choose the membership of the Central Committee and Political Bureau. Party congresses are to meet every five years, the Central Committee Plenum every year, and the Political Bureau once a week. In practice, as already noted, the Political Bureau is the party's most important entity and the only one whose actual power corresponds to the formal organization.

Party structure was simplified in the 1990s. The post of "alternate" for various posts (including Political Bureau and Central Committee member) was eliminated. The party Secretariat is no longer a separate body but simply the party's staff at various levels. The party's subnational organization matches the number of provinces and municipalities. The most rapidly replaced significant party post is that of provincial secretary; that job requires mediation between the demands of the center and the localities and is difficult to perform.

The PCC is a party of selection. Not everyone who wishes to belong to the party has the right to join it, although all party members must seek to be a member. Party members are chosen through a complex process. First, all candidates for party membership must be chosen as "exemplary workers" at assemblies held at their workplace. Then, a party commission in charge of membership scrutinizes each candidacy and is empowered to reject any and all. A variant on this procedure is through membership in the UJC, the party's youth wing. Ordinarily, the party hopes that UJC members will, in due course, also be chosen as exemplary workers, but the party commissions can bypass such procedures.

Concerned that party membership might drop in Cuba in the 1990s as it had in formerly communist Europe in the late 1980s, the Fourth Party Congress liberalized membership procedures in two ways. First, it eliminated all discrimination against religious believers; the party no longer required a person to be an atheist or an agnostic to qualify for membership. Second, the probation time for young UJC members to be eligible for party membership was cut from three to two years. As a result, in the 1990s party membership grew on average some 46,000 persons per year, compared with an annual member-

Havana Headquarters of the Union of Young Communists (Unión
de Jóvenes Comunistas—UJC), 1997
Courtesy Mark P. Sullivan

ship growth of only about 27,000 persons in the 1980s. Party
membership grew to 800,000 members by the time of the Fifth
Party Congress in 1997 out of a population of about eleven million people. In 1997 about 30 percent of the members had
joined during the 1990s. Workers constituted about one-third
of the entire party membership. Another half-million belonged
to the UJC.

The PCC's manner of filling public offices differs from how
political parties elsewhere in the world go about this pursuit.
Elected public offices wield relatively modest power in Cuba.
The National Assembly meets infrequently and has limited
powers. Provincial and municipal assemblies have limited
resources to carry on with their tasks. Although the PCC
screens who is elected to these offices, it focuses its attention
on appointed offices that wield significant power. The PCC
commission at the appropriate level must clear and endorse
every officeholder for such posts prior to appointment. Heads
of central government agencies, state enterprises, hospitals,
military commands, and so forth must all be cleared and

endorsed. This type of control is the party's principal source of power.

PCC officials, especially at the subnational level, also play key roles as problem solvers and coordinators. When difficulties arise in a province or a municipality, the party first secretary is often the only person well positioned to appeal through the party hierarchy for additional support or resources from Havana. The party first secretary in the provinces and the municipalities functions also as an arbiter in disputes that may arise in various spheres of life. More controversially, the party municipal or provincial secretary often assumes the responsibility of breaking a national policy directive on the grounds that local conditions are not propitious. This last role implies that party provincial and municipal secretaries are, in some instances, high risk-takers, but it also explains why provincial first secretaries are vulnerable to dismissal.

The PCC organs are loci for discussion and debate over national, sectoral, provincial, or municipal policies. Although the Central Committee had become less representative of Cuban society by the late 1990s, PCC cells (the party's lowest units) and various assemblies often congregate leaders from various spheres of life effectively. These fora provide opportunities to clear the air in a heated dispute and to review, understand, and influence decisions issued from on high.

The party generally orients policies at various levels and with varying degrees of specificity. In contrast to previous decades, in the 1990s the party's national staff became smaller, and party officials were instructed to interfere less in the routine running of government agencies, state enterprises, and social service entities. The party in the 1990s retained its key tasks, as outlined above, but withdrew in many cases from becoming a substitute policy executor. This behavior was consistent with turning the party into, and using it, as a political machine.

Mass Organizations

Three of Cuba's principal mass organizations were founded shortly after revolutionary victory, between late 1959 and 1961. The Federation of Cuban Women (FMC) groups women members, as might be expected. The National Association of Small Farmers (ANAP) brings together smallholders regardless of their crops of specialization. Following the 1963 agrarian reform, many such private smallholders remained. Some cultivated plots on their own or with their families; others did so as members of cooperatives. All belonged to the ANAP. The Committees for the Defense of the Revolution (CDRs) were established in every neighborhood to uncover plots against the government. "Revolutionary vigilance" was their main task. The CDRs were also responsible for rooting out common crime and, from time to time, collaborated in such activities as mass vaccination campaigns, garbage recycling, park clean-ups, and the like.

The fourth mass organization is much older: the Cuban Workers Federation (CTC) was founded in the 1930s. The CTC groups all Cubans who are gainfully employed. It is organized into federations according to sectors of economic activity, not according to professional categories or trades. The CTC has a presence in every work center, and it and the ANAP often substitute for government agencies in dispute resolution.

From the 1960s to the 1980s, these mass organizations were means by which the government and the PCC implemented policies and monitored the population. The moment of highest recognition of their role came at the Second Party Congress in 1980, when all four heads of the mass organizations became alternate members of the party's Political Bureau.

By the 1980s, however, the capacities of the mass organizations had begun to weaken. Consider the ANAP. One of the top national objectives in the rural sector was to promote Agricultural-Livestock Cooperatives (Cooperativas de Producción Agropecuaria—CPAs); the national leadership thought it more rational for smallholders to pool their resources. CPA membership jumped from 9,103 in 1978 to 82,611 in 1983, but by 1990 membership had dropped to 62,130. The number of hectares in CPAs peaked in 1986; after this high point, the organizations lost nearly a fifth of their pooled land.

A generalized weakening of the capacity of the various mass organizations became evident in the late 1980s. PCC leaders, worried that these longstanding means of control were breaking down, took decisive action in the early 1990s by replacing the leaders of three mass organizations. Thus, Orlando Lugo Fonte replaced José Ramírez Cruz, the longtime ANAP president; Juan Contino replaced Armando Acosta Cordero, the longtime national coordinator of the CDRs; and Pedro Ross Leal replaced the longtime CTC secretary-general, Roberto Veiga Menéndez. Lugo Fonte and Contino joined the PCC Central Committee in 1991; Ross Leal was elevated to the Political Bureau that same year.

Vilma Espín founded the FMC and has remained its only president. She is Raúl Castro's wife, Fidel's sister-in-law. Espín was promoted to alternate member of the Political Bureau in 1980 and to full Political Bureau membership in 1986. In 1991 she became a member of the Central Committee but remained as FMC president.

Notwithstanding these attempts to reinvigorate the mass organizations, primarily through new leadership, the FMC, the CDRs, and the ANAP remain weaker than in decades past in terms of representing and mobilizing the population. The CDRs hit bottom in the early 1990s; in the mid-1990s, they responded to their reduced capacity by concentrating on some strategic tasks where they are still capable of delivering important support for the political regime. For example, the CDRs came to play an important role in Cuba's electoral process in the 1990s. (As the 1990s closed, the CDRs counted 7.5 million people on their membership rolls.) During the 1998 National Assembly elections, the CDRs campaigned steadily and massively on behalf of a vote for the single official slate; they combated both blank voting and the process of voting selectively for some but not all candidates on the official ballot. On election day, the CDRs visited some homes repeatedly to ensure the highest possible turnout. The CDRs were literally an arm of the PCC working to achieve the desired electoral results.

The CTC, in contrast, found a new, albeit still limited, role in the 1990s: defending the interests of workers in some respects and questioning some of the recommendations of government technocrats. In this latter stance, the CTC differed from its prior role of just helping the government implement its objectives. In the 1990s, labor unions, for example, delayed legislation that would have forced recalcitrant workers to relocate to other jobs. As a result, Cuban state firms remained overstaffed and inefficient, but the government was spared from political protest and overt unemployment remained relatively low. Unions also resisted stricter sanctions against labor absenteeism (thus making it easier for workers to moonlight as self-employed), and fought off linking wages to productivity. The CTC also spoke out in late 1993 when the government adopted some of its most far-reaching economic reforms and, spurred by Finance Minister José Luis Rodríguez García, the government's leading technocrat, began to consider whether to impose taxes on self-employed and salaried workers. The CTC opposed the imposition of taxes on the payrolls of salaried workers and supported a nationwide discussion of the proposed measures in "workers' parliaments" during the first half of 1994. In the end, taxes were imposed on self-employed but not on salaried workers (see Tax Reform, ch. 3).

The changes that took place in the 1990s increased the CTC's autonomy from the state and imbued it with some claims to represent the interests of state workers. This new political role, of course, came at the expense of delaying or impeding economic reform, but it no doubt made the CTC more important. During this period, the CDRs, on the other hand, became even more closely connected to the PCC's partisan interests. The ANAP and the FMC have yet to find an effective new role.

Civil Organizations

Religion and the State

The Cuban state is secular, according to the constitution. In fact, in the 1960s government policy was designed to weaken the Roman Catholic Church and other forms of organized religious behavior, while respecting "freedom of religion" at its narrowest level: Cubans remained free to worship. Active churchgoers and their children, however, risked being discriminated against when applying to selective schools and the university and when seeking promotions in the workplace. The PCC was formally atheist until 1991, and membership in the party was often a prerequisite for jobs carrying significant responsibilities. Therefore, the Cuban leadership's decision to drop atheism as a formal requirement for party membership in 1991 and, more generally, in the 1990s to discontinue the active campaigns against organized religion were significant decisions with broad impact.

In fact, Cuba witnessed a religious revival in many faiths in the 1990s. The revival began from a fairly low baseline. A large survey (N=3105, with N meaning the size of the random poll sample) conducted in the early 1990s by Cuba's Center for Psychological and Sociological Research (Centro de Investigaciones Psicológicas y Sociológicas—CIPS) showed that 65 percent of respondents believed in the possibility of magical cures while 43 percent thought well of burial ceremonies. But only 17 percent approved of baptisms, only 6 percent attended religious services, and only 2 percent admitted to belonging to a religious grouping. In 1997 a Cuban government survey showed that more than four-fifths of Cubans believed in something transcendent, while 15 percent admitted to belonging to a religious grouping.

Although its social base of support remains modest, the Roman Catholic Church is Cuba's most hierarchically organized community of faith (see Roman Catholic Church, ch. 2). The rebuilding of the Roman Catholic Church in Cuba began in the mid-1980s in preparation for the 1986 Roman Catholic Congress, the first to be held since 1959. Congress participants reviewed the situation of the church in Cuba, through history and in the present. They formulated broad recommendations for pastoral action and provided the first sustained critique of aspects of Cuban government policy. The final document issued by the Congress complained of discrimination in job promotions suffered by Roman Catholics, criticized official atheism, and called attention to "moral deficiencies" in contemporary Cuba, including "duplicity, mendacity, fraud."

In the early 1990s, Roman Catholic bishops criticized the government and party policies more sharply. The bishops issued their pastoral letter, "Love Hopes All Things," on September 8, 1993, the feast of Our Lady of Charity of Cobre, Cuba's patroness, and coincidentally the grimmest moment in Cuba's sharp economic collapse of the early 1990s. The bishops developed several controversial themes that would resurface during the pope's visit in January 1998. In 1993 the bishops claimed the right to speak to all Cubans, including politicians. "We bishops of Cuba," they added, "reject any kind of measure that in order to punish the Cuban government serves to aggravate the problems of our people," specifically mentioning the United States embargo and other sanctions on Cuba. The bishops criticized official practice "that leads to identifying terms that cannot be made synonymous, such as *homeland* and *socialism . . . Cuban* and *revolutionary.*" They chided the authorities for limiting freedoms, for "excessive surveillance by the state security agencies that even extends into the strictly private life of individuals." They lamented the "high number of prisoners being held," including those "being punished for economic or political reasons . . . ."

In November 1996, President Fidel Castro visited Pope John Paul II at the Vatican and invited him to visit Cuba. The Roman Catholic bishops had first invited the pope in 1989, and informal discussions had been underway since earlier in the 1980s, but the Cuban government had delayed issuing its own invitation. In preparation for the papal visit that took place in Janu-

*On the occasion of the June 29, 1997, open-air mass held in
Havana, the first in almost four decades, a sign advertises
the upcoming January 1998 visit of Pope John Paul II.
Courtesy Mark P. Sullivan*

ary 1998, the first ever to Cuba by a pope, church and state
negotiated extensively. The Cuban government agreed to permit outdoor masses, not limiting them just to the period of the
pope's visit, and authorized religious processions outside
church buildings. In addition, in December 1997, Christmas
Day became an official holiday for the first time since 1969.
The Cuban mass media covered some of the preparation for
the pope's visit, and during the visit radio and television broadcast all public events live. Cardinal Jaime Ortega, archbishop of
Havana, was given a half-hour of free television time shortly
before the pope's visit to explain the meaning and significance
of the forthcoming events. The government also allowed thousands of international pilgrims, including Cuban-Americans, to
visit Cuba for the duration of the visit, and allowed the church
to import paper and other materials to publish necessary information.

Because the pope's visit took place well after a process of
social and religious change had begun, his visit may have a
longer-lasting impact on Cuban society and politics than if it

had taken place without such prior changes. Thus, the papal visit may be a catalyst or an accelerator of further changes. The Roman Catholic church in Cuba has begun to behave like its brethren in former communist countries or in former Latin American dictatorships. Some parishes sponsor book or film clubs, or other groups to discuss issues of common concern, not just exclusively religious issues. Several dioceses also publish magazines that cover a wide array of topics, not just those of religious significance. For example, the Havana archdiocesan magazine *Palabra Nueva* often publishes articles that assess and criticize government economic policy. *Vitral*, the magazine of the diocese of Pinar del Río, has been the boldest in challenging aspects of government policy.

It is difficult to assess the relative size of Cuba's various communities of faith. Nonetheless, both before the Revolution and in the 1990s it is likely that the largest such community is heir to Cuba's Afro-Cuban religious traditions. *Santería, regla de palo*, spiritualism, and other forms of Afro-Cuban religiosity command significant popular allegiance, probably more than Roman Catholicism. The already mentioned large survey from the early 1990s, for example, suggests strong support for beliefs and practices often associated with Afro-Cuban practices. According to the survey, more Cubans believed in the worth of consulting a *babalao* (an Afro-Cuban religious leader) than a priest. In the western provinces, Roman Catholic Church attendance once a month reached 20 percent by late 1994, but, even after the pope's visit in 1998, consistent weekly church attendance nationwide was only about 3 percent, although the proportion was much higher in Havana than in eastern Cuba.

During the 1990s, evangelical Protestantism reportedly grew rapidly in Cuba, as was the case elsewhere in Latin America and in former communist Europe. More traditional forms of Protestantism did not grow much, however. To the extent that religious belief and behavior remained a form of distancing oneself from the government and the PCC, then the fact that other forms of religiosity grew faster than mainstream Protestantism could be explained in political terms: Cubans were unwilling to join those communities of faith perceived as too close to the political regime, and some Protestant pastors from mainline Protestant faiths had agreed to serve on the government's single official slate for National Assembly elections.

Cuba also has a small Jewish community but no resident rabbi, although one or two are in training and rabbis from the

United States visit Cuba for services on holy days. The Jewish community has also grown, as older and younger Jews have sought to explore their religious tradition. (Some Jews, however, have used this reactivation of their community links as a means to emigrate to Israel. If they are active members of a Temple, Jews have found it more likely that Israel will accept them as immigrants and that the Cuban government will permit their emigration.)

Nongovernmental Organizations

Cuba's most important nonreligious nongovernmental organizations (NGOs) are often government operated nongovernmental organizations (GONGOs). This is the case for two reasons. The nature and extent of government and PCC control over Cuban society and political life have been very extensive. The principal forms of societal organization, for example, have been the mass organizations, already discussed. By the late 1970s and thereafter, however, the government and party found it useful to establish organizations with a greater margin of autonomy. In the 1990s, one additional motivation was that GONGOs could more readily obtain international assistance from NGOs in Western Europe and Canada.

There are many examples of GONGOs. They include sports clubs; environmental organizations; a Cuban variant of a national rifle association; professional associations of lawyers, economists, engineers, and so forth; as well as many intellectual and scientific organizations, including think tanks. The think tanks focused on political, economic, and social analysis, were founded directly by the PCC, and followed its guidelines fairly closely through the 1980s. The Center for the Study of the World Economy (Centro de Investigaciones de la Economía Mundial—CIEM), for example, conducted research principally on the Soviet Union and East European communist countries until their collapse, but also on the Cuban economy. The director and deputy director of the CIEM, Oswaldo Martínez and José Luis Rodríguez, respectively, successively held the post of minister of economy in the 1990s. In the mid-1990s, more than one-half of the publications produced by the CIPS (Center for Psychological and Sociological Research) were classified for the use of government and party officials, not for wider academic circulation.

In the mid-1990s, the most notable GONGO was the Center for American Studies (Centro de Estudios sobre América—

CEA). Founded in the late 1970s by the PCC to generate information and analysis about the United States, Canada, and Latin America, the CEA, by the early 1990s, was strikingly independent in the development of its work while remaining well connected to some high-ranking government and party officials. Central Committee members and staff, National Assembly leaders and staff, and ministers of government solicited the work of CEA staff and at times attended CEA workshops and conferences.

In the early 1990s, CEA economists working on Cuba distinguished themselves by the originality of their thought and their willingness to venture past the officially established canon for discussion of economic policy. One CEA-produced book, *Cuba: La restructuración de la economía, una propuesta para el debate*, provides a searching diagnosis and critique of Cuba's economic circumstances and proposes economic policies different from those the government was then pursuing. The CEA economists wished to accelerate the use of market incentives and instruments, although still within a socialist framework. The CEA sociologists and political scientists had also been working on domestic Cuban politics and society. In the spring of 1994, they held a conference to assess the quality of Cuban democracy. In that conference and in the resulting book that was published in 1995, some foreign authors were included as well. The publication of these two CEA books, however, alarmed some within the leadership.

In March 1996, Raúl Castro, minister of the FAR, read a wide-ranging report on behalf of the Political Bureau to the Fifth Plenum of the Central Committee. One part of the text sharply criticized the CEA, accusing its academics of parroting the line of United States scholars on Cuba and, more generally, of serving United States interests and undermining revolutionary ideology. There followed an investigation led by José Ramón Balaguer Cabrera, party secretary for ideology. The terms of the investigation resembled a witch hunt. The CEA senior staff held together, however, insisting that they were good revolutionaries and good communists. (The United States government from time to time had denied CEA academics visas to enter the United States precisely for these reasons.) Although they "confessed" to minor issues (for example, something could have been done better), they held firm in defense of their substantive ideas and professions of loyalty. In the end, although they had to leave the CEA (the institution became a

A view of Havana from Fort Spain (Fortaleza La España)
Courtesy Danielle Hayes, United Nations Development Programme

pale shadow of its former self), each of the senior academics at first found employment that, for the most part, permitted the continuation of much of their academic research. None was immediately expelled from the PCC. The survival of the CEA academics depended greatly on the expression of international support by scholars and governments in many countries that had come to value CEA researchers.

NGOs, no matter what their origin might have been, create spaces between state and society, between ruling party and private citizens. Such an occurrence has been an aspect of the Cuban experience in the 1990s. The CEA case is instructive because the CEA was able to resist more effectively than would have been the case in Cuba in previous decades.

Human Rights and Opposition Groups

It is not news that the Cuban government harasses or jails human rights activists and groups as well as the political opposition. The news in the 1990s was that the government was no longer succeeding in its repression. Since the defeat and destruction of violent counterrevolutionary forces in the mid-1960s, the government has not feared violent opposition. But, beginning slowly and haltingly in the late 1970s and gathering steam in the 1980s, a human rights movement finally blossomed in Cuba in the 1990s.

In the 1990s, when the government jailed human rights activists or opposition political leaders or destroyed some of their organizations, others, hitherto unknown, replaced them. Thus, the work of these groups has continued even if the faces and names of the people and organizations have changed.

A high-water mark for human rights groups was reached in 1995–96. On October 10, 1995 (the anniversary of the beginning of Cuba's first war of independence), an organization called the Cuban Council (Concilio Cubano) was founded. The Concilio was an attempt by some 140 small, unofficial opposition groups to coalesce around a minimal program. The Concilio's aims were a general amnesty for all political prisoners, full respect for the present constitution and fundamental laws, a call on the Cuban government to fulfill its obligations to respect human rights under the United Nations Charter, a demand for freedom of economic organization, and a call for free and direct elections on the basis of the pluralist nature of society.

In November 1995, the Concilio reaffirmed its commitment to use only peaceful means to achieve its aims. In short, the Concilio respected the country's constitution and legal framework while demanding changes within them. In December the Concilio formally asked the government for permission to hold a large gathering on February 24, 1996 (the anniversary of the beginning of Cuba's last war of independence). On February 15, however, the government launched a wave of repression against Concilio leaders and members; the next day it banned the gathering. The Concilio's principal leader and national delegate, Leonel Morejón, served a prison term for his role in the organization; several others were jailed as well.

The Concilio Cubano episode was noteworthy because it was the largest and most ambitious attempt to consolidate human rights and opposition groups. Throughout the 1990s, the repression of human rights and opposition activity and the rebirth in due course were a recurring pattern. In the late 1990s, human rights and opposition activists founded new groups, some of which created new, smaller coalitions. The government again resorted to repression, and the activists and oppositionists rebounded as well.

As in decades past, in the 1990s the government responded to opposition efforts by forcing some activists into exile and sometimes, in effect, deporting them. One means of assuring political stability since 1959 has been the government's export of its opposition. Many Concilio Cubano leaders and members went into exile after the 1996 crackdown, for example. The government often releases political prisoners only on the condition that they emigrate.

Mass Media

In the 1990s, as in decades past, the state owned and operated all mass media, except for publications of the Roman Catholic Church. Because of the high cost of importing newsprint, in the early 1990s the government sharply cut back on the publication of newspapers and magazines. Many journals and magazines were shut down; the circulation of newspapers was cut back.

The principal daily newspaper is *Granma*, official organ of the PCC. *Granma* reads like a collection of press releases. It often publishes the full texts of official speeches and is generally devoid of editorial or substantive variety. In the late 1990s, it resumed occasional publication of abbreviated "letters to the editor" along with responses to them, thereby providing a glimpse of how official Cuba addresses popular questions. *Juventud Rebelde* is the official organ of the UJC (Communist Youth Union). In the 1990s, it changed from a daily to a weekly. It is likely to feature opinion pieces that provide a slightly wider range of political and social commentary. *Bohemia* is a newsmagazine of long standing that at times presents investigative reporting of problems that government leaders wish to bring to light.

By the end of the 1950s, Cuba had an impressive nationwide network of television broadcast companies and television sets. Fidel Castro employed television extensively in 1959 and thereafter to communicate his vision and his policies to the Cuban people. The Cuban Revolution was the first revolution whose leaders made extensive use of television. In the 1990s, however, the costs of production for television led the government to reduce the number of channels and of hours of transmission. Nonetheless, television remains the principal source of communication for entertainment and news.

In the 1990s, however, radio, a lower-cost alternative to print or television media, became the more dynamic mass medium. Moreover, the Cuban government's response to the United States-sponsored Radio Martí Program led to wider freedom of programming for radio. Consequently, Cuban radio engages in investigative reporting of various misdeeds, ranging from stores that do not open when they should or that sell shoddy merchandise, to incidents of crime and corruption. Live talk shows urge listeners to call in with their questions and complaints. Some radio programs broadcast internationally popular music, instead of the establishment revolutionary or "solidarity" music favored by official Cuba. In 1993, for example, Radio Taíno was revamped to broadcast with the characteristics of commercial-style radio. It featured contemporary Cuban and international Latin dance music, and it carried advertising from foreign firms operating in Cuba.

In the 1990s, the Roman Catholic Church was allowed to accept donations to import materials and equipment to publish the texts necessary for the liturgy and to publish magazines of substantial circulation. As already mentioned, several archdioceses publish magazines and other limited-circulation publications. The most important one, *Palabra Nueva*, sponsored by the Archdiocese of Havana, features articles on religious themes, but it has also published regularly on economics and social issues, at times diverging significantly and critically from government policies.

Political Processes

Emerging Political Leaders

Cuba's political processes at the start of the twenty-first century were more complex than in decades past. President Fidel Castro remained at the pinnacle of power. Although aging (he was born in 1926) and less healthy than in prior years, his energy and talents remained extraordinary. He could still deliver multi-hour speeches with few notes; and he still kept the hours of a night owl, insisting on seeing foreign leaders at midnight or thereafter when the latter were exhausted and he was in his prime. Castro is still thoughtful, eloquent, inspiring, decisive, and charming. He is also ruthless, brutal, intolerant, egomaniacal, and manipulative. These and other traits make him a politician who is revered and feared, admired and loathed, but whom none take lightly.

Fidel's slightly younger brother Raúl Castro (born in 1931), the FAR minister, is the designated successor. Raúl Castro lacks the more attractive qualities of his brother's public personality, but he has inspired respect and loyalty among subordinates for

*A view of downtown Havana (Old Havana), including the
National Capitol (Capitolio Nacional), 1996
Courtesy National Imagery and Mapping Agency, Washington*

his painstaking and effective construction of Cuba's armed
forces. Although no longer a formidable force, the FAR won
the wars that it fought twice in Angola against South African
invasions (1975–76, 1987–88) and once on Ethiopian soil
against Somalia's invasion (1977–78).

Other important political leaders will most likely continue to
play a role in Cuba's future politics. PCC Organization Secretary José Ramón Machado was a winner in the composition of
the Central Committee chosen at the Fifth Party Congress and
positioned himself well for the future. Army Corps General
Abelardo Colomé, "Hero of the Republic of Cuba" for his combat service in overseas wars, rose through a professional career
in the army and in the late 1980s became interior minister.
National Assembly President Ricardo Alarcón revitalized
Cuba's parliament and, to some degree, political life by reaching out to a wider number of loyal "revolutionary" Cubans who
were not necessarily PCC cadres. Alarcón has remained the
government's chief of relations with the United States. Esteban
Lazo Hernández is the party's expert on subnational government, having served as first party secretary in more provinces
(including La Habana) than anyone else. Lazo (born in 1944)

is the Afro-Cuban who best combines relative youth and significant experience at the top of the leadership. Carlos Lage, vice president of the Council of State, heads the economic cabinet and, backed by Minister of Economy and Planning José Luis Rodríguez García, was the political architect of Cuba's economic reforms of the 1990s. Younger than these others, Lage portrays on national television and in person an image of quiet competence and candor. Also playing political roles wider than their ministerial portfolios imply are Culture Minister Abel Prieto, Division General and Sugar Industry Minister Ulises Rosales del Toro, and Basic Industries Minister Marcos Portal. Portal in particular was the champion of more efficient administrators in state enterprises.

In the 1990s, unlike the 1960s, Cuba had no clearly identifiable "factions" within the party, but it has witnessed varying currents of opinion. These combine and overlap. In general, PCC cadres and Secretary Machado tend to oppose most economic, political, and religious reforms. Leading military and internal security officers in contrast, favor various market reforms. FAR Minister Raúl Castro, for example, took the lead in 1994 to advocate market reforms in agriculture, contrary to what had been Fidel Castro's position. The Ministry of Interior, too, favors economic reforms to decriminalize activities that would otherwise occur illegally; ministry officials believe that they have tougher enemies to fight than parents seeking milk for their children. Vice President Lage and National Assembly President Alarcón, among others, have been more willing than other national leaders to support the various economic and political experiments that took place in the 1990s.

Political Aspects of the Security and Military Forces

Cuban state security remains effective in many ways. In the summer of 1994, it controlled and suffocated with a professional use of force a large riot that took place in downtown Havana, as thousands of Cubans protested the use of force against those seeking to emigrate without prior lawful authorization. Cuban leaders quietly pointed out that the People's Liberation Army of the People's Republic of China used massive force in Tiananmen Square, Beijing, in 1989 to put down protests. The Cuban military was not called in to put down this riot, however, because internal security forces handled the incident effectively, with restrained use of force. Internal security forces also effectively suppressed illegal job actions and attempted strikes at various moments in the 1990s.

Politically, several factors are noteworthy about the FAR. Most Cuban military officers are also PCC members. In the 1990s, military officers on active duty constituted a consistent fifth of the membership of the party's Political Bureau. Two of the key members of the Political Bureau were Generals Raúl Castro and Abelardo Colomé. And, after the 1997 Fifth Party Congress, the military represented 17 percent of the membership of the party's Central Committee, continuing a slide evident over the decades but retaining significant clout (see also The Military in the Government and Party, ch. 5).

In the 1990s, the FAR became a pale shadow of its former self, as regards combat readiness and effectiveness. Cuba stopped receiving weaponry free of charge from the Soviet Union at the beginning of the decade, and it could not afford to import sufficient new equipment or even spare parts. As a result, the FAR had to reduce the frequency and scope of its military exercises. Its size shrank greatly, downsizing to not more than 65,000 regular troops. From 1989 to 1997, the size of the military and internal security budget (in pesos) was cut by 45 percent. The leadership's downsizing of the FAR was a major political and budgetary contribution to any future government of Cuba.

To facilitate the demobilization of personnel and to supplement the meager peso-denominated pensions, the government created semi-private companies (they operate as private companies, but the state is the sole shareholder) to employ former officers. The military-run tourist firm Gaviota is one example; many of its taxi drivers, former military officers, are paid in dollars by tourists. However, military officers on active duty are prohibited from moonlighting and discouraged from receiving funds from their overseas relatives. As a result, the standard of living of military officers dropped appreciably relative to other Cubans who enjoyed lawful access to self-employment or to dollar remittances. Some officers moonlighted, nonetheless, and in so doing broke the law they were sworn to uphold.

The Widening of Public Space

The most notable change in elite political processes in the 1990s was that some disputes could no longer be resolved just in private as had hitherto been quite common. In the 1990s, some disputes became quite public. The new Foreign Investment Law 77 of 1995 was vigorously debated and its approval consequently delayed. Another publicly debated case, that relating to the imposition of payroll taxes, was the first instance in which an economic initiative advocated by the leadership was defeated. Fidel Castro's need to explain and defend publicly his invitation to Pope John Paul II both at the Fifth Party Congress and in the days prior to the pope's arrival was yet another example.

The widening of public space was most closely associated, however, with the weakening of the government's control. The boom of illegal markets in the 1990s, discussed in previous chapters, is the best example of weakened control. The government had been an intrusive micromanager of economic life, shaping the work place and earnings decisions and outcomes for every Cuban. In the 1990s, that changed. Lawfully or not, many Cubans took hold of their economic lives and became largely independent of the state for their livelihood. Given the context of past decades, this was a major political change, not just an economic change.

Moreover, President Fidel Castro repeatedly made it clear that he detested authorizing the limited market-oriented policies that he felt compelled to authorize in the 1990s to ensure his government's survival. For Cubans long-accustomed to a ruler who had governed with vast discretion, this, too, was a stunning political change. Fidel Castro could no longer govern his way.

Human rights and opposition activists understood this new modest but nonetheless real opening. Each of them might suffer repression, abuse, or imprisonment, but they were newly confident that others would pick up their fallen standard to continue to press for wider spaces for democratic liberties. Cuba's government could no longer prevail even in the one area that had always mattered the most, namely, the capacity to eliminate all organized opposition.

The academics associated with the Center for American Studies (CEA) did not consider themselves dissidents or oppositionists but loyal PCC members; nonetheless, the party leadership came down hard on them. And yet, these academics resisted, as well, in ways unlike in the past. They did not break ranks. They did not betray each other. And, to a surprising degree, they succeeded in continuing at least some aspects of their academic work.

"Do not be afraid," said Pope John Paul II during his visit to Cuba in January 1998. Posters with the pope's photograph, plastered all over the country, reiterated this fundamental message. Cubans took the pope's message to heart in their participation in the events associated with his visit. The pope's pilgrimage to Cuba, as already noted, was likely to have some lasting impact because it rode the crest of a wave of renewed interest in religiosity.

The political attitudes of Cubans also changed. In the spring of 1990, Cuba's newsmagazine *Bohemia* conducted a nationwide public opinion poll (N=957). Asked about municipal government, more than 40 percent of respondents failed to express trust in the delegate elected from their district; nearly 60 percent believed that improvements needed to be made in Cuba's local government structures and procedures. In the spring of 1990, the PCC also sponsored a nationwide survey. Only 20 percent of respondents said that the food supply was good, and only 10 percent said that the quality of transportation was good. Having thus reported criticism on certain matters, the poll was believable when it reported that 77 percent of respondents thought that health services were good and 83 percent believed in the efficacy of the country's schooling. Cubans were, therefore, unhappy with the capacity of their government institutions and leaders to represent and serve many of their interests, but they continued to be impressed by performance in education and health care. This legacy of at least partial public support was crucial for regime survival at its moment of greatest peril, when so many Cubans had come to feel free to express their severe unhappiness even to PCC pollsters.

In late 1994, an affiliate of the Gallup Poll conducted a large survey in Cuba's western provinces. A large proportion of respondents had no difficulty reporting complaints. Only a quarter of Cubans believed that their needs for food were fully met, although half believed their health care needs were being met and nearly three-quarters were satisfied with Cuba's education programs. Only one in ten Cubans called themselves "communists" although half thought of themselves as "revolutionaries"; a quarter said that they were not supporters of the regime. Half of those surveyed were interested in setting up small businesses, if the government were to authorize them. More Cubans supported the value of equality than the value of freedom.

These views suggest that Cubans had absorbed—and supported—a number of socialist values but that many also disagreed significantly with the government and were not afraid to voice those disagreements to pollsters. Support for the PCC was quite low even though, as noted before, many individual party members were highly regarded by their neighbors.

Cuban politics changed slowly but decisively in the 1990s. Political leaders could not and did not govern as had been their custom. They were forced to authorize some changes and permit others, even when they disapproved of them. Cubans began to act through the market, legally or not, and chose to explore new political, religious, and intellectual alternatives.

The PCC and government leaders, in turn, had enacted important changes on their own to shape Cuba's present and future. The leadership was substantially overhauled in the early 1990s. New, younger people were appointed to significant posts. The armed forces were downsized sharply. After a period of decline and deinstitutionalization early in the 1990s, the government took some steps to strengthen and rearticulate regime institutions as the decade closed. The regime's leaders and institutions, however, had changed in perceptible ways even if their purpose continued to be the retention of power.

Cuba in the 1990s was in the throes of a political transition, although its end point was uncertain. This "transition to somewhere" did not imply a transition to a liberal democratic regime as had occurred elsewhere in Latin America or in much of the former communist world. It was associated with more open spaces for a private and public life autonomous from government and party power, and with rules that enabled market processes to operate. Whether Cuba's transition would evolve toward democratization remained unclear as the decade reached a close.

Foreign Relations

With the collapse of the Soviet Union and the communist governments of Central and Eastern Europe, Cuba was bereft of international allies. Its trade, investments, military support, and political relations had been disproportionately concentrated and dependent on governments that no longer existed. As 1990 opened, the Soviet Union required that all bilateral trade be conducted at international market prices by whatever private or state enterprises engaged in pertinent activities. No

*The North East Gate, Marine Barracks, Ground Defense Force,
U.S. Naval Base, Guantánamo Bay, Cuba, 1993*

longer would bilateral trade be mandated and carried out by
the central government in Moscow.

During the 1990s, Cuban economic relations with Central
and Eastern Europe plummeted. Cuban economic relations
with Russia focused principally on barter trade, at market
prices, exchanging sugar for petroleum (see The Economic
Crisis of the 1990s, ch. 3). Cuba refused to service its large
accumulated international debt to the Russian Federation, but
that was no different from its general policy on nonservicing of
any debts. Russian ground troops, who had been stationed in
Cuba since the 1962 Cuban Missile Crisis, also departed in
1992.

Russia and Cuba retained two somewhat more complicated
relationships. The Russian government paid rent to Cuba for
the use of electronic eavesdropping facilities set up south of
Havana at Lourdes (see Relations with Russia, ch. 5) at the
height of the Cold War. And Russia and Cuba continued to
negotiate over the fate of the nearly completed but mothballed
nuclear power plant near Cienfuegos in south central Cuba.
The investment costs of completing the nuclear power plant,
however, were beyond the capacities of both governments.

Cuba accepted international inspection of these facilities by the International Atomic Energy Agency.

Cuban relations with China recovered only gradually from the sharp bilateral split that had become manifest in 1966. With the collapse of European communism, however, political relations warmed more quickly between these two remaining communist governments. The Cuban government sought to learn fast and well the magic secrets of China's creation of market Leninism. Economic relations between the two countries remained basically what they had been, however: significant for Cuba, modest for China, and conducted at international market prices. Sino-Cuban military relations are modest in scope.

Between 1989 and 1991, Cuba repatriated its overseas troops from all countries to which they had been deployed. In 1992 it announced that it had stopped providing military support to revolutionary movements seeking to overthrow governments in other countries.

The international dimensions of the Cuban government's strategy for survival required the active cultivation of foreign investment and, therefore, of better political relations with market-economy countries. To resist the increased United States economic and political pressures on Cuba, Fidel Castro's government needed to find some international support.

United States actions led to some sympathy for Cuba. In October 1992, the United States Congress enacted the Cuban Democracy Act (see Glossary), whose principal sponsor was Representative Robert G. Torricelli. The new law prohibited United States subsidiaries in third countries from trading with Cuba. Other governments deemed it an extraterritorial secondary boycott in violation of the rules under the General Agreement on Tariffs and Trade (GATT—see Glossary). In March 1996, the United States Congress enacted the Cuban Liberty and Democratic Solidarity Act (also known as the Helms-Burton Act), sponsored by Senator Jesse Helms and Representative Dan Burton. However, invoking procedures in the law itself, President William Jefferson Clinton suspended the enforcement of the act's key feature, Title III, which authorizes United States citizens and firms to sue in United States courts those firms from other countries that "traffic" with Cuba. The law is broadly written to affect most foreign investment in Cuba as well as trade.

These laws provoked strong opposition from Canada, the European Union (EU—see Glossary), the Caribbean, and

Latin American countries, among others. The EU, Canada, Argentina, and Mexico enacted blocking legislation to prevent their firms from complying with these United States laws and to protect them if they were sued in United States courts. At the annual Iberoamerican summits of heads of state, opposition to these United States policies rose markedly. Although the Iberoamerican summits endorsed democracy and human rights strongly, President Fidel Castro was welcomed at each of these events, and his government's authoritarian practices were never explicitly criticized.

Within days of the enactment of the Cuban Democracy Act, in November 1992, for the first time ever Cuba gained overwhelming support in the United Nations General Assembly for a resolution condemning United States policies toward Cuba. The enactment of the Helms-Burton Act further tilted the vote in the General Assembly against the United States. In 1992 the vote was fifty-nine in favor of Cuba's resolution; three nations, including the United States, voted against the motion; and seventy-one abstained. In November 1997, 143 countries voted to condemn United States policy, three voted against, and only seventeen abstained. United States policy served Cuba's purposes well. (In separate motions, however, the General Assembly repeatedly criticized the Cuban government's violations of human rights.)

Cuban policy was most effective within the Anglophone Caribbean. Cuba was admitted to the Caribbean Tourism Organization in 1992, and in 1994 became a founding member of the Association of Caribbean States (see Glossary) led by the Anglophone Caribbean. Caribbean countries became among the most vocal opponents of United States policy toward Cuba.

In September 1993, the European Parliament (see Glossary) condemned the Cuban Democracy Act, and in September 1994 it called upon Cuba to enact democratic reforms. Also in 1993, the European Commission (see Glossary) created for the first time a humanitarian aid program for Cuba, although Cuba remained the only Latin American country with which the EU had not concluded a formal cooperation agreement. In response to the enactment of the Helms-Burton Act, European governments challenged the United States and refused to accept its imposition on European firms.

The government of Canada, along with those of various Caribbean countries, went the farthest in opposing United States policies. Canada strengthened its legislation to block the impact of United States law on Canadian firms, established a program of official development assistance in addition to humanitarian aid, and financed the business activities of Canadian firms with Cuba. It facilitated the work of Canadian NGOs in Cuba. And in 1998, Canada's Prime Minister Jean Chrétien visited Havana.

Cuban relations with the United States featured three key events in the 1990s. In the aftermath of the riot in Havana in the summer of 1994, the Cuban government lifted all requirements for an exit permit to emigrate and encouraged unauthorized emigration by boat or raft to the United States. Tens of thousands of Cubans took to the seas. Many were seized by United States Coast Guard and Navy ships and held for months at the United States base at Guantánamo Bay. Eventually, the United States and Cuba reached agreements in September 1994 and May 1995 to end the crisis. The United States accepted almost all Cubans who had emigrated illegally in 1994, although a few criminals were excluded and returned to Cuba, which accepted them. The United States promised to accept no fewer than 20,000 legal immigrants per year for the indefinite future. The United States also undertook to intercept on the high seas and return to Cuba those seeking to enter the United States illegally and without a credible claim to refugee status; this policy has been enforced. Cuba agreed to accept those whom the United States had intercepted and not to discriminate against them. It also agreed to reimpose its barriers on unlawful exit.

The next significant episode occurred on February 24, 1996, when at least one, perhaps three, unarmed civilian aircraft piloted by Cuban-American members of a group called Brothers to the Rescue flew into Cuban airspace. (On a prior trip, Brothers to the Rescue airplanes had dropped antigovernment leaflets over Havana.) As they were fleeing the pursuit of Cuban Air Force jets, two of the planes were shot down over international waters. This Cuban action, condemned by the International Civil Aviation Association, triggered the enactment of the Helms-Burton Act.

In November 1999, a five-year-old boy, Elián González, was rescued in the Straits of Florida, hanging on a raft after his mother had drowned. At first, the United States Immigration and Naturalization Service allowed his great-uncle to obtain provisional custody. Soon, however, the boy's father, Juan Miguel González, claimed custody, requesting the boy's return to Cuba. An intense seven-month legal and political battle developed over the child's custody, engaging both national governments, various local governments in southern Florida as well as state and Federal courts, including the Supreme Court. Consistent with their new migration relations, the United States and Cuban governments assumed similar positions on the issue and ultimately prevailed: Elián González, accompanied by his father, returned to Cuba in June 2000. In the United States, the political battle over Elián was fierce; in Cuba, the government used the incident to mobilize nationalist support. In the end, the Cuban American community's insistence that the boy should remain in the United States, and not with his father in Cuba, received little support. The Elián González case may have begun a re-thinking of United States policy toward Cuba.

During the 1990s, the United States and Cuba also constructed modest confidence-building measures to prevent accidental war and minimize the likelihood of accidents. These included frequent contact between the two countries' coast guards to enforce the migration agreements and carry out search-and-rescue operations. Regular procedures for contact were also established between both sides at the Guantánamo base. In anticipation of potential trouble, both governments inform each other in great detail and, to the extent possible, coordinate their actions.

Outlook

As the twenty-first century began, Cuba's communist leadership believed that it had survived the collapse of the Soviet Union and the European communist world. It had overcome increased United States sanctions on Cuba. And it had stemmed the economy's decline. Cuban leaders were conscious that popular support had dipped seriously, but they believed that they retained enough support, and wider tolerance, from their people to rebuild the political bases of the regime and to live through the next and perhaps most decisive crisis: Fidel Castro's death. Although Castro remained firmly in charge, his health had begun to fail and, for the first time since 1959, regime loyalists began to contemplate seriously a Cuba without Fidel.

Much has already changed in Cuba in anticipation of that future. Cuba's political institutions from the mid-1960s to the mid-1980s had been marked by very slow rotation of personnel.

The circulation of elites accelerated dramatically in the early 1990s and then stabilized somewhat later in the decade. Most members of the party's Political Bureau in place in 2000 had joined the bureau after the collapse of the Berlin Wall. In effect, a much younger, more dynamic set of leaders was in place, ready for the regime's future battles for political survival. The armed forces had also changed. In particular, the forces were downsized, a move that reduced the political burden on future governments to do more downsizing.

Cuba's political institutions, however, were weaker, more brittle, and enjoyed much less political support than in the past. The National Assembly, despite its partial revitalization in the 1990s, remained a toothless institution. The PCC's members were well regarded by their fellow citizens, but the party as such was not. The PCC as an institution weakened also in the early to mid-1990s, although an attempt was made to reinvigorate it in time for the Fifth Party Congress. The strengthening of the PCC in 1997 may have set the basis for a future "renewed communist" party, as in Poland, Lithuania, or Hungary in the mid-1990s.

Ordinary Cubans were ready for change and were already seizing the reins of the future. They sought and found jobs on their own. A growing number discovered the value of religion to their lives. Some courageous ones joined human rights and opposition groups, and did not desist despite repression. Intellectuals were more willing to challenge the government and the party. And even Fidel Castro grudgingly and publicly confessed that he could no longer pursue the policies he preferred most.

The future of Cuba lies also in part with the United States. It will be made easier or more difficult by United States government policies regarding the claims of American citizens and firms seeking compensation for the property expropriated in 1959 and 1960. And it will also be greatly affected by the generosity or the revenge of returning Cuban-Americans.

Cuba is an island archipelago, battered by hurricanes, natural and political. There is absolute certainty that real as well as metaphorical hurricanes will strike it in the years to come. The only doubt is when and with what force.

*   *   *

Much of the literature on Cuban government and politics in the 1990s was polemical or speculative, that is, it denounced the Cuban political regime and imagined a post-Castro future. As a result, there is less careful analytical and empirical work on Cuba in the 1990s than there is for previous times. Most of the material for this chapter had to be constructed from primary sources. Various books do, however, ably place the early 1990s within the broader sweep of Cuban politics since 1959. Among them are Irving Louis Horowitz's *Cuban Communism*, Carollee Bengelsdorf's *The Problem of Democracy in Cuba*, Marifeli Pérez-Stable's *The Cuban Revolution*, and Susan Eckstein's *Back from the Future*. Perhaps the single most comprehensive analytical and empirical work about Cuban politics and economics in the 1990s remains unpublished, however. It is *Cuba in Transition*, sponsored by the Cuban Research Institute of Florida International University (for the series, see http://www.lanic.utexas.edu/la/cb/cuba/asce/index.html). The journal *Cuban Studies* continues to provide valuable articles, book reviews, and bibliographies.

The good news is that significant social scientific work has been published in Cuba in the 1990s. Until 1996, Cuba's leading scholarly institution for political analysis was the Center for American Studies (CEA). The works of then-CEA scholars, such as Julio Carranza, Haroldo Dilla, Rafael Hernández, and Pedro Monreal, among others, contributed much to the understanding of Cuba in the 1990s. So, too, did the center's journal, *Cuadernos de Nuestra América*. Important work was also produced, although infrequently published, at the Center for Psychological and Sociological Research (CIPS) and at various research centers within the University of Havana. Cuba's premier social science publication is *Temas*, edited by Rafael Hernández.

Indispensable primary sources remain the daily newspaper *Granma*, the weekly newsmagazine *Bohemia*, and the panoply of journals published, sometimes just occasionally, by Cuba's universities and think tanks. The official legal gazette is the *Gaceta Oficial de la República*. The official Cuban government web site (http://www.cubaweb.cu) is also informative and useful. (For further information and complete citations, see Bibliography.)

Chapter 5. National Security

The marble obelisk and statue at the José Martí Memorial (Monumento a José Martí) in the center of Revolution Plaza (La Plaza de la Revolución), formerly Republic Plaza (La Plaza de la República), 1997
Courtesy Mark P. Sullivan

AT THE CLOSE OF THE 1990s, Cuba's Revolutionary Armed Forces (Fuerzas Armadas Revolucionarias—FAR) was a shadow of its former self. The decline of the Cuban military institution during the 1990s was in stark contrast to the FAR's position in the mid-1980s, when it was one of the largest and most formidable militaries in the Latin American region, if not in the entire developing world.

The pre-1990 development of the military institution owed much to Soviet aid, a benefit from the Cuban leadership's close ties with the former Soviet Union that dated to the early years of the Revolution. These ties made possible not only the FAR's intensive professionalization, which was deepened in the early 1970s, but also the extension several years later of Cuban military involvement to other developing world nations. By the time that Cuba's military "internationalism" (see Glossary) in Africa ended in 1991, 300,000 FAR personnel had served as trainers, advisers, and combatants. Throughout the 1970s and 1980s, the most promising young Cuban officers were trained at the Soviet Union's top military schools; foreign assistance worth millions of dollars was channeled each year to help support the Cuban institution; and the FAR's inventory was replete with many of the Soviet Union's most sophisticated, state-of-the-art weapons and equipment.

By the early 1990s, the erosion of the FAR's image as one of the premier military institutions of the developing world was already underway. With the collapse of the Soviet Union and the deepening of the island's economic crisis, the Cuban military found itself confronted with some of the most serious challenges in the history of the institution. By 1989, with the demise of the East European bloc imminent, the Cuban military leadership was already making plans to "go it alone" without the help they had long received. As the era of Cuba's military "internationalism" drew to a close, the combat troops once deployed abroad and hailed as heroes returned home only to be tasked to menial agricultural labor. In the difficult years that followed, the size of the armed forces was halved, the term of military service shortened, and the defense budget reduced sharply. On top of these cuts, much of the FAR's equipment—from its supersonic jet fighters to its aging main battle tanks—was put into storage because of the continuing shortages of fuel and spare parts.

By the mid-1990s, there were signs that the FAR was successfully defining a new course. The post-Cold War thaw made possible the establishment of closer ties with fellow military officers in Latin America and Europe, which helped somewhat to mitigate the institution's isolation. Even more significant were the reforms introduced on the island that provided an opening for the FAR to assume a more prominent role in the economy. This provided the military the opportunity to serve as an exemplary model for the rest of the nation, as suggested by the "experiments" with the System for Managerial Improvement (Sistema de Perfeccionamiento Empresarial—SPE) that were first conducted within the FAR's production enterprises. Of no small import, this economic involvement was also motivated by the FAR's interest in economic survival, which was facilitated by the expansion of the military-linked Gaviota Tourism Group, S.A., in the burgeoning tourism industry. Toward the close of the decade, although a United States Department of Defense study affirmed that the weakened FAR no longer posed a serious threat, it appeared equally unlikely that the military institution, still professional and staunchly supportive of the regime, might wither away.

The latter half of the 1990s heralded a period of new and different security-related concerns for the Cuban leadership. These concerns—stimulated, in part, by the dynamic set underway by the economic reforms carried out only years before—led to a higher profile for the police forces of the Ministry of Interior. In an effort to stem the growth of common crime, the regular police found themselves the beneficiaries of increased budgets, new equipment, and training programs, occasionally carried out with modest assistance from European police authorities. At the same time, the political police—as the members of the Ministry of Interior's Department of State Security are often called—were tasked to monitor and do what was necessary to rein in the increasingly bold activities of dissidents and members of the nascent independent press. One serious crackdown, which began in earnest in late 1998, brought changes in the Penal Code that codified new offenses and established harsher sentences for many crimes already on the books. The crackdown included the issuance of harsher sentences for what foreign observers might recognize as offenses that were political in nature, as well as the more frequent application of the death penalty.

Cuba's security environment of the 1990s thus appeared quite different from what it did in the 1980s. In some respects, it resembled more the difficult years of the 1960s than either of the two succeeding decades. With the collapse of the Eastern bloc, the Cuban government's focus was redirected from ambitious military efforts to bolster socialist allies abroad to efforts simply to maintain domestic order and the regime's own socialist foundation. Despite continuing economic problems in the final years of the decade, the FAR appeared to be adapting to its new position and economic role. As well, the deterrent measures aimed at halting the surge in common crime appeared to be achieving some success. At the same time, however, there were few indications that the regime's harsher treatment for political offenders had led dissidents and independent journalists to cease efforts to press for changes.

At the close of the twentieth century, various aspects of Cuban internal security had clearly been challenged, whether directly or indirectly, as a result of the crisis of the past decade. Yet despite the frequent forecasts of impending collapse that were heard throughout the 1990s, the Cuban regime maintained its stability. This was made possible in part by the continuing loyalty and support of the security forces under the Ministry of the Revolutionary Armed Forces (Ministerio de las Fuerzas Armadas Revolucionarias—MINFAR). Moreover, the regime appeared ready to take on the new security challenges that were sure to arise in the coming years.

Background of the Revolutionary Armed Forces, 1959–91

Institutional Consolidation in the 1960s

One of the greatest challenges faced by the revolutionary government when it assumed power in January 1959 was that of organizing a new military. Fidel Castro Ruz, who initially had no formal role in the civilian government, was recognized as the commander in chief of the armed forces. In turn, the troops of the Rebel Army formed the core of the new military, and the Rebel Army's top field commanders became the new institution's leaders. However, the issue remained as to what to do with the remnants of Fulgencio Batista Zaldívar's (president, 1940–44; dictator, 1952–59) old armed forces and with the poorly prepared peasants who had joined the Rebel Army's ranks during the final phases of the struggle in 1958.

Batista had left behind a 40,000-man military consisting of 35,000 members of the army and 5,000 members of the naval and air forces, including several thousand new recruits. The armed forces also had received new equipment from the United States shortly before the cutoff of aid to the regime. With Batista gone, the armed forces fell into complete disarray. Many officers quickly fled the island upon learning of Batista's departure, and members of army units throughout the country refused to continue fighting, with some abandoning their posts. Although the victorious rebels initially professed plans to unite the two armies into a single large force, the difficulties in building a new military organization composed of both guerrillas and their former enemies may have been recognized. In the months that followed the rebels' arrival in Havana, very few of the old military's officers who remained in Cuba were kept on active duty, and thousands were dismissed peremptorily. Hundreds of others were accused of war crimes, court martialed, and publicly executed in fulfillment of what Fidel Castro termed "revolutionary justice."

The MINFAR was created on October 16, 1959, to replace the Batista-era Ministry of Defense. Headed by Raúl Castro, the MINFAR quickly became the dominant organization in the new government. At first, the new MINFAR's leaders planned to have a military of 15,000 to 25,000 well-trained troops, whose hierarchy would be built around the few hundred individuals who had been the Rebel Army's leaders, were hardened combatants, and were known for their loyalty to Fidel and Raúl Castro. This aim was never fully realized, however, because, despite their low level of professionalism, it was seen as politically unwise to dismiss the many who had joined the rebels in the latter days of the revolutionary struggle. Organized in October 1959, the FAR numbered 40,000 troops and officers by early 1961, making it comparable in size to Batista's old military. The FAR was supported by the National Revolutionary Militias (Milicias Nacionales Revolucionarias—MNR), a civilian organization formed in October 1959.

Although maintaining a large force posed a problem, the FAR proved useful in helping the regime counter two threats that developed in the early 1960s. The first was the internal security problem posed by the activities of the counterrevolutionaries, who opposed the new government and Fidel Castro

Cuban soldiers wearing Soviet helmets and armed with Czech-made automatic rifles stand guard outside the U.S. Naval Base at Guantánamo in September 1962.
Courtesy National Imagery and Mapping Agency, Washington

and were roaming the countryside in central Cuba. The Castro government's campaign against the counterrevolutionaries, known as the "fight against bandits" (*lucha contra bandidos*), began in 1960 and continued until victory was declared five years later. Working together in coordinated operations to defeat the antigovernment rebels were members of at least four organizations—the military, the Ministry of Interior's Department of State Security (Departamento de Seguridad del Estado—DSE), the MNR, and the Committee for the Defense of the Revolution (Comité de Defensa de la Revolución—CDR). By the end of 1964, 500 soldiers had died in the campaign, and a total of 3,500 counterrevolutionaries had been killed or captured.

The United States Government's efforts to bring about the regime's overthrow perhaps posed a more serious threat. On April 17, 1961, the first major United States-sponsored military action against the Castro government was carried out with the landing of an army of Cuban exiles organized by the United States Central Intelligence Agency (CIA) on Playa Girón in the Bay of Pigs on the south-central Cuban coast. This ostensibly covert invasion, which came only fourteen weeks after Washington had broken off diplomatic relations with Cuba, presented the first real test of the ability of the regime's security forces, including the militia and the FAR's newly organized air force, to repel external aggression. About 300 of the invaders were killed outright, and 1,179 others were captured and held for twenty-two months. The exile force's ready defeat turned into a propaganda victory for the FAR and the regime. The following year, initiation of the United States-sponsored Operation Mongoose, which was aimed at sparking a popular revolt, obliged the FAR to continue to maintain a high state of readiness. This readiness continued until the declarations of victory in 1965, at which time the Cuban leadership turned its attention to developing the armed forces' professional capabilities (see Revolutionary Adventurism and Institutionalization, ch. 1).

This effort began with steps taken in early 1963, when the MNR was disbanded. Also at that time, the armed forces' ranks were trimmed, and several professional military schools were opened to improve the training and competency of the senior officer corps as well as of the various service arms. In addition, the universal conscription system known as Obligatory Military Service (Servicio Militar Obligatorio—SMO) was instituted so that draftees completing their three-year term of service might help fill the scaled-down military's manpower requirements. In 1965 the military budget, which had been reduced along with the manpower cuts, was increased. But the truly capping achievement during this period was the delivery of state-of-the-art MiG–21 supersonic fighters, which lent the FAR the prestige of being the first military in Latin America to have such advanced aircraft.

Despite the Soviet contributions to the Cuban arsenal during the first half of the 1960s, tensions in Soviet-Cuban relations persisted over Cuban efforts to "export the Revolution" to other developing countries (at a time when the Soviets were pursuing "peaceful coexistence" with the West). After the capture and execution by Bolivian army troops of Ernesto "Che" Guevara in October 1967, the regime's radical ardor was tempered. One of the Revolution's heroes, Guevara had left Cuba in a vain attempt to fulfill his revolutionary theory by sparking a peasant-led insurgency in that distant nation.

With Cuba's decision to return to the Soviet fold, the FAR's professional development was intensified, a move that set the course that the institution would follow for the next two decades. In mid-1969, in one of the first outward signs that the rapprochement would likely extend to the FAR, a Soviet naval squadron entered Caribbean waters on a flag-showing visit to Cuba. Such visits by the Soviet Navy continued on at least an annual basis well into the 1980s.

The Era of "Internationalism," 1970–91

Through the 1970s and into the 1980s, the FAR enjoyed a reputation as one of the developing world's preeminent military institutions, and its troops participated in various international combat missions. This reputation and foreign involvement were made possible in part as a result of the extensive Soviet military assistance that the FAR began receiving during the early 1970s. By the end of that decade, "internationalist service," as the foreign military duty was known, had become an important part of the institution's professional identity and was counted among the FAR's official missions.

The Soviet role in Cuba during the first half of the 1970s was aimed at developing the FAR's professional training and capabilities as well as Cuban military installations that the Soviets could use. The latter included Soviet construction of a deepwater submarine support facility at Cienfuegos on Cuba's southern coast. The construction of this militarily significant facility prompted a minor crisis in United States-Soviet relations in 1970. According to a former Soviet diplomat, the Cubans had agreed to the facility's construction in exchange for the promise of modern Soviet fighter aircraft. There were also efforts to model the FAR's development on that of the Soviet military, an aim that included routinely sending FAR officers for training at Soviet military schools. In keeping with this emphasis on training, the Youth Labor Army (Ejército Juvenil de Trabajo—EJT) was created in 1973. As a result, thousands of enlisted troops and officers were relieved of their duty to work in agriculture and construction in order that they might dedicate themselves to their professional development. During this period, military ranks and insignia were also revised to resemble more closely the Soviet style. In addition, the size of the FAR was cut by half between 1970 and 1974, bringing it to 100,000. An attempt was made to improve the combat readiness of these forces through constant training and exercises.

This professionalization helped to prepare the FAR for its extensive international involvement in Africa, which began with the surreptitious dispatch of Cuba's elite Special Troops (Tropas Especiales) to the newly independent nation of Angola in 1975 (see Special Troops, this ch.). Although made possible by Soviet aid, this extension of the FAR's international role was principally a reflection of the Cuban regime's abiding interest in providing political and military support to allies abroad. During the early 1960s, Che Guevara had traveled throughout Africa in hopes of building a support network between African nationalists and Cuban revolutionaries. In October 1963, in the first international action in which FAR troops took part, 686 soldiers, including a battalion of 400 tank troops (*tanquistas*), were deployed to Algeria to aid in its border war with Morocco and remained there for six months. Elsewhere in Africa during the 1960s, small numbers of Cuban military personnel were reportedly involved in guerrilla fighting in territory encompassing Congo (present-day Zaire), Tanzania, and Guinea-Bissau. Within the Western Hemisphere as well, the regime also sought to provide aid and military training to members of leftist guerrilla movements and to organize insurgencies where such groups were lacking. In early 1973, Cuban advisers, eventually numbering 600 and 700 personnel, were sent to South Yemen to train its military and their guerrilla allies who were fighting in the Dhofari rebellion. In October and November 1973, with the outbreak of the Yom Kippur War, Cuba's deployment of an 800-man tank brigade to fight for Syria against Israel heralded the more prominent foreign role that the FAR would shortly assume.

On the heels of the Special Troops' arrival in Angola, the first large-scale commitment of Cuban combat personnel abroad came in late 1975 when tens of thousands of forces arrived to fight in the civil war on the side of the ruling Popular Movement for the Liberation of Angola (Movimento Popular de Libertação de Angola—MPLA), then under the leadership of Agostinho Neto. For the next sixteen years, Cuban troop strength in Angola varied according to the ebbs and flows in the prolonged conflict. The FAR's air and ground forces, equipped by the Soviets, were pitted at different times against personnel of the South African Defence Force; the rebels fighting for the National Union for the Total Independence of Angola (União Nacional para la Independência Total de Angola—UNITA), led by Jonas Savimbi; and members of a lesser known rebel group, the National Front for the Liberation of Angola (Frente Nacional de Libertação de Angola—FNLA), which, despite United States covert funding, soon fell apart. In mid-1976, 33,000 to 36,000 FAR combat troops began to be deployed in Angola during one of the early peaks in the fighting; as many as 80 percent were thought to be activated reserve troops.

When fighting intensified again in the late 1980s, the Cuban deployment in Angola grew to 50,000 personnel. The Battle of Cuito Cuanavale in early 1988 was the final major clash in which Cuban forces participated. It was hailed by the Cuban leadership as the great victory that paved the way for negotiations to end the war and Cuba's withdrawal from the conflict. These negotiations led to the signing of the United States-mediated Tripartite Agreement by representatives of Angola, South Africa, and Cuba in December 1988. In addition, to providing for an end to the Angolan war and Namibian independence, the agreement set a timetable for the phased withdrawal of Cuban forces over a thirty-month period. In May 1991, the last combat troops returned home to Cuba, two months ahead of schedule.

The second major theater to which Cuban troops were deployed was in eastern Africa, where several thousand combat personnel were sent in early 1978 to aid Ethiopia in its war with Somalia. During the peak of the fighting that year, 12,000 FAR troops were involved in the conflict. Following Somalia's decision to end hostilities, the number of Cuban combatants in Ethiopia was reduced to 5,000 personnel, and this number remained relatively constant for most of the next decade. At the time of the decision to withdraw Cuban forces from Ethiopia in 1989, the Cuban contingent numbered 3,000 personnel.

Toward the end of the 1980s, because of economic difficulties at home as well as the shifting international environment, Soviet support for the Cubans' continuing involvement abroad was beginning to wane. Nevertheless, the FAR clearly had benefitted greatly from the considerable Soviet aid it had received over the past years. At the conclusion of the 1980s, the Cuban military was one of the largest in the Western Hemisphere, with an estimated 180,500 personnel, of whom more than three-fourths were ground troops. The FAR was also one of the best-equipped armed forces in the Latin American region, if not the entire developing world, counting in its inventory more than 100 MiG fighter jets (including new MiG–29s, which were then being delivered), several submarines, more than 1,000 main battle tanks, and an array of missiles and other armaments. FAR personnel also remained beneficiaries of the extensive Soviet training program, with the most upwardly mobile officers sent either to Moscow's M.V. Frunze Military Academy or the K.E. Voroshilov General Staff Academy. Others received technical training, often in Eastern Europe, to operate and maintain the sophisticated equipment that the FAR had received.

The United States military's intervention in Grenada in late October 1983 ended Cuban activities on that island nation. After the takeover of Grenada's government by the Marxist-Leninist New Jewel Movement in 1979, Cuban military advisers and labor brigades were brought in to help build an international airport capable of landing large military transports. After only brief skirmishes with the Cubans, the 13,000 United States troops accepted the surrender of the fifty Cuban military advisers to Grenada's then-collapsing regime and of the approximately 600 armed construction workers.

The Grenada intervention was the last incident in the twentieth century in which armed United States and Cuban personnel directly confronted each other. In 1990, following the electoral defeat of Nicaragua's Sandinista government, the Cuban military advisers who had been active there since 1979 and who had once numbered several thousand were sent home. FAR advisers who were involved in training missions in various other developing world nations also returned home, including the 1,500 personnel who were withdrawn from Congo in 1991.

As of the end of 1991, with all Cuban troops at home, the FAR's "internationalist" mission was effectively over. The members of the military who served abroad had gained valuable combat experience. In addition, the institution's inventory of matériel was expanded by the equipment and weapons that the troops brought back with them. Overall, the FAR's prestige was enhanced as a result of its "internationalist" role, in which the Cuban forces were generally considered to have acquitted themselves well. Both this "internationalist" experience and the ethos of professionalism instilled over the past two decades were important in the FAR's development as an institution, one that might be capable of managing the changes that it would have to embrace during the course of the 1990s (see Challenges Faced by the Institution in the 1990s, this ch.).

Ministry of the Revolutionary Armed Forces

Organizational Changes of 1989

Toward the end of the 1980s, the political and economic changes already taking place at home and abroad had begun to place strains on the Cuban military institution. The withdrawal of troops from Angola, Ethiopia, and elsewhere marked the beginning of the end for the FAR's "internationalist" mission and obliged the institution's leadership to seriously consider what the future might hold for the armed forces. At the same time, the military's domestic economic role and interest in economic involvement were also beginning to change, largely as a result of decisions implemented following the 1986 Third Party Congress, when several select FAR enterprises were authorized to initiate experiments in allowing plant managers greater autonomy in decision-making as a means to spur efficiency and productivity. Only two years later, with the collapse of the eastern bloc regimes already imminent, the leadership announced its decision, with seeming abruptness, to commit Cuban military troops, including many returning combat veterans, to agricultural production in order to help ensure the country's continuing food supply during the difficult times it saw ahead.

By mid-1989, the changes then taking place on the island and abroad had already likely resulted in a shared sense among the Cuban leadership that a crisis might be at hand. The shake-up of Cuba's security apparatus later that same year, together with the events that preceded it, seemed to confirm this. As a result of the shake-up, the prestige of the Ministry of Interior was diminished and its capabilities weakened as many career intelligence officers were forced out of the institution and replaced by military personnel. The events surrounding this shake-up, in which Army Corps General Abelardo Colomé Ibarra, the FAR's ranking officer under Raúl Castro, was installed as minister of interior, has continued to be debated among scholars who follow Cuban security issues. Because of the secrecy related to these changes in the security apparatus, it remains one of the least understood actions undertaken by the regime (see Ministry of Interior, this ch.).

The most important reason for this lack of understanding is linked to what has become popularly known as the Ochoa affair, named after Division General Arnaldo T. Ochoa Sánchez. Although it involved the detention and trial of a number of ranking officers of the country's security forces, nearly all of them Ministry of Interior personnel, it was named the Ochoa affair because it began with the court martial and execution of Ochoa, along with three other officers. Ochoa was a widely respected FAR officer who was not only popular among his men but, as the recipient of the MINFAR's highest decoration, a Hero of the Republic. At the time, the Ochoa affair raised widespread speculation about support within the military for the regime, given Fidel Castro's resistance to implementing any political or economic reforms similar to those then being carried out in the Soviet Union under President Mikhail Gorbachev and recurring rumors that Ochoa was somehow involved in plotting against the leadership. It also raised questions yet to be answered concerning the regime's underlying motives in singling out Ochoa for punishment and in joining his case with that made against the Ministry of Interior officials implicated.

In June 1989, six months after his return from a tour of duty as the commander of Cuba's "internationalist" forces in Angola, General Ochoa was slated to take over as the chief of the Western Army, the most important of the FAR's three territorial commands (see The Revolutionary Armed Forces, this ch.). Instead, on June 13, the well-regarded general was arrested and charged with "serious acts of corruption and illegal use of economic resources." Within weeks, a Military Honor Tribunal, composed of forty-seven fellow general officers, was convened. The Honor Tribunal stripped Ochoa of his rank and honors, recommended that he be tried for high treason, and expressed its support for the application of the "full weight" of the law against him, if convicted, by a Special Military Tribunal.

The court martial by the Special Tribunal began on June 30, 1989. In addition to Ochoa, the government identified three other officers, each also stripped of rank, as the key players in a wide conspiracy of self-enrichment that included trafficking in drugs, diamonds, and other contraband, and money laundering. Another ten individuals, who had backgrounds in either the Ministry of Interior or the MINFAR, were tried on related charges at the court martial, but were convicted of lesser crimes. Many foreign observers at the time described the hastily convened Special Tribunal, the proceedings of which were

The Ministry of the Revolutionary Armed Forces building at Revolution Plaza (Plaza de la Revolución), October 1991
Courtesy National Imagery and Mapping Agency, Washington

broadcast on state television, as a "show trial" that was reminiscent of the Stalinist era in the Soviet Union. In July, following the Council of State's review and approval of the sentences handed down, the four former officers were executed by firing squad.

Well beyond the proceedings that were known formally as Case Number 1 of 1989, the Ochoa affair continued to have repercussions within the state's security apparatus. Only shortly before the court martial began, the government announced that the minister of interior, Division General José Abrantes Fernández, a man who had long been responsible for Fidel Castro's personal guard and was counted among his most trusted aides, had been removed from office for failing to discover the illegal activities that were carried out by the soon-to-be convicted officials under his charge. Abrantes was immediately replaced as minister by General Colomé Ibarra.

Through the ensuing month, a succession of MINFAR officers were appointed to fill the vacated posts of the top Ministry of Interior officials who resigned. Then, on July 30, Abrantes and a number of those who had worked closely under him were arrested. The crimes with which they were charged included negligence, illegal use of government resources, corruption and/or toleration of corruption by others, and the manipulation and concealment of information of interest to the government. On August 24, a second Special Military Tribunal was convened for Case Number 2 of 1989, to consider the charges against Abrantes and six other former Ministry of Interior officials. At the conclusion of this secret court martial, Abrantes, who was then in his late fifties, was sentenced to twenty years in prison, where he died of a heart attack in January 1991. The other former officials were given prison terms ranging from five to fifteen years.

By the end of 1989, with Abrantes gone and a trusted career FAR officer in his place, hundreds of Ministry of Interior officials, including many who had spent their entire careers in the organization, had been retired, dismissed, or otherwise replaced by FAR officers. These new Ministry of Interior personnel, according to some analysts, often had little training or background in intelligence matters, and as a result, the institution's effectiveness was thought to have suffered during the 1990s. In 2001 Colomé Ibarra remained head of the Ministry of Interior.

Challenges Faced by the Institution in the 1990s

The decade of the 1990s brought important political and economic changes for the FAR that were associated with the end of the armed forces' "internationalist" mission and the break-up of the Soviet Union and its East European bloc. These changes presented formidable challenges for the Cuban military, perhaps the most critical of which was simply continuing to maintain the FAR as a professional military institution despite a serious lack of resources. During the course of the decade, the FAR leadership's responses to the continuing challenges led the military to become more involved in national life and to assume a more prominent role as a domestic economic actor. This shift appeared to be driven both by the FAR's financial need, given the institution's efforts to become "self-financing" as its share of the national budget was pared, and by the regime's prevailing concern about being able to maintain domestic order should a security crisis develop.

Well before Fidel Castro's September 1990 declaration of the "special period in peacetime" (*período especial en tiempo de paz*; hereafter Special Period—see Glossary), the FAR had already begun efforts to cut spending and otherwise help minimize the impact of what it saw as an impending crisis. Troops returning from "internationalist" service were sent to work in agriculture in order to help boost the national food supply; still others were discharged from active duty, often placed on inactive reserve and left to fend for themselves, despite the promise that they would have jobs to return to after completing their foreign military duty. Within the FAR, meetings were routinely convened among service personnel in order to brainstorm on ways to conserve fuel and make do with fewer expenditures. Paramount among the military leadership's planning efforts at that time was the formulation of contingency plans for what was known as the "zero option," which was to be implemented if all foreign aid and supplies were cut off.

Changing Ties with the Former Soviet Union

By mid-1991, less than a year after Cuba's formal declaration of its economic crisis, the Soviet commitment to the island under President Mikhail Gorbachev had already clearly weakened. However, even in the face of the Castro regime's adamant refusal to implement any Soviet-style reforms, the longstanding ties between the FAR and the conservative-leaning Soviet Armed Forces might have suggested some slight hope for continuing close military-to-military relations, despite tensions between the two countries' political leaders. There appeared some basis for this hope: United States Department of State estimates of Soviet military assistance to Cuba, although said by some scholars to be inflated amounts, had reached US$1.5 billion in 1990, which turned out to be the final year of Soviet aid to the island. In addition, in early 1990, the first six of what was expected to be a squadron of thirty-six state-of-the art MiG–29 jet fighters had arrived on the island.

The failed coup attempt against President Mikhail Gorbachev in August 1991 and Cuba's resounding silence after the fact marked an irreversible shift in relations between the two countries. In September Gorbachev announced plans to withdraw the Soviet military's "special training brigade," which had been based on the island since the Cuban Missile Crisis. According to Fidel Castro, this decision was announced without the courtesy of informing him beforehand. The Soviet training brigade, more formally known as an independent motorized infantry brigade, numbered only 2,800 troops in 1991, but it had once had an estimated 20,000 troops. Despite a drawdown in personnel that had already taken place, the brigade was considered in Cuba, as well as abroad, as one of the enduring symbols of the Soviet Union's commitment to the regime. The announcement of its formal withdrawal appeared to confirm that it would not be possible for the FAR's ties with their Soviet counterparts to remain close. In September 1992, months after the formation of the new Commonwealth of Independent States (CIS), the Cubans reluctantly agreed to the Russians' schedule for the departure of the brigade's last troops. In 1993, as the Cuban economy bottomed out, the final brigade members departed the island.

The Military's Economic Role

Since the beginning of the economic crisis in the early 1990s, the military has become increasingly involved in the nation's economy. Such involvement was officially denoted as a new responsibility for the MINFAR in early 1991, when Fidel Castro declared, "[O]ne of the Armed Forces' missions at this time is to help the economy." The military's interest in this economic involvement has been spurred as much by concerns over the loss of the military aid and training once provided by the Soviet Union as by the weakness of the civilian economy, which has forced reduced government spending on the armed forces and the inception of the MINFAR's efforts to "self-finance" a portion of its budget. In addition, this involvement has helped the military avoid further reductions in personnel that might otherwise have been necessary. Toward the end of the 1990s, some reports estimated that the MINFAR had managed to provide for as much as 80 percent of its spending needs through self-financing.

The MINFAR's efforts to achieve heightened efficiency and productivity through management innovations in its enterprises, known as the SPE (System for Managerial Improvement), can be traced to policies embraced as early as 1987. The severity of the economic crisis, however, spurred the military to become more extensively involved in agricultural production. During the most difficult years of the economic crisis in the early 1990s, the military's troops, often having just returned from "internationalist" duty, were routinely deployed in the fields in intensive efforts to boost crop yields, and its trucks were used to help farmers transport their goods to the newly opened farmers' markets. The participation of MINFAR troops in the annual sugar harvest (*zafra*) and in planting or picking other crops was not unprecedented; however, it did mark the first time in twenty years that regular troops had been assigned to such tasks. During this period, the military is generally considered to have achieved self-sufficiency in terms of its ability to feed its troops, and surplus produce from the military farms (*granjas*) was sold to bring in additional revenue.

Perhaps the most important facet of the military's economic involvement came about after the government's 1990 decision to legalize joint investment ventures, when the military became a dominant partner in the state tourism company known as the Gaviota Tourism Group, S.A. Gaviota was originally formed in 1988 in order to provide support for vacations by Cuban and Soviet military personnel on the island. In its new incarnation, Gaviota has teamed with such foreign partners as Spain's Sol Meliá and Tryp hotel chains and France's Club Med in order to bring in significant hard-currency earnings for the MINFAR. Gaviota has been active in both the management and the administration of the tourism projects funded by foreign capital, which include four- and five-star hotels and resorts located in prime tourism spots, such as Varadero. It has also established subsidiary operations, such as AeroGaviota, which operates domestically to fly tourists to their vacation destinations.

Although the exact connection between Gaviota and the armed forces hierarchy has not yet been publicly clarified, it is widely acknowledged that, since the early 1990s, the firm has been routinely used as a source of employment for loyal officers who are formally retired from active duty. Some direction is provided through the MINFAR's Vice Ministry for Economic Affairs, which in the late 1990s was headed by a Politburo member, Division General Julio Casas Regueiro, the former commander of the Antiaircraft Defense and Revolutionary Air Force (Defensa Antiaérea y Fuerza Aérea Revolucionaria—DAAFAR).

The Military in the Government and Party

From almost the beginning of the Revolution, the Cuban military has played a prominent role in both the government of the nation and, since its founding in 1965, the Communist Party of Cuba (Partido Comunista de Cuba—PCC). The most notable aspects of this role are the key leadership duties of Fidel and Raúl Castro, who exercise overlapping national authority as heads of the government, the military, and the PCC. Other senior military officials may also be found in positions of authority and influence elsewhere within the regime, particularly within the cabinet and in the top councils of the PCC. Their most significant single unifying trait continues to be their record of loyalty to the Castros, often dating back to the era of the guerrilla struggle.

The military's influence within the national government can be most clearly seen in the composition of the Council of Ministers (Consejo de Ministros). In addition to Fidel and Raúl Castro, five other men with military backgrounds were members of the Council of Ministers in the late 1990s. These included General Colomé Ibarra, the minister of interior; Division General Ulises Rosales del Toro, the FAR's former Chief of General Staff, who was appointed minister of the sugar industry in late 1997; Brigade General Silvano Colas Sánchez, the minister of communications; Captain (Capitán de Navío) Orlando Felipe Rodríguez Romay, the minister of the fishing industry; and Colonel Álvaro Pérez Morales, the minister of transportation. In addition, another prominent military official in the government is retired Brigade General Juan Escalona Reguera, the Attorney General of the Republic (Fiscal General de la República). Although not a member of the Council of Ministers, Escalona, as attorney general, serves as the country's top law enforcement official and sits on the Governing Council of the Supreme People's Tribunal, the Cuban state's top judicial body.

The MINFAR has been under Raúl Castro's leadership since its organization in 1959. By the time of the shake-up in 1989, however, the Ministry of Interior had been led by three different individuals, who, although members of the guerrillas' Rebel Army, did not necessarily build careers within the FAR. Since 1989 the Ministry of Interior has been led by a FAR officer (see Organizational Changes of 1989, this ch.). In addition to the other ministerial posts now held by military officials, the ministries of communications and transportation have previously been headed by military officers, a record that suggests not only the military's expertise in logistics but also that the leadership likely considers these to be important resources to control in the event of a security crisis. Similarly, some analysts believed that Rosales's appointment as minister of the sugar industry signaled the military's expanded influence in domestic economic affairs. It should also be noted, however, that Rosales's ministerial post has previously been held by a military man, most recently in the early 1980s. Escalona's appointment as attorney general, a post he has held during the 1990s, is somewhat unusual despite the general's legal background, as none of his predecessors were known to be military officials. It

SS-N2 STYX missile on parade in Havana, December 2, 1986
Courtesy National Imagery and Mapping Agency, Washington

may be explained by his prominent role in 1989 as the lead prosecutor in the Ochoa affair.

The military also wields considerable influence within the top echelons of the PCC. Yet, throughout the 1990s, a consistent decline in the number of officers elected to the PCC's Central Committee took place. In 1981, following the PCC's Second Congress, officers, all with commissioned ranks, were elected to just over a quarter of the Committee's 225 seats. By contrast, after the Fourth Congress in 1991, their representation in the Central Committee had declined by half.

At the same time, the FAR has retained its dominance within the Political Bureau (Politburo), the PCC's top decision-making organ. After the 1997 Party Congress, although the overall size of the Politburo was cut by one member, an additional military officer was named, which brought to seven the number of officials in the twenty-four-member body. They included Commander-in-Chief Fidel Castro, General of the Army Raúl Castro, Army Corps General Colomé Ibarra, and Division Generals Julio Casas Regueiro, Leopoldo Cintra Frias, Rosales del Toro, and the more recently appointed Ramón Espinosa Martín. Given the hierarchical nature of the Cuban regime, the military's continuing domination at this top level within the Party suggests that its declining representation on the Central Committee may not be a matter that greatly concerns the military institution and its leadership.

Constitutional Provisions and Treaty Obligations

Cuba's 1976 constitution, as amended in July 1992, establishes in Article 43 the right of all Cubans to ascend to any rank in the country's security forces, "according to their merits and capabilities." In turn, as described in Article 134, the members of the armed forces and of other security forces also have the same right to vote and to be elected to office as do other citizens. In Article 65, the "defense of the socialist homeland" is recognized as "the greatest honor and the supreme duty of every Cuban citizen." As stipulated in this article, military service is to be regulated by law. Treason is recognized as "the gravest of all crimes," with the person committing it to be "subject to the most severe sanctions." These sanctions, although not specified in the constitution, might include capital punishment or life imprisonment (see Penal System, this ch.).

The articles guaranteeing Cuban citizens the right to serve in the security forces and setting the primacy of defense as a citizen's duty have remained unchanged since 1976. However, the 1992 reforms created a new Chapter 8 in the constitution, composed of a single article, that was added to address provisions for a state of emergency. In that chapter, Article 67 sets out the right of the president of the Council of State to declare a state of emergency in case of developments or imminent developments—whether "natural disasters or catastrophes or other circumstances"—which may affect "domestic order, the security of the country or the stability of the State." This state of emergency may be applied to all the republic or a part of it, and the president is authorized to mobilize the population while the state of emergency is in effect. Article 67 also states that the manner in which the state of emergency is declared, its enforcement, and its termination are to be regulated by law. Similarly, although still to be subject to law, Article 67 stipulates that the exercise of "the rights and fundamental duties recognized by the constitution" during normal times "must be regulated differently" while the state of emergency is in force.

In complementing the authority granted the president of the Council of State to declare a state of emergency, the National Assembly of People's Power (Asamblea Nacional del

Poder Popular—ANPP; hereafter, National Assembly), Cuba's national legislature, formally bears constitutional responsibility to "declare a state of war in case of military aggression and to approve peace treaties." However, as the National Assembly meets in regular session only briefly each year, Article 89 establishes that the Council of State, a body elected by the National Assembly, has the right to represent it between sessions or, according to Article 90, to convene extraordinary sessions. Among other provisions, Article 90 further explicitly assigns the Council of State the right "to decree a general mobilization when required for national defense, to declare war in case of aggression, or to approve peace treaties when the Assembly is in recess and cannot be convened with the necessary security and urgency."

According to Article 93, the president of the Council of State, the office held by Fidel Castro that establishes him as chief of the Cuban state and government, has expansive responsibilities in terms of the security forces and national defense. The Council's president serves as the supreme commander of the country's security forces, which include the FAR's troops as well as the forces under the immediate supervision of the Ministry of Interior, and is authorized to determine their general organization. As noted above, the president also has the authority to declare a state of emergency in situations addressed by Article 67 of the constitution, and as soon as circumstances permit, to give an accounting of that declaration to the National Assembly or, if the legislature cannot be convened, to the Council of State. Further, the president of the Council of State also presides over the National Defense Council (Consejo de Defensa Nacional), the body established to oversee the defense planning and coordination system adopted in the 1980s. In addition, Article 94 establishes that in case of "the absence, sickness, or death of the president of the Council of State," authority is delegated to the first vice president of the Council of State, an office held by Raúl Castro.

As the nation's supreme executive and administrative body, the Council of Ministers, whose president is also Fidel Castro, is also invested by the constitution with security-related responsibilities. As enumerated under Article 98, these responsibilities include "providing for national defense, the maintenance of domestic order and security, the protection of citizens' rights, and the protection of lives and property in the event of natural disaster." To support these responsibilities, among others, the

Council of Ministers is charged with formulating the national budget and, following its approval by the National Assembly, its oversight. All government ministers, including the heads of the MINFAR and of the Ministry of Interior, are members of the Council of Ministers. Further, because Raúl Castro serves as the first vice president of the Council of State, he would remain a member of the Council of Ministers even if he no longer served as the MINFAR's chief.

Lastly, Article 101 addresses the role of the National Defense Council. This body is charged with the responsibility to direct the country during "conditions of a state of war, during the war, the general mobilization, and the state of emergency." It is required to maintain its readiness to assume responsibility for any of these duties at any time. As noted above, the National Defense Council's president is the president of the Council of State—again, Fidel Castro. According to Article 101, the Council's organization and functions are to be regulated by law. Related to this, Article 119 elaborates the responsibilities of the Provincial Defense Councils, the Municipal Defense Councils, and the neighborhood-based Defense Zones, which within their respective territories mirror those assigned to the National Council. In accordance with the law, the National Council is charged with determining these bodies' organization and functions. The specific execution of their duties during a crisis, however, is to be defined by the nation's general defense plan and the role and responsibility assigned each body by one of the country's three regional military councils, which cover geographic territories that correspond to the areas under each of the MINFAR's three regional army commands.

In terms of Cuba's security-related treaty obligations, Fidel Castro's government has been reluctant to enter into multilateral and bilateral pacts that might limit the scope of its actions either domestically or in the international arena. This stance is underscored in Article 11 of the 1992 constitution, which states that "The Republic of Cuba repudiates and considers illegal and null the treaties, pacts, or concessions that were signed in conditions of inequality or that disregard or diminish its sovereignty and territorial integrity."

In March 1960, shortly after the victory of the Revolution, Cuba withdrew from the 1947 Inter-American Treaty of Reciprocal Assistance (more commonly known as the Rio Treaty— see Glossary), which provides for collective hemispheric defense against external aggressors. In August 1960, months before diplomatic relations with the United States were broken off, Cuba terminated its participation in the United States Mutual Defense Assistance Program, which provided military aid and had been endorsed by Batista in 1952. Cuba's participation in the Organization of American States (OAS—see Glossary) was formally suspended on January 31, 1962, after the member states determined that the Marxist-Leninist ideology of the Castro government was "incompatible with the interests of the hemisphere." Consequently, Cuba does not have a representative on the Inter-American Defense Board, nor are its military personnel eligible to attend the Inter-American Defense College, located at Fort McNair in Washington, D.C.

Until recently, Cuba also resisted entering into any agreements aimed at controlling the spread of nuclear weapons. It remains the only country in the hemisphere that has not joined the 1968 Nuclear Non-Proliferation Treaty (NPT), which a former Cuban United Nations ambassador said would require Cuba to give up "its inalienable right to defend itself using weapons of any kind." Nevertheless, in March 1995, Cuba did finally sign the 1967 Treaty for the Prohibition of Nuclear Weapons in Latin America, more commonly known as the Treaty of Tlatelolco (see Glossary), which, like the NPT, establishes a commitment to nuclear nonproliferation. Cuba also reached an agreement with the International Atomic Energy Agency (IAEA) in May 1980 with respect to implementing safeguards and allowing inspections at its nuclear power facilities then under construction (and now abandoned) at Juraguá, near Cienfuegos on Cuba's southern coast.

Despite its avowals, the Castro government has shown an inclination to join other pacts related to the conduct of warfare and the treatment of its victims. In June 1966, Cuba ratified the 1925 Geneva Protocol that prohibits the wartime use of poisonous gases or bacteriological agents. It also has ratified the four international agreements of the 1949 Geneva Convention for the protection of war victims. In 1976 the Cuban government ratified the 1972 Bacteriological (Biological) and Toxic Weapons Convention. Cuba has refused to sign the 1997 Ottawa Convention on the Prohibition of the Use, Stockpiling, Production and Transfer of Anti-Personnel Mines and on Their Destruction, however, largely because of the use of these devices throughout the Cuban side of the no-man's-land that separates the United States Naval Station at Guantánamo Bay from the rest of the mainland.

The United States Naval Station at Guantánamo Bay

The United States Naval Station at Guantánamo consists of a seventy-three-kilometer area (including land and water), four kilometers wide, located east of the Sierra Maestra in Cuba's southeastern Guantánamo Province. United States Marines first landed at this site during the Spanish-American War in 1898. The United States leased the territory in 1903 as a coaling station for United States naval vessels transiting the Caribbean.

A 1934 treaty with the United States replaced the 1901 Platt Amendment (see Glossary), which had authorized United States military intervention in Cuba. Several of the principal provisions of both treaties were identical, however. For example, the 1934 treaty also grants a lease to the Guantánamo Naval Station area "in perpetuity" and free maritime access to the land through Guantánamo Bay. In exchange, the United States agreed to continue to pay the Cuban government an annual rent of $2,000, an amount tied to the gold standard that was equivalent in the late 1990s to just over US$4,000. The main difference was that under the 1934 treaty the United States agreed to forego the discretionary right to intervene in Cuba's domestic affairs. The United States also agreed in both 1901 and 1934 to terminate the lease by the joint consent of both governments.

In terms of its strategic role, Guantánamo serves as a supply and logistics base for the United States Navy's Atlantic Fleet. Although the base's strategic value to the United States has declined over the years, it would still likely be a platform for operations in the event of war or natural disaster in the Caribbean or Latin America. For more mundane purposes, the United States Navy uses the base for exercises and maneuvers, the maintenance of United States naval vessels, and the monitoring of Cuban airspace. From time to time, it has also been used to temporarily house refugees, including 34,000 Haitian refugees in 1991 and many of the 30,000 Cubans who attempted to leave the island during the *balsero* (rafter) crisis in the summer of 1994. During 1999, the base was briefly considered as a possible temporary shelter for the estimated 20,000 Kosovo refugees left homeless as a result of the war. Although it serves as a permanent "home" to approximately 1,080 United States military personnel and possibly about 2,500 American civilian personnel, as well as 300 foreign nationals, the base is believed to be capable of providing temporary housing for up to 50,000. Since the 1960s, it has been self-sufficient in terms of its water supply and electrical needs. In the late 1990s, approximately 1,000 United States Navy personnel and 640 United States Marines were stationed at Guantánamo. The number of American personnel stationed there is expected to continue to decline over the foreseeable future as a result of ongoing efforts to pare military expenditures.

The base, described by Fidel Castro as a "dagger plunged into the heart of Cuban soil," has remained a point of tension in bilateral relations. As a sign of its defiance of the United States' right to use the territory, Castro's government has refused the funds paid annually by the United States Department of the Navy over the past decades under the terms of the lease. Beginning in 1961, after President Dwight D. Eisenhower broke diplomatic relations with the Castro government, Cuban and United States military troops began patrolling opposite sides of a twenty-eight-kilometer barb-wire-fenced stretch of the perimeter that separates the base from Cuban territory, and watchtowers were constructed on both sides. Since then the base has remained separated from the rest of the island by barbed-wire fencing and a no-man's-land filled with antipersonnel and antitank mines that are designed as much to keep Cubans out of the base as to keep the American personnel there isolated. Since the onset of Cuba's economic crisis in the early 1990s, tourists on the Cuban side of the perimeter have been able to pay for visits to some of the look-out points used by the FAR's Border Brigade (Brigada de la Frontera) to monitor the base's activities.

Despite Cuba's continuing adamant demand for the departure of American troops from Cuban territory, the tensions between Cuba and the United States over the base have been reduced in recent years, especially since the bilateral Migratory Accords were signed in August 1994 and May 1995 and the final Cuban refugees left the base. The accords establish that Washington grant 20,000 visas a year to Cubans who wish to reside in the United States and that Cubans picked up at sea be returned to Cuba, with no reprisals by Cuba. The last time that shots were fired by troops stationed on either side of the perimeter was in December 1989. In 1996 the United States began removing antipersonnel mines from its side of the no-man's-land that separates the base from the rest of the island; the task was completed in 1999. These mines were replaced by motion and sound detectors to warn of any incursion onto the base.

The Cubans, on the other hand, have not made public any plans to begin de-mining their side of the 100-kilometer perimeter. Rather, the Cuban government maintains that these mines are needed for defensive purposes, and will be removed only after the United States gives up its base on Cuba's national territory. Thirteen American soldiers and five Cubans have been killed by the mines since their installation. Between 50,000 and 70,000 mines were placed in the no-man's-land between Cuba and the Guantánamo base beginning in 1961.

The Revolutionary Armed Forces

By the end of the twentieth century, the profile of the FAR had changed significantly from that of only a decade before. The change was brought about largely as a result of a change in the armed forces' missions: the abandonment of military "internationalism" and the embrace of a new domestic economic role; the loss of the extensive financial assistance and training support for the military that was once provided by the Soviet Union; and the continuation of the island's economic crisis, also a product of the loss of Soviet support. As a consequence of these changes, the FAR has had to make do with far fewer resources, both in terms of getting by on a reduced budget and with reduced manpower, yet all the while attempting to maintain itself as a professional military organization.

In the late 1990s, the FAR was composed of three major armed services, as it had been for the past four decades: the Revolutionary Army (Ejército Revolucionario), the aforementioned DAAFAR (Antiaircraft Defense and Revolutionary Air Force), and the Revolutionary Navy (Marina de Guerra Revolucionaria—MGR). Of these, the army, as the historical successor to the guerrillas' Rebel Army, is generally recognized as the main force; not until 1972 were separate commands established for the DAAFAR and the MGR. All three services are under the authority of the MINFAR's General Staff. At the end of 2000, the chief of the MINFAR's General Staff continued to be Division General Álvaro López Miera, also MINFAR vice minister. López Miera assumed the General Staff post in late 1998 on succeeding Division General Ulises Rosales del Toro, who, at that time, had only recently been promoted from the rank of brigade general (see Ranks, Insignia, and Uniforms, this ch.). As General Staff chief, López Miera also serves as the commander of the Revolutionary Army. The DAAFAR was commanded by Division General Rubén Martínez Puentes, and the MGR, by Vice Admiral Pedro Miguel Pérez Betancourt.

During the course of the 1990s, the FAR's manpower was reduced by more than half from what had been an estimated 180,500 active-duty troops in 1990. This reduction, with the most severe cuts having been carried out between 1993 and 1995, was the result of efforts to trim expenditures as well as adjust to a greatly reduced need for military manpower following the end of the "internationalist" mission. According to the London-based International Institute for Strategic Studies (IISS), the FAR was composed of 65,000 personnel in 2000. This number included an estimated 45,000 members of the Revolutionary Army, 10,000 of the DAAFAR, and 5,000 of the MGR. The ratio of Cuba's army in proportion to the island's population dropped from twenty-nine soldiers per 1,000 inhabitants in 1987 to only five soldiers per 1,000 inhabitants in 1997, based on data compiled by the Stockholm International Peace Research Institute. This ratio was comparable on a per capita basis to that found in such countries as Colombia, Bolivia, Ecuador, and El Salvador. Moreover, the FAR's present force strength is even lower than it was prior to the adoption of the military's "internationalist" mission in the mid-1970s, a period when its manpower needs were roughly comparable yet its budget was subsidized by Soviet aid. At that time, the FAR was able to maintain an active-duty force strength of 120,000 troops and officers.

These regular military forces under the FAR's command, which include conscripts and activated reservists, are supported by yet other organizations that are assigned duties related to defense and the maintenance of internal order. Of these, the EJT (Youth Labor Army) and the Territorial Troops Militia (Milicias de Tropas Territoriales—MTT) are the most important. The members of the EJT are primarily engaged in agriculture and military construction projects. The MTT consists of civilian volunteers who are trained and led by the members of the regular military. A Civil Defense (Defensa Civil) force, also made up of civilians and led by military officers, rounds out the nation's defense organization (see Territorial Troops Militia; Civil Defense, this ch.).

The FAR's two main missions in the late 1990s consisted of providing for the island's external defense and the maintenance of internal order. These have remained the FAR's principal missions since the beginning of the Revolution. In 1976 the

FAR's "internationalist" mission was added, which provided a basis for the military's deployment of troops to foreign combat. However, after the return home of the last "internationalist" forces in 1991, the sixteen-year "internationalist" mission was replaced with a new charge for the military to help the ailing economy. During the course of the 1990s, this newest mission led to the FAR's expanded activities in the economic sphere that extend from the military's role in agricultural production, to manufacturing, and even to providing services for the burgeoning tourism industry.

Doctrine of the War of All the People

The military doctrine that guides the FAR in the execution of its traditional defense-related missions is known as the War of All the People (Guerra de Todo el Pueblo—GTP). This doctrine has been in force since the early 1980s, around the time that the MTT was established. The GTP centers on the key role assigned to the Cuban population in helping defend the island in the event of an attack. Its objective is to deter such an attack by so raising the costs for an invader, in terms of the casualties inflicted, that the action is deemed unacceptable. The doctrine is built around the defense-related duties assigned to the members of the MTT, who would be armed in order to support the regular armed forces. Under this doctrine, the country's entire population has been organized into defense zones, which exist at the local and provincial level and which are presided over by the National Defense Council. In the event of a crisis, the local defense zones and the militia would be mobilized and their command taken over by the armed forces. In the Cubans' defensive strategy, the regular military is conceived of as only a "professional vanguard" of the mobilized citizenry, and any ensuing struggle would be waged by means of conventional warfare as well as unconventional or guerrilla warfare. The regime's ability to rely on an armed population for the island's defense, at least rhetorically, has helped to compensate slightly for the loss of capabilities, especially in terms of diminished manpower, that the FAR has suffered since the early 1990s.

Territorial Troops Militia

The Territorial Troops Militia (Milicias de Tropas Territoriales—MTT), a body composed exclusively of civilian volunteers, was established on May 1, 1980, and placed under the command of the MINFAR. Its creation is recognized as having

A fire station in Old Havana, 1999
Courtesy National Imagery and Mapping Agency, Washington

marked the beginning of Cuba's official embrace of the military doctrine of the War of All the People, which has remained in force since then. Like the MNR (National Revolutionary Militia) of the early 1960s, the MTT's formation reinforced the notion of the popular will to defend the Revolution.

Most members of the MTT are women, the elderly, or retirees. Male teenagers who are too young or have not yet been called for military service are also eligible to join the MTT, as are men who are not obligated to serve as reservists. The MTT expanded from 500,000 members in 1982 to 1.2 million by mid-1984. The size of the force has remained at about 1 million, despite the economic crisis.

The MTT's mission during a crisis would be to fight alongside, and provide replacements for, the personnel of the regular armed force; to help protect such strategic infrastructure as bridges, highways, and railroads; and to carry out any other measures that might be needed to immobilize, wear down, or ultimately destroy the enemy. By the beginning of the 1980s, MTT members were extensively involved in the construction of tunnels throughout the island, which would be used as shelter for the population in the event of an attack. As a result of Cuba's continuing economic difficulties during the 1990s, the time that MTT members have spent in training and preparing for their various defense-related activities has been reduced. The reduction includes a decrease in the time that MTT mem-

313

bers have spent in carrying out joint exercises and maneuvers with regular FAR troops.

The MTT is supported through the MINFAR's budget as well as through "voluntary" donations made by citizens. Most of these donations come from workplace contributions, which are paid through weekly deductions from workers' salaries. According to the MINFAR, between 1981 and 1995, the expenses incurred for the MTT's training averaged approximately 35 million Cuban pesos (for value of peso, see Glossary) per year. During this same period, popular contributions toward the force averaged about 30 million pesos per year. Just over half of the training expenditures went toward the purchase of study supplies and other training materials; just over one-third were dedicated for the purchase of weapons, communication equipment, uniforms, and spare parts. Other organizations also set annual funding goals with respect to their own MTT contributions. Among such organizations were the CDR (Committee for the Defense of the Revolution), the Federation of Cuban Women (Federación de Mujeres Cubanas—FMC), the National Association of Small Farmers (Asociación Nacional de Agricultores Pequeños—ANAP), and even the Organization of José Martí Pioneers (Organización de Pioneros José Martí—OPJM).

According to reforms for allocating MTT funds made in the system in 1995, the funds collected for the MTT are no longer sent to a central government account but remain within each municipality to support local MTT activities. Despite the country's economic hardships, the amount of funds collected through popular contributions to the MTT continued to increase after the beginning of the Special Period in the early 1990s. As of 1995, the MINFAR was paying only 14 percent of the MTT's total expenditures.

Civil Defense

Civil Defense was organized in 1966, following the disbandment of the Popular Defense Force, which was the immediate successor to the MNR (National Revolutionary Militias), after the MNR's dissolution in 1963. The mission of the civilian-based Civil Defense, which falls under the command of the MINFAR, is, in some respects, similar to that of the MTT, as the militia's modern incarnation. During a national crisis or wartime, Civil Defense members would be responsible for helping provide for local defense and rear-area security.

Civil Defense's more routine duties, however, are to aid the civilian population and help protect economic resources in the event of a peacetime disaster. In practice this has most often meant that the force has been active in helping safeguard the population and property, including livestock, when the island has been threatened or hit by hurricanes or affected by other natural disasters, such as droughts or earthquakes. In 1999 Civil Defense had an estimated 50,000 members, including both men and women. Members are often PCC members or local government officials and are active in their local defense zones. Civil Defense units are often organized at schools as well as at workplaces.

Revolutionary Army

In 1999 the Revolutionary Army (Ejército Revolucionario) represented approximately 70 percent of Cuba's regular military manpower. According to the IISS, the Army's estimated 45,000 troops included 39,000 members of the Ready Reserves who were completing the forty-five days of annual active-duty service necessary for maintaining their status, as well as conscripts who were fulfilling their military service requirement. These personnel were under the command of one of three territorial armies, which are under the authority of the FAR's General Staff. These commands roughly divide the island into thirds, corresponding with territory under either the Western, Central, or Eastern Armies. Since 1993 the commands have been unified, with the units of the DAAFAR and MGR having been brought under the operational control of the territorial army chiefs. By the beginning of the 1990s, the Isla de la Juventud Military Region—which was established in 1962 and in the 1980s was an independent command, with a single infantry division—had been brought under the authority of the Western Army.

The Western Army, organized in 1970, is the largest of the three territorial commands, and is generally considered the most strategically important because its troops are responsible for the defense of the nation's capital as well as Cuba's most important military installations. In addition to the Isla de la Juventud, the territory under the Western Army includes the provinces of Pinar del Río, La Habana, and Ciudad de La Habana, where its headquarters is shared with the MINFAR. The Western Army is also thought to be subdivided into three army corps—the Havana Eastern Corps, the Havana Western

Corps, and the Pinar del Río Corps—plus the Isla de la Juventud Military Region. Since 1989 the Western Army has been led by Division General Leopoldo "Polo" Cintra Frias, a Politburo member, former commander of Cuban forces in Angola, and Hero of the Republic. Each of the provinces under the Western Army's command has its own general staff. This organizational pattern at the provincial level is replicated in the Central and Eastern Armies.

The Central Army was established in April 1961, only thirteen days before the Bay of Pigs landing at Playa Girón in the province of Matanzas. In addition to Matanzas, the provinces under the Central Army's command include Cienfuegos, Santa Clara, and Sancti Spíritus. Its headquarters is in Santa Clara, the capital of Villa Clara Province. The Central Army is further subdivided into three army corps, consisting of the Matanzas Corps, the Central Corps (which has command over troops stationed in Villa Clara, Cienfuegos, and Sancti Spíritus provinces), and the Ciego de Ávila Corps. In 1999 the chief of the Central Army was Division General Joaquín Quintas Solá, who has held that post since 1984.

The Eastern Army, established in April 1961, held command over personnel stationed in the provinces of Camagüey, Las Tunas, Holguín, Granma, Santiago de Cuba, and Guantánamo from its headquarters in Santiago de Cuba. In 1999 the chief of the Eastern Army was Division General Ramón Espinosa Martín, who has held that command for the past fifteen years. The Eastern Army is also organized into three army corps, consisting of the Camagüey, the Northern, and the Southern Army Corps. The Northern Army Corps had authority over troops in the provinces of Las Tunas and Holguín. The Southern Army Corps had command over units deployed in the provinces of Granma, Santiago de Cuba, and Guantánamo. Also under the Eastern Army's command is the elite Border Brigade (Brigada de la Frontera), which maintains watch over the United States Naval Station at Guantánamo Bay (see The United States Naval Station at Guantánamo Bay, this ch.).

The IISS reported in 1999 that the army's troop formations consisted of four to five armored brigades; nine mechanized infantry brigades; an airborne brigade; fourteen reserve brigades; and the Border Brigade. In addition, there is an air defense artillery regiment and a surface-to-air missile brigade. Each of the three territorial armies is believed to be assigned at least one armored brigade—usually attached to the army's

A Cuban army colonel inspects an infantry squad and tank crew on
April 17, 1993.
A front-side view of a BMP-1 armored infantry fighting vehicle at
Battalion 2721 in San José de las Lajas, January 1998
Courtesy National Imagery and Mapping Agency, Washington

headquarters—as well as a mechanized infantry brigade. As well, it is known that the Border Brigade in Guantánamo and at least one ground artillery regiment (attached to a mechanized infantry brigade), based in Las Tunas, are under the Eastern Army's command. Unfortunately, there is relatively little public information available with respect to the organization of the ground forces within the three armies, let alone the equipment that pertains to each of these commands (see table 19, Major Army Equipment, 1999, Appendix). Nevertheless, the Western Army is known to have the greatest priority for the FAR leadership, and is also likely to be assigned the most personnel and the most equipment; this would be followed, according to defense priorities, by the Eastern Army, and, lastly, by the Central Army.

Assessing the situation of Cuba's ground forces has been further complicated by the leadership's decision to put into storage three-fourths of the FAR's equipment. The mothballing of so much of the military's equipment began with the onset of the economic crisis in the early 1990s, and was prompted by the lack of spare and replacement parts for the Soviet-era matériel as well as the shortage of the hard currency needed to pay for the fuel for training and exercises. Much of this equipment is stored in tunnels and caves throughout the island, but it is not thought to be withstanding well the island's tropical environment. Especially vulnerable are the equipment and weaponry that rely on more sophisticated technology. According to the United States Department of Defense's 1998 report entitled, "The Cuban Threat to U.S. National Security," the mothballed matériel would not be available for defense on short notice. The same report also concludes that, owing to severely reduced training, the ground forces' overall state of readiness is low and notes that the FAR generally is not capable of mounting effective operations above the battalion level.

The Cuban military has long maintained its own secret base for intercepting electronic communications. Operated by the FAR's Electronic Warfare Battalion, this smaller, relatively unknown base is located at El Wajay, 14.5 kilometers southwest of Havana, near the Russian operation at Lourdes. Although not as powerful as the Russian facility, the Cuban military's signals intelligence (SIGINT) facility is thought to be capable of monitoring telephone and radio signals at least as far away as Florida. The Electronic Warfare Battalion reportedly has the equipment necessary to jam United States communications, but is not thought to have used it for this end.

Antiaircraft Defense and Revolutionary Air Force

The Antiaircraft Defense and Revolutionary Air Force (Defensa Antiaérea y Fuerza Aérea Revolucionaria—DAAFAR) traces its origins to the single aircraft that constituted the guerrillas' Rebel Air Force in April 1958. It was established as a branch of service separate from the Revolutionary Army, with its own command structure, in April 1972, a change that was likely influenced by the then ongoing efforts by the Soviet Union to help professionalize Cuba's armed forces. The DAAFAR's responsibilities encompass providing for the nation's air defense as well as tactical and airlift support for the FAR's ground forces. According to the IISS, in 1999 the DAAFAR had 10,000 personnel, including conscripts, and represented 15 percent of total regular military manpower.

The DAAFAR's territorial commands parallel those of the three territorial armies and consist of the Western, Central, and Eastern Air Force brigades. In addition, the DAAFAR also maintains Air Defense Artillery and Missile Forces. Although their locations are not publicly disclosed, it is reasonable to surmise that they are stationed in a position to defend the capital of Havana. The major air installations under the command of the Western Air Force Brigade include bases at San Julián in Pinar del Río Province and San Antonio de los Baños, as well as the Baracoa Air Base and the José Martí International Airport in La Habana Province. Under the Central Brigade are air bases at Güines, Matanzas; Cienfuegos, Cienfuegos; Santa Clara, Villa Clara; and Sancti Spíritus, Sancti Spíritus. The Western Brigade maintains its key installations at the provincial capitals of Camagüey, Holguín, and Santiago de Cuba in the respective provinces of Camagüey, Holguín, and Santiago de Cuba. Of all these, the base at San Antonio de los Baños is considered to be the military's most important airport. It is the only airport that, as of the early 1990s, had three airstrips, one of which was 4,000 meters in length.

The operational readiness and effectiveness of the DAAFAR have been severely compromised by the economic crisis and the loss of Soviet aid. Although Cuba is formally acknowledged as having one of the better equipped air forces in Latin America, consisting of several hundred combat aircraft and armed helicopters, the reality is that, by the late 1990s, a significant part of the fleet was no longer deemed operational (see table 20, Appendix). To become more self-sufficient, the DAAFAR's Research and Development Center is also seeking to build its own aircraft, such as the AC–001 multi-use "Comas" planes that were first produced at the Yuri Gargarin Military Industrial Enterprise in 1992.

The United States Department of Defense estimated in 1998 that fewer than two dozen of the DAAFAR's MiGs remain operational. Despite the access to spare parts established by an accord with the Russians as rent for the signals intelligence facility at Lourdes, which is located south of Havana in La Habana Province, the DAAFAR's state of readiness is expected to continue to worsen. The mothballed equipment continues to deteriorate, and pilot training and flight hours, which are essential for flying the more sophisticated MiGs in the Cuban inventory, remain limited because of the cost of fuel.

Revolutionary Navy

The Revolutionary Navy (Marina de Guerra Revolucionaria—MGR), which has always been the smallest and least prestigious of the FAR's three armed services since its establishment in August 1963, is the service that has been most severely affected by the economic crisis. As of late 2000, it barely managed as an independent force. The MGR's formal mission has traditionally been to provide for shore-based coastal defense as well as to conduct offshore naval operations. By the end of the 1990s, however, the MGR had no major ships that were still seaworthy and no longer was considered to be a blue-water navy. It remained capable only of patrolling Cuba's territorial waters, and even that responsibility was shared with the Ministry of Interior's Border Guard Troops (Tropas Guardafronteras—TGF).

In 1999 the IISS estimated that the MGR was composed of 5,000 personnel, which represented just over 7.5 percent of total regular military manpower. Of these 5,000 personnel, an estimated 3,000 were conscripts. Another 550 were members of the Naval Infantry, a battalion-size force that was created in the late 1970s. This force, which was assigned to coastal defense, gave the MGR a limited ground combat capability. Although the MGR has no reserve force, it would presumably be supplemented by members of the Cuban Merchant Marine in the event of a crisis. Naval aviation is a function of the DAAFAR.

The MGR's headquarters is located in Havana. Its operational commands are divided in accordance with the three territorial armies, each of which holds ultimate authority over the MGR's forces within its geographic boundaries. The MGR's western headquarters is believed to be at Cabañas, located approximately 48.4 kilometers west of Ciudad de La Habana Province on the coast in Pinar del Río Province; and its eastern headquarters, at Holguín, an inland city in the province of the same name. The location of the central headquarters—or even if the headquarters is still maintained, given the cutbacks—is unclear. During the 1990s, the MGR's principal installations were said to include facilities at the Bahía de Cienfuegos, Cienfuegos; the Bahía de Cabañas, Pinar del Río; the Bahía de Mariel, Havana; the Bahía de La Habana, Ciudad de La Habana; the Bahía de Matanzas, Matanzas; the Bahía de Nuevitas, Camagüey; and the Bahía de Nipe, Holguín. With the exception of that at the Bahía de Cienfuegos, all of these bases were located along the northern coast. Some of the installations may have been closed as a result of the continuing cutbacks that were carried out during the course of the 1990s. The naval academy was one of the installations closed. Located just west of Ciudad de La Habana Province on the northern coast at Punta Santa Ana, the MGR's principal training school was converted into a hospital in the 1990s.

As recently as a decade ago, the MGR counted in its inventory three submarines, which had been delivered by the Soviets between 1979 and 1984, and two frigates, the last of which was also received in 1984. It was one of the few countries in the region to have such an ocean-going fleet (see table 21, Appendix). But by the end of the 1990s, none of these vessels remained in operation, and only just over a dozen of the MGR's remaining surface vessels were held to be combat capable. The fast-attack boats that are equipped with Styx (SS–N–2B) surface-to-surface antiship missiles provide the MGR with a continuing, yet weak, antisurface warfare capability. The MGR's shore-based naval infantry reportedly is armed with approximately fifty Samlet (SSC–2B) and two Styx (SSC–3) surface-to-surface missiles. According to the United States Naval Institute, auxiliary ships that remained in operation as late as 1998 included a replenishment oiler, an intelligence collector, a cargo ship, and several hydrographic survey vessels.

Conscription and Personnel Resources

Until 1991, Cuban men were required to perform three years of compulsory military service under the SMO (Obligatory Military Service) system. The three-year obligation had been in force since the first Law of Military Service was promulgated in November 1963. In August 1991, however, the Active Military Service (Servicio Militar Activo—SMA) requirement was reduced to two years, beginning at age sixteen, under the General Military Service Law (Ley de Servicio Militar General—SMG), formerly the SMO. Young Cubans usually are not called to service until age seventeen.

The compulsory service duty reflects the interest of the military and Cuban leadership in having a large proportion of the island's population prepared to contribute to the defense of the Revolution. By the end of the 1990s, 1.7 million young Cuban men had completed their SMA requirement as conscripts. Since the onset of the economic crisis, Cuban youth carrying out such compulsory military service continue to play an important role in the military. Although now at reduced numbers because of overall cutbacks in military manpower, they have become most important in providing a source of cheap labor for the MINFAR's efforts to become a self-sustaining institution.

In terms of overall personnel resources, in 1999 a total of 6.08 million Cubans between the ages of fifteen and forty-nine were considered to be "available" for military service, according to the Central Intelligence Agency's *World Factbook*. Of this total, only 3.76 million Cubans, or just under two-thirds, were judged to be "fit" for military service. In this latter category, 1.9 million of the Cubans were males and 1.86 million were females.

The fulfillment of SMA for conscripts entails their assignment to one of the services of the regular armed forces, to the 65,000-member EJT (Youth Labor Army), or to the Ministry of Interior. Cuban males between the ages of sixteen and fifty are required to perform a minimum of two years' service as an active-duty member of one of the country's security forces, a member of the military reserves, or in some combination of both forms of service. Young men are required to register locally for the draft after reaching their sixteenth birthday, and are then issued a certificate that shows they have registered. According to population statistics, just under 75,000 young Cuban males were becoming eligible for conscription each

The barracks at Battalion 2721 in San José de las Lajas,
La Habana Province, January 1998
A view of the sleeping quarters in the Battalion 2721 barracks
in San José de las Lajas, January 1998
Courtesy National Imagery and Mapping Agency, Washington

year during the late 1990s. Induction calls are held twice a year, with the youth to be inducted selected by lottery. Young men between the ages of sixteen and twenty-eight who have not been called for Active Military Service are known as prerecruits (*prereclutados*). During the late 1980s, new draftees received six to eight months of basic training before being formally inducted into the armed forces. It is likely that the extent and nature of the training given draftees in the 1990s were limited as a result of the economic crisis.

Since the end of the FAR's "internationalist" mission, during which tens of thousands of draftees were sent to fight abroad, the military's need for conscripted manpower has fallen markedly. The decreased need was likely one of the considerations behind the 1991 decision to reduce the SMA term from three to two years, a move that brought the Cuban system more closely in line with the military service requirements maintained by other Latin American countries. The official explanation for the reduction was that the overall educational level of draftees had so improved over the years that they now needed less training. This explanation does not appear to be wholly without merit, given that since 1987, graduates of preuniversity programs who are drafted are required to perform only one year of service. In addition, the military maintains policies that reflect an interest in supporting the educational accomplishments of its draftees, as reflected in a provision known as Order 18. According to this order, youth who were initially not admitted to a university but who distinguish themselves during their term of service are given a second opportunity to pursue their higher education. By the end of 1998, 14,000 graduates of Cuban universities had been beneficiaries of this program.

Cuban women are not subject to conscription. After turning sixteen years of age, however, they are eligible to enlist in the armed forces under the program known as Voluntary Female Military Service (Servicio Militar Voluntario Feminimo), which was established in 1986. (Women served in the FAR well before that date, however.) Their applications for enlistment are coordinated by the FMC (Federation of Cuban Women), the mass organization that has long been headed by Vilma Espín, Raúl Castro's wife. During the 1980s, new female volunteers were accepted twice a year and signed up for two-year tours of duty, in contrast to the five-year commitment that was then required of male enlistees. Those who did not reenlist upon completion of their tour of duty automatically became members of the

FAR's reserve forces; they were eligible to remain active in the reserve until reaching forty years of age.

Women who enlist in the FAR are formally eligible to ascend within the ranks of the armed forces, yet they are believed to face limited opportunities for the advanced military education that might qualify them for such promotions. At the pre-university level, women were reported to be subject to meeting more restrictive entrance requirements than male applicants. At the more advanced levels of military education, it was believed that the only professional program open to women was that offered by the Military Technical Institute (Instituto Técnico Militar—ITM). The prevalence of traditional attitudes regarding sex roles also appeared as an impediment to women's career advancement within the armed forces. Between 1986 and early 1999, more than 18,000 young women had volunteered for military service.

Men who have completed their Active Military Service automatically pass to the ranks of the reserves, where they are expected to continue to train annually until reaching age fifty. Reservists are divided into various groups, according to their state of readiness and training. The members of the Ready Reserves are assigned to army units, serve on active duty for at least forty-five days each year, and could reportedly be mobilized on a few hours' notice. In 1999 these reserve forces numbered approximately 39,000 troops. The next tier consists of men who have completed at least one year of Active Military Service and could be mobilized on a few days' notice. The final group consists of those who either have not completed a year of active service or who were deemed unfit for duty, whether for reasons ascribable to their physical condition or political unreliability. Members of this last group appear to be "reservists" only in name, and reportedly are not required to undergo regular military training.

Professional Training and Education

Cuba's system of military training and education has been developed over the decades to support the specialized needs of a highly professional military force. These schools and training centers are under the authority of a separate directorate within the MINFAR. This directorate is dedicated exclusively to overseeing the education system and reports to the FAR General Staff. During the late 1970s, as a result of efforts to improve educational standards, the upper-level military educational institutions were granted university status. The extent to which these schools, their admission standards, and their curricula were affected by the economic crisis of the 1990s and by the downsizing of the armed forces is unclear.

The preparation of potential future members of the armed forces may be seen as beginning with the Camilo Cienfuegos Military Schools (Escuelas Militares Camilo Cienfuegos—EMCC), which are open to youth (both males and females) between the ages of eleven and seventeen. The first Camilo Cienfuegos school was opened in Matanzas in 1966. By the 1980s, eleven such schools had been established and were located throughout the island. Each was under the authority of a particular branch of military service, with the army controlling seven of the schools. They offered a five-year course of study that was considered comparable to a preuniversity education. Yet in addition to the general curriculum that paralleled that offered by civilian schools, the Camilitos—as the school's students are known—were also given introductory classes on military tactics, the handling of light weapons, topography, chemical defense, and engineering. The students were also expected to adhere to military discipline and participate in drills. Most students gained admission either through their own participation in PCC-related youth organizations—namely, the OPJM (Organization of José Martí Pioneers) or the Union of Young Communists (Unión de Jóvenes Comunistas—UJC)—or through their parents' membership in the FAR or PCC. The graduates of the EMCC were believed to be given preference in admission to the MINFAR's more advanced schools and training programs. The extent to which these schools and their curricula were affected by the economic crisis of the 1990s remained unclear at the time of writing.

Beyond this level, each branch of the armed forces has, until recently, operated its own schools and service academies. The exception is the MGR, whose naval academy at Punta Santa Ana, near Havana, was closed in the 1990s and converted into a hospital. The DAAFAR's Aviation Pilots Military School (Escuela Militar de Pilotos de Aviación—EMPA) is located at the San Julián airbase in western Pinar del Río Province. During the 1980s, the DAAFAR also operated its own technical school, the DAAFAR Technical School (Escuela Técnica de la DAAFAR). The Ministry of Interior also operates separate schools for training its personnel.

The General Antonio Maceo Joint-Service School (Escuela de Cadetes Interarmas General Antonio Maceo—ECAM) has traditionally been the Army's service academy. This school, located at Ceiba del Agua, a short distance southeast of the capital, was first opened in 1963. By the 1980s, admission requirements had been stiffened to stipulate that entrants must have a minimum of a tenth-grade education and be between the ages of fifteen and twenty-one. ECAM's three- and four-year programs of study emphasize the preparation and training of tactical and technical command officers; the curriculum is designed for members of armored and mechanized infantry units and for engineering and logistics personnel.

The Major Camilo Cienfuegos Revolutionary Armed Forces Artillery School (Escuela de Artillería de las FAR Comandante Camilo Cienfuegos) was founded in 1963 and is located at La Cabaña Fortress in Havana harbor. It provides advanced training for field and antiaircraft artillery officers, who upon completion of their studies are awarded a degree in either science or engineering. Those admitted to the school's engineering program, which is a five-year course of study, are required to have graduated from a preuniversity preparatory school, technical institute, or high school, and must be between the ages of seventeen and twenty-one. A four-year program, with similar admission requirements, is offered that focuses on preparing future officers who will command field and antiaircraft artillery, reconnaissance, and radio-technical units.

The Military Technical Institute (ITM), founded in 1966 and located in Havana, offers the most advanced technical training programs available to MINFAR personnel. Unlike the other academies, the ITM is open to women. It offers enrollment in either four- or five-year training programs. Those admitted to the more stringent five-year program must be graduates of a preuniversity preparatory school and be between the ages of seventeen and twenty-one. The five-year program provides for instruction in field artillery, infantry, weapons, tanks, and transport; those graduating from the program become qualified mechanical engineers. The two four-year programs offer training for electromechanical and mechanical technicians. The admission requirements for the four-year courses of study are slightly less stringent than for the five-year program. So long as an applicant has a minimum tenth-grade education and is between the ages of sixteen and twenty-one, he or she is eligible for admission. As with the other schools and courses of study already discussed, the demonstration of political loyalty was considered a relevant factor in determining an applicant's qualifications.

The MINFAR's senior service school is the General Máximo Gómez Revolutionary Armed Forces Academy (Academia de las FAR General Máximo Gómez), which was founded in July 1963 and is located in western La Habana Province. This school provides training for middle-to upper-ranking MINFAR officers. During the 1980s, attendance at the school became a requisite for those hoping to be assigned to the General Staff. The school's curriculum is roughly comparable to that offered at advanced officer training schools in the United States, such as the United States Army's Command and General Staff College at Fort Leavenworth, Kansas, or the United States Army War College at Carlisle Barracks, Pennsylvania.

During the 1990s, the most advanced institution for military education was the National Defense College. This recently established college, which was modeled on Canada's senior officer school, offers a curriculum that is roughly comparable to that of the United States' National Defense University at Fort McNair in Washington, D.C. Its primary focus, as reflected in the curriculum, is on strategic security issues. Although organized mainly for the benefit of senior military professionals, some civilians—most of whom are government functionaries— also are invited to attend the courses. The faculty of the college includes military officials as well as civilian professors. During the 1990s, a period when the military became increasingly involved in the national economy and was often identified as an advocate for further reforms in that arena, the college's faculty members included civilian economists, some of whom also favored economic reforms in line with those envisioned by the MINFAR's leaders.

Ranks, Insignia, and Uniforms

Since 1976 the MINFAR's system of military ranks has been basically patterned after that used by most Western armed forces (see fig. 9; 10). Prior to that time, the system of ranks was far from conventional, a factor that complicated relations with the Soviet military, which pressed Cuba to carry out such changes as part of its professionalization. In about 1998, a minor revision to the FAR's rank insignia was made when chevrons were reintroduced to replace the stars on the insignia of junior officers. Two decades earlier, in 1978, the stars had replaced the chevrons. Another minor change, also made in 1978, was the creation of a new rank, adding the warrant officer class for all three services.

The lack of conventionality in the MINFAR's system of ranks may be traced to the earliest days of the Revolution, and may be understood as a gesture that reflected the rebels' egalitarian nature. Following the victory of the Revolution in 1959, this unconventionality continued, and the only military ranks recognized were those inherited from the Rebel Army. They consisted of lieutenant, first lieutenant, captain, and major (*comandante*). At that time, three dozen men—nearly all of them Rebel Army veterans—held the rank of *comandante*, including Fidel Castro (even though he was clearly recognized as the others' superior).

Between 1959 and 1973, no sweeping overhauls were carried out, but new ranks were gradually introduced. In late 1959, the rank of second lieutenant was the first addition to the military echelons. Between 1963 and 1973, other new ranks were added, including brigade commander, division commander, corps commander, army commander, and commander-in-chief. First-class officers included the ranks of first commander, commander, and major; and junior officers, the ranks of first and second lieutenant and first and second captain.

In November 1976, Law No. 1315 created the system of ranks that remained basically unchanged for the next twenty-odd years. These ranks are held by personnel assigned to the FAR and by personnel under the Ministry of Interior. Personnel assigned to the Revolutionary Army, the DAAFAR, and the Ministry of Interior may have similar rank titles, differentiated only by their uniforms and insignia colors. Fidel Castro holds the rank of commander in chief; his brother, MINFAR Minister Raúl Castro, as army general (*general de ejército*), is the second-ranking officer in the hierarchy of the armed forces. Minister of Interior Abelardo Colomé Ibarra, as army corps general (*general de cuerpo de ejército*), is the third-ranking officer.

The vice ministerial slots within the MINFAR as well as the commands of the FAR's general staff and of its three territorial armies are filled by officers having the rank of division general (*general de división*). The remaining rank at the general officer level is that of brigade general (*general de brigada*).

First-class officer ranks are composed of, in descending order, colonel (*coronel*), lieutenant colonel (*teniente coronel*), and major (*mayor*); junior officers' ranks include captain (*capitán*),

CUBAN RANK	SUB-TENIENTE	TENIENTE	PRIMER TENIENTE	CAPITÁN	MAYOR	TENIENTE CORONEL	CORONEL	GENERAL DE BRIGADA	GENERAL DE DIVISIÓN	GENERAL DE CUERPO DE EJÉRCITO	GENERAL DE EJÉRCITO	COMANDANTE EN JEFE
ARMY AND AIR FORCE[1]												
U.S. RANK TITLES	2D LIEUTENANT	1ST LIEUTENANT		CAPTAIN	MAJOR	LIEUTENANT COLONEL	COLONEL	BRIGADIER GENERAL	MAJOR GENERAL	LIEUTENANT GENERAL	GENERAL	COMMANDER IN CHIEF
CUBAN RANK (NAVY)	ALFÉREZ	TENIENTE DE CORBETA	TENIENTE DE FRAGATA	TENIENTE DE NAVÍO	CAPITÁN DE CORBETA	CAPITÁN DE FRAGATA	CAPITÁN DE NAVÍO	CONTRA ALMIRANTE	VICE ALMIRANTE	ALMIRANTE	NO RANK	
U.S. RANK TITLES	ENSIGN	LIEUTENANT JUNIOR GRADE		LIEUTENANT	LIEUTENANT COMMANDER	COMMANDER	CAPTAIN	REAR ADMIRAL LOWER HALF	REAR ADMIRAL UPPER HALF	VICE ADMIRAL	ADMIRAL	

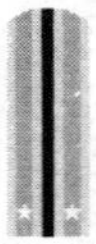

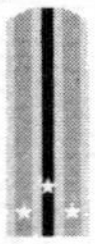

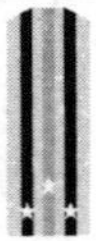

NOTE—United States equivalents represent ranks of relatively comparable authority and are not necessarily the corresponding ranks for protocol purposes.

[1]Army and air force officers at the rank of colonel and below are distinguished by red piping and light blue piping, respectively, on their rank insignia. Insignia for army and air force officers at the rank of brigadier general and above are the same for both services.

Figure 9. Officer Ranks and Insignia, 1999

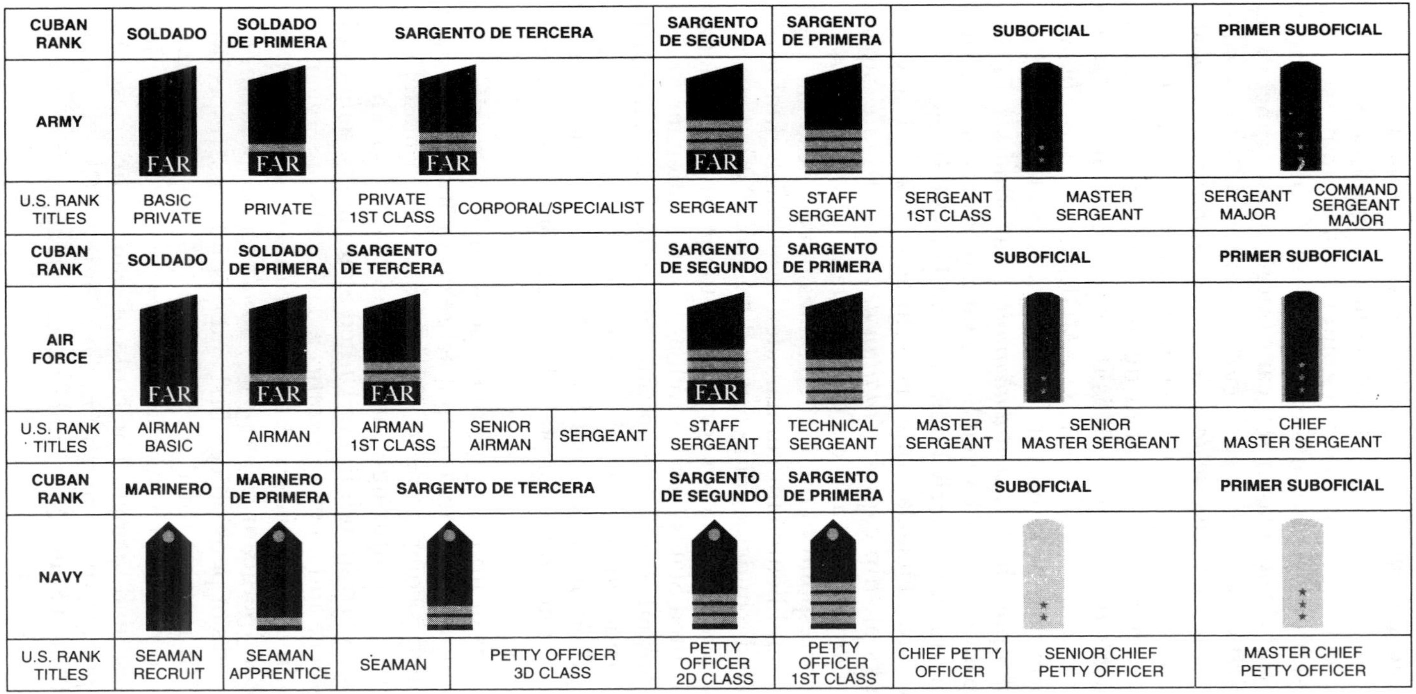

CUBAN RANK							
ARMY	SOLDADO	SOLDADO DE PRIMERA	SARGENTO DE TERCERA	SARGENTO DE SEGUNDA	SARGENTO DE PRIMERA	SUBOFICIAL	PRIMER SUBOFICIAL
U.S. RANK TITLES	BASIC PRIVATE	PRIVATE	PRIVATE 1ST CLASS / CORPORAL/SPECIALIST	SERGEANT	STAFF SERGEANT	SERGEANT 1ST CLASS / MASTER SERGEANT	SERGEANT MAJOR / COMMAND SERGEANT MAJOR
CUBAN RANK	SOLDADO	SOLDADO DE PRIMERA	SARGENTO DE TERCERA	SARGENTO DE SEGUNDO	SARGENTO DE PRIMERA	SUBOFICIAL	PRIMER SUBOFICIAL
AIR FORCE	AIRMAN BASIC	AIRMAN	AIRMAN 1ST CLASS / SENIOR AIRMAN / SERGEANT	STAFF SERGEANT	TECHNICAL SERGEANT	MASTER SERGEANT / SENIOR MASTER SERGEANT	CHIEF MASTER SERGEANT
U.S. RANK TITLES							
CUBAN RANK	MARINERO	MARINERO DE PRIMERA	SARGENTO DE TERCERA	SARGENTO DE SEGUNDO	SARGENTO DE PRIMERA	SUBOFICIAL	PRIMER SUBOFICIAL
NAVY	SEAMAN RECRUIT	SEAMAN APPRENTICE	SEAMAN / PETTY OFFICER 3D CLASS	PETTY OFFICER 2D CLASS	PETTY OFFICER 1ST CLASS	CHIEF PETTY OFFICER / SENIOR CHIEF PETTY OFFICER	MASTER CHIEF PETTY OFFICER
U.S. RANK TITLES							

Figure 10. Enlisted Ranks and Insignia, 1999

331

first lieutenant *(primer teniente)*, lieutenant *(teniente)*, and second lieutenant *(subteniente)*. The noncommissioned ranks of warrant officers and enlisted personnel include, in descending order, senior warrant officer *(primer suboficial)* and warrant officer *(suboficial)*, master sergeant (sargento de primera), sergeant first class *(sargento de segunda)*, sergeant *(sargento de tercera)*, private first class *(soldado de primera)*, and private *(soldado)*.

Establishing comparability for the highest ranks of MGR personnel remains somewhat difficult inasmuch as the Cuban rank of *almirante* (admiral) is the equivalent of the United States rank of vice admiral. The MGR rank of *vice almirante* (vice admiral) is comparable to the United States rank of rear admiral, upper half. A *contra almirante* (rear admiral), in turn, is comparable to the United States rank of rear admiral, lower half (the rank formerly known in the United States Navy as commodore). First-class officers include, in descending order, the ranks of ship captain *(capitán de navío)*, frigate captain *(capitán de fragata)*, and corvette captain *(capitán de corbeta)*, which correspond to the United States ranks of captain, commander, and lieutenant commander, respectively. Junior officers include, in descending order, the ranks of ship lieutenant *(teniente de navío)*, which is comparable to the rank of lieutenant in the United States Navy, as well as frigate lieutenant *(teniente de fragata)* and corvette lieutenant *(teniente de corbeta)*, which are both considered comparable to the single rank of lieutenant junior grade in the United States Navy. The rank of ensign *(alférez)* is comparable for both the United States Navy and the MGR.

In terms of noncommissioned personnel in the MGR, the most senior rank is that of first sergeant major *(primer suboficial)*, which is comparable to a United States Navy master chief petty officer. Confusingly, however, an MGR sergeant major *(suboficial)* corresponds to two United States ranks, senior chief petty officer and chief petty officer. The ranks of sergeant are divided into three classes: A first sergeant *(sargento de primera)* and second sergeant *(sargento de segunda)* correspond directly to the ranks of petty officer, first and second class, respectively. The MGR rank of third sergeant *(sargento de tercera)* corresponds to the two United States Navy ranks of petty officer, third class, and seaman. The ranks of seaman, first class *(marinero de primera)* and seaman *(marinero)* in the MGR correspond to the United States Navy ranks of seaman apprentice and seaman recruit, respectively.

With respect to uniforms, the olive-drab fatigues made famous by Castro continue to be the standard field uniform for the FAR's ground and air forces. Other uniforms issued to FAR personnel include various styles of service, parade, and ceremonial parade uniforms. The parade uniforms of the Revolutionary Army are olive-drab; those of the DAAFAR are blue; and those of the MGR are either blue-black, for winter, or white, for summer. Notwithstanding changes that might be ordered by commanders, summer uniforms are generally worn from mid-March through mid-November. In addition, special uniforms are also issued. For the ground forces, they include paratrooper, chemical warfare, and tanker uniforms. For the DAAFAR, special pilot uniforms include an antigravity uniform and a pressurized uniform.

Relations with Russia

Following the departure of the last Russian troops in 1993, the SIGINT facility at Lourdes remained one of the only practical vestiges (apart from the extensive Soviet-origin matériel in the FAR's inventory) of the once-close security relationship between Cuba and the former Soviet Union. Nevertheless, it provided a reason for continuing regular interaction between the leaders of the two countries on issues related to security concerns through the remainder of the 1990s. During this period, the Lourdes facility was maintained and staffed by Russian intelligence personnel of the Federal Security Service (Federal'naya Sluzhba Bezopasnosti—FSB), a successor entity to the Soviet-era Committee for State Security (Komitet Gosudarstvennoi Bezopastnosti—KGB). An estimated 810 Russian military personnel were in Cuba in 1999.

Under the first bilateral agreement pertaining to Lourdes that was reached in 1993, it was agreed that the facility would remain in operation and that "rent" would be paid in the form of spare parts for the FAR. At that time, the Russians agreed to pay Cuba for the next twenty years for both the Lourdes operation and for a since-closed submarine support facility at Cienfuegos on the southern Cuban coast, but the amount of the rent was not set. In March 1995, the agreement finalizing the terms for remuneration for Lourdes was signed in Moscow by FAR First Vice Minister Division General Julio Casas Regueiro. It provided for an annual rent in the range of US$200 million, much of which would be in the form of bartered military materials. Although the Russians, owing to their own domestic problems, had difficulties in providing the Cubans with the bartered goods during the first years that followed the agreement's signing, the supply problems were thought to have been resolved by the end of the 1990s.

According to the Russians, the "listening post" is used to monitor compliance with international arms-control agreements. Yet notwithstanding its likely utility in this regard, the Lourdes facility also is capable of intercepting and monitoring communications along the eastern coast of the United States as well as the circum-Caribbean region. Although the Cubans do not have access to the "raw" intelligence data obtained by the Russians, they are routinely provided intelligence summaries on issues that are thought to affect their interests.

Relations with Other Armed Forces

The onset of the economic crisis, the end of military "internationalism," and the loss of Soviet support appeared to bring about a heightened awareness within the Cuban armed forces with respect to the institution's potential isolation. As a result, the Cuban military's efforts to build contacts with foreign militaries were stepped up during the 1990s. In terms of other countries' receptivity, the Cuban military's efforts were aided by the end of the Cold War and Fidel Castro's 1992 declaration that Cuba would no longer support revolutionary movements abroad.

The Cuban military has long maintained contacts with the armed forces of developing world nations that are considered nonaligned or, at least, not ideologically hostile toward the Castro regime. The changed situation of the 1990s, however, helped open the way for broader international contacts. The Cuban interest in reducing the FAR's ideological isolation in the post-Cold War era spurred its efforts to increase cooperation and regular contacts with other militaries in the Latin American region. By mid-decade, these efforts appeared to have been somewhat successful. In 1996 Cuba served as host of the biennial meeting of Ibero-American Military Academies, a gathering whose participants included military officials from Argentina, Bolivia, Colombia, Ecuador, Guatemala, and Nicaragua. In this new environment, the Cuban military has also sought to build ties and expand cooperation with militaries in Canada and Western Europe. Among the latter group of countries with whose militaries the Cubans have been most publicly engaged are Britain, France, and, most significantly, Spain, which in 1996 announced its decision to become the first European Union (EU—see Glossary) nation to assign a permanent military attaché to Havana. The contacts with these European countries have included hosting visits of students from their military schools as well as conducting discussions on mutual concerns and exploring areas of possible future cooperation.

Despite the importance of Cuba's renewed military ties with Latin America and Europe, perhaps the most important tie with a foreign military service to develop since the Soviet Union's demise has been the FAR's relationship with the Chinese Popular Liberation Army (PLA). On various occasions during the 1990s, FAR leaders have traveled to the People's Republic of China (PRC) to meet with military officials; and those officials, in turn, have reciprocated in visiting the island. In February 1999, the Chinese defense minister and a delegation of military officials paid a three-day visit to Cuba. The FAR's interest in these contacts is believed to stem from the desire to have a powerful ally. In addition, the MINFAR leadership's view—and, in particular, Minister Raúl Castro's view—that elements of the Chinese model of economic reform may be relevant for Cuba also likely contributed to the interest in broadening ties with their military colleagues, who during the 1990s had a prominent role in the Chinese economy. The PLA, at the same time, may be recognized to have a geostrategic interest with respect to its Cuban ally in the Caribbean, an interest that has raised some concerns in the United States. In late 1999, for example, Cuban officials were obliged to deny a report published by a Miami newspaper that the PRC had established a military communications facility on the island.

Ministry of Interior

Leadership and Organization

The Ministry of Interior was created in June 1961 and charged with maintaining Cuba's internal security, with responsibilities ranging from counterintelligence to firefighting. Between that time and 1989, the Ministry of Interior was often pitted against the MINFAR in the bureaucratic competition for primacy in ensuring national security. In contrast to the MINFAR, which since its organization has remained under the sole authority of Raúl Castro, the Ministry of Interior has been variously headed by Ramiro Valdés Menéndez, a Rebel Army veteran and the founder of the ministry, and by Sergio del Valle

Jiménez, also a longtime revolutionary supporter. Perhaps owing to his background as a physician, del Valle launched rehabilitation programs and efforts to curtail torture. In the years immediately preceding the trial involving Division General Arnaldo Ochoa, the ministry's head was its former first vice minister, Division General José Abrantes Fernández, who was a close associate of Valdés, a trusted aide to Fidel Castro, and who had also played a key role in the organization of Cuba's intelligence community, beginning in the early 1960s (see Organizational Changes of 1989, this ch.).

Following the events of mid-1989 that were associated with the Ochoa affair, Abrantes was sentenced to jail. The post of minister of interior was then assigned to the second-ranking officer in the FAR, Army Corps General Abelardo Colomé Ibarra, a close associate of Raúl Castro. During the ensuing months, the top layers of leadership of the ministry's various directorates were purged and their officials replaced by men who had a background as loyal officers in the FAR. By the late 1990s, a few reports suggested that some of the once-purged Ministry of Interior officials, mainly those who had had backgrounds in intelligence, were being invited back on a selective basis. Nevertheless, some analysts maintained that even a decade later the ministry had still not recovered from the shake-up that followed the Ochoa affair. As of 1999, Colomé Ibarra continued to head the ministry and served as its representative on the Council of Ministers (see The Military in the Government and the Party, this ch.).

At the time of the shake-up, the Ministry of Interior was organized with six vice ministries, each of which was in turn responsible for various directorates and departments. Despite some name changes, this basic structure is thought to have remained intact since 1989. The most important of the vice ministries is that of the first vice minister. The first vice minister has authority over a number of key directorates and departments, including the General Directorate of Personal Security (Dirección General de Seguridad Personal—DGSP), which is responsible for safeguarding the life of the Cuban leader; the General Directorate of Special Troops (Dirección General de Tropas Especiales—DGTE); the General Directorate of Border Guards (Dirección General de Guardafronteras—DGG); the Technical Directorate; and the directorates of immigration, control, codes (sometimes referred to as the Eighth Directorate), and weapons. The Central Laboratory of Criminology is also under the first vice minister's jurisdiction.

The remaining five vice ministries have more specific responsibilities. They include the Vice Ministry of Counterintelligence, which is responsible for the Directorate of Counterintelligence (Dirección de Contra Inteligencia); the Vice Ministry of Intelligence, which oversees the Directorate of Intelligence (Dirección de Inteligencia—DI); and the Vice Ministry of Political Affairs, which reportedly is jointly subordinate to the head of the PCC Central Committee's national security commission, as well as to the minister of interior. The Vice Ministry of Internal Order has authority over the following directorates: National Revolutionary Police, Penitentiary Establishments, Prevention and Extinction of Fires, and Identity Cards. Lastly, the Vice Ministry of the Economy is responsible for overseeing the ministry's administrative functions, including planning, budgeting, and exercising inventory control over motor vehicles and warehouses.

Other ministry subdivisions that are organizationally independent of the vice ministries include the directorates of Cadres, Personnel, and Instruction; Information; and International Relations. The ministry's Secretariat, a body established in the 1980s and which maintains the central archives, is thought to still be responsible for overseeing the aforementioned directorates. In addition to the personnel who may be stationed abroad, the ministry also maintains delegations in each provincial capital that work closely with the local PCC in helping to carry out the charges of the sundry directorates and departments.

Special Troops

The Special Troops (Tropas Especiales) are considered the elite of Cuba's security forces. Under the nominal authority of the first vice minister of the Ministry of Interior, they are thought to receive their orders directly from Fidel Castro. Established in the mid-1960s, the Special Troops consist of two battalions made up of an estimated 1,200 highly trained and politically reliable personnel. Despite the economic crisis of the 1990s, the Special Troops are considered to remain capable of executing selected military and internal security missions.

The Special Troops' mission is to serve as a highly mobile shock force that can provide protection for high-ranking officials, conduct special military operations, and help support other special security requirements that the leadership might have. During the 1980s, several foreign advisers, all of whom were from Vietnam, were brought in to aid with the Special Troops' training, especially in survival techniques; in turn the Special Troops are also known to have provided training to selected foreign forces. Roughly comparable to the United States Green Berets or the *spetznaz* of the former Soviet Union, the Special Troops are trained to operate as commando-style units. Most members of the force are both parachute- and scuba-qualified and trained in the martial arts for hand-to-hand combat. In terms of their publicly known operations, members of the Special Troops were the surreptitious "advance" forces sent by Fidel Castro to Angola in 1975, whose arrival there prior to Angolan independence preceded the formal beginning of Cuba's military involvement in that African conflict. Few details are available with respect to the deployment of these forces throughout the island. Most personnel belonging to the Special Troops are believed to be stationed in or near Havana, although at least one unit was reportedly stationed near the United States Naval Base at Guantánamo.

Border Guard Troops

The Border Guard Troops (Tropas Guardafronteras—TGF) are under the authority of the Ministry of Interior's Directorate of Border Guards, an entity that falls under the jurisdiction of the first vice minister. In 1999 the TGF had an estimated 6,500 personnel, as compared with an estimated 3,500 in the late 1980s. The TGF was originally established under the Ministry of Interior in March 1963 as the Department of Coastal and Port Vigilance. During the counterrevolutionary campaign of the 1960s known as the "fight against bandits," the members of this force engaged in the maritime-oriented "fight against pirates." Their principal mission remains coastal surveillance. Correspondingly, they are charged with helping ensure the security of the country's borders, both in preventing unauthorized incursions into Cuban territory and in preventing unauthorized departures by Cubans attempting to leave the island. Although responsible primarily for patrolling Cuba's inland waterways, shores, and coastal waters, their members would be the first line of defense against any external invading force. Up until the significant weakening of Cuba's naval forces during the 1990s, it was expected that the TGF's forces would fall under the operational command of the MGR during a national

A Soviet-built Cuban Foxtrot-class patrol submarine, August 1, 1986
New Cuban patrol boats at the Boquerón port facility, August 1992
Courtesy National Imagery and Mapping Agency, Washington

security crisis. According to a 1996 report, the TGF is thought to have at least one antisubmarine unit. The TGF is equipped with twenty Soviet-era Zhuk patrol craft as well as various fast launches and utility boats. TGF forces also regularly use motorcycles for helping patrol the shoreline as well as canines for tracking.

At the time of the 1994 *balsero* crisis, the TGF was widely condemned for its role in the sinking of the tugboat *13 de marzo*, which was carrying Cubans seeking to leave the island illegally. As a result of the TGF's ramming and fire-hosing of the vessel, forty-one of the boat's seventy-two passengers drowned, deaths that included women and twenty-three children. Because of the international outcry that the incident provoked, the leadership instructed the TGF to no longer use force in preventing such departures.

During the late 1990s, by contrast, no reports emerged that cited significant brutality on the part of the TGF. Rather, in helping Cuba comply with the terms of the May 1995 immigration accord signed with the United States, members of the TGF are routinely in contact with their counterparts in the United States Coast Guard. Their main role is to cooperate in the repatriation of Cuban émigrés who are intercepted at sea by United States Coast Guard personnel.

National Revolutionary Police

The National Revolutionary Police (Policía Nacional Revolucionaria—PNR) fall under the authority of the Vice Ministry of Internal Order. As Cuba's primary uniformed law enforcement body, they are responsible for handling routine criminal and law enforcement matters and are also occasionally called on by other security forces to help with what are deemed to be political matters. The force was established on January 5, 1959, only days after the victory of the Revolution, and in the mid-1980s numbered 10,000. It is unclear how the size of the force may have been affected by the economic crisis of the 1990s.

The regime's increased concern over the growing crime problem on the island prompted greater attention to the PNR's professional development during the late 1990s. As a result, the PNR received improved training, was assigned new French Citroën cruisers to replace the old Soviet-era Ladas, and also was provided new, more modern communications equipment. During this period, the presence of the uniformed PNR officers on the street was also increased, especially with respect to the patrols, often accompanied by canines, assigned to areas frequented by foreign tourists. According to Cuban officials, the increases in security-related government expenditures in 1999 were largely attributable to the attention dedicated to beefing up the country's police forces.

During the late 1990s, numerous reports by human rights groups also stated that PNR officers routinely assisted the non-uniformed personnel of the DSE in matters related to the activities of Cuban dissidents. On occasion, political detainees have been taken to PNR precinct stations, where they have been held briefly before being released or transferred to other facilities associated with the DSE. The PNR's forces have also been criticized for failing to act to break up the so-called spontaneous demonstrations that often erupted outside the home of dissidents and others considered to be antagonistic toward the regime, such as members of the small yet vocal independent press. The participants in these demonstrations, which are known as acts of repudiation (*actos de repudio*), are usually members of the officially sanctioned Rapid Response Brigades (Brigadas de Respuesta Rápida—BRR) or of the local CDRs. The BRR, composed of civilian volunteers, were initially organized in mid-1991 to deal with possible problems that could develop in relation to Cuba's hosting of the Pan-American Games in the midst of the then new economic crisis (see Human Rights and Political Prisoners, this ch.).

In addition, to assist the regular police in their increased responsibilities in light of Cuba's tourism boom of the 1990s, a new black-bereted force known as the Special Brigade (Brigada Especial) was created in 1998. The main role of the Special Brigade has been preventive, often in helping identify and arrest the hustlers and pimps who prey on foreign tourists. The force members have also worked closely with the PNR in coordinating the neighborhood-based, anticrime groups under the Unified Prevention and Vigilance System (Sistema Unificado de Prevención y Vigilancia—SUPV). The SUPV was conceived during the early 1990s and placed under the PNR's supervision as part of the effort to stem the surge in economic-related crime that accompanied the onset of the crisis and at the same time improve vigilance in relation to "antisocial" behavior.

Intelligence Directorate

The key organization responsible for Cuba's foreign intelligence is the Intelligence Directorate (Dirección de Inteligencia). Before its name was changed in 1989, this body was long known as the General Intelligence Directorate (Dirección General de Inteligencia—DGI). Prior to the collapse of the Soviet Union, the DGI was closely aligned with and organized along the lines of the former Soviet Union's KGB, from which it also received training. During the Soviet era, foreign intelligence gained by either organization was occasionally shared.

The United States and the resident Cuban exile community in this country have been the two principal foci of the Intelligence Directorate's collection and analytical efforts. The collection activities include the infiltration of exile organizations, an effort that is relatively easy given the common language and culture and the large numbers of exiles resident in the United States. Following the February 1996 downing of two aircraft piloted by members of the exile organization Brothers to the Rescue, it became known that one of the group's pilots who did not fly that day, Juan Pablo Roque, had infiltrated the organization on behalf of the Cuban government. Shortly after the aircraft were shot down, Roque disappeared from his home in Florida and resurfaced in Havana. Other United States-based groups and paramilitary organizations reportedly targeted by the Intelligence Directorate include the Democracy Movement, the Alpha 66, the Democratic National Unity Party (Partido de Unidad Nacional Democrático—PUND), and even the Latin American Chamber of Commerce.

Cuban intelligence operatives are believed to have been somewhat less successful in other United States penetration efforts. On various occasions, members of the Cuban Interests Section in Washington, D.C., have been identified as intelligence agents, declared persona non grata, and sent home. In September 1998, an extensive effort to penetrate the United States government was revealed, when ten Cubans residing in Florida were arrested for espionage. Related to these arrests, in December 1998, three Cuban diplomats from Cuba's United Nations mission were ordered to leave the United States because of their ties to the ten individuals. The Miami spy ring was the largest single group of Cubans charged with spying by the United States since the Castro government came to power. According to the United States Federal Bureau of Investigation (FBI), the ten arrested were tasked with spying on military installations in Florida, including the Boca Chica Naval Air Station, the United States Southern Command, and MacDill Air Force Base.

With respect to the Intelligence Directorate's interests, this shift to military targets was deemed by some observers to reflect a new Cuban intelligence concern, namely its interest in regaining access to the kind of strategic information on the United States military that had once been provided by the Soviet Union. However, the directorate is also active elsewhere in the world, where its operatives are often tasked to collect intelligence related to investments in the island or other business-related endeavors. Still, even beyond North America, the Cubans have demonstrated a continuing interest in military-related targets, as was suggested by the revelation in early 1999 that the directorate had infiltrated Spanish military intelligence. At the time, Intelligence Directorate agents were thought to be seeking details regarding Spain's participation in the North Atlantic Treaty Organization (NATO), as well as information pertaining to investments in Cuba's tourism industry. Spain's capital, Madrid, is believed to serve as the "home base" for the directorate's agents assigned to Europe.

By the end of the 1990s, the Intelligence Directorate appeared to be stepping up its overseas activities, apparently having recovered from the shake-up in 1989, when, as occurred in the other bureaucratic entities under the Ministry of Interior's authority, a large number of the directorate's long-time personnel were fired or retired, and were replaced with military personnel. This extensive changeover in personnel was believed to have negatively affected Cuban intelligence during most of the 1990s, given that scores of operatives with many years of experience were peremptorily dismissed. During the mid-1990s, in an effort to recoup its capabilities, the directorate was reported to have asked some of these career intelligence officers to return to active service. The directorate remained dominated by military personnel, however.

In the late 1990s, the Intelligence Directorate reportedly had six divisions, or bureaus, which were divided into two categories of roughly equal size, consisting of operational divisions and support divisions. The operational divisions include the Political-Economic Intelligence Division, which is subdivided into regional sections, including a separate one for North America; the Military Intelligence Division, and the External Counterintelligence Division, which is tasked with penetrating foreign intelligence services and the surveillance of exiles. The support divisions include the Technical Division, the Information Division, and the Preparation Division. The first is responsible for the production of false documents, maintenance of the communications systems that support clandestine operations, and the development of clandestine message capabilities. The Ministry of Interior's Intelligence Directorate maintains a radio listening and transmitting post on the island that is used primarily to maintain contact with its operatives abroad. The information and preparation divisions assist in matters related to intelligence analysis. During the 1970s and 1980s, the operatives of the America Department (Departamento América—DA), an entity formally under the PCC's jurisdiction, worked closely with the DGI (as the Intelligence Directorate was then known) in managing covert activities and support for national liberation movements throughout the world.

Crime and Punishment

General Crime Trends

By the end of the 1990s, the growing national crime problem had become a focal point for the regime. During the early 1990s, economic crimes—often committed by average citizens trying to *resolver,* or make do, during the most difficult years of the crisis—became the focus of official attention. By the end of the 1990s, however, the types of crimes being committed, as well as those committing them, had changed, prompting heightened concerns. These concerns stemmed from what was recognized as a sudden, alarming increase in violent crime, including armed robbery and murder, that occurred in 1998. In late 1998, a special section in one of the nation's leading weekly newspapers, *Juventud Rebelde*, identified crime as "one of the great new challenges" facing the regime and said that it even was emerging as a threat to the socialist system. In a major speech made in January 1999 to the country's National Revolutionary Police (PNR), Fidel Castro called for urgent measures to preserve law and order. These measures included changes to the country's Penal Code, with the addition of new crimes as well as increasing sentences for a number of offenses.

Throughout most of the Revolution, Cuba has traditionally had low rates of violence and juvenile delinquency, and has been counted among the nations in Latin America that could boast of having "safe streets." During the 1990s, however, this situation appeared to be changing. Many Cuban citizens responded to the increasing incidence of crime by installing bars on the windows and balconies of their homes in order to keep intruders out; others reportedly turned to attack dogs and alarm systems. The government maintains that the increase in crime is "temporary" and blames it on the difficulties caused by the longstanding United States embargo. The cause, however, is generally acknowledged to be linked with the long economic crisis, the dollarization of the economy, and the many changes associated with the growth of the tourism industry on the island during the 1990s. Apart from the incidence of violent crime, the general trends in crime reflected a rise in all kinds of theft during the late 1990s, whether break-ins, car theft, or livestock theft. Lastly, the theft, usually by employees, of goods and manufacturing materials from state-run industries for sale in dollars on the black market remained a problem that interfered with the government's efforts to achieve greater productivity.

In addition to theft, prostitution has increased since the legalization of dollars in 1992 and the growth of the tourism industry on the island during the decade, as Cubans have turned to this profession as a way to earn hard currency. Although prostitution itself is not recognized as a criminal offense, it is viewed as morally reprehensible, and Cuban authorities have instituted periodic campaigns against it. Those who profit from prostitution, whether pimps or those who rent rooms used by the prostitutes, are subject to prosecution and several years' imprisonment. During the 1998 campaign, police patrols in areas frequented by foreigners, such as Varadero Beach and the Cuban Keys, were stepped up in efforts to discourage the prostitutes' open solicitation of tourists; yet some reports indicated that the prostitutes were often able to bribe the officers to look the other way.

The government has been anxious to keep the increase in crime from negatively affecting the tourism industry, one of the primary sources of the nation's hard currency earnings. (One of the incidents that may have contributed to the suddenly heightened official concern in late 1998 was the fatal shooting of two Italian tourists during a robbery.) As a result, the government has attempted to increase police training, patrols, and manpower, and to put other resources at the disposal of the police (see National Revolutionary Police, this ch.). In this last regard, a special new police force, the aforementioned Special Brigade, was created in 1998 to deter crime in tourist areas. Cuban authorities have also called on the population for assistance in the anticrime campaign. At the Fifth

Congress of the Committees for the Defense of the Revolution (CDRs) in September 1998, CDR members—whose political fervor was generally thought to have diminished as the daily difficulties of economic life increased in the 1990s—were assigned a new role in helping improve anticriminal vigilance in their neighborhoods. As part of this vigilance program, which is coordinated by the PNR, joint patrols by neighborhood residents and police were increased in Cuba's urban areas.

Drug Trafficking and Narcotics-Related Problems

During the late 1990s, the issue of drug trafficking became a heightened concern for Cuban officials. During this period, the island had become an important transshipment point for illicit drugs destined for sale either in Europe or, most often, the United States. With increasing frequency, Cuba was being used for airdrops of South American-produced drugs, usually cocaine, bundles of which were then retrieved and carried by fast launches to the United States. Cuba's ability to prevent the traffickers' operations is limited by its own strategic inability to fully monitor national airspace, particularly the skies over central Cuba, the air corridor most often favored by the traffickers. Similarly, severe resource shortages have hampered the ability of the Ministry of Interior's Border Guard Troops, which are assigned to patrol the island's coastal waters, to interdict shipments, and to apprehend traffickers at sea.

Cuban authorities appear to have had mixed success in their interdiction efforts. By the end of 1999, the use of Cuban airspace by traffickers was believed to be on the decline, the reason for which may have been their relatively easier access to the skies over the neighboring island of Hispaniola. Still, Cuban officials reported that in 1999 they seized two tons of cocaine that had washed up on the country's north shore. This cocaine, part of failed airdrops at sea, was intended to be picked up by the small speedboats, known colloquially as "go-fasts," that ferry the drugs to the United States. Some analysts maintain that the unconfiscated drugs that have washed ashore have been the source of the island's nascent domestic drug problem. Cuban authorities also have achieved some success in apprehending individuals who tried to smuggle drugs through one of the island's eleven international airports. Foreigners apprehended for attempted drug smuggling have included Canadian, Jamaican, and British nationals, among others. During

1998 alone, a Ministry of Interior report stated that arrests and seizures had doubled over the previous year. Cuban authorities arrested 1,216 individuals for possession and trafficking and seized a total of 106 kilos of cocaine and eighty kilos of marijuana.

Despite Cuba's efforts, a notable drug seizure made in Colombia in December 1998 suggested a possible new aspect to the island's strategic role in the international narcotics trade. That seizure was of 7.2 tons of cocaine found packed in shipping containers aboard a vessel bound for Cuba that had an ultimate destination in Spain. It raised the possibility that the maritime transit of containerized cargo was a new tactic in trafficking via Cuba because, as one police official observed, it was unlikely that so large a shipment would have been sent along an untested route. Following the broad negative publicity that the incident generated, President Fidel Castro announced in January 1999 that international traffickers apprehended and convicted by Cuban authorities would be subject to the death penalty.

Within the Cuban government, the Ministry of Interior and the Ministry of Justice are the two principal entities charged with antinarcotics responsibilities. As a reflection of Cuba's concern over what is perceived as a growing problem, the minister of justice, Roberto Díaz Sotolongo, also served as the head of the country's National Drug Commission (Comisión Nacional de Drogas). Within the Ministry of Interior, the National Antidrug Division, which in 1999 was led by Colonel Oliverio Montalvo, is responsible for coordinating the antinarcotics efforts of its personnel, which include the police, the Border Guard Troops, and Customs authorities. Also, in recognition of this relatively new national problem and its extension well beyond national borders, Cuba has signed pacts with twenty-five foreign governments in an effort to combat international narcotics trafficking and the associated money laundering that often accompanies it. Included are pacts with Spain, Britain, and even Colombia. Training assistance provided by European governments includes helping the Cubans improve their investigative and ship-searching techniques as well as their airport control measures.

Cuban officials have also sought to increase cooperation on antinarcotics issues with the United States, in particular with the United States Coast Guard. These have included efforts to establish and maintain routine communications and contacts between the Coast Guard and their counterparts in the Border Guard Troops, particularly among lower-ranking officials and on a "case-by-case" basis (see Border Guard Troops, this ch.). In one of the most notable cases involving successful cooperation between Cuba and the United States to deter drug trafficking, the United States informed the Cuban government in late 1996 of a suspicious disabled freighter, the *Limerick*, which had drifted into Cuban waters. The Cubans searched the vessel and found six tons of cocaine. Cuban officials later testified at the United States trial in which the traffickers were convicted.

Despite official concern with narcotics trafficking, Cuban government authorities officially maintained that the domestic consumption of drugs had not become a broad social problem by the end of the 1990s, but they did acknowledge a trend toward growing use. It was also recognized that drug use had increased, in particular in areas frequented by foreign tourists, suggesting that the tourists themselves either were bringing illicit drugs to the island or were a target market for Cubans selling the drugs.

The use of illegal drugs has been discouraged in Cuba since the very beginning of the Revolution, when under Order 6, which was issued by Fidel Castro while still a guerrilla in the Sierra Maestra, the use and consumption of marijuana was prohibited. Despite the paucity of statistical data on the subject, drug consumption within the Cuban population, especially by youth, is believed to have increased markedly during the late 1990s. Frequently, unretrieved drug shipments that accidentally wash ashore are recovered by Cubans, who often choose to sell the drugs and may save some for their own use. The Cubans have favored a community-based, educational approach in addressing this potential problem, as spelled out in their Integrated Drug Prevention Plan. According to a fine line drawn by the Penal Code, drug consumption itself is not a crime, but possession is. An individual with a record of illegal drug consumption or identified as exhibiting behavior that suggests drug use may be subject to "preventive detention."

Despite the Cuban government's belief that the country is not a target market for such common illegal narcotics as cocaine, marijuana, or heroin, it does acknowledge that Cuba is one of the largest illegal markets in the hemisphere for the pharmaceutical tranquilizer known as meprobamate, which is medically prescribed to relieve anxiety, tension, and muscle spasms. In terms of the classification of illicit drugs, Cuba adheres to the schedule elaborated by the U.N.'s Vienna Commission. The government officially supports international efforts to fight narcotics trafficking. For example, Cuba's minister of justice represented Cuba at the mid-1998 U.N. Anti-Drug Summit in New York.

Yet notwithstanding present efforts to build cooperation in this area, the issue of illicit narcotics remains a somewhat sensitive subject for the Cuban government, a number of whose officials have in the past been accused of engaging in international drug trafficking. During the 1989 trial of Division General Arnaldo Ochoa, one of the key charges that government prosecutors highlighted as having threatened the Revolution was the defendants' involvement and contacts with Carlos Lehder Rivas, the one-time head of Colombia's Medellín Cartel, with whom the defendants were said to have discussed collaboration. Some critics of the Castro government maintain that the regime's own concern over being exposed for participating in the international drug trade prompted it at that time to convict and "sacrifice" several of its leading security officers in order to save itself.

Allegedly, Cuba's interest in facilitating international drug trafficking can be dated to the late 1970s, when the government first realized that it could gain by providing safe haven and other support for the major drug cartels and independent traffickers that operated in and around the Caribbean. In addition, in supporting the introduction of illicit drugs into the United States, the regime enjoyed an insidious side benefit: the ability to "corrupt" the country from within by promoting drug use. Some of the money obtained was thought to have been used to finance revolutionary activities in Central and South America as well as to help support the sending of Cuban troops to Africa. According to one former Cuban intelligence officer, these operations were initially managed through what was known as Department "Z" of the Ministry of Interior's Special Troops Directorate. They were later transferred to Department "MC," which was under the Ministry of Interior's Vice Ministry of Information. (The initials "MC" are said to stand for *moneda convertible* (convertible currency), and the generation of *moneda convertible* was the main purpose of that department.)

The heyday of Cuba's covert role in the international drug trade was presumably between 1979 and 1989. At this point, only six weeks before Ochoa's arrest in June 1989, it became known that two traffickers who were in the custody of United

States authorities in Miami were preparing to provide details on Cuba's role in narcotics trafficking and to testify against regime authorities for their involvement. Earlier, in November 1982, four Cuban government officials, including Admiral Aldo Santamaría Cuadrado, then the chief of the Revolutionary Navy, were indicted by a United States grand jury for allowing Cuba to be used as a drug transshipment point by foreign traffickers. United States prosecutors' plans in 1993 to indict MINFAR chief Raúl Castro along with several top Ministry of Interior officials for their role in facilitating the transit of Colombian cocaine to the United States market over a ten-year period were never carried out. Many of the critics who have cited the Cuban government's role in narcotics trafficking argue that the leadership continues to be deeply involved in trafficking and money laundering. Despite the successful limited cooperation involved in the 1996 *Limerick* case and the fact that no Cuban authorities have ever been detained based on the indictments handed down, this alleged record of long-time involvement in international narcotics trafficking left some United States officials reluctant in the late 1990s to engage in more extensive cooperation with the Cubans in this area. As of the late 1990s, however, United States intelligence had never publicly revealed any evidence that high-level Cuban government officials are engaged in drug trafficking.

The Problem of Illegal Emigration and Refugee Smuggling

By the end of the 1990s, illegal emigration and alien smuggling had become a growing problem for the regime. Given that Cubans are not free to leave the country without government-provided exit visas, illegal emigration has long plagued the regime, yet it has also provided a political "relief valve" in that those most dissatisfied with their situation on the island have left. Nevertheless, the incidence of alien smuggling—in which professional smugglers are paid to help Cubans surreptitiously leave the country—is a relatively new and growing phenomenon. By 1999 United States authorities believed that the majority of the Cubans arriving illegally had been brought in by smugglers. This developing problem was in part spurred by the terms of the 1995 immigration accord, which provides that most Cuban refugees who make it to United States soil are not turned away from this country but that those intercepted at sea by the United States Coast Guard are picked up and repatriated to Cuba. This accord reflected a change in United States policy inasmuch as for decades the United States had welcomed all Cubans. In turn, under the accords, the Cuban regime agreed that it would attempt to stem the uncontrolled flow of Cubans illegally departing the island, as had occurred on various occasions in the past. Two such incidents were the Mariel Boatlift of 1980, in which 125,000 Cubans left the island, and the 1994 *balsero* crisis, when 30,000 Cubans attempted to leave the island on rafts.

Since 1994, thousands of Cubans have attempted to leave the island, often on their own, setting off on makeshift rafts or other unseaworthy vessels. During good weather, the number of Cubans attempting to make the trip across the shark-infested Straits of Florida to United States soil generally increases. From January to July 1999 alone, the United States Coast Guard reported that it had apprehended at sea 1,039 Cubans, who—with the Coast Guard working in coordination with Cuba's Border Guard Troops—were returned to the island. This figure reflects a significant increase over prior years, given that from May 1995 to July 1999, a total of 2,195 Cubans were reported to have been intercepted at sea and repatriated. By contrast, the United States Border Patrol, which assumes jurisdiction once the Cubans reach United States soil, reported that between October 1998 and July 1999, 1,943 Cubans had made it to Florida, thus enabling them to seek permanent resident status in the United States. Based on the physical condition of those arriving and the absence of vessels or other likely means of transport, the Border Patrol estimated that 80 percent had been ferried to the United States by smugglers. The number of those who have perished at sea in attempting to make the 145-kilometer trip to the shores of Florida, however, is unknown and perhaps incalculable. In one of the more noted cases to come to public attention in the late 1990s, a six-year-old boy, Elián González, was found clinging to a tire's inner tube and rescued by fishermen in November 1999; he was the sole survivor of a raft sinking in which his mother perished.

There is little debate that the 1994 *balsero* crisis, which came as Cuba's economic decline was near its worst, so raised concerns on the part of both the United States and Cuban governments that it paved the way for the new agreement on immigration. Yet the unintended consequence appears to have been that the agreement, which also set up a lottery system for the granting to Cubans of only 20,000 United States visas annually, raised the stakes for leaving the island to the point that

Cubans became more willing to pay a smuggler for assistance. In most cases, the smugglers are paid by the Cubans' relatives who reside in the United States and wish to help their family members join them. Occasionally, Cubans are not transported directly from the island, but must first travel to the Bahamas where they are picked up by the smugglers whose networks operate from there. During the late 1990s, the professional smugglers' fees reportedly ranged from a low of US$1,000 to as much as US$8,000 or US$10,000 per person; they often make their trips using fast boats that can outrun the United States Coast Guard's vessels. According to one estimate, a single boat-load that might carry two dozen Cubans could bring the smugglers more than US$200,000 per trip.

Alien smuggling stands as a criminal offense in both the United States and Cuba. Although smugglers apprehended by United States authorities have long been subject to prosecution, not until the late 1990s did Cuba begin instituting laws that were specifically targeted against the smuggling of its citizens. According to United States regulations aimed at deterring these smugglers' activities, the United States Coast Guard requires that boats up to 45.5 meters in length obtain a United States permit to travel to Cuba from a Florida port. If it is found that a boat intercepted by the Coast Guard has made a trip without permission, the Coast Guard can seize the vessel and subject those aboard to prosecution. For those convicted of smuggling by United States courts, sentences might range from five to ten years' imprisonment.

In early 1999, in light of this growing problem, Cuba announced its intent to crack down on those involved in smuggling. In a widely publicized anticrime speech to the PNR in January, Fidel Castro urged that smugglers who are apprehended and convicted be "at least" imprisoned for life (*cadena perpetua*) (see Penal System, this ch.). In July 1999, in a more direct attempt to deter Cubans from leaving, Decree–Law 194 also established a 500 to 10,000 peso fine (payable in hard currency for foreigners) for those who buy, transport, or repair vessels without first gaining official approval. Despite Cuba's efforts to crack down on this crime, alien smuggling remains very lucrative; its continuation suggests the smugglers may deem their possible apprehension and prosecution by Cuban authorities to be unlikely and worth the risk. As of July 1999, Cuba was holding thirty United States residents arrested for alien smuggling, twenty-six of whom it had offered to send back to the United States for trial.

Human Rights and Political Prisoners

Cuba is widely recognized as being among the nations of the world whose governments have a poor human rights record. This general assessment is offered by entities as diverse as the United Nations Commission on Human Rights, the United States Department of State, Amnesty International, Human Rights Watch, and Freedom House. The Cuban leadership does not accept this assessment; rather, it maintains that any definition of "human rights" should consider a government's efforts to provide for such basic needs of its citizens as food, health care, and education. In this respect, the regime deems it has fared well. Notwithstanding this view of its own performance, Cuban authorities routinely interfere with the citizens' exercise of political and civil rights to the extent that Canada and member states of the EU have sought to use their diplomatic and economic ties, most often in vain, to sway the regime toward improving its human rights record.

The nature of Cuba's political system, which follows a totalitarian model according to which the PCC remains the sole legal political party, appears at the core of the issue. Unlike the situation in many countries identified as having poor human rights records, the incidence of politically related "disappearances" of individuals has not been reported as problematic in Cuba. However, since almost the beginning of the Revolution, the government has not tolerated active opposition, albeit nonviolent, by any who challenge its leadership and political program. In recognizing such activity as counterrevolutionary, the leadership has developed a sophisticated system to deal with such opposition, often using the Ministry of Interior for support. As a result, those recognized as challenging the regime have for decades been subject to harassment, loss of employment, or even imprisonment, and many have sought exile in the United States or other countries, rather than continue to face oppressive political conditions (see Human Rights and Opposition Groups, ch. 4).

According to the Cuban Committee for Human Rights and National Reconcilation (Comité Cubano Pro Derechos Humanos y Reconciliación Nacional—CCDRN), Cuban jails held 344 political prisoners in July 1999. This Cuba-based organization—headed by Elizardo Sánchez, himself a former political prisoner—is generally recognized by those abroad as being a reliable source of information about both the number of political prisoners and internal political conditions. Because the government refuses to release statistics relating to how many Cubans are imprisoned for political crimes, the CCDRN's estimates are based largely on information confirmed through interviews with the detainees' families. Reports by some human rights advocates in Cuba suggest that many of these detainees are young men who have been imprisoned for their refusal to carry out their obligatory military service. According to the CCDRN, the number of individuals arrested and imprisoned for political offenses began to increase after 1997. This trend continued through the balance of the decade, in contrast to the decline in arrests and detentions that occurred for several years in a row during the early years of the economic crisis.

The watershed event that marked this minor shift in the regime's tolerance of political activism and dissent was the detention of four prominent citizens, leaders of what was known as the Internal Dissidents' Working Group (Grupo de Trabajo de la Disidencia Interna), in what became one of the most noted human rights-related cases of the 1990s. These individuals were arrested in mid-July 1997, only weeks after signing and circulating a document entitled "The Homeland Is for All" ("La Patria es de todos") just prior to the convening of the PCC's Fifth Congress in October 1997. This document offered an analysis of the Cuban economic crisis that discouraged foreign investment, discussed the problem of human rights, and proposed reforms to the constitution that would end the PCC's monopoly on power. They were accused of inciting sedition and "other acts against the security of the state." Despite the international concern provoked by the detention of these four respected professionals and the request for their release by many foreign dignitaries, including Pope John Paul II, the regime ignored the pleas and held the four without trial for nearly two years. They were not formally charged with any crimes until September 1998, after they had spent more than a year in prison. In March 1999, they were finally tried behind closed doors, convicted, and given prison sentences ranging from three-and-one-half to five years. However, only one remained in prison as of early 2001.

Individuals who have been considered by human rights groups to be political prisoners have occasionally been released in response to requests by foreign officials. The Cuban government has done this as a means to generate goodwill and, in demonstrating its presumed responsiveness to foreign concerns, has used the occasional releases as a tactic to gain political advantages in its foreign relations. The largest group released during the 1990s consisted of approximately 300 detainees, about half of whom were considered to be political prisoners, who were freed in response to the clemency appeal made by Pope John Paul II during his January 1998 visit to the island. According to human rights monitors, many of those released in response to the papal request were at or nearing the end of their sentences. Shortly thereafter, in late November 1998, in response to a request made to Fidel Castro by the Spanish foreign minister, who had traveled to the island in preparation for King Juan Carlos' upcoming trip, two more prisoners were released. The men, one of whom had already served nearly half of his fourteen-year term, had been convicted of disseminating "enemy propaganda." According to Cuban officials, they were pardoned for "humanitarian reasons," and released to foreign exile in Spain. Frequently, political prisoners who are released from detention before completion of their sentences are required to accept exile abroad as a condition for their release.

These recent instances of the detention of dissidents and occasional prisoner releases in response to outsiders' requests also reflect the regime's methods during the decades preceding the 1990s. In 1979, for example, 3,600 political prisoners were released from detention as a result of negotiations between the Cuban and United States governments. Many of those released in 1979 remained on the island for a number of years because of migration-related problems that arose after the 1980 Mariel exodus. In mid-1984, twenty-seven political detainees, along with twenty-two United States citizens who were serving prison sentences in Cuba, were released and granted entry to this country following the intervention of the Reverend Jesse Jackson. In late 1984, under an immigration accord reached between Cuba and the United States, the United States agreed to accept during the following year up to 20,000 Cuban emigres, a figure that included former political detainees still residing on the island.

In dealing with its imprisoned dissidents, the Cuban government routinely seeks to obtain the prisoners' participation in reeducation and rehabilitation efforts as part of the terms of their confinement. Those convicted of politically related offenses are required to perform wage labor and participate in other prison-sponsored activities. Frequently, however, political prisoners are known to refuse to join in, an act of disobedience that may be interpreted as a sign of continuing defiance. These prisoners, who usually also refuse to wear prison uniforms (as they maintain they are not common criminals), are known as *plantados* (literally, the planted ones). Human rights monitors report that *plantados* are often accorded the harshest treatment by prison officials. This treatment may include the denial of contact with visitors or fellow prisoners and of basic privileges and needs, such as medical treatment, or the restriction of already meager food rations. Further, depending on the situation, political prisoners are reported to often be intentionally placed in cells with prisoners convicted of violent crimes or held for long periods in solitary confinement, or sealed cells (*celdas tapiadas*). A 1985 report issued by the American Association for the Advancement of Science noted that such tactics are generally recognized to be methods of physical and psychological torture. In May 1995, Cuba ratified the United Nations Convention against Torture and Other Cruel, Inhuman or Degrading Treatment or Punishment, but by the end of the decade it had not yet established criminal penalties for acts of torture.

Penal System

The revisions in the Penal Code carried out during the 1990s suggested the regime's intent to toughen its stance on crime and tighten political control by recognizing as criminal some offenses that could be deemed to be basically political in nature. These revisions stood in contrast to the trend evident during the preceding decade, when changes in the code carried out between roughly 1979 and 1988 deleted some acts previously considered criminal and reduced the length of sentence for a number of common crimes. The revisions of the 1990s appeared to be prompted by a variety of new pressures generated in relation to the economic crisis, including those associated with the dollarization of the economy, the legalization of foreign investment, and the growth of tourism. They may also be seen as the regime's response to security-related concerns spurred by the efforts of dissidents and the nascent independent press to expand and deepen their contacts with foreign sympathizers, especially those in the United States.

As a result, during the latter half of the 1990s, a number of existing code provisions were being enforced more vigorously while new provisions were established in what the regime recognized an the ongoing effort to "adequately respond to the present situation." Specifically, in early 1999, three new crimes were recognized and incorporated in the code. They were the crimes of money laundering (*lavado de dinero*), of trafficking in humans (*tráfico de personas*), and of the sale and trafficking of minors (*venta y tráfico de menores*). Crimes in Cuba are broadly categorized as either felonies or misdemeanors, for which anyone aged sixteen or above may be convicted. Felony crimes may carry either a potential sentence of greater than one year's imprisonment or a fine above a threshold of 300 *cuotas*, a variable unit that is loosely linked with the Cuban peso. Misdemeanor crimes carry either a potential sentence of less than one year or a fine under or at the 300-*cuota* threshold. Crimes categorized as felony offenses consist of murder, rape, and robbery. Other crimes, including assault, death or injury by vehicle, burglary, larceny, vehicle theft, arson, and drug trafficking, may variously be classified as felonies or misdemeanors depending on the severity of the offense.

According to the Penal Code, acts that are recognized to be offenses against socialist organization are also subject to criminal prosecution. These crimes have become the focus of heightened state scrutiny during the 1990s, especially in light of the exigencies related to the economic crisis. They include the misuse of employment in a state enterprise for illegal personal gain (*malversación*), obtaining money or property illegally channeled from a state economic venture (*receptación*), trading in foreign currency (*tráfico de divisas*), slaughter and distribution of livestock outside the socialist distribution system (*sacrificio ilegal*), and attempting to leave the country without complying with formal emigration requirements (*salida ilegal*).

Of the existing code provisions that were more vigorously enforced during the late 1990s, many were targeted against individuals who were deemed hostile to the regime. Among these offenses are included contempt for authority (*desacato*), dangerousness (*peligrosidad*), defamation, resisting authority, association to commit criminal acts (*asociación para delinquir*), and a vaguely defined, catch-all category of other acts against state security (*otros actos contra la seguridad del estado*).

Under some of these provisions, it was recognized that the commission of what might normally be considered a criminal act was not necessarily a prerequisite for arrest. The offense of dangerousness, for example, is recognized under the code as the "special inclination of a person to commit crimes, demonstrated by his conduct in manifest contradiction of socialist norms." Thus, as defined, the code allows for arrests to be made on a preventive basis. According to critics of the current human rights situation on the island, such arrests—which may call for up to several years' imprisonment if an individual is convicted—have reportedly resulted in the detention of thousands of Cubans. Lastly, the new Law for the Protection of the National Independence and Economy of Cuba, enacted in February 1999 and sometimes referred to simply as Law 88, appeared specifically directed against dissidents and independent journalists. Law 88 identifies a broad range of activities as undermining state security, with sanctions of up to twenty years' imprisonment established for contacts or collaboration with the United States or other foreign media aimed at destabilizing the country or destroying the socialist state.

According to Cuba's Law of Penal Procedures, once an arrest is made police are required to file formal charges within the next ninety-six hours and to provide those detained with access to a lawyer within seven days. Between the arrest and the filing of formal charges, in what is known as the preparatory phase (*fase preparatoria*), the police, possibly in conjunction with the government prosecutor (*fiscal*), gather the witnesses and evidence considered necessary to demonstrate that a crime has been committed. Police and other security officers are permitted to exercise their discretion in stopping, detaining, and interrogating probable offenders, who during such a period are often not provided access to counsel. The individuals detained may then be released without charges. According to the Law of Penal Procedures, those suspected of having committed an offense may be held no more than twenty-four hours before their case must be submitted to an investigator. Human rights monitors report that such methods are frequently used to intimidate political dissidents. In addition, as occurred with the members of the aforementioned Working Group, individuals may sometimes be held for long periods without formal charges being filed.

According to the Cuban constitution, the state reserves the right to deny the civil rights of anyone who actively opposes the "decision of the Cuban people to build socialism." The state invokes this right to justify its detention of some individuals, even though doing so stands in violation of the penal procedures law. Once a determination is made that a crime has been committed, the prosecutor issues a bill of indictment (*conclusiones provisionales*) that details the charges and circumstances surrounding the crime. The case is then sent to trial, with a copy of the criminal indictment being provided to the defense attorney, if one has been identified. Lawyer collectives (*bufetes colectivos*), whose members charge fees set by the state, exist to provide the accused with legal counsel. All criminal cases are required to be adjudicated; no provisions exist for plea bargaining. Pretrial incarceration (*prisión provisional*) is permitted for those charged with serious felony offenses, those charged with multiple crimes, or those who are deemed likely to flee prosecution. The determination regarding the need for such incarceration in relation to any specific case is made by the court of first instance.

Penal Code

The Penal Code delineates the range of sentences that might be handed down. They include probation, public chastisement (*amonestacíon*), fines, correctional labor without confinement, correctional labor with confinement to the worksite, incarceration, and execution. A conviction for first-degree murder, for example, might warrant a sentence in the range of fifteen to twenty years' imprisonment. The maximum prison term is twenty to thirty years. During the crackdown on crime initiated at the end of the 1990s, Cuban leader Fidel Castro called for harsher sentences for a number of other crimes, including drug trafficking, alien smuggling, and robbery; life sentences were also to be recommended for repeat offenders.

Unlike many countries in the region, Cuba does carry out capital punishment, as it has since the beginning of the Revolution. From the 1980s to the early 1990s, death sentences were not handed down as frequently as during the first twenty years of the Revolution. However, by the end of the 1990s, this trend appeared to be reversing. Under the Penal Code, the death penalty has traditionally been reserved for particularly heinous offenses, or exceptional cases (*casos excepcionales*), whether represented by crimes against individuals or against state security. In 1999 the Penal Code recognized 112 different types of offenses for which capital punishment could potentially be applied, two-thirds of which involved crimes against state security. As a result of revisions in the Penal Code that became effective in March 1999, the death penalty was established as a possible punishment for convictions of drug-trafficking, corruption of minors, and armed robbery. The mode of execution in Cuba is by firing squad. Persons either under twenty years of age or pregnant at the time of the crime or at sentencing cannot be condemned to death. Cuban law stipulates that all death sentences are automatically appealed to the Supreme Court and subject to review by the Council of State, which has the authority to commute the sentences to life imprisonment. Although on occasion executions have been carried out within weeks after a judgment is rendered, the appeal and review process can sometimes continue for months.

It is believed that eleven individuals were executed in Cuba between 1989 and the end of 1997. Included in this group were the four MINFAR and Ministry of Interior officers who were put to death in 1989. A trend toward more frequent application of the death penalty was apparent during the final years of the 1990s. Based on data released by Amnesty International, although no executions were carried out during 1997, "at least" five individuals were executed during 1998. Then, during 1999 alone, "at least" thirteen Cubans were executed, and nine others were under sentence. Among the individuals sentenced to death in 1999 were two Cubans convicted for the murder of four foreign tourists. In addition, two Salvadoran nationals, tried in entirely separate cases, were convicted of terrorism and sentenced to death for a string of hotel bombings carried out in 1997, in one of which a foreign tourist was killed. According to the prosecutors, both Salvadorans were acting on behalf of anti-Castro exiles in an effort to sabotage Cuba's tourism industry. As of the close of 1999, the sentences had not been carried out.

Penal Institutions

Cuba's prison system falls under the authority of the Ministry of Interior's Directorate of Penitentiary Establishments. In 1998 there were 294 prisons and correctional work camps located throughout the island. These prisons included forty maximum security facilities, thirty minimum security prisons, and more than 200 work camps or farms (*granjas*) where those convicted of less serious offenses might complete their sentences. Of the prisons, nineteen were reported to be "closed," meaning that the detainees are not allowed contact with outsiders. In addition to these facilities, police stations, offices of the

Ministry of Interior's Department of State Security, and even the headquarters of the Ministry of Interior at Villa Marista are often used as prisons. The Ministry of Interior supervises the administration of these various places of confinement, and provides guards, work camp and farm overseers, and other staff for the facilities.

Cuba in the late 1990s was believed to have one of the highest per capita confinement ratios in all of Latin America and the Caribbean. In 1996 one estimate placed the island's prison population at between 100,000 and 200,000 prisoners of all categories. This number stood in marked contrast to a 1990 estimate that indicated a prison population of only 19,000. Although the Cuban government reportedly maintains a computerized database to keep track of its prison population, it does not release or allow any public access to statistics regarding it. In addition to those serving time for their convictions, large numbers of pretrial detainees are also held in the prisons, many of whom, according to human rights critics, may be confined six to nine months or longer before being brought to trial. Darker-skinned Cubans are reportedly overrepresented in Cuba's prisons. Separate penal establishments are maintained for women; delinquent youth under sixteen years of age might be sent to school-like facilities. Conjugal visits with spouses are formally permitted once every two months, yet might occur more or less frequently, based on a prisoner's conduct.

In the late 1990s, the conditions for prisoners at many of the island's facilities were generally considered to be substandard, unhealthy, and not in compliance with the United Nations' Standard Minimal Rules for the Treatment of Prisoners. Problems frequently noted by those knowledgeable of prison conditions included inadequate food, overcrowding, inadequate or denied medical attention, and forced participation in "re-education" programs for all detainees. In tacit recognition of these oft-cited problems, the Cuban government made some efforts during the late 1990s to improve the state of confinement. In May 1997, the Ministry of Interior promulgated several new regulations designed to achieve this end. Further revisions in the Penal Code in early 1999 explicitly prohibited the use of corporal punishment by guards and other security officials against detainees. However, the code set no penalties for violating that provision.

Outlook

The Cuban military in 2001 is a very different institution from what it was when the regime first came to power. At least three distinct generations have been through the institution since the Revolution, from the veterans of the guerrilla war to the young professional technicians of the present generation. Recognizing the different formative experiences of these individuals is as important as considering how their varied backgrounds may relate to the effectiveness of political control. The officers who are now prepared to move into positions of leadership in the institution have spent their careers as military professionals. Their perspective on the future of the Cuban military institution is likely to be quite different from that of the guerrilla leaders who led the Revolution in the late 1950s. And the mechanisms necessary to ensure their continuing subordination to political authority may be quite different as well.

*　　*　　*

The study of the Cuban military and national security is seriously hampered by the lack of publicly available information. The Cuban government rarely makes public any details regarding the status of its security forces and related security concerns; rather, it tends to view efforts to obtain and relate such information, whether by private Cuban or foreign citizens, as inimical to the interests of the Revolution. Consequently, of the information garnered, most is gathered by United States or foreign government authorities and obtained in such a manner that leads it to be classified. Despite these difficulties, the careful monitoring of the press and other open-source documents and reports can often yield fragmentary details that help fill out the picture. Defectors are also an often valuable source, particularly when the details they provide help to corroborate other information.

The PCC's official daily newspaper, *Granma,* is the single best source to consult. Within the United States, the *Miami Herald* and its Spanish-language counterpart, *El Nuevo Herald,* have the most regular coverage of Cuban affairs, and offer the best chance for finding information related to Cuban military and security affairs. Digital versions of these newspapers can be found on the Internet (*Miami Herald* at http://www.herald.com; *El Nuevo Herald* at http://www.elherald.com). The

Cuban Armed Forces Review (http://www.cubapolidata.com/ cafr/cafr.html) is a private website containing military-related details and photographs compiled from other public sources. Lastly, an excellent resource for general information is the Cuba Today e-mail list operated by political scientist Nelson Valdés at the University of New Mexico. This list tracks daily media coverage related to Cuba and often includes reporting on security-related concerns.

Studies by academics also have contributed to an improved understanding of the FAR and its role in national life. Among the important authors of such studies are Domingo Amuchastegui, Jorge I. Domínguez, Edward Gonzalez, and Jaime Suchlicki. Rafael Fermoselle's comprehensive study, *The Evolution of the Cuban Military*, and the biographies of the officers provided in his *Cuban Leadership after Castro* should also be noted. The text, *Cuban Communism*, now in its ninth edition and whose primary editor throughout the years has been Irving Louis Horowitz, has regularly included a section on the military composed of previously published articles. Lastly, mention must be made of the important 1996 volume that profiles the prominent members of the FAR. Cuban journalist Luis Báez's *Secretos de generales: Desclasificado*, a collection of his interviews with the officers, provides not only insights into the lives and career paths of the military's top officials but also the organization of the institution.

Unfortunately, finding information on the forces under the Ministry of Interior is even more difficult than locating information on the FAR. The little to be found is often based on defectors' recollections that date to the period preceding the economic crisis and the ministry's 1989 shake-up. Nevertheless, two good starting points to be noted are José Luis Llovio-Menéndez's *Insider: My Hidden Life as a Revolutionary in Cuba* and Juan Antonio Rodríguez-Menier's *Inside the Cuban Interior Ministry*.

For information related to human rights, penal procedures, and prison conditions, the best sources are the annual human rights reports published by the United States Department of State and those of the widely recognized nongovernmental organizations, Amnesty International and Human Rights Watch. On the Internet, the daily reports by independent Cuban journalists available on the Website maintained by CubaNet (http://www.cubanet.org) offer unusual perspectives on the difficulties that life on the island may pose for those who fail to go along with the regime.

Appendix

Table 1. *Metric Conversion Coefficients and Factors*[1]

When you know	Multiply by	To find
Millimeters............................	0.04	inches
Centimeters...........................	0.39	inches
Meters................................	3.3	feet
Kilometers............................	0.62	miles
Hectares (10,000 m?)[2]	2.47	acres
Square kilometers......................	0.39	square miles
Cubic meters..........................	35.3	cubic feet
Liters	0.26	gallons
Kilograms.............................	2.2	pounds
Metric tons[3]..........................	0.98	long tons
....	1.1	short tons
....	2,204	pounds
Degrees Celsius (Centigrade)..............	1.8	degrees Fahrenheit
	And add 32	

[1] Cuba uses the metric system, but old Spanish units are also used.
[2] For area measurement, one Cuban *caballeria* equals 13.4 hectares or 33.16 acres.
[3] Sugar is often measured in Spanish tons of 2,271 pounds, and there is a Cuban *quintal* of 101.4 pounds made up of four *arrobas*.

Table 2. *Demographic Trends in Cuba, Selected Years, 1950–2000*

Year	Population			Population Density (in square kilometers)	Total Fertility Rate[1]	Infant Mortality Rate[1]	Life Expectancy at Birth[2]
	Size (in thousands)	Growth Rate (in percentages)	Median Age				
1950	1,850	n.a.[3]	23.3	53	n.a.	n.a.	n.a.
1955	6,417	1.85	23.2	58	4.10	81	59.3
1960	6,985	1.70	23.4	63	3.68	70	62.3
1965	7,754	2.09	22.7	70	4.67	59	65.2
1970	8,520	1.88	22.3	77	4.29	50	68.3
1975	9,306	1.77	22.7	84	3.55	38	70.7
1980	9,710	.85	24.2	88	2.13	22	72.6
1985	10,615	.82	25.7	91	1.83	17	73.4
1990	10,828	.99	27.8	96	1.83	13	74.1
1995	10,964	.62	30.2	99	1.60	12	74.9
2000[4]	11,177	.38	33.0	101	1.50	9	75.7

[1] Rates refer to the quinquennium preceding the reference period.
[2] Both sexes combined.
[3] n.a.—not available.
[4] Projection.

Source: Based on information from United Nations, *World Population Prospects: The 1998 Revision*, New York, 1998, 602–03.

Table 3. Trends in Urban and Rural Population Change, Selected Years, 1970–95

Year	1970	1975	1980	1985	1990	1995
Population size (in thousands)						
TOTAL..........	8,520	9,306	9,710	10,102	10,598	11,041
Urban...........	5,122	5,962	6,605	7,237	7,927	8,560
Rural............	3,398	3,343	3,105	2,865	2,671	2,481
Percent urban	60	64	68	72	75	78
Quinquennial growth rates (in percent)[1]						
TOTAL..........	n.a.[2]	1.8	.85	.79	.96	.82
Urban...........	n.a.	3.03	2.05	1.83	1.82	1.54
Rural............	n.a.	-.32	-1.48	-1.61	-1.40	-1.48

[1] Rates refer to the quinquennium preceding the reference period.
[2] n.a.—not available.

Source: Based on information from Centro Latinoamericano de Demografía, "América
  Latina: Proyecciones de población urbana-rural," *Boletín Demográfico* [Santi-
  ago, Chile], 28, 1995, 31, 35.

Table 4. Enumerated Population Classified by Race, Selected Years, 1899–1981
(in percentages)

Census Year	White	Black	Mulatto or Mestizo	Asian
1899	66.9	14.9	17.2	1.0
1907	69.7	13.4	16.3	0.6
1919	72.3	11.2	16.0	0.5
1931	72.1	11.0	16.2	0.7
1943	74.3	9.7	15.6	0.4
1953	72.8	12.4	14.5	0.3
1981	66.0	12.0	21.9	0.1

Source: Based on information from Cuban censuses provided by Sergio Díaz-Briquets.

Table 5. Gross Domestic Product (GDP) by Economic Activity, 1989–98 (in millions of pesos at 1981 prices)

	1989	1990	1991	1992	1993	1994	1995	1996	1997	1998
Gross domestic product.	19,585.8	19,008.3	16,975.8	15,009.9	12,776.7	12,868.3	13,184.5	14,218.0	14,572.4	14,754.1
Agriculture, hunting, forestry, and fishing	1,924.5	1,756.3	1,334.9	1,197.1	924.9	879.4	915.5	1,075.4	1,073.7	1,017.5
Mining and quarrying	123.0	91.6	81.6	105.7	96.4	97.5	152.1	177.3	181.9	184.1
Manufacturing industries	4,886.8	4,640.2	4,199.7	3,506.5	3,103.6	3,340.6	3,555.2	3,835.4	4,154.5	4,290.7
Electricity, gas, and water.	452.0	454.6	426.5	378.2	335.2	350.0	384.2	398.0	421.8	426.8
Construction	1,349.7	1,508.1	1,085.2	603.7	385.7	383.9	412.1	538.5	556.0	587.9
Trade, restaurants, and hotels.	5 150.6	4,936.3	4,396.4	4,050.2	2,936.4	2,935.2	2,984.8	3,250.8	3,175.8	3,089.6
Transport, warehousing, and communications	1,352.6	1,202.3	1,058.9	911.6	733.3	708.7	748.4	813.4	845.4	855.4
Finance, real estate, and business services.	584.9	603.2	639.2	543.9	513.4	492.4	483.8	518.6	544.5	599.3
Community, social, and personal services.	3,761.7	3,815.7	3,753.4	3,713.0	3,747.8	3,680.6	3,548.4	3,610.6	3,618.8	3,702.8

Source: Based on information from Banco Nacional de Cuba, *Economic Report, 1994*, Havana, August 1995, Appendix A; Oficina Nacional de Estadísticas, *Anuario estadístico, 1997*, Havana, 1999, 82; and Oficina Nacional de Estadísticas, *Cuba en cifras, 1998*, Havana, 1999, 30.

Table 6. Cuban Foreign Merchandise Trade, 1989–98
(in millions of pesos)

Year	Exports	Imports	Turnover	Balance
1989	5,399.9	8,139.8	13,539.7	-2,739.9
1990	5,414.9	7,416.5	12,831.4	-2,001.6
1991	2,979.5	4,233.8	7,213.3	-1,254.3
1992	1,779.4	2,314.9	4,094.3	-535.5
1993	1,156.7	2,008.2	3,164.9	-851.5
1994	1,330.8	2,016.8	3,347.6	-686.0
1995	1,491.6	2,882.5	4,374.1	-1,390.9
1996	1,865.5	3,569.0	5,434.5	-1,703.5
1997	1,819.1	3,996.0	5,815.1	-2,176.9
1998	1,443.7	4,181.2	5,624.9	-2,737.5

Source: Based on information from Banco Nacional de Cuba, *Economic Report, 1994*, Havana, August 1995, 11; Oficina Nacional de Estadísticas, *Anuario estadístico, 1997*, Havana, 1999, 119; and Oficina Nacional de Estadísticas, *Cuba en cifras, 1998*, Havana, 1999, 38.

Table 7. *Selected Categories of the State Budget, 1989–98 (in millions of pesos)*

	1989	1990	1991	1992	1993	1994	1995	1996	1997	1998
Total revenues	12,501	12,255	10,949	9,263	9,516	12,757	11,593	12,249	12,307	12,502
Circulation tax	5,138	5,017	3,979	3,968	3,310	5,097	5,684	5,079	4,876	5,076
Profits	1,888	1,125	1,066	1,193	1,400	1,847	1,409	n.a.[1]	n.a.	n.a.
Contribution by state enterprises	850	1,465	2,026	1,309	1,516	1,488	1,057	2,685	2,015	1,908
Total expenditures	13,904	14,213	14,714	14,132	14,567	14,178	12,359	12,814	12,663	1,306.2
Education	1,651	1,620	1,504	1,427	1,385	1,335	1,359	1,421	1,454	1,510
Health	905	937	925	938	1,077	1,061	1,108	1,190	1,265	1,345
Defense and internal order	1,259	1,149	882	736	713	651	610	497	638	537
Social security	1,039	1,164	1,226	1,348	1,452	1,532	1,594	1,630	1,636	1,705
Administration	490	453	400	362	413	365	366	398	431	438
Housing and community services	406	383	281	248	260	315	411	462	488	566
Productive sphere	388	351	209	204	166	179	166	165	165	169
Culture and arts	191	201	203	178	173	160	163	114	109	104
Science and technology	124	124	126	122	125	123	125	114	189	184
Sports	116	117	125	100	104	106	112	118	122	126
Welfare	101	96	88	98	94	94	119	128	135	145
Subsidies to loss-making enterprises	2,654	2,975	3,882	4,889	5,434	3,447	1,803	1,624	1,350	1,139

Table 7. (Continued) Selected Categories of the State Budget, 1989–98 (in millions of pesos)

	1989	1990	1991	1992	1993	1994	1995	1996	1997	1998
Price subsidies.................	673	737	554	921	735	510	676	867	758	1,352
Investment expenses.............	3,060	2,886	3,625	2,356	2,038	2,683	2,296	2,043	1,839	1,581
Surplus or Deficit.............	-1,404	-1,958	-3,765	-4,869	-5,051	-1,615	-766	-570	-459	-560

[1] n.a.—not available.

Source: Based on information from Comisión Económica para América Latina y el Caribe (CEPAL), *La economía cubana: Reformas estructurales y desempeño en los noventa*, Mexico, 1997, Table A7; Oficina Nacional de Estadísticas, *Anuario estadístico, 1997*, Havana, 1999, 93; and Oficina Nacional de Estadísticas, *Cuba en cifras, 1998*, Havana, 1999, 35.

Table 8. *Selected Indicators of Production: Agriculture, 1989, 1993–97* (in thousands of tons, unless otherwise indicated)

Product	1989	1993	1994	1995	1996	1997	Percent change 1989–97
Tubers	681.2	568.7	484.5	624.2	742.3	679.4	-0.3
Potatoes	281.7	235.2	188.3	281.6	365.0	330.0	17.1
Sweet potatoes	194.8	130.4	133.4	151.6	149.4	145.7	-25.2
Vegetables	610.2	392.9	322.2	402.3	493.6	471.5	-22.7
Tomatoes	260.0	127.8	95.9	140.4	162.9	146.2	-43.8
Grains	584.0	226.2	299.7	303.8	472.9	544.9	-6.7
Rice	536.4	176.8	226.1	222.9	368.6	418.9	-21.9
Corn	47.1	49.5	73.6	81.0	104.3	126.0	167.5
Beans	14.1	8.8	10.8	11.5	14.0	15.8	12.1
Plantains	291.4	400.0	360.7	400.0	539.4	382.3	31.2
Citrus fruits	825.7	644.5	505.0	536.5	662.2	808.4	-2.1
Other fruits	218.9	68.3	89.1	112.3	102.6	117.4	-46.4
Tobacco	41.6	19.9	17.1	25.0	31.5	30.9	-25.7
Eggs[1]	2,522.6	1,362.2	1,376.1	1,224.0	1,091.2	1,264.6	-49.9
Milk[2]	924.1	316.7	167.6	117.7	123.2	132.2	85.7

[1] In millions of units.

[2] In millions of tons. State sector only.

Source: Based on information from Consultores Asociados, S.A., *Cuba: Inversiones y negocios, 1995–1996*, Havana, 1995, 41; Comisión Económica para América Latina y el Caribe (CEPAL), *La economía cubana: Reformas estructurales y desempeño en los noventa*, Mexico, 1997, Table A36; and Oficina Nacional de Estadísticas, *Anuario estadístico, 1997*, Havana, 1999, 189–98.

Table 9. Selected Indicators of Production: Manufacturing, 1989, 1993–98
(in thousands of tons, unless otherwise indicated)

Product	1989	1993	1994	1995	1996	1997	1998	Percent change 1989–98
Electricity[1]	15.2	11.0	12.0	12.5	13.2	14.2	14.2	-6.6
Steel	314	98	131	201	229	334	278	-11.5
Nickel plus cobalt (mineral content)	46.6	30.2	26.9	42.7	53.7	61.6	67.7	45.3
Automotive batteries[2]	360	153	164	179	149	185	198	-45.0
Automotive tires	315	63	112	194	212	233	165	-47.6
Oxygen gas[3]	21	16	20	21	21	24	21	0
Complete fertilizers	899	95	136	218	242	184	157	-17.5
Cement[4]	3.8	1.0	1.1	1.4	1.4	1.7	1.7	-55.3
Crushed stone[3]	12.5	1.9	2.3	2.4	2.9	2.9	2.9	-77.8
Concrete blocks[5]	103	27	32	48	49	45	43	-58.3
Cotton yarn	33	5	6	5	7	6	5	-84.8
Textiles[6]	220	51	56	45	48	54	54	-75.5
Raw sugar[4]	8.1	4.1	3.9	3.3	4.4	4.2	3.2	-56.2
Rice	249	85	75	79	141	145	90	-63.9
Wheat flour	398	215	265	268	245	282	291	-26.9
Milk	762	328	295	269	273	270	272	-64.3
Pork	67	12	16	16	19	17	19	-71.6
Poultry	76	16	19	19	23	20	18	-76.3
Canned meats	68	68	67	72	74	79	81	19.1
Canned fruits and vegetables	166	66	742	113	136	144	144	-13.3
Pasta	52	13	24	25	28	31	29	-44.2

Table 9. (Continued) Selected Indicators of Production: Manufacturing, 1989, 1993–98 (in thousands of tons, unless otherwise indicated)

Product	1989	1993	1994	1995	1996	1997	1998	Percent change 1989–98
Lard[7]	2,077	31	46	19	23	20	n.a.[8]	-99.0*
Vegetable oil[7]	1,923	463	661	555	577	478	289	-85.0
Powdered milk	2.4	0.6	0.5	0.4	0.3	0.1	0.1	-95.8
Bread.	497	327	353	354	362	370	389	-21.7
Fish catch	142	67	57	74	95	106	n.a.	-25.4*
Rum[9]	514	388	441	528	476	499	54.0	5.1
Beer[9]	3,333	1,304	1,201	1,330	1,504	1,639	1,759	-47.2
Soft drinks[9]	2,391	1,511	1,721	1,941	1,938	2,097	253.7	6.1
Cigars[5]	304	208	186	192	194	215	264	-13.2
Cigarettes[10]	17	12	14	13	11	11	12	-29.4
Mixed animal feed	1,904	668	723	798	713	680	59.3	-68.9

* 1989–97.
[1] In thousands of gigawatt hours.
[2] In thousands of units.
[3] In millions of cubic meters.
[4] In millions of tons.
[5] In millions of units.
[6] In millions of square meters.
[7] In tons.
[8] n.a.—not available.
[9] In thousands of hectoliters.
[10] In billions of units.

Source: Based on information from Consultores Asociados, S.A., *Cuba: Inversiones y negocios, 1994–95*, Havana, 1995, 40; Comisión Económica para América Latina y el Caribe (CEPAL), *La economía cubana: Reformas estructurales y desempeño en los noventa*, Mexico, 1997, Table A49 and others; Oficina Nacional de Estadísticas, *Anuario estadístico, 1997*, Havana, 1999; and Oficina Nacional de Estadísticas, *Cuba en cifras, 1998*, Havana.

Table 10. Tourism Industry Indicators, 1990–97

	1990	1991	1992	1993	1994	1995	1996	1997
Number of visitors (thousands)	340	424	461	546	619	742	1,004	1,170
Length of average stay (days)	8.7	8.7	9.1	9.6	9.1	8.7	7.3	n.a.
Stock of hotel rooms (thousands)	n.a.[1]	31.8	32.9	35.5	34.5	37.5	39.5	40.7
Stock of hotel rooms suitable for international tourism (thousands)	12.9	16.6	18.7	22.1	23.3	24.2	26.9	n.a.
Occupancy rate of hotel rooms (percent)	n.a.	69.8	60.4	57.9	59.1	62.9	64.9	75.4
Occupancy rate of hotel rooms suitable for international tourism (percent)	39.7	43.0	42.0	43.8	46.0	52.6	55.9	n.a.
Gross income (in millions of United States dollars)..........	243.4	387.4	567.0	720.0	850.0	1,100.0	1,333.1	1,543.3
Average daily income per visitor (in United States dollars)	82.5	105.3	135.6	137.9	150.3	170.3	187.8	n.a.

[1] n.a.—not available.

Source: Based on information from Comisión Económica para América Latina y el Caribe (CEPAL), *La economía cubana: Reformas estructurales y desempeño en los noventa*, Mexico, 1997, Table A23; and Oficina Nacional de Estadísticas, *Anuario estadístico, 1997*, Havana, 1999, 230–37.

Table 11. Employed and Unemployed Economically Active Population, 1989–96 (in thousands of people)

	1989	1990	1991	1992	1993	1994	1995	1996[1]
Economically active population	4,728.2	4,741.6	4,736.8	4,635.3	4,597.0	4,495.9	4,483.6	4,550.0
Employment	4,355.8	4,393.5	4,374.3	4,523.3	4,312.5	4,194.5	4,131.0	4,240.0
State sector	4,126.6	4,153.5	4,119.3	4,072.3	3,969.9	3,465.9	3,256.0	3,225.0
Non-state	229.2	240.0	255.0	280.0	342.6	728.6	875.0	1,015.0
Cooperatives and UBPCs[2]	64.6	60.0	60.0	60.0	59.7	324.1	420.0	440.0
Private farmers	123.1	130.0	130.0	130.0	144.2	163.7	170.0	175.0
Self-employed	25.2	30.0	40.0	60.0	101.5	180.0	225.0	340.0
Salaried	16.3	20.0	25.0	30.0	37.1	60.8	60.0	60.0
Unemployed population	372.4	348.1	362.5	283.0	284.5	301.4	352.1	310.0
Dislocated from previous job	299.9	276.2	291.1	212.1	214.2	231.6	283.3	241.2
First-time job seekers	72.5	71.9	71.4	70.9	70.3	69.8	69.3	68.8

[1] Estimated.
[2] Basic Unit of Cooperative Production Unit (Unidad Básica de Producción Cooperativa—UBPC).

Source: Based on information from Comisión Económica para América Latina y el Caribe (CEPAL), *La economía cubana: Reformas estructurales y desempeño en los noventa*, Mexico, 1997, Table A28; and Oficina Nacional de Estadísticas, *Anuario estadístico, 1997*, Havana, 1999.

Table 12. State Civilian Employment, by Economic Sector, 1990–97 (in thousands of employees)

	1990	1991	1992	1993	1994	1995	1996	1997
State Civilian Employment	3,569.4	3,579.3	3,542.3	3,469.9	2,972.8	2,822.3	2,708.9	2,703.5
Agriculture, hunting, forestry, and fishing	785.3	831.0	838.1	845.8	453.5	419.7	321.5	334.8
Mining	38.8	40.0	42.5	40.0	34.3	32.7	30.6	38.2
Manufacturing	685.2	663.1	654.8	646.4	637.9	619.3	616.8	561.8
Electricity, gas, and water	40.5	40.1	42.7	44.2	47.1	50.2	50.4	52.0
Construction	309.8	304.8	287.7	231.7	201.8	200.7	196.9	202.8
Commerce, restaurants, and hotels	431.2	420.2	416.3	412.9	373.3	329.4	326.6	336.0
Transportation, warehousing, and communications	232.6	229.4	215.0	198.4	187.2	150.3	146.6	124.2
Finance, insurance, real estate, and business services	65.2	65.5	56.5	55.2	54.7	49.2	48.7	41.6
Community, social, and personal services	920.8	985.2	988.7	995.3	983.0	970.8	970.8	1,012.1

Source: Based on information from Oficina Nacional de Estadísticas, *Anuario estadístico, 1997*, Havana, 1999, 104.

Table 13. Foreign Debt in Convertible Currency, 1993–98 (in millions of United States dollars)

	1993	1994	1995	1996	1997	1998
Total Debt.........	8,785	9,083	10,504	10,465	10,146	11,209
Official bilateral.........	4,067	3,992	4,550	6,035	5,853	6,248
Intergovernmental loans.........	40	44	47	1,376	1,512	1,601
Credits for development aid.........	151	164	181	222	209	220
Export credits with government guarantee.........	3,855	3,784	4,321	4,437	4,132	4,426
Official multilateral.........	438	503	601	561	521	575
Suppliers.........	1,867	2,058	2,403	1,199	1,169	1,673
Financial institutions.........	2,406	2,501	2,919	2,640	2,577	2,687
Bank loans and deposits.........	2,156	2,254	2,602	2,361	2,297	2,573
Medium- and long-term bilateral and consortium loans.........	1,027	1,135	1,222	1,133	1,116	1,362
Short-term deposits.........	1,130	1,119	1,380	1,229	1,181	1,211
Credits for current imports.........	249	248	317	279	280	113
Other credits.........	27	29	31	30	26	27

Source: Based on information from Banco Nacional de Cuba, *Economic Report 1994*, Havana, August 1995, 25; Banco Nacional de Cuba, *Informe económico, 1995*, Havana, May 1996, 24; and Banco Central de Cuba, *Informe económico, 1998*, April 1999, 33.

Table 14. Balance of Payments, 1993–98 (in millions of pesos)

	1993	1994	1995	1996	1997	1998
Current Account	-371.6	-260.2	-517.7	-166.8	-436.7	-396.3
Goods and Services	-370.7	-307.6	-639.1	-417.9	-745.5	-617.1
Goods	-847.4	-971.4	-1,483.3	-1,790.3	-2,264.5	-2,785.3
Exports	1,136.6	1,381.4	1,507.3	1,866.2	1,823.1	1,444.4
Imports	1,984.0	2,352.8	2,991.6	3,656.5	4,087.6	4,229.7
Services	476.7	663.8	845.2	1,372.4	1,519.0	2,168.2
Income	-263.8	-422.8	-524.8	-492.6	-482.9	-599.2
Current Transfers	262.9	470.2	646.2	743.7	791.7	820.0
Capital Account	356.1	262.4	596.2	174.4	457.4	413.3
Long-term Capital	118.4	817.4	24.2	307.9	786.9	632.7
Direct Investment	54.0	563.4	4.7	82.1	442.0	206.6
Other	64.4	254.0	19.5	225.8	344.9	426.1
Other Capital	237.7	-555.0	572.0	-133.5	-329.5	-219.4
Change in Reserves	15.5	-2.2	-78.5	-7.6	-20.7	-17.0

Note: By convention, a negative change in international reserves is a gain in such reserves.

Source: Based on information from Oficina Nacional de Estadisticas, *Anuario estadístico de Cuba, 1997*, Havana, 1999, 117; and Oficina Nacional de Estadisticas, *Cuba en cifras, 1998*, Havana, 1999, 36.

Table 15. Foreign Joint Ventures in Cuba, by Country of Origin, 1988, 1990–95 (in numbers of joint ventures)

	1988	1990	1991	1992	1993	1994	1995	Total
Spain...........	1		3	9	10	14	10	47
Mexico.........			2	3	3	4	1	13
Canada.........				2	8	16		26
Italy...........				1	5	4	7	17
France..........		1		3	5	2	2	13
Netherlands.....				1	2	3	3	9
Tax havens......		1	3	10	5	12		31
Other Latin American countries..			2	3	11	9	4	29
Other countries..			1	1	11	10	4	27
TOTAL.........	1	2	11	33	60	74	31	212

Source: Based on information from Consultores Asociados, S.A., *Cuba: Inversiones y negocios, 1995–1996*, Havana, 1995, 18.

Table 16. Foreign Joint Ventures in Cuba, by Economic Sector, 1988, 1990–95 (in numbers of joint ventures)

	1988	1990	1991	1992	1993	1994	1995	Total
Agriculture			1	1	3	3	2	10
Mining			1		10	17		28
Oil		1	1	11	8	4		25
Industry			5	9	17	12	13	56
Tourism	1			4	9	16	4	34
Transportation						1	4	5
Construction and construction materials			2	3	6	10	1	22
Communications		1		1		1		3
Other			1	4	7	10	7	29
TOTAL	1	2	11	33	60	74	31	212

Source: Based on information from Consultores Asociados, S.A., *Cuba: Inversiones y negocios, 1995–1996*, Havana, 1995, 19.

Table 17. Voters in National Assembly Elections, 1993

Province (from west to east)	Number of Voters Casting Ballots	Voting for Full Official Slate (percentage)	Voting for Some But Not All Candidates (percentage)	Voting Blank or Void (percentage)
Pinar del Río.............	510,551.0	89.5	3.8	6.6
Ciudad de La Habana......	1,607,173.0	77.3	8.0	14.7
La Habana	503,211.0	82.2	5.1	12.6
Matanzas.................	476,600.0	88.0	5.0	7.0
Cienfuegos	281,053.0	90.8	4.2	5.0
Villa Clara..............	613,616.0	88.5	4.6	6.9
Sancti Spíritus..........	327,692.0	91.8	4.2	4.0
Ciego de Ávila...........	276,274.0	91.1	4.6	4.3
Camagüey.................	537,557.0	90.4	4.6	5.0
Las Tunas	356,172.0	96.5	1.6	1.9
Holguín..................	718,815.0	92.0	3.5	4.5
Granma...................	560,646.0	97.0	1.6	1.4
Santiago de Cuba.........	692,228.0	94.2	3.1	2.7
Guantánamo...............	333,471.0	95.7	2.3	2.0
Isla de la Juventud	57,056.0	88.3	5.7	5.9
TOTAL...................	7,852,315.0	88.4 (average)	4.6 (average)	7.0 (average)

Source: Based on information compiled by Jorge I. Domínguez from *Granma* [Havana], March 11, 1993.

Table 18. Percentage of Null and Blank Votes Cast in Elections, 1993, 1997, and 2000

Provinces	1993 National Elections	1997 Municipal Elections	2000 Municipal Elections
Pinar del Río	6.6	8.3	6.7
Ciudad de La Habana	14.7	9.9	7.9
La Habana	12.6	11.2	8.8
Matanzas.	7.0	8.5	6.6
Cienfuegos	5.0	7.9	6.4
Villa Clara.	6.9	8.0	7.1
Sancti Spíritus	4.0	6.3	4.9
Ciego de Ávila	4.3	5.3	4.4
Camagüey.	5.0	6.2	4.8
Las Tunas	1.9	4.4	4.0
Holguín	4.5	6.2	5.3
Granma	1.4	4.0	3.4
Santiago de Cuba.	2.7	4.4	3.5
Guantánamo	2.0	3.9	3.4
Isla de la Juventud	5.9	5.9	5.3
Countrywide	7.0	7.2	5.9

Source: Based on information computed by Jorge I. Domínguez from *Granma* [Havana], March 11, 1993, and April 25, 2000.

Table 19.   Major Army Equipment, 1999[1]

Type and Description	Country of Origin	In Inventory
Medium battle tanks		
T–34, T–54/–55, T–62..............	Soviet Union	1,500 (including 400 T–34, 600 T–54/–55, 400 T–62)
Light tanks		
PT–76	n.a.[2]	A relatively small number.
Reconnaissance		
BRDM–1/–2.....................	n.a.	250
Armored infantry fighting vehicle		
BMP–1	n.a.	400
Armored personnel carrier		
BTR–40/–50/–60/–152.............	n.a.	700
Towed artillery	n.a.	700
76mm ZIS–3......................		
122mm M–1938, D–30..............		
130mm M–46		
152mm M–1937, D–1..............		
Self-propelled artillery	n.a.	40
122mm 2S1......................		
152mm 2S3......................		
Multiple rocket launcher	n.a.	300
122mm BM–21....................		
140mm BM–14....................		
Mortars	n.a.	1,000
82mm M–41/–43.................		
120mm M–38/–43................		
Static defense artillery	n.a.	n.a.
122mm JS–2 heavy tank............		
85mm T–34		
Antitank guided weapon	n.a.	n.a.
AT–1 Snapper....................		
AT–3 Sagger		
Artillery guns.......................	n.a.	n.a.
85mm D–44		
100mm SU–100 self-propelled, T–12................		100 SU–100
Air defense guns	n.a.	400 ZU–23, 36 ZSU–23–4
23mm ZU–23, ZSU–23–4 self-propelled...................		
30mm M–53 (twin)/BTR–60P self- propelled		100
37mm M–1939		300

Table 19. *(Continued) Major Army Equipment, 1999*[1]

Type and Description	Country of Origin	In Inventory
57mm S–60 towed, ZSU–57–2 self-propelled		200 S–60, 25 ZSU–57–2
85mm KS–12		100
100mm KS–19		75
Surface-to-air missile	n.a.	n.a.
SA–6/–7/–8/–9/–13/–14/–16		

[1] Most equipment in storage and not available on short notice.
[2] n.a.—not available.

Source: Based on information from *The Military Balance, 1999–2000*, London, 1999, 228–29; and "The 1999–2000 World Defence Almanac," *Military Technology* [Bonn], 24, No. 1, 2000, 51.

Table 20.   Major Air Force Equipment, 1999[1]

Type and Description	Country of Origin	In Inventory
Air Force		
Fighter ground attack (two squadrons)		
MiG–23 BN	Soviet Union	10
Fighters[2] (four squadrons)		
MiG–21F	Soviet Union	30
MiG–21bis	Soviet Union	50
MiG–23MF	Soviet Union	20
MiG–29	Soviet Union	6
Attack helicopters		
Mi–8 and Mi–17	Soviet Union	45
Mi–24	Soviet Union	12
Mi–25	Soviet Union	35
Antisubmarine warfare		
Mi–14 helicopters	Soviet Union	5
Transport (four squadrons)		
An–2	Soviet Union	8
An–24	Soviet Union	1
An–26	Soviet Union	15
An–30	Soviet Union	1
An–32	Soviet Union	2
Yak–40	Soviet Union	4
Il–76 (Air Force aircraft in civilian markings)	Soviet Union	2
Helicopters		
Mi–8/–17	Soviet Union	40
Training		
L–39C Albatros	Soviet Union	25
MiG–15	Soviet Union	30
MiG–21U	Soviet Union	8
MiG–23U	Soviet Union	4
MiG–29UB	Soviet Union	2
Z–326	Soviet Union	20
Missiles		
Antisubmarine missiles AS–7	Soviet Union	n.a.[3]
Antiaircraft missiles AA–2, AA–7, AA–8, AA–10, AA–11	Soviet Union	n.a.
Surface-to-air missiles Active SA–2, SA–3 sites	Soviet Union	13
Civil Airline		
Aircraft used as troop transports		
Il–62	Soviet Union	10

Table 20. (Continued) Major Air Force Equipment, 1999[1]

Type and Description	Country of Origin	In Inventory
Tu–154	Soviet Union	7
Yak–42	Soviet Union	12
An–30	Soviet Union	1

[1] Most aircraft are in storage for lack of spare parts and as a cost-saving measure.
[2] The International Institute for Strategic Studies estimates that probably only about three MiG– 29, ten MiG–23, and five MiG–21bis are in operation.
[3] n.a.—not available.

Source: Based on information from *The Military Balance, 1999–2000*, London, 1999, 229; and "The 1999–2000 World Defence Almanac," *Military Technology* [Bonn], 24, No. 1, 2000, 51.

Table 21. Major Naval Equipment, 1999[1]

Type and Description	Country of Origin	In Inventory
Navy		
Submarines		
Foxtrot with 533mm and 406mm torpedo tube (nonoperational)	Soviet Union	1
Frigates		
Koni-class with two antisubmarine warfare rocket launchers (nonoperational)	Soviet Union	2
Patrol and coastal combatants missile craft		
Osa I/II with four SSN–2 Styx surface-to-surface missiles......................	Soviet Union	4
Pauk II fast patrol craft with two anti-submarine warfare rocket launchers and four anti-submarine torpedo tubes.........	Soviet Union	1
Mine countermeasures		
Sonya coastal minesweeper......	Soviet Union	2
Yevgenya inshore minesweeper	Soviet Union	4
Support and miscellaneous intelligence collection		
vessel	n.a.[2]	1
survey.................................	n.a.	1
Naval Infantry		
Artillery		
122mm M–1931/37	n.a.	n.a.
130mm M–46...........................	n.a.	n.a.
152mm M–1937........................	n.a.	n.a.
Surface-to-surface missiles		
SS–C–3 systems	n.a.	n.a.
Mobile Bandera IV	n.a.	n.a.
Naval Aviation		
Ka–28s................................	Soviet Union	4
Mi–4s.................................	Soviet Union	4
MiG–29...............................	Soviet Union	6

[1] The Cuban Navy is no longer an operational force.
[2] n.a.—not available.

Source: Based on information from *The Military Balance. 1999–2000*, London, 1999, 229; and "The 1999–2000 World Defence Almanac," *Military Technology* [Bonn], 24, No. 1, 2000, 50.

Bibliography

Chapter 1

Aguila, Juan del. *Cuba: Dilemmas of a Revolution*. Colorado: Westview Press, 1984.

Aguilar, Luis E. *Cuba 1933: Prologue to Revolution*. Ithaca: Cornell University Press, 1972.

Barrera, Elsa. *Reajustes y reformas en la economía cubana, 1994*. Series: Dossier. Havana: Centro de Estudios sobre América, Sección de Información Científica, 1995.

Batista, Fulgencio. *The Growth and Decline of the Cuban Republic*. New York: Devin-Adair, 1964.

Benglesdorf, Carollee. *The Problem of Democracy in Cuba: Between Vision and Reality.* New York: Oxford University Press, 1994.

Benjamin, Jules R. *The United States and Cuba: Hegemony and Dependent Development, 1880–1934*. Pittsburgh: University of Pittsburgh Press, 1977.

Blight, James G., and David A. Welch. *On the Brink: Americans and Soviets Reexamine the Cuban Missile Crisis*. New York: Hill and Wang, 1989.

Bonachea, Rolando, and Nelson Valdes, eds. *Che: Selected Works of Ernesto Che Guevara*. Cambridge: MIT Press, 1969.

Bonsal, Philip W. *Cuba, Castro, and the United States*. Pittsburgh: University of Pittsburgh Press, 1971.

Brown Castillo, Gerardo. *Cuba Colonial.* Havana: Jesús Montero, 1952.

Buell, Raymond L. *Problems of the New Cuba: Report of the Commission on Cuban Affairs*. New York: Foreign Policy Association, 1935.

Bunck, Julia Marie. *Fidel Castro and the Quest for a Revolutionary Culture in Cuba*. University Park: Pennsylvania State University Press, 1994.

Carbonell, Nestor T. *And the Russians Stayed: The Sovietization of Cuba*. New York: Morrow, 1989.

Carbonell y Rivero, José M. *Evolución de la cultura cubana*. 18 vols. Havana: Montalvo y Cardenas, 1928.

Chapman, Charles E. *A History of the Cuban Republic.* New York: Macmillan, 1927.

Corwin, Arthur. *Spain and the Abolition of Slavery in Cuba, 1817–1886.* Austin: University of Texas Press, 1967.

Dewart, Leslie. *Christianity and Revolution: The Lesson of Cuba.* New York: Herder and Herder, 1963.

Díaz-Briquets, Sergio. *The Health Revolution in Cuba.* Austin: University of Texas Press, Institute of Latin American Studies, 1983.

Domínguez, Jorge I. *Cuba: Order and Revolution.* Cambridge: Harvard University Press, 1978.

Domínguez, Jorge I. *To Make a World Safe for Revolution: Cuba's Foreign Policy.* Cambridge: Harvard University Press, 1989.

Draper, Theodore. *Castroism: Theory and Practice.* New York: Praeger, 1965.

Dumont, René. *Socialism and Development.* New York: Grove Press, 1970.

Duncan, Raymond W. *The Soviet Union and Cuba: Interests and Influence.* New York: Praeger, 1985.

Fagen, Richard R. *The Transformation of Political Culture in Cuba.* Stanford: Stanford University Press, 1969.

Falk, Pamela S. *Cuban Foreign Policy: Caribbean Tempest.* Lexington, Massachusetts: Lexington Books, 1986.

Fauriol, George, and Eva Loser, eds. *Cuba: The International Dimension.* New Brunswick, New Jersey: Transaction, 1990.

Fermoselle, Rafael. *The Evolution of the Cuban Military, 1492–1986.* Miami: Ediciones Universal, 1987.

Fernández, Damián J. *Cuba's Foreign Policy in the Middle East.* Boulder, Colorado: Westview Press, 1988.

Fitzgibbon, Russel H. *Cuba and the United States, 1900–1935.* Menasha, Wisconsin: Banta, 1935.

Foner, Philip S. *A History of Cuba in Its Relations with the United States.* 2 vols. New York: International Publishers, 1963.

Foreign Policy Association Commission on Cuban Affairs. *Problems of the New Cuba.* New York: Little and Ives, 1935.

Franco, José. *Antonio Maceo.* 3 vols. Havana: 1975.

Franqui, Carlos. *Diary of the Cuban Revolution.* Trans., Georgette Félix. New York: Viking Press, 1976.

Franqui, Carlos. *Family Portrait with Fidel.* New York: Random House, 1984.

Geyer, Georgie Anne. *Guerrilla Prince: The Untold Story of Fidel Castro.* Boston: Little Brown, 1991.

Goldenberg, Boris. *The Cuban Revolution and Latin America.* New York: Praeger, 1965.

Gonzalez, Edward. *Cuba: Clearing Perilous Waters.* Santa Monica, California: Rand, 1996.

Gonzalez, Edward. *Cuba Under Castro: The Limits of Charisma.* Boston: Houghton Mifflin, 1974.

Gray, Richard B. *José Martí: Cuban Patriot.* Gainesville: University of Florida Press, 1962.

Grupo Cubano de Investigaciones Económicas. *Un estudio sobre Cuba.* Coral Gables, Florida: University of Miami Press, 1965.

Guerra y Sánchez, Ramiro. *Sugar and Society in the Caribbean.* New Haven, Connecticut: Yale University Press, 1964.

Guerra y Sánchez, Ramiro, et al. *Historia de la nación cubana.* 10 vols. Havana: Editorial Historia de la Nación Cubana, 1952.

Guiteras, Pedro José. *Historia de la isla de Cuba.* 3 vols. Havana: Colección de Libros Cubanos, 1928.

Halperin, Ernst. *Castro and Latin American Communism.* Cambridge: MIT, Center for International Studies, 1963.

Halperin, Ernst. *The Ideology of Castroism and Its Impact on the Communist Parties of Latin America.* Cambridge: MIT, Center for International Studies, 1961.

Halperin, Maurice. *The Rise and Decline of Fidel Castro.* Berkeley and Los Angeles: University of California Press, 1972.

Horowitz, Irving Louis. *Cuban Communism.* New Brunswick, New Jersey: Transaction, 1996.

International Bank for Reconstruction and Development. *Report on Cuba.* Washington: 1951.

Jackson, D. Bruce. *Castro, The Kremlin, and Communism in Latin America.* Baltimore: Johns Hopkins Press, 1969.

James, Daniel. *Che Guevara: A Biography.* New York: Stein and Day, 1969.

Jenks, Leland. *Our Cuban Colony.* New York: American Fund for Public Service Studies in American Investment Abroad, American Imperialism Series, 1928.

Johnson, Haynes. *The Bay of Pigs.* New York: Norton, 1964.

Johnson, Willis F. *The History of Cuba.* 5 vols. New York: B. F. Buck, 1920.

Kiple, Kenneth T. *Blacks in Colonial Cuba.* Gainesville: University of Florida Press, 1976.

Kirk, John. *Between God and the Party: Religion and Politics in Revolutionary Cuba.* Gainesville: University of Florida Press, 1989.

Knight, Franklin W. *Slave Society in Cuba During the Nineteenth Century.* Madison: University of Wisconsin Press, 1970.

Kuethe, Allen J. *Cuba, 1753–1815.* Knoxville: University of Tennessee Press, 1986.

Langley, Lester D. *The Cuban Policy of the United States: A Brief History.* New York: Wiley and Sons, 1968.

Le Riverend Brusone, Julio. *Economic History of Cuba.* Havana: Havana Book Institute, 1967.

Lévesque, Jacques. *The USSR and the Cuban Revolution: Soviet Ideological and Strategic Perspectives, 1959–77.* New York: Praeger, 1978.

Liss, Sheldon B. *Fidel! Castro's Political and Social Thought.* Boulder, Colorado: Westview Press, 1994.

Lizaso, Felix. *Martí: Martyr of Cuban Independence.* Albuquerque: University of New Mexico Press, 1953.

Llerena, Mario. *The Unsuspected Revolution: The Birth and Rise of Castroism.* Ithaca: Cornell University Press, 1978.

Lockmiller, David A. *Magoon in Cuba: A History of the Second Intervention, 1906–1909.* Chapel Hill: University of North Carolina Press, 1938. Reprint. New York: Greenwood Press, 1969.

MacGaffey, Wyatt, and Clifford R. Barnett. *Cuba: Its People, Its Society, Its Culture.* New Haven, Connecticut: Human Relations Area Files, 1962.

Mallin, Jay, ed. *Che Guevara on Revolution.* Coral Gables, Florida: University of Miami Press, 1969.

Manach, Jorge. *Indagación al choteo.* Havana: Editorial Lex, 1936.

Manach, Jorge. *Martí: Apostle of Freedom.* New York: Devin-Adair, 1950.

Marrero, Leví. *Cuba: La forja de un pueblo.* 16 vols. Puerto Rico: Editorial San Juan, 1971.

Mazarr, Michael J. *Semper Fidel: America and Cuba, 1776–1988.* Baltimore: Nautical and Aviation Publishing Company of America, 1988.

Mesa-Lago, Carmelo. *The Economy of Socialist Cuba*. Albuquerque: University of New Mexico Press, 1981.

Mesa-Lago, Carmelo, ed. *Revolutionary Change in Cuba*. Pittsburgh: University of Pittsburgh Press, 1971.

Millet, Allan Reed. *The Politics of Intervention: The Military Occupation of Cuba, 1906–1909*. Columbus: Ohio State University Press, 1968.

Montaner, Carlos Alberto. *Fidel Castro and the Cuban Revolution*. New Brunswick, New Jersey: Transaction, 1989.

Moreno Fraginals, Manuel. *The Sugarmill*. New York: Monthly Review Press, 1976.

Nelson, Lowry. *Cuba: The Measure of a Revolution*. Minneapolis: University of Minnesota Press, 1972.

Nelson, Lowry. *Rural Cuba*. Minneapolis: University of Minnesota Press, 1950.

Ortiz Fernández, Fernando. *Las cuatro culturas indias de Cuba*. Havana: Arellano, 1943.

Ortiz Fernández, Fernando. *Cuban Counterpoint: Tobacco and Sugar*. New York: Knopf, 1947.

Ortiz Fernández, Fernando. *Los negros esclavos: Estudio sociológico y de derecho público*. Havana: Editorial de Ciencias Sociales, 1975.

Paterson, Thomas G. *Contesting Castro*. New York: Oxford University Press, 1994.

Payne, Richard J. *Opportunities and Dangers of Soviet-Cuban Expansion: Toward a Pragmatic U.S. Policy*. New York: State University of New York Press, 1988.

Pérez, Louis A. *Army Politics in Cuba, 1898–1958*. Pittsburgh: University of Pittsburgh Press, 1976.

Pérez, Louis A. *Cuba Between Reform and Revolution*. New York: Oxford University Press, 1995.

Pérez-Stable, Marifeli. *The Cuban Revolution: Origins, Course, and Legacy*. New York: Oxford University Press, 1993.

Pratt, Julius. *Expansionists of 1898: The Acquisition of Hawaii and the Spanish Islands*. New York: P. Smith, 1964.

Portell-Vilá, Herminio. *Historia de la guerra de Cuba y los Estados Unidos contra España*. Havana: 1949.

Portuondo del Prado, Fernando. *Historia de Cuba*. Havana: Molina, 1953.

Ratliff, William E. *Castroism and Communism in Latin America: 1959–1976.* Washington: American Enterprise Institute, 1976.

Roca, Sergio. *Cuban Economic Policy and Ideology.* Beverly Hills, California: Sage, 1976.

Santovenia, Emeterio S., and Raúl Shelton. *Cuba y su historia.* Miami: Rema Press, 1966.

Seers, Dudley, ed. *Cuba: The Economic and Social Revolution.* Chapel Hill: University of North Carolina Press, 1964.

Smith, Robert F., ed. *Background to Revolution: The Development of Modern Cuba.* New York: Knopf, 1966.

Stone, Elizabeth. *Women and the Cuban Revolution.* New York: Pathfinder Press, 1981.

Suárez, Andrés. *Cuba: Castroism and Communism, 1959–1966.* Trans., Joel Carmichael and Ernst Halperin. Cambridge: MIT Press, 1967.

Suchlicki, Jaime. *Cuba: From Columbus to Castro and Beyond.* 4th ed. Washington: Brassey's, 1997.

Suchlicki, Jaime. *Historical Dictionary of Cuba.* Metuchen, New Jersey: Scarecrow Press, 1988.

Suchlicki, Jaime. *University Students and Revolution in Cuba.* Coral Gables, Florida: University of Miami Press, 1969.

Suchlicki, Jaime, ed. *Cuba, Castro and Revolution.* Coral Gables, Florida: University of Miami Press, 1972.

Suchlicki, Jaime, ed. *The Cuban Military under Castro.* Coral Gables, Florida: University of Miami Press, 1989.

Suchlicki, Jaime, ed. *Problems of Succession in Cuba.* Coral Gables, Florida: University of Miami Press, 1985.

Suchlicki, Jaime, and Antonio Jorge, eds. *Investing in Cuba: Problems and Prospects.* New Brunswick, New Jersey: Transaction, 1994.

Szulc, Tad. *Fidel: A Critical Portrait.* New York: Morrow, 1986.

Thomas, Hugh. *Cuba: The Pursuit of Freedom.* New York: Harper and Row, 1971.

Truslow, Francis A. *Report on Cuba.* Baltimore: Johns Hopkins Press, 1951.

Varona Guerrero, Miguel A. *La guerra de independencia de Cuba.* 3 vols. Havana: Editorial Lex, 1946.

Vitier, Medardo. *Las ideas en Cuba: Proceso del pensamiento político, filosófico y crítico en Cuba.* Havana: Editorial Trópico, 1938.

Wilkerson, Loree. *Fidel Castro's Political Programs: From Reformism to Marxism-Leninism.* Gainesville: University of Florida Press, 1965.

Wright, Irene A. *The Early History of Cuba, 1492–1586.* New York: Macmillan, 1916.

Wyden, Peter. *Bay of Pigs: The Untold Story.* New York: Simon and Shuster, 1979.

Chapter 2

Academia de Ciencias de Cuba. *Nuevo atlas nacional de Cuba.* Havana: Instituto de Geografía, 1989.

Aguirre, Benigno E. "The Conventionalization of Collective Behavior in Cuba," *The American Journal of Sociology,* 90, 1985, 541–66.

Alvarez, José, and William A. Messina, Jr. "Cuba's New Agricultural Cooperatives and Markets: Antecedents, Organization, Early Performance and Prospects." Pages 175–95 in *Cuba in Transition,* 6. Washington: Association for the Study of the Cuban Economy, 1996.

Amaro, Nelson. "Decentralization, Local Government, and Citizen Participation in Cuba." Pages 262–82 in *Cuba in Transition,* 6. Washington: Association for the Study of the Cuban Economy, 1996.

American Association for World Health. *The Impact of the U.S. Embargo on Health and Nutrition in Cuba.* Washington: March 1997.

Borhidi, A. *A Phytogeography and Vegetation Ecology of Cuba.* Budapest: Akadémia Kiadó, 1991.

Brundenius, Claes. "Measuring Income Distribution in Pre- and Post-revolutionary Cuba," *Cuban Studies,* 9, 1979, 29–44.

Bunck, Julie Marie. "The Cuban Revolution and Women's Rights." Pages 443–63 in Irving Louis Horowitz, ed., *Cuban Communism.* 8th ed. New Brunswick, New Jersey: Transaction, 1995.

Bunck, Julie Marie. *Fidel Castro and the Quest for a Revolutionary Culture in Cuba.* University Park: Pennsylvania State University Press, 1994.

Castellanos, Jorge, and Isabel Castellanos. *Cultura Afrocubana 3: Las religiones y las lenguas.* Miami: Ediciones Universal, 1992.

Catholic Church of Cuba. *La voz de la iglesia en Cuba.* Mexico City: Obra Nacional de la Buena Prensa, A.C., 1995.

Centeno, Miguel Angel, and Mauricio Fout, eds. *Toward a New Cuba? Legacies of a Revolution.* Boulder, Colorado: Lynne Rienner, 1997.

Centro Latinoamericano de Demografía. "América Latina: Proyecciones de población urbana-rural," *Boletín Demográfico* [Santiago, Chile], 28, 1995.

Clark, Juan. *Mito y realidad: Testimonios de un pueblo.* Miami: Ediciones Saeta. 1992.

Comisión Económica para América Latina y el Caribe (CEPAL). *La economía cubana: Reformas estructurales y desempeño en los noventa.* Mexico City: Fondo de Cultura Económica, 1997.

Comité Estatal de Estadísticas. *Anuario estadístico de Cuba, 1989.* Havana: 1990.

Cuba Neuropathy Field Investigation Team. "Epidemic Optic Neuropathy in Cuba: Clinical Characterization and Risk Factors," *New England Journal of Medicine,* 333, 1995, 1176–82.

Cuéllar, Roberto. "Human Rights: The Dilemmas and Challenges Facing the Non-Governmental Organization Movement During a Transition in Cuba." Pages 153–95 in Lisandro Pérez, ed., *Transition in Cuba: New Challenges for U.S. Policy.* Miami: Florida International University, Cuban Research Institute, 1994.

Danielson, Ross. *Cuban Medicine.* New Brunswick, New Jersey: Transaction, 1979.

Del Aguila, Juan M. *Cuba: Dilemmas of a Revolution.* Rev. ed. Boulder, Colorado: Westview Press, 1988.

Del Aguila, Juan M. "The Politics of Dissidence: A Challenge to the Monolith." Pages 164–88 in Enrique A. Baloyra and James A. Morris, eds., *Conflict and Change in Cuba.* Albuquerque: University of New Mexico Press, 1993.

Díaz-Briquets, Sergio. *The Health Revolution in Cuba.* Austin: University of Texas Press, Institute of Latin American Studies, 1983.

Díaz-Briquets, Sergio, and Jorge Pérez-López. *Conquering Nature: The Environmental Legacy of Socialism in Cuba.* Pittsburgh: University of Pittsburgh Press, 2000.

Díaz-Briquets, Sergio, and Jorge Pérez-López. "Internationalist Civilian Assistance: The Cuban Presence in Sub-Saharan Africa." Pages 48–77 in Sergio Díaz-Briquets, ed., *Cuban Internationalism in Sub-Saharan Africa.* Pittsburgh: Duquesne University Press, 1989.

Díaz-Briquets, Sergio, and Jorge Pérez-López. "Refugee Remittances: Conceptual Issues and the Cuban and Nicaraguan Experiences," *International Migration Review,* 31, 1997, 411–37.

Domínguez, Jorge I. Cuba: *Order and Revolution.* Cambridge: Harvard University Press, 1978.

Espino, María Dolores. "Tourism in Cuba: A Development Strategy for the 1990s?," *Cuban Studies,* No. 23, 1993, 49–69.

Espinosa, Juan Carlos. "The 'Emergence' of Civil Society in Cuba," *Journal of Latin American Affairs,* 4, Spring–Summer 1996, 24–33.

Feinsilver, Julie M. *Healing the Masses: Cuban Health Politics at Home and Abroad.* Berkeley and Los Angeles: University of California Press, 1993.

Fernández, Damián J. "Civil Society in Transition." Pages 97–152 in Lisandro Pérez, ed., *Transition in Cuba: New Challenges for U.S. Policy.* Miami: Florida International University, Cuban Research Institute, 1994.

Fernández, Damián J. "Youth in Cuba: Resistance and Accommodation." Pages 189–211 in Enrique A. Baloyra and James A. Morris, eds., *Conflict and Change in Cuba.* Albuquerque: University of New Mexico Press, 1993.

Fuller, Linda. *Work and Democracy in Socialist Cuba.* Philadelphia: Temple University Press, 1992.

Grupo Cubano de Investigaciones Económicas. *Un estudio sobre Cuba.* Coral Gables, Florida: University of Miami Press, 1963.

Gunn, Gillian. *Cuba's NGOs: Government Puppets or Seeds of Civil Society?* Cuba Briefing Paper Series, No. 7. Washington:

Georgetown University, Center for Latin American Studies, 1995.

Horowitz, Irving Louis, ed. *Cuban Communism, 1959–1995.* 8th ed. New Brunswick, New Jersey: Transaction, 1995.

Horowitz, Irving Louis, and Jaime Suchlicki, eds. *Cuban Communism.* 9th ed. New Brunswick, New Jersey: Transaction, 1998.

Horowitz, Irving Louis, and Jaime Suchlicki, eds. *Cuban Communism.* 10th ed. New Brunswick, New Jersey: Transaction, 2001.

Instituto de Demografía y Censos. *La población cubana en 1953 y 1981.* Havana: Comité Estatal de Estadísticas, 1984.

Kirk, John M. *Between God and the Party: Religion and Politics in Revolutionary Cuba.* Tampa: University of South Florida Press, 1989.

Levins, Robert M. *Tropical Diaspora: The Jewish Experience in Cuba.* Gainesville: University of Florida Press, 1993.

Lutjens, Sheryl. *The State, Bureaucracy, and the Cuban Schools: Power and Participation.* Boulder, Colorado: Westview Press, 1996.

Luzón, José Luis. *Economia, población y territorio en Cuba, 1899– 1983.* Madrid: Instituto de Cooperación Iberoamericana, Ediciones Cultura Hispánica, 1987.

Marrero, Leví. *Geografía de Cuba.* Havana: La Moderna Poesía, 1950.

Mesa-Lago, Carmelo. *The Economy of Socialist Cuba.* Albuquerque: University of New Mexico Press, 1981.

Mesa-Lago, Carmelo. *Market, Socialist and Mixed Economies: Comparative Policy and Performance, Chile, Cuba, and Costa Rica.* Baltimore: Johns Hopkins University Press, 2001.

Mesa-Lago, Carmelo. "The Social Safety Net in the Two Cuban Transitions." Pages 601–70 in Lisandro Pérez, ed., *Transition in Cuba: New Challenges for U.S. Policy.* Miami: Florida International University, Cuba Research Institute, 1994.

Ministerio de Ciencia, Tecnología y Medio Ambiente. *Estrategía Ambiental Nacional.* Havana: 1997.

Moore, Carlos. *Castro, the Blacks, and Africa.* Los Angeles: University of California, Center for Afro-American Studies, 1988.

Moses, Catherine. *Real Life in Castro's Cuba.* Wilmington, Delaware: Scholarly Resources, 2000.

Mújal-León, Eusebio. *The Cuban University under the Revolution.* Washington: Cuban American National Foundation, 1988.

Oficina Nacional de Estadísticas. *Estudios y datos sobre la población cubana.* Havana: May 1997.

Oro, José R. *The Poisoning of Paradise: The Environmental Crisis in Cuba.* Miami: The Endowment for Cuban American Studies, 1992.

Pérez, Lisandro, ed. *Transition in Cuba: New Challenges for U.S. Policy.* Miami: Florida International University, Cuban Research Institute, 1994.

Pérez-López, Jorge F. *Cuba's Second Economy: From Behind the Scenes to Center Stage.* New Brunswick, New Jersey: Transaction, 1995.

Rosendahl, Mona. *Inside the Revolution: Everyday Life in Socialist Cuba.* Ithaca, New York: Cornell University Press, 1997.

Sáez, Héctor R. "Resource Degradation, Agricultural Policies, and Conservation in Cuba," *Cuban Studies,* No. 27, 1997, 40–67.

Salas, Luis. *Social Control and Deviance in Cuba.* New York: Praeger, 1979.

Simon, Françoise L. "Tourism Development in Transition Economies: The Case of Cuba," *Columbia Journal of World Business,* 30, 1995, 26–41.

Suchlicki, Jaime, ed. *The Cuban Military.* Coral Gables: University of Miami, 1989.

United Nations. Economic Commission for Latin America and the Caribbean (Comisión Económica para América Latina y el Caribe). *La economía cubana: Reformas estructurales y desempeño en los noventa.* Mexico City: Fondo de Cultura Económica, 1997.

United Nations. *The Sex and Age Distribution of the World Populations: The 1996 Revision.* New York: 1997.

United Nations. *World Population Prospects.* New York: 1998.

Walker, Phyllis Greene. "The Cuban Military Service System: Organization, Obligations, and Pressures." Pages 99–128 in Jaime Suchlicki, ed., *The Cuban Military under Castro.* Coral Gables, Florida: University of Miami, North-South Center, Institute of Interamerican Studies, 1989.

(Various issues of the following periodicals also were used in the preparation of this chapter: *Granma* [Havana]; *Granma International* [Havana]; *New York Times*; *El Nuevo Herald* [Miami]; and *Washington Post.*)

Chapter 3

Alligood, Arlene. "Cuba's Seaports and Airports: Can They Handle a Post-Embargo Cargo Boom?," *Columbia Journal of World Business*, 30, No. 1, Spring 1995, 71–72.

Bekarevich, A. "Cuba y el CAME: El camino de la integración." Pages 115–24 in *Cuba: 25 años de construcción del socialismo.* Moscow: Redacción Ciencias Sociales Contemporáneas, 1986.

Business International Corporation. *Developing Business Strategies for Cuba.* New York: 1992.

Cabello, Roque, Marta Beatriz, and Arnaldo Ramos Lauzurique. "PIB (Producto Interno Bruto)." Pages 1–5 in *Documentos del Instituto Cubano de Economistas Independientes.* Miami: Cuban Studies Association, 1997.

Carranza Valdés, Julio, Luis Gutiérrez Urdaneta, and Pedro Monreal Gutiérrez. *Cuba: La restructuración de la economía: Una propuesta para el debate.* Havana: Editorial de Ciencias Sociales, 1995.

Castro Ruz, Fidel. "Discurso pronunciado en la inauguración del IV Congreso del Partido Comunista de Cuba, Santiago de Cuba, 10 de octubre de 1991," in *Independientes hasta siempre.* Havana: Editora Política, 1991.

Comisión Económica para América Latina y el Caribe (CEPAL). *La economía cubana: Reformas estructurales y desempeño en los noventa.* Mexico: Fondo de Cultura Económica, 1997.

Constitución de la República de Cuba (1976). Havana: Editorial de Ciencias Sociales, 1985.

Constitución de la República de Cuba (1992). Havana: Editora Política, 1992.

Consultores Asociados, S.A. *Cuba: Inversiones y negocios, 1994–95.* Havana: CONAS, 1994.

Consultores Asociados, S.A. *Cuba: Inversiones y negocios, 1995–96.* Havana: CONAS, 1995.

Cuba. "Acuerdo IV–24, Asamblea Nacional del Poder Popular," *Gaceta Oficial,* May 2, 1994.

Cuba. Aduana General de la República. "Resolución No. 34/ 96—Sobre el Régimen Especial Aduanero en las Zonas Francas y Parques Industriales," October 18, 1996.

Cuba. Banco Central de Cuba. *Informe económico, 1997.* Havana: May 1998.

Cuba. Banco Central de Cuba. *Informe económico, 1998.* Havana: April 1999.

Cuba. Banco Nacional de Cuba. *Economic Report, 1994.* Havana: August 1995.

Cuba. Banco Nacional de Cuba. *Informe económico, 1994.* Havana: August 1995.

Cuba. Banco Nacional de Cuba. *Informe económico, 1995.* Havana: May 1996.

Cuba. Comité Estatal de Estadísticas. *Anuario estadístico de Cuba, 1986.* Havana: 1988.

Cuba. Comité Estatal de Estadísticas. *Anuario estadístico de Cuba, 1989.* Havana: 1991.

Cuba. "Decreto-Ley No. 73—Del sistema tributario," *Gaceta Oficial,* August 5, 1994.

Cuba. "Decreto-Ley No. 76—Ley de minas," *Gaceta Oficial,* January 23, 1995.

Cuba. "Decreto-Ley No. 77—Ley de inversión extranjera," *Gaceta Oficial,* September 6, 1995.

Cuba. "Decreto-Ley No. 140," *Gaceta Oficial,* August 13, 1993.

Cuba. "Decreto-Ley No. 141—Sobre el ejercicio del trabajo por cuenta propia," *Gaceta Oficial,* September 8, 1993.

Cuba. "Decreto-Ley No. 141—De la reorganización de los organismos de la administración central del estado," *Gaceta Oficial,* April 21, 1994.

Cuba. "Decreto-Ley No. 142—Sobre las Unidades Básicas de Producción Cooperativa," *Gaceta Oficial,* September 21, 1993.

Cuba. "Decreto-Ley No. 149—Sobre confiscación de bienes e ingresos obtenidos mediante enriquecimiento indebido," *Gaceta Oficial,* May 4, 1994.

Cuba. "Decreto-Ley No. 165—Ley sobre zonas francas y parques industriales," *Gaceta Oficial,* September 6, 1995.

Cuba. "Decreto-Ley No. 191—Sobre el mercado agropecuario," *Gaceta Oficial,* September 20, 1994.

Cuba. "Decreto-Ley No. 192—Sobre el mercado de artículos industriales y artesanales," *Gaceta Oficial,* October 21, 1994.

Cuba. Ministerio para la Inversión Extranjera y la Colaboración Económica. "Resolución No. 66/96—Sobre el registro oficial de concesionarios y operadores de zona franca," October 24, 1996. (Website: http://www.tips.cu)

Cuba. Oficina Nacional de Estadísticas. *Anuario estadístico de Cuba, 1996.* Havana: 1998.

Cuba. Oficina Nacional de Estadísticas. *Anuario estadístico de Cuba, 1997.* Havana: 1999.

Cuba. Oficina Nacional de Estadísticas. *Cuba en cifras 1998.* Havana: 1999.

Cuba. "Resolución Conjunta No. 1 CETSS-CEF," *Gaceta Oficial,* September 8, 1993.

Díaz-Briquets, Sergio, and Jorge Pérez-López. "Cuba's Labor Adjustment Policies During the Special Period." Pages 118–46 in Jorge Pérez-López, ed., *Cuba at a Crossroads: Politics and Economics after the Fourth Party Congress.* Gainesville: University of Florida Press, 1994.

Díaz-Briquets, Sergio, and Jorge Pérez-López. "Internationalist Civilian Assistance: The Cuban Presence in Sub-Saharan Africa." Pages 48–77 in Sergio Díaz-Briquets, ed., *Cuban Internationalism in Sub-Saharan Africa.* Pittsburgh: Duquesne University Press, 1989.

Espino, María Dolores. "Tourism in Cuba: A Development Strategy for the 1990s?" Pages 147–66 in Jorge Pérez-López, ed., *Cuba at a Crossroads: Politics and Economics after the Fourth Party Congress.* Gainesville: University of Florida Press, 1994.

González, Gerardo. "Transición y recuperación económica en Cuba." Pages 162–77 in *Cuba in Transition,* 7. Washington: Association for the Study of the Cuban Economy, 1997.

Jatar-Hausmann, Ana Julia. *The Cuban Way: Capitalism, Communism, and Confrontation.* West Hartford, Connecticut: Kumarian Press, 1999.

Martino, Orlando D. *Mineral Industries of Latin America.* Washington: United States Department of the Interior, Bureau of Mines, 1998.

Meléndez Bachs, Ernesto. "Relaciones económicas de Cuba con el CAME," *América Latina* [Moscow], 7, 1987, 95–96.

Mesa-Lago, Carmelo. *Are Economic Reforms Propelling Cuba to the Market?* Coral Gables, Florida: University of Miami, North-South Center, 1994.

Mesa-Lago, Carmelo. *Breve historia económica de la Cuba socialista: Política, resultados y perspectivas.* Madrid: Alianza Editorial, 1994.

Mesa-Lago, Carmelo. "La dolarización de la economía cubana," *Estudios Internacionales*, 27, July–September/October–December 1994, 375–88.

Mesa-Lago, Carmelo. "The Economic Effects on Cuba of the Downfall of Socialism in the USSR and Eastern Europe." Pages 133–96 in Carmelo Mesa-Lago, ed., *Cuba after the Cold War.* Pittsburgh: University of Pittsburgh Press, 1993.

Mesa-Lago, Carmelo. "¿Recuperación económica en Cuba?," *Encuentro de la Cultura Cubana*, 3, Winter 1996/97, 54–61.

Mesa-Lago, Carmelo, and Fernando Gil. "Soviet Economic Relations with Cuba." Pages 193–232 in Eusebio Mújal-León, ed., *The USSR and Latin America: A Developing Relationship.* Boston: Unwin Hyman, 1989.

Mesa-Lago, Carmelo, and Jorge Pérez-López. *A Study of Cuba's Material Product System, Its Conversion to the System of National Accounts, and Estimation of Gross Domestic Product and Growth Rates.* World Bank Staff Working Paper No. 770. Washington: World Bank, 1985.

Messina, William A. "Agricultural Reform in Cuba: Implications for Agricultural Production, Markets and Trade." Pages 433–42 in *Cuba in Transition*, 9. Washington: Association for the Study of the Cuban Economy, 1999.

Pérez, Lisandro. "The Population of Cuba: The Growth and Characteristics of Its Labor Force," *Columbia Journal of World Business*, 30, No. 1, Spring 1995.

Pérez-López, Jorge F. "The Cuban Economy in the Age of Hemispheric Integration," *Journal of Interamerican Studies and World Affairs*, 39, No. 3, Fall 1997, 3–47.

Pérez-López, Jorge F. "Cuba's Oil Reexports: Significance and Prospects," *Energy Journal*, 8, 1987, 18–19.

Pérez-López, Jorge F. *Cuba's Second Economy: From Behind the Scenes to Center Stage.* New Brunswick, New Jersey: Transaction, 1995.

Pérez-López, Jorge F. "Cuba's Transition to Market-Based Energy Prices," *Energy Journal,* 13, No. 4, 1992, 18–27.

Pérez-López, Jorge F. *The Economics of Cuban Sugar.* Pittsburgh: University of Pittsburgh Press, 1991.

Pérez-López, Jorge F. "Energy Production, Imports, and Consumption in Revolutionary Cuba," *Latin American Research Review,* 16, No. 3, 1981, 111–37.

Pérez-López, Jorge F. "Foreign Investment in Socialist Cuba: Significance and Prospects," *Studies in Comparative International Development,* 31, No. 4, Winter, 1996–97, 3–28.

Pérez-López, Jorge F. "Islands of Capitalism in an Ocean of Socialism: Joint Ventures in Cuba's Development Strategy." Pages 190–219 in Jorge F. Pérez-López, ed., *Cuba at a Crossroads: Politics and Economics after the Fourth Party Congress.* Gainesville: University of Florida Press, 1994.

Pérez-López, Jorge F. *Odd Couples: Joint Ventures Between Foreign Capitalists and Cuban Socialists.* Agenda Papers No. 16. Coral Gables, Florida: University of Miami, North-South Center, 1995.

Pérez-López, Jorge F. "Swimming Against the Tide: Implications for Cuba of Soviet and Eastern European Reforms in Foreign Relations," *Journal of Interamerican Studies and World Affairs,* 33, No. 2, Summer 1991, 81–139.

Peters, Philip. *Cuban Agriculture: Slow Road to Recovery.* Arlington, Virginia: Alexis de Tocqueville Institution, March 1999.

Peters, Philip. *A Different Kind of Workplace: Foreign Investment in Cuba.* Arlington, Virginia: Alexis de Tocqueville Institution, March 1999.

Pollitt, Brian H. "The Cuban Sugar Economy: Collapse, Reform, and Prospects for Recovery," *Journal of Latin American Studies* [London], 29, No. 1, February 1997, 171–210.

Press, Larry. "Cuban Telecommunication Infrastructure and Development." Pages 145–54 in *Cuba in Transition,* 6. Washington: Association for the Study of the Cuban Economy, 1996.

Ritter, Archibald R.M. "Cuba's Convertible Currency Debt Problem," *CEPAL Review,* 36, December 1988, 117–40.

Ritter, Archibald R.M. "La dualidad del tipo de cambio de la economía cubana en los noventa," *Revista de la CEPAL* [Santiago, Chile], 57, December 1995, 113–31.

Roca, Sergio G. "Reflections on Economic Policy: Cuba's Food Program." Pages 94–117 in Jorge F. Pérez-López, ed., *Cuba at a Crossroads: Politics and Economics after the Fourth Party Congress.* Gainesville: University of Florida Press, 1994.

Rodríguez, José Luis. *Estrategía del desarrollo económico en Cuba.* Havana: Editorial de Ciencias Sociales, 1990.

Simon, Françoise. "Tourism Development and Transition Economies: The Cuban Case," *Columbia Journal of World Business*, 30, No. 1, Spring 1995, 26–41.

Suddaby, Charles. "Cuba's Tourism Industry." Pages 123–30 in *Cuba in Transition, 7.* Washington: Association for the Study of the Cuban Economy, 1997.

United Nations. Economic Commission for Latin America and the Caribbean. Asociación Latinoamericana de Integración. Secretaría General, Asociación Latinoamericana de Integración. *La economía cubana: Reformas estructurales y desempeño en los noventa.* Montevideo, Uruguay: 1998.

United Nations. *Statistical Yearbook, 1993.* New York: 1993.

United Nations. *World Statistics Pocketbook, 1995.* World Statistics in Brief Series, 5, No. 16. New York: 1995.

United States. Directorate of Intelligence, Central Intelligence Agency. *Cuba: Handbook of Trade Statistics, 1997.* Washington: 1997.

United States. Directorate of Intelligence, Central Intelligence Agency. *Cuba: Handbook of Trade Statistics, 1998.* Washington: 1999.

Werlau, María C. "Foreign Investment in Cuba: The Limits of Commercial Engagement." Pages 456–95 in *Cuba in Transition, 6.* Washington: Association for the Study of the Cuban Economy, 1996.

Werlau, María C. "Update on Foreign Investment in Cuba, 1996–97." Pages 72–98 in *Cuba in Transition, 7.* Washington: Association for the Study of the Cuban Economy, 1997.

(Various issues of the following periodicals were also used in the preparation of this chapter: *CubaNews*; *Daily Report: Latin America* of the Foreign Broadcast Information Service; *Diario las Américas* [Miami]; *Economic Report*; *Granma* [Havana];

Granma International Electronic Edition; *Informe económico trimestral/ Quarterly Economic Report*; *Journal of Commerce*; *New York Times*; *El Nuevo Herald* [Miami]; *Quarterly Report*; *Trabajadores* [Havana]; and *Washington Post*. In addition, numerous publications of the Banco Nacional de Cuba were consulted.)

Chapter 4

Ackerman, Holly. "The *Balsero* Phenomenon, 1991–1994," *Cuban Studies*, 26, 1996, 169–200.

Alvarado Ramos, Juan. "Relaciones raciales en Cuba: Notas de investigación," *Temas* [Havana], 7, July–September 1996, 37–43.

Alvarez, José, and William A. Messina, Jr. "Cuba's New Agricultural Cooperatives: Antecedents, Organization, Early Performance, and Prospects." Pages 175–95 in *Cuba in Transition, 6*. Washington: Association for the Study of the Cuban Economy, 1996.

Amnesty International. *Cuba: Government Crackdown on Dissent*. London: International Secretariat, 1996.

Amnesty International. *Cuba: Renewed Crackdown on Peaceful Government Critics*. London: International Secretariat, 1997.

Arboleya, Jesús. *La contrarrevolución cubana*. Havana: Editorial de Ciencias Sociales, 1997.

Azcuy, Hugo. *Derechos humanos: Una aproximación a la política*. Havana: Editorial de Ciencias Sociales, 1997.

Azcuy, Hugo. "Los derechos humanos en la política norteamericana y el caso cubano," *Cuadernos de Nuestra América*, 10, No. 20, July–December 1993, 4–19.

Báez, Luis. *Secretos de generales: Desclasificado*. Havana: Editorial Si-Mar, 1996.

Baloyra, Enrique, and James A. Morris, eds. *Conflict and Change in Cuba*. Albuquerque: University of New Mexico Press, 1993.

Barrera, Elsa. *Reajustes y reformas en la economía cubana, 1994*. Series: Dossier. Havana: Centro de Estudios sobre América, Sección de Información Científica, 1995.

Bengelsdorf, Carollee. *The Problem of Democracy in Cuba: Between Vision and Reality*. New York: Oxford University Press, 1994.

Blight, James G., Bruce J. Allyn, and David A. Welch. *Cuba on the Brink: Castro, the Missile Crisis, and the Soviet Collapse.* New York: Pantheon, 1993.

Bobes, Velia Cecilia. "Cuba y la cuestión racial," *Perfiles latinoamericanos,* 5, No. 8, January–June 1996, 115–39.

Braga, Michael. "Cuban Labor and Economic Reform," *Cuba News,* 2, No. 4, April 1994, 2 and 8.

Bunck, Julie Marie. *Fidel Castro and the Quest for a Revolutionary Culture in Cuba.* University Park: Pennsylvania State University, 1994.

Bunck, Julie Marie. "Market-Oriented Marxism: Post-Cold War Transition in Cuba and Vietnam," *Cuban Studies,* 26, 1996, 35–59.

Carranza, Valdés Julio. "Cuba: Los retos de la economía," *Cuadernos de Nuestra América,* 9, No. 19, July–December 1992, 131–58.

Carranza, Valdés Julio, Luis Gutiérrez Urdaneta, and Pedro Monreal Gutiérrez. *Cuba: La restructuración de la economía. Una propuesta para el debate.* Havana: Editorial de Ciencias Sociales, 1995.

Castañeda Donate, Susana. "Proceso electoral cubano," *Dossier,* 1. Havana: Centro de Estudios sobre América, 1993.

Centeno, Miguel Angel, and Mauricio Font, eds. *Toward a New Cuba? Legacies of a Revolution.* Boulder, Colorado: Lynne Rienner, 1997.

Centro de Investigaciones Psicológicas y Sociológicas. *La religión: Estudios de investigadores cubanos sobre la temática religiosa.* Havana: Editora Política, 1993.

Céspedes, Carlos Manuel de. "¿Puede afirmarse que el pueblo cubano es católico o no?," *Temas* [Havana], 4, October–December 1995, 13–22.

Colectivo de Autores. *Desarrollo rural y participación.* Havana: Universidad de Havana, 1996.

Comisión Económica para América Latina y el Caribe. *La economía cubana: Reformas estructurales y desempeño en los noventa.* Mexico: Fondo de Cultura Económica, 1997.

Cuban Research Institute. *Transition in Cuba: New Challenges for US Policy.* Miami: Florida International University, 1993.

Deere, Carmen Diana, Mieke Meurs, and Niurka Pérez. "Toward a Periodization of the Cuban Collectivization Process: Changing Incentives and Peasant Response," *Cuban Studies*, 22, 1992, 115–49.

Del Aguila, Juan M. "A Retrospective Analysis of Cuba's Role During the Persian Gulf Crisis of 1990–1991," *Cuban Studies*, 26, 1996, 97–119.

Dilla, Haroldo, Gerardo González, and Ana Vincentelli. "Cuba: La crisis de la rearticulación del consenso político (notas para un debate socialista)," *Cuadernos de Nuestra América* [Havana], 10, No. 20, July–December 1993, 20–45.

Dilla, Haroldo, Gerardo González, and Ana Teresa Vincentelli. "Cuba's Local Governments: An Experience Beyond the Paradigms," *Cuban Studies*, 22, 1992, 151–70.

Dilla, Haroldo, Gerardo González, and Ana Vincentelli. *Participación popular y desarrollo en los municipios cubanos*. Havana: Centro de Estudios sobre América, 1993.

Dilla, Haroldo, Gerardo González, and Ana Vincentelli, eds. *La democracia en Cuba y el diferendo con Estados Unidos*. Havana: Ediciones Centro de Estudios sobre América, 1995.

Dilla, Haroldo, Gerardo González, and Ana Vincentelli, eds. *La participación en Cuba y los retos del futuro*. Havana: Ediciones Centro de Estudios sobre América, 1996.

Domínguez, Jorge I. "¿Comienza una transición hacia el autoritarismo en Cuba?," *Encuentro*, 6–7, Fall–Winter 1997, 7–23.

Domínguez, Jorge I. "Cuba in the International Community in the 1990s: Sovereignty, Human Rights, and Democracy." Pages 297–315 in Tom Farer, ed., *Beyond Sovereignty: Collectively Defending Democracy in the Americas*. Baltimore: Johns Hopkins University Press, 1996.

Domínguez, Jorge I. "International and National Aspects of the Catholic Church in Cuba," *Cuban Studies*, 19, 1989, 43–60.

Domínguez, Jorge I. "La política exterior de Cuba: 1989–1994." Pages 50–70 in Alberto van Klaveren, ed., *América Latina en el mundo: Anuario de políticas externas Latinoamericanas y del Caribe*. Santiago, Chile: Editorial Los Andes, 1997.

Domínguez, Jorge I. "The Secrets of Castro's Staying Power," *Foreign Affairs*, 72, No. 2, Spring 1993, 97–107.

Domínguez, Jorge I. "La transición política en Cuba," *Encuentro*, 1, Summer 1996, 5–12.

Domínguez, Jorge I. "United States-Cuban Relations: From the Cold War to the Colder War," *Journal of Interamerican Studies and World Affairs*, 39, No. 3, Fall 1997, 49–75.

Dominguez, Jorge I., and Raimundo López. "Prela Report on PCC Membership, Percentages," October 8, 1997. Foreign Broadcast Information Service.

Domínguez, María Isabel. "Las investigaciones sobre la juventud," *Temas* [Havana], 1, January–March 1995, 85–93.

Domínguez, María Isabel. "La mujer joven en los 90," *Temas* [Havana], 5, January–March 1996, 31–37.

Eckstein, Susan E. *Back from the Future: Cuba under Castro.* Princeton: Princeton University Press, 1994.

Elizalde, Rosa Miriam. *Flores desechables: ¿Prostitución en Cuba?* Havana: Ediciones Abril, 1996.

Erisman, H. Michael. "Evolving Cuban-CARICOM Relations: A Comparative Cost-Benefit Analysis," *Cuban Studies*, 25, 1995, 207–27.

Feinsilver, Julie M. *Healing the Masses: Cuban Health Politics at Home and Abroad.* Berkeley and Los Angeles: University of California Press, 1993.

Feinsilver, Julie M. "Will Cuba's Wonder Drugs Lead to Political and Economic Wonders? Capitalizing on Biotechnology and Medical Exports," *Cuban Studies*, 22, 1992, 79–111.

Fernández, Damián J. *Cuban Studies and the Revolution.* Gainesville: University of Florida Press, 1992.

Fernández, Damián J. "Opening the Blackest of Black Boxes: Theory and Practice of Decision Making in Cuba's Foreign Policy," *Cuban Studies*, 22, 1992, 53–78.

Ferriol, Angela. "Cuba: Situación social y transformaciones en la política social," *Cuba: Investigación económica* [Havana], 3, No. 1, January–March 1997, 51–79.

Ferriol, Angela. "El empleo en Cuba," *Cuba: Investigación económica* [Havana], 2, No. 1, January–March 1996, 1–23.

Fitzgerald, Frank. T. *The Cuban Revolution in Crisis: From Managing Socialism to Managing Survival.* New York: Monthly Review Press, 1994.

Giuliano, Maurizio. *El caso CEA: Intelectuales e inquisidores en Cuba.* Miami: Ediciones Universal, 1998.

Gonzalez, Edward. *Cuba: Clearing Perilous Waters.* Santa Monica, California: Rand, 1996.

Gonzalez, Edward, and David Ronfeldt. *Storm Warnings over Cuba.* Santa Monica, California: Rand, 1994.

Gunn, Gillian. *Cuba in Transition: Options for U.S. Policy.* New York: Twentieth Century Fund Press, 1993.

Halebsky, Sandor, and John Kirk. *Cuba in Transition: Crisis and Transformation.* Boulder, Colorado: Westview Press, 1992.

Hernández, Rafael. *Mirar a Cuba: Ensayos sobre cultura y sociedad civil.* Havana: Editorial Letras Cubanas, 1999.

Hernández, Rafael. "El ruído y las nueces II: El ciclo en la política de los Estados Unidos hacia Cuba," *Cuadernos de Nuestra América,* 9, No. 18, January–June, 1992, 4–21.

Hernández, Rafael. "Sobre las relaciones con la comunidad cubana en los Estados Unidos," *Cuadernos de Nuestra América,* 8, No. 17, July–December 1991, 149–60.

Hernández, Rafael, and Alfredo Prieto. *Cuba en las Américas: Una perspectiva sobre Cuba y los problemas hemisféricos.* Havana: Ediciones CEA, 1995.

Horowitz, Irving Louis. *Political Pilgrimage to Cuba, 1959–1996.* Miami: University of Miami, Cuban Studies Association, 1996.

Horowitz, Irving Louis, ed. *Cuban Communism, 1959–1995.* 8th ed. New Brunswick, New Jersey: Transaction, 1995.

Human Rights Watch. *Cuba's Repressive Machinery: Human Rights Forty Years after the Revolution.* New York: 1999.

Instituto de Relaciones Europeo-Latinoamericanas. *Cuba: Apertura económica y relaciones con Europa.* Madrid: 1994.

Jatar-Hausman, Ana Julia. *The Cuban Way: Capitalism, Communism, and Confrontation.* West Hartford, Connecticut: Kumarian Press, 1999.

Jatar-Hausman, Ana Julia. "Through the Cracks of Socialism: The Emerging Private Sector in Cuba." Pages 202–18 in *Cuba in Transition,* 6. Washington: Association for the Study of the Cuban Economy, 1996.

Kaplowitz, Donna Rich, ed. *Cuba's Ties to a Changing World.* Boulder, Colorado: Lynne Rienner, 1993.

Krinsky, Michael, and David Golove. *United States Economic Measures Against Cuba: Proceedings in the United Nations and International Law Issues.* Northampton, Massachusetts: Aletheia Press, 1993.

Lutjens, Sheryl. "Fixing *Filtraciones*: Decentralization, the State, and the 1990s in Cuba," *Cuban Studies*, 26, 1996, 1–33.

Lutjens, Sheryl. *The State, the Bureaucracy, and the Cuban Schools: Power and Participation.* Boulder, Colorado: Westview Press, 1996.

Machado, Darío. "¿Cuál es nuestro clima socio-político?," *El militante comunista*, 9, September 1990, 2–12.

Martín Fernández, Consuelo, Maricela Perera, and Maiky Díaz Pérez. "La vida cotidiana en Cuba: Una mirada psicosocial," *Temas* [Havana], 7, July–September 1996, 92–98.

Mesa-Lago, Carmelo. *Are Economic Reforms Propelling Cuba to the Market?* Miami: University of Miami, North-South Center, 1994.

Montaner, Carlos Alberto. *Cuba hoy: La lenta muerte del castrismo.* Miami: Ediciones Universal, 1996.

Nazario, Olga. "Overcoming Political Isolation and Responding to International Pressures: Cuba's New Independent Foreign Policy," *Cuban Studies*, 26, 1996, 75–96.

Oppenheimer, Andrés. *Castro's Final Hour: The Secret Story Behind the Coming Downfall of Communist Cuba.* New York: Simon and Schuster, 1992.

Partido Comunista de Cuba, Departamento de Orientación Revolucionaria. *Constitución de la República de Cuba, tesis, y resolución.* Havana: 1976.

Partido Comunista de Cuba, Departamento de Orientación Revolucionaria. *IV Congreso del Partido Comunista de Cuba: Discursos y documentos.* Havana: Editora Política, 1992.

Pérez, Santiago. "El fin de la URSS y Cuba," *Cuadernos de Nuestra América* [Havana], 10, No. 20, July–December 1993, 83–98.

Pérez-López, Jorge F. *Cuba's Second Economy: From Behind the Scenes to Center Stage.* New Brunswick, New Jersey: Transaction, 1995.

Pérez-López, Jorge, F., ed. *Cuba at a Crossroads: Politics and Economics after the Fourth Party Congress.* Gainesville: University of Florida Press, 1994.

Pérez-Stable, Marifeli. "Charismatic Authority, Vanguard Party Politics, and Popular Mobilization: Revolution and Socialism in Cuba," *Cuban Studies*, 22, 1992, 3–26.

Pérez-Stable, Marifeli. *The Cuban Revolution: Origins, Course, and Legacy.* New York: Oxford University Press, 1993.

Quirk, Robert E. *Fidel Castro.* New York: Norton, 1993.

Rabkin, Rhoda P. "Cuban Socialism: Ideological Responses to the Era of Socialist Crisis," *Cuban Studies,* 22, 1992, 27–50.

República de Cuba. Asamblea Nacional del Poder Popular. *Ley electoral.* Havana: Ediciones Entorno, 1992.

República de Cuba. *Constitución de la República de Cuba.* Havana: Editorial de Ciencias Sociales, 1996.

Ritter, Archibald R.M., and John M. Kirk, eds. *Cuba in the International System: Normalization and Integration.* New York: St. Martin's Press, 1995.

Rodríguez Chávez, Ernesto. *Cuba: Derechos humanos.* Havana: Editorial José Martí, 1991.

Rosendahl, Mona. *Inside the Revolution: Everyday Life in Socialist Cuba.* Ithaca, New York: Cornell University Press, 1997.

Roy, Joaquín. "The Helms-Burton Law: Development, Consequences, and Legacy for Inter-American and European-US Relations," *Journal of Interamerican Studies and World Affairs,* 39, No. 3, Fall 1997, 77–108.

Sagebien, Julia. "The Canadian Presence in Cuba in the Mid-1990s," *Cuban Studies,* 26, 1996, 143–68.

Segre, Roberto, Mario Coyula, and Joseph L. Scarpaci. *Havana: Two Faces of the American Metropolis.* New York: Wiley, 1997.

Shultz, Donald E., ed. *Cuba and the Future.* Westport, Connecticut: Greenwood Press, 1994.

Smith, Lois M., and Alfred Padula. *Sex and Revolution: Women in Socialist Cuba.* New York: Oxford University Press, 1996.

Sweeney, John P. "Why the Cuban Trade Embargo Should Be Maintained," *Heritage Foundation Backgrounder,* No. 1010, November 10, 1994, 1–13.

Tulchin, Joseph S., and Rafael Hernández, eds. *Cuba and the United States: Will the Cold War in the Caribbean End?* Boulder, Colorado: Lynne Rienner, 1991.

United States. Department of Defense. Defense Intelligence Agency. *The Cuban Threat to U.S. National Security.* Washington: 1998.

Valdés Paz, Juan. "La política exterior de Cuba hacia América Latina y el Caribe en los años 90: Los temas," *Cuadernos de*

Nuestra América [Havana], 9, No. 19, July–December 1992, 108–30.

Valdés Paz, Juan. *Procesos agrarios en Cuba, 1959–1995.* Havana: Editorial de Ciencias Sociales, 1997.

Vázquez Penelas, Aurora, and Roberto Dávalos Domínguez, eds. *Participación social: Desarrollo urbano y comunitario.* Havana: Universidad de La Habana, 1998.

Walker, Phyllis Greene. "Cuba's Revolutionary Armed Forces: Adapting in the New Environment," *Cuban Studies*, 26, 1996, 61–74.

Whitefield, Mimi, and Mary Beth Sheridan. "Cuba Poll: The Findings," *Miami Herald*, December 18, 1994.

Chapter 5

Alonso, José. "The Ochoa Affair and Its Aftermath." Pages 629–66 in Irving Louis Horowitz, ed., *Cuban Communism, 1959–1995.* 8th ed. New Brunswick, New Jersey: Transaction, 1995.

Amuchastegui, Domingo. "Cuba's Armed Forces: Power and Reforms." Paper presented at the annual meeting of the Association for the Study of the Cuban Economy, Coral Gables, Florida, August 1999.

Aspaturian, Vernon V. "Gorbachev's New Political Thinking and the Angolan Conflict." Pages 3–54 in Owen Ellison Kahn, ed., *Disengagement from Southwest Africa: The Prospects for Peace in Angola and Namibia.* New Brunswick, New Jersey: Transaction, 1991.

Báez, Luis. *Secretos de generales: Desclasificado.* Havana: Editorial Si-Mar, 1996.

Beschloss, Michael R. *The Crisis Years: Kennedy and Khrushchev, 1960–1963.* New York: Harper Collins, 1991.

Betancourt, Ernesto. *Revolutionary Strategy: A Handbook for Practitioners.* New Brunswick, New Jersey: Transaction, 1992.

Biliary, Enrique. "The Frustration of Cuban Nationalism." Pages 13–58 in Jaime Suchlicki, Antonio Jorge, and Damián J. Fernández, eds., *Cuba: Continuity and Change.* Coral Gables, Florida: University of Miami, North-South Center, Institute of Interamerican Studies, 1985.

Biliary, Enrique A., and Roberto Lozano. "Soviet-Cuban Relations: The New Environment and Its Impact." Pages 265–86 in Enrique A. Biliary and James A. Morris, eds., *Conflict and Change in Cuba.* Albuquerque: University of New Mexico Press, 1993.

Blank, Stephen. "The End of the Affair: Moscow and Havana, 1989–1992." Pages 97–115 in Donald E. Schulz, ed., *Cuba and the Future.* Westport, Connecticut: Greenwood Press, 1994.

Blanksten, George I. "Fidelismo and Its Origins." In Robert D. Tomasek, ed., *Latin American Politics: Studies of the Contemporary Scene.* Garden City, New York: Doubleday, 1966.

Blight, James G., and David A. Welch. *On the Brink: Americans and Soviets Reexamine the Cuban Missile Crisis.* New York: Noonday Press, Farrar, Straus and Giroux, 1990.

Blight, James G., Bruce J. Allyn, and David A Welch, eds. *Cuba on the Brink: Castro, the Missile Crisis, and the Soviet Collapse.* New York: Pantheon, 1993.

Bonachea, Ramón, and Marta San Martín. *The Cuban Insurrection, 1952–1959.* New Brunswick, New Jersey: Transaction, 1974.

Bonitos Manaut, Raúl, Lucrecia Lozano, Ricardo Córdova, and Antonio Cavalla. "Armed Forces, Society, and the People: Cuba and Nicaragua." Pages 131–62 in Augusto Varas, ed., *Democracy under Siege: New Military Power in Latin America.* New York: Greenwood Press, 1989.

Brenner, Philip. From *Confrontation to Negotiation: U.S. Relations with Cuba.* Boulder, Colorado: Westview Press, 1988.

Carrillo, Justo. "Could Cuba Have Been Different?," *Caribbean Review,* 10, December 1981, 38–40.

Castro Ruz, Fidel. *La revolución cubana*: Selección, prólogo y notas de Gregorio Selser. Buenos Aires, Argentina: Editorial Palestra, 1960.

Casuso, Teresa. *Cuba and Castro.* Trans., Elmer Grossberg. New York: Random House, 1961.

Causa 1/89: Fin de la conexión cubana. Havana: Editorial José Martí, 1989.

Chaffee, Wilber A., Jr. "Poder Popular and the Buro Político: Political Control in Cuba." Pages 19–35 in Wilber A. Chaffee, Jr. and Gary Prevost, eds., *Cuba: A Different America.* Lanham, Maryland: Rowman and Littlefield, 1992.

Chilcote, Ronald, ed. *The Challenge for Cuba in the 1990s: Cuban Perspectives.* Boulder, Colorado: Westview Press, 1991.

Del Aguila, Juan M. "The Changing Character of Cuba's Armed Forces." Pages 27–60 in Jaime Suchlicki, ed., *The Cuban Military under Castro.* Coral Gables, Florida: University of Miami, North-South Center, Research Institute for Cuban Studies, 1989.

Del Aguila, Juan M. *Cuba: Dilemmas of a Revolution.* Rev. ed. Boulder, Colorado: Westview Press, 1988.

Del Pino Días, Rafael. *General del Pino Speaks: An Insight into Elite Corruption and Military Dissension in Castro's Cuba.* Washington: Cuban American National Foundation, 1987.

Domínguez, Jorge I. "The Civic Soldier in Cuba." Pages 209–38 in Catherine McArdle Kelleher, ed., *Political-Military Systems: Comparative Perspectives.* Beverly Hills, California: Sage, 1974.

Domínguez, Jorge I. *Cuba: Order and Revolution.* Cambridge: Harvard University Press, 1978.

Domínguez, Jorge I. "Racial and Ethnic Relations in the Cuban Armed Forces: A Non-Topic," *Armed Forces and Society,* 2, February 1976, 273–90.

Domínguez, Jorge I. "Revolutionary Politics: The New Demands for Orderliness." Pages 19–70 in Jorge I. Domínguez, ed., *Cuba: Internal and International Affairs.* Beverly Hills, California: Sage, 1982.

Domínguez, Jorge I. "Succession in Cuba: Institutional Strengths and Weaknesses." Pages 29–37 in Jaime Suchlicki, ed., *Problems of Succession in Cuba.* Coral Gables, Florida: University of Miami, North-South Center, Institute of Interamerican Studies, 1985.

Domínguez, Jorge I. *To Make a World Safe for Revolution: Cuba's Foreign Policy.* Cambridge: Harvard University Press, 1989.

Domínguez, Jorge I., and Rafael Hernández. *U.S.-Cuban Relations in the 1990s.* Boulder, Colorado: Westview Press, 1989.

Draper, Theodore. *Castroism: Theory and Practice.* New York: Praeger, 1965.

Erisman, H. Michael. *Cuba's International Relations: The Anatomy of a Nationalistic Foreign Policy.* Boulder, Colorado: Westview Press, 1985.

Escalante Font, Fabián. *The Secret War: CIA Covert Operations Against Cuba, 1959–1962.* Ed., Mirta Muñiz; trans., Maxine

Shaw. Melbourne, Australia: Ocean Press; New York: Talman, 1995.

Falk, Pamela S. *Cuban Foreign Policy: Caribbean Tempest.* Lexington, Massachusetts: Lexington Books, 1986.

Falk, Pamela S. "Cuba's Role in Southern Africa: The Angola-Namibia Negotiations and the Future of Superpower Conflict in the Region." Pages 95–114 in Owen Ellison Kahn, ed., *Disengagement from Southwest Africa: The Prospects for Peace in Angola and Namibia.* New Brunswick, New Jersey: Transaction, 1991.

Fermoselle, Rafael. *Cuban Leadership after Castro: Biographies of Cuba's Top Commanders.* 2d ed. New Brunswick, New Jersey: Transaction, 1992.

Fermoselle, Rafael. *The Evolution of the Cuban Military: 1492–1986.* Miami: Ediciones Universal, 1987.

Fernández, Damián J. "Historical Background: Achievements, Failures, and Prospects." Pages 1–26 in Jaime Suchlicki, ed., *The Cuban Military under Castro.* Coral Gables, Florida: University of Miami, North-South Center, Research Institute for Cuban Studies, 1989.

Fitzgerald, Frank T. *The Cuban Revolution in Crisis: From Managing Socialism to Managing Survival.* New York: Monthly Review Press, 1994.

Franqui, Carlos. *Diary of the Cuban Revolution.* Trans., Georgette Félix. New York: Viking, 1990.

Gonzalez, Edward. *Cuba: Clearing Perilous Waters.* Santa Monica, California: Rand, 1996.

Gonzalez, Edward. *Cuba under Castro: The Limits of Charisma.* Boston: Houghton Mifflin, 1974.

Gonzalez, Edward, and David Ronfeldt. *Cuba Adrift in a Postcommunist World.* Report No. R–4231–USDP. Santa Monica, California: Rand, 1992.

Gonzalez, Edward, and David Ronfeldt. *Storm Warnings for Cuba.* Santa Monica, California: Rand, 1994.

Gouré, Leon. "Cuban Military Doctrine and Organization." Pages 61–97 in Jaime Suchlicki, ed., *The Cuban Military under Castro.* Coral Gables, Florida: University of Miami, North-South Center, Research Institute for Cuban Studies, 1989.

Gouré, Leon. "Soviet-Cuban Military Relations." Pages 165–97 in Jaime Suchlicki, ed., *The Cuban Military under Castro.* Coral Gables, Florida: University of Miami, North-South Center, Research Institute for Cuban Studies, 1989.

Greig, Ian. *The Communist Challenge to Africa: An Analysis of Contemporary Soviet, Chinese, and Cuban Policies.* Richmond, Surrey, United Kingdom: Foreign Affairs, 1977.

Habel, Janette. *Cuba: The Revolution in Peril.* Trans., Jon Barnes. London: Verso, 1991.

Halebsky, Sandor, and John M. Kirk, eds. *Cuba: Twenty-Five Years of Revolution, 1959–1984.* New York: Praeger, 1985.

Halebsky, Sandor, Richard Harris, John M. Kirk, Andrew Zimbalist, and Carollee Bengelsdorf, eds. *Cuba's Struggle for Development.* Boulder, Colorado: Westview Press, 1991.

Hernández, José M. "The Role of the Military in the Making of the Cuban Republic." Ph.D. dissertation. Washington: Georgetown University, 1976.

Hernández, Rafael. "Cuban Security Interests in Perspective." Pages 47–49 in Joseph S. Tulchin and Rafael Hernández, eds., *Cuba and the United States: Will the Cold War in the Caribbean End?* Boulder, Colorado: Lynne Rienner, 1991.

Hinckle, Warren, and William Turner. *The Fish Is Red: The Story of the Secret War Against Castro.* New York: Harper and Row, 1981.

Horowitz, Irving Louis. "Castrology Revisited: Further Observations on the Militarization of Cuba," *Armed Forces and Society,* 3, August 1977, 617–31.

Horowitz, Irving Louis. "Military Origins and Outcomes of the Cuban Revolution." Pages 617–54 in Irving Louis Horowitz, ed., *Cuban Communism.* 5th ed. New Brunswick, New Jersey: Transaction, 1984.

Horowitz, Irving Louis, ed. *Cuban Communism, 1959–1995.* 8th ed. New Brunswick, New Jersey: Transaction, 1995.

Hudson, Rex A. *Castro's America Department: Coordinating Cuba's Support for Marxist-Leninist Violence in the Americas.* Washington: Cuban American National Foundation, 1988.

Judson, C. Fred. *Cuba and the Revolutionary Myth: The Political Education of the Cuban Rebel Army, 1953–1963.* Boulder, Colorado: Westview Press, 1984.

Karol, K.S. *Guerrillas in Power: The Course of the Cuban Revolution.* Trans., Arnold Pomeranz. New York: Hill and Wang, 1970.

Kelleher, Catherine McArdle, ed. *Political-Military Systems: Comparative Perspectives.* Beverly Hills, California: Sage, 1974.

LeoGrande, William. "A Bureaucratic Approach to Civil-Military Relations in Communist Political Systems: The Case of Cuba." Pages 201–18 in Dale R. Herspring and Ivan Volgyes, eds., *Civil-Military Relations in Communist Countries.* Boulder, Colorado: Westview Press, 1978.

LeoGrande, William. "Civil-Military Relations in Cuba." Pages 655–77 in Irving Louis Horowitz, ed., *Cuban Communism.* 5th ed. New Brunswick, New Jersey: Transaction, 1984.

LeoGrande, William. "The Politics of Revolutionary Development: Civil-Military Relations in Cuba," *Journal of Strategic Studies,* 1, December 1978, 260–95.

Lévesque, Jacques. *The USSR and the Cuban Revolution: Soviet Ideological and Strategical Perspectives.* New York: Praeger, 1978.

Llovio-Menéndez, José Luis. *Insider: My Hidden Life as a Revolutionary in Cuba.* Trans., Edith Grossman. Toronto: Bantam, 1988.

Mesa-Lago, Carmelo. *Are Economic Reforms Propelling Cuba to the Market?* Coral Gables, Florida: University of Miami, North-South Center, 1994.

Mesa-Lago, Carmelo. *Cuba in the 1970s: Pragmatism and Institutionalization.* Rev. ed. Albuquerque: University of New Mexico Press, 1978.

Mesa-Lago, Carmelo, and June S. Belkin. *Cuba in Africa.* Pittsburgh: University of Pittsburgh Press, 1982.

Mesa-Lago, Carmelo, ed. *Cuba after the Cold War.* Pittsburgh: University of Pittsburgh Press, 1993.

The Military Balance, 1999–2000. London: International Institute for Strategic Studies, 1999.

Millett, Richard L. "From Triumph to Survival: Cuba's Armed Forces in an Era of Transition." Pages 133–56 in Richard L. Millett and Michael Gold-Biss, eds., *Beyond Praetorianism: The Latin American Military in Transition.* Coral Gables, Florida: University of Miami, North-South Center, 1996.

Montes, Ana B. *The Military's Response to Cuba's Economic Crisis.* Washington: Defense Intelligence Agency, August 1993.

"The 1999–2000 World Defense Almanac," *Military Technology* [Bonn], 24, No. 1, 2000, 51.

Oppenheimer, Andrés. *Castro's Final Hour: The Secret Story Behind the Coming Downfall of Communist Cuba.* New York: Simon and Schuster, 1992.

Pavlov, Yuri. *Soviet-Cuban Alliance, 1959–1991.* New Brunswick, New Jersey: Transaction, 1994.

Pérez, Louis A. *Army Politics in Cuba, 1898–1958.* Pittsburgh: Pittsburgh University Press, 1976.

Pérez, Louis A. "Army Politics in Socialist Cuba," *Journal of Latin American Studies* [London], 8, No. 2, November 1976.

Pérez Betancourt, Armando, and Berto González Sánchez. "El perfeccionamiento empresarial en el MINFAR," *Cuba Socialista*, 36, No. 6, November–December 1988.

Pérez-López, Jorge F. *The Cuban State Budget: Concepts and Measurement.* New Brunswick, New Jersey: Transaction, 1992.

Pérez-Stable, Marifeli. *The Cuban Revolution: Origins, Course, and Legacy.* New York: Oxford University Press, 1993.

Preston, Julia. "The Trial That Shook Cuba," *New York Review of Books*, December 7, 1989, 24–32.

Quirk, Robert E. *Fidel Castro.* New York: Norton, 1993.

Riefe, Robert H. *Moscow, Havana, and National Liberation in Latin America: Three Decades of Guerrillas and Terrorists, 1959–1990.* New Brunswick, New Jersey: Transaction, 1992.

Rodríguez-Menier, Juan Antonio. *Inside the Cuban Interior Ministry.* Ed., William Ratliff. Washington: Jamestown Foundation, 1994.

Roque, Juan Pablo. *Desertor.* Miami: Cuban American National Foundation, 1995.

Samuels, Michael A., and Chester A. Crocker. *Implications of Soviet and Cuban Activities in Africa for U.S. Policy.* Washington: Georgetown University, Center for Strategic and International Studies, 1979.

Sánchez Pérez, Manuel. *Quién manda en Cuba: Estructuras del poder.* Miami: Ediciones Universal, 1989.

San Martín, Marta, and Ramón L. Bonachea. "The Military Dimension of the Cuban Revolution." Pages 585–616 in Irving Louis Horowitz, ed., *Cuban Communism.* 5th ed. Rutgers, New Jersey: Transaction, 1984.

Schuyler, George W. "Perspectives on Canada and Latin America: Changing Context . . . Changing Policies," *Journal of Interamerican Studies and World Affairs*, 33, Spring 1991, 19–58.

Special Operations Research Office. *Special Warfare Area Handbook for Cuba.* Washington: American University, 1961.

Suárez, Andrés. "Civil-Military Relations in Cuba." Pages 129–64 in Jaime Suchlicki, ed., *The Cuban Military under Castro.* Coral Gables, Florida: University of Miami, North-South Center, Research Institute for Cuban Studies, 1989.

Suárez, Andrés. *Cuba: Castroism and Communism, 1959–1966.* Trans., Joel Carmichael and Ernst Halperin. Cambridge: MIT Press, 1967.

Suárez, Andrés. "Cuba: Ideology and Pragmatism." Pages 129–46 in Jaime Suchlicki, Antonio Jorge, and Damián J. Fernández, eds., *Cuba: Continuity and Change.* Coral Gables, Florida: University of Miami, North-South Center, Institute of Interamerican Studies, 1985.

Suárez Hernández, Georgina. "Political Leadership in Cuba: Background and Current Projections," *Latin American Perspectives*, 18, Spring 1991, 55–68.

Suchlicki, Jaime. *Cuba: From Columbus to Castro.* 2d ed. New York: Pergamon-Brassey's, 1986.

Suchlicki, Jaime, ed. *Problems of Succession in Cuba.* Coral Gables, Florida: University of Miami, Institute of International Studies, 1985.

Suchlicki, Jaime, Antonio Jorge, and Damián J. Fernández, eds. *Cuba: Continuity and Change.* Coral Gables, Florida: University of Miami, North-South Center, Institute of Interamerican Studies, 1985.

Szulc, Tad. *Fidel: A Critical Portrait.* New York: Morrow, 1986.

Thomas, Hugh. *The Cuban Revolution.* London: Weidenfeld and Nicholson, 1986.

United States. Department of Defense. Defense Intelligence Agency. *The Cuban Threat to U.S. National Security.* Washington: May 6, 1998. (Website: http://www.fas.org/irp/dia/product/980507-dia-cubarpt.htm)

United States. Department of Defense. Defense Intelligence Agency. *Handbook on the Cuban Armed Forces.* No. DDB–2680–

62–79. Washington: Defense Intelligence Agency, April 1979.

United States. Department of Defense. Defense Intelligence Agency. *Handbook on the Cuban Armed Forces.* No. DDB–2680–62–86. Washington: Defense Intelligence Agency, May 1986.

United States. Department of State. Bureau of Public Affairs. "Agreements for Peace in Southwestern Africa." Pages 223–35 in Owen Ellison Kahn, ed., *Disengagement from Southwest Africa: The Prospects for Peace in Angola and Namibia.* New Brunswick, New Jersey: Transaction, 1991.

United States. United States Information Agency. Voice of America. Radio Martí Program. Office of Research and Policy. *Cuba Annual Report: 1989.* New Brunswick, New Jersey: Transaction, 1991.

Valladares, Armando. *Against All Hope: The Prison Memoirs of Armando Valladares.* Trans., Andrew Huxley. New York: Knopf, 1986.

Vellinga, M.L. "The Military and the Dynamics of the Cuban Revolutionary Process," *Comparative Politics*, 8, January 1976, 245–71.

Wyden, Peter. *The Bay of Pigs: The Untold Story.* New York: Simon and Schuster, 1979.

Walker, Phyllis Greene. "Challenges Facing the Cuban Military." Cuba Briefing Paper Series, No. 12. Washington: Georgetown University, Center for Latin American Studies, The Cuba Project, October 1996.

Walker, Phyllis Greene. "The Cuban Armed Forces and Transition." Pages 53–68 in Donald E. Schulz, ed., *Cuba and the Future.* Westport, Connecticut: Greenwood Press, 1994.

Walker, Phyllis Greene. "The Cuban Military Service System: Organization, Obligations, and Pressures." Pages 99–128 in Jaime Suchlicki, ed., *The Cuban Military under Castro.* Coral Gables, Florida: University of Miami, North-South Center, Research Institute for Cuban Studies, 1989.

Walker, Phyllis Greene. "Cuba's Revolutionary Armed Forces: Adapting in the New Environment." Pages 61–74 in Jorge I. Domínguez, ed., *Cuban Studies*, 26. Pittsburgh: University of Pittsburgh Press, 1996.

Walker, Phyllis Greene. "National Security." Pages 225–91 in James D. Rudolph, ed., *Cuba: A Country Study.* Washington: GPO, 1985.

Walker, Phyllis Greene. "Political-Military Relations from 1959 to the Present." Pages 527–50 in Irving Louis Horowitz, ed., *Cuban Communism, 1959–1995.* 8th ed. New Brunswick, New Jersey: Transaction, 1995.

Walker, Phyllis Greene. "Political-Military Relations since 1959." Pages 110–33 in Enrique A. Baloyra and James A. Morris, eds., *Conflict and Change in Cuba.* Albuquerque: University of New Mexico Press, 1993.

Walker, Phyllis Greene. "Political-Military Relations under a Revolutionary Regime: The Case of Cuba." Ph.D. dissertation. Washington: Georgetown University, 1998.

Zimbalist, Andrew. "Dateline Cuba: Hanging on in Havana," *Foreign Policy,* 92, Fall 1993, 151–67.

Zimbalist, Andrew, and Claes Brundenius. *The Cuban Economy: Measurement and Analysis of Socialist Performance.* Baltimore: Johns Hopkins University Press, 1991.

acopio—Compulsory system of state agricultural procurement established in 1962. Nonstate agricultural producers are required to sell a certain percentage of their output to the state at fixed prices. Fulfillment of these quotas is a condition for private farmers to continue to receive access to agricultural services, fertilizer, and other inputs from the state. Output in excess of *acopio* quotas is used by nonstate producers for self-consumption, for barter or black market sales, or for sale in government-authorized markets (which were allowed during the period 1980–86 and again since 1993).

agros—Short for *agromercados*, or agricultural markets. A network of farm-produce markets opened across the island in 1994. These markets allow vendors, rather than the state, to set prices for their products. The *agros* have helped to ease chronic food shortages.

Association of Caribbean States—An association of twenty-five Caribbean Basin countries formed in 1994 under the sponsorship of the Caribbean Community and Common Market (Caricom—*q.v.*) for the purpose of promoting regional integration, economic cooperation, and a common approach to regional political problems. In addition to the fifteen members of Caricom, it includes Belize, Colombia, Costa Rica, Cuba, the Dominican Republic, Honduras, Mexico, Nicaragua, Panama, and Venezuela. Its creation was seen largely as a reaction to the North American Free Trade Agreement (NAFTA) among the United States, Canada, and Mexico, although its far smaller market raised doubts about its viability.

audiencia—A high court of justice, exercising some administrative and executive functions in the colonial period.

balance of payments—An annual statistical summary of the monetary value of all economic transactions between one country and the rest of the world, including goods, services, income on investments, and other financial matters, such as credits or loans.

black market—Illegal activities related to trade in goods, services, and currencies.

Bourbon Reforms—Throughout the eighteenth century, the

Bourbons reorganized the government structure, the economic system, and church-state relations in Latin America. The reforms introduced centralized government, in which ministries and a Council of State replaced the council system.

cabildo—Presided over by the governor or his lieutenant and composed of *alcaldes* (judges), *regidores* (councilmen), and other minor officials, the *cabildo* was the political, judicial, and administrative unit of each new settlement. It imposed local taxes, provided for local police, and maintained public buildings, jails, and roads.

capital-intensive—A high ratio of capital to labor and other resources used in the production process.

Caribbean Community and Common Market (Caricom)—The successor to the British West Indies Federation that was formed in 1958 and ended in 1962, Caricom officially came into effect on August 1, 1973, and by mid-1995 had fourteen member states. From its inception, Caricom has focused on promoting economic integration and foreign policy coordination among the independent member states.

Casa de Contratación (House of Trade)—A colonial-era institution located in Seville, Spain, and devoted to finance, taxation, and maritime operations between Spain and America.

caudillista—Dictatorial. Derived from the term *caudillo* (*q.v.*).

caudillo—A Spanish or Latin American dictator. An adaptation of an Arab word meaning *leader.*

central bank—Usually a government institution that is entrusted with control of the commercial banking system and with the issuance of the currency. Responsible for setting the level of credit and money supply in an economy and serving as the banker of last resort for other banks. Also has a major impact on interest rates.

centrally planned economy—An economy where crucial economic processes are determined not by market forces but by an economic planning board. In a planned economy such as Cuba's, production and consumption goals are set largely in specific quantities, without regard to factors such as profitability and efficiency; production successes supposedly reflect the superiority of socialism, and therefore have high ideological and political values; and much importance is placed on achieving high output targets within a short deadline.

Comecon (CMEA)—*See* Council for Mutual Economic Assistance.

consumer durables—Consumer items used for several years, such as automobiles, appliances, or furniture.

Contadora Support Group—A diplomatic initiative launched by a January 1983 meeting on Contadora Island off the Pacific coast of Panama, by which the "Core Four" mediator countries of Mexico, Venezuela, Colombia, and Panama sought to prevent through negotiations a regional conflagration among the Central American states of Guatemala, El Salvador, Honduras, Nicaragua, and Costa Rica. The governments of Argentina, Brazil, Peru, and Uruguay formed the Contadora Support Group in 1985 in an effort to revitalize the faltering talks.

convertible currency—Currencies that are freely exchanged in international markets and are generally acceptable as a medium of payment in international transactions. Examples of convertible currencies are the United States dollar, the German deutsche mark, the Japanese yen, and the French franc. Currencies of the socialist countries (including the peso—*q.v.*) were not convertible. Because their currencies were not convertible, transactions among the socialist countries relied heavily on commodity bartering.

convertible peso—The official term for a new currency introduced in 1995. It denotes a kind of money that has no value outside of Cuba, but which circulates on the island as a parallel hard currency alongside the domestic peso. The value of the convertible peso is fixed at one per United States dollar.

Cortes—The Spanish parliament to which Cuba was allowed to send representatives beginning in 1820. After the Ten Years' War (1868–78), Cubans were again represented in the Cortes, although with a very restrictive franchise.

Council for Mutual Economic Assistance (CMEA or Comecon)—An intergovernmental council headquartered in Moscow and established on January 25, 1949, to promote the development of socialist countries and to further economic cooperation among member countries. Membership included the centrally planned economies of Eastern Europe (Bulgaria, Czechoslovakia, Hungary, Poland, and Romania), the Soviet Union, the Mongolian People's Republic, Vietnam, and Cuba. Cuba joined Comecon in

1972. The organization was abolished on January 1, 1991.

Cuban Democracy Act (CDA)—Sponsored by Congressman Robert G. Torricelli (D-New Jersey). Signed into law on October 23, 1992, reversing the 1975 decision to allow third-country companies owned or controlled by United States firms to engage in licensed trade with Cuba. An exception allowed special licenses to be granted for the sale of medicines or medical equipment by these firms or their parent companies.

Cuban Liberty and Democratic Solidarity Act (Helms-Burton)—Enacted on March 12, 1996, mandates full enforcement of criminal penalties for those who knowingly violate the embargo, enables claimants on properties expropriated by the Cuban government after January 1, 1959, to sue for compensation in United States Federal Court those international investors employing those properties for their profit, mandates the denial of United States visas to executives of business firms trafficking with Cuba, and prescribes United States policy during post-Castro transition.

Economic Commission for Latin America and the Caribbean (ECLAC; more commonly known in Latin America as the Comisión Económica para la América Latina y el Caribe—**CEPAL)**—A United Nations regional economic commission established on February 25, 1948, as the Economic Commission for Latin America (ECLA). In 1984 ECLA expanded its operations and title to include the Caribbean. Main functions are to initiate and coordinate policies aimed at promoting economic development. In addition to the countries of Latin America and the Caribbean, ECLAC's forty-one members include Britain, Canada, France, the Netherlands, Portugal, Spain, and the United States. There are an additional five Caribbean associate members.

encomenderos—Colonial grantees, usually large landowners, who were given rights over Native American labor and tribute in exchange for assuming responsibility to protect and Christianize these indigenous subjects.

encomienda—A system or legal arrangement that entailed assigning Indian families or other inhabitants of a town to a Spaniard, who would extract labor and tribute from them while providing for their Christianization. The granting of an *encomienda* did not carry with it title to the land on which the Indians lived and labored or ownership of the Indians. The crown took the position that the natives were "free" subjects, although they could be compelled to pay tribute and to work like other such subjects. Many *encomenderos* (*q.v.*), however, interested only in exploiting the resources of the island, disregarded their moral, religious, and legal obligations to the Indians, as did others elsewhere in the New-World.

Enlightenment—An eighteenth-century European philosophical movement influenced by the seventeenth-century Scientific Revolution and the ideas of John Locke and Issac Newton. Its basic belief was the superiority of reason as a guide to all knowledge and human concerns. From this flowed the idea of progress and a challenging of traditional Christianity.

European Commission (EC)—The twenty-member executive body of the European Union (*q.v.*) responsible for implementing and managing EU policies and the EU's annual budget, among other responsibilities.

European Parliament—The directly elected (since 1979) assembly of the European Union (*q.v.*), with limited legislative and juridical competence. It has the right of scrutiny and supervision of EC executives and participates in the legislative and budgetary processes, advising the EC and reviewing all legislative proposals.

European Union (EU)—Successor organization to the European Community, the EU was officially established on November 1, 1993, when the Treaty on European Union went into effect. The goal of the EU is a closer economic union of its member states and the European Monetary Union, a greater unity in matters of justice and domestic affairs, and the development of a common foreign and security policy. To the members of the EC, the EU added Austria, Finland, and Sweden, effective January 1, 1995.

fiscal year (FY)—Coincides with Cuban calendar year.

General Agreement on Tariffs and Trade (GATT)—A 123-member international organization created on October 30, 1947, to provide a continuing basis for nations to negotiate and regulate commercial policies and promote international trade on a nondiscriminatory basis. Its principal activity is multinational negotiation for tariff reductions. Its seventh and final round of negotiations, held on April 15, 1994, was the Uruguay Round (*q.v.*), which had the aim of liberalizing the world market and promoting intellectual property. GATT was subsumed by the World Trade Organization (*q.v.*) on January 1, 1995.

global social product (GSP)—The broadest measure of an economy's output under the Material Product System (*q.v.*). The GSP accumulates the value of goods and "material" services produced by the economy in a given time frame, typically a year. The GSP differs from the gross domestic product (*q.v.*) in two main respects. First, the GSP tends to inflate value because it is based on gross value. For example, GSP includes the value of output of a furniture factory as well as the value of wood and other inputs that were used to produce the furniture. Thus, the GSP is subject to double-counting because the cost of inputs is not deducted from final output at each stage of the production process. Second, whereas the GDP includes nonproductive services, the GSP does not.

gross domestic product (GDP)—The most commonly used broad measure of an economy's output under the System of National Accounts (*q.v.*). The GDP aggregates the value added at each stage of the production process for goods and services and therefore avoids double counting. In the 1990s, Cuba reported economic performance on the basis of GDP growth rates, while earlier it did so on the basis of global social product (*q.v.*) growth rates.

gross national product (GNP)—Total market value of all final goods (those sold to the final user) and services produced by an economy during a year, plus the value of any net changes in inventories. Measured by adding the gross domestic product (GDP—*q.v.*), net changes in inventories, and the income received from abroad by residents less payments remitted abroad to nonresidents. Real GNP is the value of GNP when inflation has been taken into account.

Group of Eight—A permanent mechanism for consultation and political coordination that succeeded the Contadora Support Group in December 1986. It consisted of Argentina, Brazil, Colombia, Mexico, Panama, Peru, Uruguay, and Venezuela. It advocated democracy and a negotiated solution to the Central American insurgencies. Its name was changed in 1990 to the Rio Group (*q.v.*).

Group of Seventy–Seven (G–77)—Established on June 15, 1964, by seventy-seven developing countries that signed the "Joint Declaration of the Seventy-Seven Countries" issued at the end of the first session of the United Nations

Conference on Trade and Development (UNCTAD) in Geneva. Although the membership of the G–77 has increased to 133 countries, the original name has been retained because of its historic significance. As the largest developing-world coalition in the UN, the G–77 provides the means for the developing world to articulate and promote its collective economic interests and enhance its joint negotiating capacity on all major international economic issues in the UN system and promote economic and technical cooperation among developing countries.

Helms-Burton Act—*See* Cuban Liberty and Democratic Solidarity Act.

Inter-American Treaty of Reciprocal Assistance of 1947—*See* Rio Treaty.

internationalism—Starting in 1959, Cuba actively engaged in dispatching overseas missions involving support for insurgencies, combat troops, or members of construction and medical brigades to support developing countries in Africa, Asia, and Latin America for diplomatic, military, political, ideological, or other reasons. In the 1990s, Cuba continued to send nonmilitary internationalists abroad. In May 1998, Cuba had 2,759 internationalist technical workers, professionals, and specialists in eighty-six countries.

latifundio—A large landed estate. A legacy of the Spanish Empire and the Roman Catholic Church, latifundia provided the foundation for the small upper class and huge peasant class in the New World colonies.

Latin American Economic System (Sistema Económico Latinoamericano—SELA)—A regional intergovernmental organization, headquartered in Caracas, Venezuela, that groups twenty-seven Latin American and Caribbean countries. SELA was established on October 17, 1975, by the Panama Convention, and currently consists of the following member countries: Argentina, Barbados, Belize, Bolivia, Brazil, Chile, Colombia, Costa Rica, Cuba, Dominican Republic, Ecuador, El Salvador, Grenada, Guatemala, Guyana, Haiti, Honduras, Jamaica, Mexico, Nicaragua, Panama, Paraguay, Peru, Suriname, Trinidad and Tobago, Uruguay, and Venezuela. SELA provides a consultation and coordination system for consensus on joint positions and common strategies for the Latin American and Caribbean regions on economic issues vis-à-vis countries, groups of countries, and international organizations.

Latin American Free Trade Association (LAFTA)—A regional group founded by the Montevideo Treaty of 1960 to increase trade and foster development. LAFTA was replaced in 1980 by the Latin American Integration Association (Asociación Latinoamericana de Integración—ALADI—*q.v.*).

Latin American Integration Association (Asociación Latinoamericana de Integración—ALADI)—An organization that was established by the Treaty of Montevideo (August 1980) and became operational in March 1981. ALADI replaced the Latin American Free Trade Association (LAFTA—*q.v.*), which had been established in 1960 with the aim of developing a common market in Latin America. LAFTA made little progress, and ALADI was created with a more flexible and more limited role of encouraging free trade but with no timetable for the institution of a common market. Members approved the Regional Tariff Preference Program in 1984 and expanded upon it in 1987 and 1990. ALADI seeks economic cooperation among its eleven members—Argentina, Bolivia, Brazil, Chile, Colombia, Ecuador, Mexico, Paraguay, Peru, Uruguay, and Venezuela.

liberation theology—An activist movement led by Roman Catholic clergy who trace their inspiration to Vatican Council II (1965), when some church procedures were liberalized, and the Latin American Bishops' Conference in Medellín, Colombia (1968), which endorsed greater direct efforts to improve the lot of the poor.

Material Product System (MPS)—A national income accounting methodology used by the centrally planned economies. Cuba adopted the MPS in the early 1960s and used it through about 1992 to produce national product statistics. The MPS covers the value of output of goods and of so-called material services, which include freight transport, communications, and trade. In Cuban statistics, the MPS indicator most commonly available is the global social product (*q.v.*).

mestizaje—According to this ideology, the fusion of various cultural traditions (including language, religion, food, music, and so forth) in the Americas created a new and better mestizo race. This idea gained strength after the Mexican Revolution, and José Vasconcelos popularized it in his 1925 essay "La raza cósmica" (The Cosmic Race). Also refers to a process of racial amalgamation.

microbrigade—Started in 1971, microbrigades consist of "voluntary" workers from a given workplace—such as factories, ministries, commerce, education—who labor full time, typically in construction projects, while the rest of the workers at the original workplace cover the tasks abandoned by their comrades. These efforts are supplemented on weekends, when all workers can join in "voluntary work" in order to increase the pace of construction.

Nonaligned Movement (NAM)—Established on September 1, 1961, in Belgrade, with the aim of promoting political and military cooperation apart from the traditional East and West blocs. By 1999 NAM included 112 members plus the Palestine Liberation Organization (PLO), nineteen observer nations and organizations, and twenty-one "guest" nations. NAM experienced considerable difficulty in establishing a unified policy on many issues in international affairs. With the end of the Cold War and the breakup of the Soviet Union (1991), neutralism lost much of its usefulness as a guiding principle in many nations' foreign relations.

North American Free Trade Agreement (NAFTA)—A multilateral agreement negotiated by the United States, Canada, and Mexico setting forth agreements to lower and/or eliminate unfair trade barriers that affect the trade of goods and services among the three countries. NAFTA entered into force on January 1, 1994.

oficiales reales—The royal budget officers, of whom there were four in each Spanish colony. The *oficiales reales* worked very closely, discussing ways to increase royal revenue, with both the governor and the Casa de Contratación (*q.v.*).

Organization of American States (OAS)—Established by the Ninth International Conference of American States held in Bogotá on April 30, 1948, and effective since December 13, 1951. Has served as a major inter-American organization to promote regional peace and security as well as economic and social development in Latin America. Composed of thirty-five members, including most Latin American states and the United States and Canada. Determines common political, defense, economic, and social policies and provides for coordination of various inter-American agencies. Responsible for implementing the Inter-American Treaty of Reciprocal Assistance (Rio

Treaty—*q.v.*), when any threat to the security of the region arises.

Organization of the Eastern Caribbean States (OCES)—A regional body founded on June 18, 1981, by the seven former members of the West Indies Association (WISA), which had been created in 1966. Original members were Antigua and Barbuda, Dominica, Montserrat, St. Christopher and Nevis, St. Lucia, and St. Vincent and the Grenadines. The British Virgin Islands later became an associate member. Administered by a Central Secretariat located on the Morne, near Castries, St. Lucia, the OCES is designed to coordinate economic, foreign policy, and defense matters among its members and to facilitate their relations with various international organizations. The OCES is an associate institution of the Caribbean Community and Common Market (*q.v.*).

Ostend Manifesto—A confidential dispatch in October 1854 to the United States Department of State from United States ambassadors in Europe. It suggested that if Spain refused to sell Cuba to the United States, the United States would be justified in seizing the island. Northerners claimed it was a plot to expand slavery, and the Manifesto was disavowed.

paladares (singular, *paladar*)—The popular name given to home restaurants that sprang up in Cuba as a result of the legislation legalizing self-employment. The name originates from a chain of restaurants in a popular Brazilian soap opera shown on Cuban television in the late 1980s.

peninsulares—A term widely used throughout the Spanish Empire to refer to individuals born in Spain who were residing, usually temporarily, in one of the overseas colonies. *Peninsulares* were usually associated with important officials in the colonial bureaucracy, the military, or the Roman Catholic Church.

peso—The national currency, consisting of 100 centavos. Between 1914 and 1971, the peso was exchanged at parity with the United States dollar. Since the early 1960s, the peso has not been exchanged freely in the international market. The official exchange rate during the 1972–86 period averaged 1.23 (in pesos per United States dollar) and since 1987 has been reported by the Cuban National Bank to be 1.00. Since the 1960s, there has been an active black market for dollars in Cuba, with the black-market exchange rate fluctuating between six and fifteen pesos per United States dollar. In the 1990s, the value of the peso in the black market fell drastically. The unofficial exchange of the peso for the U.S. dollar has been estimated (in pesos per United States dollar) as follows: 1991, twenty; 1992, thirty-five; 1993, sixty; June 1994, 100; August 1994, 150; December 1994, forty-five; July 1995, thirty; September 1995, twenty-five; July 1996, twenty-one; December 1996, twenty. In the late 1990s, the exchange rate in government-operated Casas de Cambio was twenty to twenty-two pesos for one United States dollar.

Platt Amendment—In 1901, shortly after cessations of hostilities in the Spanish-American War, Washington Senator Orville Platt introduced legislation allowing the United States to intervene whenever it wished in order to protect life and property and "assure Cuban independence." The amendment was included in the Cuban constitution of 1901. On May 29, 1934, it was abrogated under the Treaty of Relations with Cuba, which continued to permit the United States to lease the site of its naval base at Guantánamo.

Rio Group—A permanent mechanism for consultation and political coordination that succeeded the Group of Eight (*q.v.*), formerly the Contadora Support Group, in 1990. The Group of Eight's predecessors had been involved in Central American peacekeeping negotiations. In 1993 the Rio Group (or Group of Rio) had twelve members: Argentina, Bolivia, Brazil, Chile, Colombia, Ecuador, Mexico, Panama, Paraguay, Peru, Uruguay, and Venezuela.

Rio Treaty (Inter-American Treaty of Reciprocal Assistance)—A regional alliance, signed in Rio de Janeiro in 1947, that established a mutual security system to safeguard the Western Hemisphere from aggression from within or outside the zone. Signatories include the United States and twenty Latin American republics. In 1975 a special conference approved, over United States objections, a Protocol of Amendment to the Rio Treaty that, once ratified, would establish the principle of "ideological pluralism" and would simplify the rescinding of sanctions imposed on an aggressor party.

santería—A syncretic cult, widely practiced in Cuba, in which Roman Catholic saints are equated with African deities. Its main practitioners are among the poorer strata of Cuban society, both black and white, but practitioners even include some of the white middle class.

special period in peacetime (*período especial en tiempo de paz;* hereafter Special Period)—A government euphemism for an emergency "wartime" economic program launched by President Castro in 1990 to deal with the onset of the economic crisis. The name reflects the Cuban leadership's view of the escalating recession as a kind of siege economy without outright war. The emphasis of Special Period policies has been on austerity measures.

sustainable development—A concept that emerged in the 1990s, based on the premise that development must meet the need of the present generation without compromising the ability of future generations to meet their own needs.

System of National Accounts (SNA)—The national income accounting methodology used by all nations other than the centrally planned economies. The SNA covers the value of output of goods and services, including "nonmaterial" services that are excluded under the Material Product System (*q.v.*), such as education, health services, culture and art, housing, government administration, and national defense. The most commonly available SNA indicator is the gross domestic product (*q.v.*). Cuba began to publish national product statistics based on the SNA in the 1990s.

tariff—A tax levied by a government in accordance with its tariff schedule, usually on imported products, but sometimes also on exported goods. May be imposed to protect domestic industries from competitive imported goods and/or to generate revenue. Types include ad valorem, variable, or some combination.

terms of trade—The ratio of a country's index of average export prices and average import prices. In international economics, the concept of "terms of trade" plays an important role in evaluating exchange relationships between nations: The terms of trade shift whenever a country's exports will buy more or fewer imports. An improvement in the terms of trade occurs when export prices rise relative to import prices. The terms of trade turn unfavorable in the event of a slump in export prices relative to import prices.

Treaty of Tlatelolco—On being ratified by Cuba in April 1995, the treaty took effect, binding the thirty-three Latin American and Caribbean signatory nations to the peaceful use of nuclear power. Under the treaty, Latin America became the world's first region to prohibit nuclear weapons. The treaty covers all of Latin America, including the Caribbean, from the Mexican border with the United States to Antarctica. It bans the testing, use, manufacture, production, or acquisition of nuclear weapons. Each participating country must negotiate accords with the International Atomic Energy Agency (IAEA) to facilitate verification.

underemployment—According to the dual-labor market hypothesis, there are many workers in the secondary labor market who either already possess skills that would enable them to function satisfactorily within the primary market or who could be trained for skilled jobs at no more than the usual costs. Given the obstacles to entering the primary labor market, however, they are required to take up unskilled secondary-sector jobs and are in this sense underemployed.

United Nations Commission on Human Rights (UNCHR)— Primary responsibility for the promotion of human rights under the UN Charter rests in the General Assembly and, under its authority, in the Economic and Social Council and its subsidiary body, the UNCHR, an intergovernmental body that serves as the UN's central policy organ in the human rights field. The UNCHR annually establishes a working group to consider and make recommendations concerning alleged "gross violations" of human rights. The UNCHR and its subcommission meet annually in Geneva to consider a wide range of human rights issues.

United Nations Development Programme (UNDP)—A thirty-six-member organization, established on November 22, 1965, to provide technical assistance to stimulate economic and social development.

United States-Cuba Trade and Economic Council (USTEC)— A United States-based organization that has collaborative relations with the Chamber of Commerce of the Republic of Cuba, Cuba's ministries of Foreign Trade, Foreign Investment and Economic Cooperation, Tourism, Public Health, Metallurgy Industry, and Foreign Relations, as well as with the National Assembly.

Uruguay Round—Refers to multilateral trade negotiations under the General Agreement on Tariffs and Trade (*q.v.*) that began at Punta del Este, Uruguay, in September 1986 and concluded in Geneva in December 1993 with an agreement signed by ministers in Marrakesh, Morocco, in April 1994. The Uruguay Round led to the World Trade Organization (*q.v.*).

World Trade Organization (WTO)—An international agency overseeing the rules of international trade of member countries. It was established on January 1, 1995, as a result of the Uruguay Round (*q.v.*) to replace the General Agreement on Tariffs and Trade (*q.v.*) dealing with trade in goods. The latter agreement is now part of the WTO agreements. The WTO has more than 130 members.

Index

ABC, 42, 48
abortion, 114, 129
Abrantes Fernández, José, 297, 336
acidification (of soil), 104
Acosta Cordero, Armando, 257
acquired immunodeficiency syndrome (AIDS), 143
Africa: Cuban military involvement in, 5, 292–94, 295; withdrawal from, lvii
Afro-Cuban religions, 131–32, 134–35, 137, 262
Afro-Cubans, 236
age structure, 115–16
agrarian reform, 46, 65–66, 68, 102–103, 122, 182–83, 256
agricultural development, 52, 100–101, 102–103
agricultural markets, 159, 160, 171–72, 175, 206
agriculture (*see also* cooperatives, agricultural), 67, 92, 103–105, 165, 169, 174–75, 180–85, 204–205
air force. *See* Antiaircraft Defense and Revolutionary Air Force
airports, 195
Alarcón de Quesada, Ricardo, lxxii, 233, 269, 270
Aldana Escalante, Carlos, 247
Allende Gossens, Salvador, 74
Almeida Bosque, Juan, 236, 249, 251
Almendares River, 98
Angola: Cuban military involvement in, li, 75, 292–93
Antiaircraft Defense and Revolutionary Air Force (Defensa Antiaérea y Fuerza Aérea Revolucionaria—DAA-FAR), 301, 310, 315, 319–20
Antilla, 193
Arawak, 6
Archipiélago de Camagüey, 93
Archipiélago de los Canarreos, 93
Archipiélago de los Colorados, 93
Archipiélago de los Jardines de la Reina, 93
Archipiélago de Sabana, 93

Ariguanabo (lake), 98
armed forces. *See* Revolutionary Armed Forces
army. *See* Revolutionary Army
artisan markets, 159, 160, 172, 206
Association of Caribbean States, 277
audiencia, 11, 12
austerity measures, 79, 109, 150, 159, 168
Authentic Organization, 59–60
Authentic Party, 4, 50, 53, 54, 55, 56, 57, 60, 63
autonomismo, 28
Autonomous Liberal Party, 28

Bacteriological (Biological) and Toxic Weapons Convention (1972), 307
Bahía de Cabañas, 94, 321
Bahía de Cienfuegos, 321
Bahía de La Habana (Havana Bay), 94, 109, 321
Bahía del Mariel, 94, 321
Bahía de Matanzas, 94, 321
Bahía de Nipe, 94, 321
Bahía de Nuevitas, 94, 321
Bahía de Puerto Padre, 94
Bahía de Santiago, 94
Bahía Honda, 94
Balaguer Cabrera, José Ramón, 264
balance of payments, 215, 216–18
Banco de los Jardines, 93
banking system, 160, 177–78
Baracoa, 10, 319
Barnet y Vinageras, José, 50
Basic Secondary Schools in the Countryside, 146–47
Basic Units of Cooperative Production (Unidades Básicas de Producción Cooperativa—UBPC), 103, 128, 171, 175, 180, 183, 185, 204, 206, 248
Batabanó, 107
Batista y Zaldívar, Fulgencio, xlvii, 4, 44, 45–46, 48, 49, 50, 51, 52, 55–64, 65, 125, 287–88, 307
Bay of Pigs invasion, xlix, l, lvi, 70, 71,

Contributors

Sergio Díaz-Briquets is Senior Division Director, Casals and Associates, Arlington, Virginia. He has written extensively on Cuban social and environmental issues.

Jorge I. Domínguez is Director, Weatherhead Center for International Affairs, and Clarence Dillon Professor of International Affairs, Harvard University, Cambridge, Massachusetts. He has written extensively on Cuban political affairs and foreign relations.

Rex A. Hudson is Senior Research Specialist in Latin American Affairs with the Federal Research Division of the Library of Congress. His earlier research on Cuba focused on Cuban support for insurgency in Latin America and Cuban diplomatic relations in the region.

Enrique J. López is an international information technology consultant and President, AKL Group, Inc., Coral Cables, Florida.

Jorge Pérez-López is Director, Office of International Economic Affairs, Bureau of International Labor Affairs, United States Department of Labor, Washington, D.C. He has written extensively on the Cuban economy.

Jaime Suchlicki is Professor of History, Graduate School of International Studies, and Director, Institute for Cuban and Cuban-American Studies (ICCAS), University of Miami, Coral Gables, Florida. He has written extensively on Cuban history.

Phyllis Greene Walker is a Washington-area political scientist who has written extensively on Cuban military and security affairs.

Published Country Studies

(Area Handbook Series)

550–65	Afghanistan		550–36	Dominican Republic and Haiti
550–98	Albania			
550–44	Algeria		550–52	Ecuador
550–59	Angola		550–43	Egypt
550–73	Argentina		550–150	El Salvador
550–111	Armenia, Azerbaijan, and Georgia		550-113	Estonia, Latvia, and Lithuania
550–169	Australia		550–28	Ethiopia
550–176	Austria		550–167	Finland
550–175	Bangladesh		550–173	Germany
550–112	Belarus and Moldova		550–153	Ghana
550–170	Belgium		550–87	Greece
550–66	Bolivia		550–78	Guatemala
550–20	Brazil		550–174	Guinea
550–168	Bulgaria		550–82	Guyana and Belize
550–61	Burma		550–151	Honduras
550–50	Cambodia		550–165	Hungary
550–166	Cameroon		550–21	India
550–159	Chad		550–154	Indian Ocean
550–77	Chile		550–39	Indonesia
550–60	China		550–68	Iran
550–26	Colombia		550–31	Iraq
550–33	Commonwealth Caribbean, Islands of the		550–25	Israel
			550–182	Italy
550–91	Congo		550–30	Japan
550–90	Costa Rica		550–34	Jordan
550–69	Côte d'Ivoire (Ivory Coast)		550–114	Kazakstan, Kyrgyzstan, Tajikistan, Turkmenistan, and Uzbekistan
550–152	Cuba			
550–22	Cyprus			
550–158	Czechoslovakia		550–56	Kenya

550–81	Korea, North	550–115	Russia
550–41	Korea, South	550–37	Rwanda and Burundi
550–58	Laos	550–51	Saudi Arabia
550–24	Lebanon	550–70	Senegal
550–38	Liberia	550–180	Sierra Leone
550–85	Libya	550–184	Singapore
550–172	Malawi	550–86	Somalia
550–45	Malaysia	550–93	South Africa
550–161	Mauritania	550–95	Soviet Union
550–79	Mexico	550–179	Spain
550–76	Mongolia	550–96	Sri Lanka
550–49	Morocco	550–27	Sudan
550–64	Mozambique	550–47	Syria
550–35	Nepal and Bhutan	550–62	Tanzania
550–88	Nicaragua	550–53	Thailand
550–157	Nigeria	550–89	Tunisia
550–94	Oceania	550–80	Turkey
550–48	Pakistan	550–74	Uganda
550–46	Panama	550–97	Uruguay
550–156	Paraguay	550–71	Venezuela
550–185	Persian Gulf States	550–32	Vietnam
550–42	Peru	550–183	Yemens, The
550–72	Philippines	550–99	Yugoslavia
550–162	Poland	550–67	Zaire
550–181	Portugal	550–75	Zambia
550–160	Romania	550–171	Zimbabwe